THE TRUE STORY
OF JAPANESE ESPIONAGE

SECRET SERVANTS

"By one who has made a full study of Japanese espionage, here is the dramatic, intensely interesting story of it, drawing on documents never before made public." —The Montgomery Advertiser

". . . these revelations of Japanese successes in compiling information about America's armed forces and industries are nothing less than shocking . . . liberally spiced with suspense and sex, they are also easy to read." —Saga Magazine

". . . so carefully documented there is no question of the truth behind it . . ." —World Telegram and Sun

"Few mystery writers could conceive situations so improbable, or ventures so daring. . . . SECRET SERVANTS is a tightly written, dramatic account of a spy system that went too far, too fast, although not before our discovery of it came too late."

—New York Times

"First-rate. . . ." —Greensboro Daily News

"A hair-raising book. . . ." —New York Mirror

SECRET SERVANTS

A History of Japanese Espionage

Ronald Seth

PAPERBACK LIBRARY, INC.

NEW YORK

To Sepha,
with private implications,
and with all my love

CONTENTS

ACKNOWLEDGMENTS

While I was collecting material for my short history of world espionage, *Spies at Work,* I was struck by the almost complete lack of information concerning the espionage activities of Japan and I decided that, if I could, I would try to fill the gap. I therefore approached the Japanese Embassy in London, who referred my request for assistance to Tokyo. The Japanese Foreign Office replied, regretfully, that those intelligence records which had not been destroyed by Allied bombing appeared to be irretrievably lost.

I was on the point of abandoning my project when the Japanese Embassy in London informed me that the American government were holding a large number of Japanese Foreign Office documents in Washington, and that the Library of Congress had published a check list. Thereupon I switched my attention to the American Embassy in London, and through the vigorous and untiring efforts of my very good friend Dr. Bowen Evans of the United States Information Service, who has placed me deeply in his debt, I was able to consult this check list.

The list told me that it would be very well worth my while to pay a visit to Washington. This was arranged, and here I must acknowledge with gratitude the assistance of the Librarian of Congress and of various members of his staff, particularly Dr. Edwin Beale of the Department of Orientalia, which was given me with unfailing courtesy and without stint. I owe a similar acknowledgment to the staff of the State Department in Washington, D. C., and to the British Foreign Office in London.

The major part of my early material is taken from the Japanese documents to which I have already referred. In the latter part of my account I am indebted to about a dozen printed sources. In the bibliography at the end I have acknowledged both the documentary material (under the reference numbers provided by the Library of Congress check list) and the printed sources by the name of the work and the author.

R. S.

CHAPTER 1

The Beginning of the End

It was 7:55 on the morning of Sunday, December 7th, 1941.

In the attic of a small house overlooking Pearl Harbor, the great Pacific base of the American Navy, Ruth Kühn spoke to her father as she trained her binoculars on the eighty-six United States warships riding peacefully and unsuspectingly at one of the largest natural anchorages in the world.

"They are coming!" she said.

Dr. Bernard Julius Otto Kühn gave a slight involuntary shiver of excitement. "All I hope is that they've managed to get the submarine inside the defenses," he replied. "If not . . ."

"They will do it," the girl said sharply. "Here they are! Be ready!"

From the northeast, out of the sky, it seemed, three formations of aircraft appeared. At first small specks against the deep blue, cloudless, sun-inflamed Pacific heavens, they grew momently as the drone of their engines crescendoed.

Through the finely precisioned Zeiss glasses, the girl saw the three groups presently veer away from one another. One made for the United States Army bases at Wheeler and Hickham Field. Another swung toward the United States Naval Airfield at Kaneohe Bay. The third came steadily on toward the ships below.

Except for the noise of the aircraft, Pearl Harbor was silent.

In the ships, in the barracks and in the houses, officers, men and civilian workers of the base were breakfasting or standing formation or going on shift. Only here and there could Ruth Kühn discern casual groups of men.

Her mother came into the room.

"What do you want?" the girl snapped, without turning from the window.

"Are you sure we should not take clothes?" her mother asked.

"Nothing . . . only the money!" the girl retorted. "Go back to Hans! It is going to begin!"

Even as she spoke the windows of the little house rattled and the walls themselves seemed to tremble. Split seconds later came the roar of the first salvos of the aerial torpedoes, the thunder of bombs exploding and the sinister whine of diving bombers as the 105 aircraft of the Imperial Japanese Air Force launched themselves against the Pacific might of America in the harbor below and, farther off, at Wheeler and Kaneohe Bay.

Ruth Kühn spoke incisively to her father. Clearly he repeated what she said, and as he spoke he translated his words into light signals, which he flashed through the window by which he was standing.

"Direct hit on battleship . . . one destroyer on fire," Otto Kühn flashed on his signal lamp.

And on the other side of the town a clerk from the Japanese Consulate tapped out to the Japanese naval commander on his key the retranslation of the signals at the dictation of his chief, Consul Otojiro Okudo, who had his binoculars trained on the Kühns' attic window.

As soon as the Japanese attack began confusion assailed the American forces. But it was only momentary. Despite the fact that the aircraft warning system was not working and that not a single regular reconnaissance or inshore patrol had been maintained by the army or navy, the ship-borne antiaircraft batteries had come into action.

But none of the land-based antiaircraft and coastal batteries came to their support, for they were unmanned; and even if they had been manned, they would have been totally ineffective, for not one of them was supplied with a single round of ammunition.

They did have the assistance of the few planes which were able to become air-borne and of eighteen Navy dive bombers from the aircraft carrier *Enterprise* which arrived fortuitously while the battle was in progress. But the aid these unprepared fliers could give was not very great.

With one fifteen-minute pause, the Japanese pressed their attack until 9:45. When at last they broke off, out of their total force they had lost only forty. But the losses they inflicted were such that besides immobilizing the United States Pacific Fleet, in their ninety-five minutes of attack they had given Japan naval and air supremacy in the Far East by making any immediate combination of American and British Far Eastern naval forces an impossibility.

During eighty of those ninety-five minutes Ruth Kühn had reported every success to her father, who flashed them to Otojiro Okudo, who tapped them on to the Japanese commander, who, on the strength of them, issued his orders.

Why did she stop fifteen minutes too soon?

A little before 9:30 the door of the attic opened.

Ruth heard it. So did her father. Believing it to be her mother again, she neither turned nor spoke, but continued to scan the harbor which lay now under a pall of smoke.

Even when she heard the noise of a small scuffle she did not turn. Only when she heard her father exclaim: "My God!" and at once a strange voice, a man's voice, snap: "Put up your hands!" did she whip around and find herself face to face with two American intelligence officers.

In the confusion that reigned in Pearl Harbor that morning—and only those who were there know what it was like—at least two men kept their heads. Hurrying to headquarters to discover how they might best help, these two men saw the light flashing from the attic window, realized that it was some sort of signal and decided to investigate. On the way they picked up a colleague.

Arrived at the little house, which the Kühns used as a week-end retreat, they surprised Frau Kühn as she soothed her frightened thirteen-year-old son, Hans, in the sitting room. While one of them guarded mother and son, the other two mounted quickly to the attic and took father and daughter even as they worked.

With their prisoners they took the packed suitcases standing ready in the hallway. At headquarters, when they were opened, the cases were found to contain only money—bundles and bundles of money, among them wads of Japanese currency.

Besides the forty Japanese aircraft the Americans destroyed they also sank three Japanese submarines which had been able to penetrate the harbor defenses. One of them was the submarine which had been sent to bear away Otojiro Okudo and his staff—and the Kühns.

How had the Kühns come to be spying for the Japanese?

Bernard Julius Otto Kühn joined the German Imperial Navy at the age of eighteen and was assigned to service in a cruiser. In 1915 his ship was sunk by the British and he was picked up and taken to England as a prisoner of war. To pass the dreary hours behind the wire he began to learn English, and made excellent progress.

After the armistice he returned to Germany and, having no profession, decided to take up medicine. Like so many of the disillusioned young in Germany during the twenties, the conditions which made it more than difficult for him to earn a living in his chosen profession turned him bitter. So when the Nazis came strutting into the streets proclaiming their promises to change all the harsh struggle for very existence in Weimar Germany into a utopia of National Socialism, they found in him a ready listener, and then an ardent adherent.

He met and became a personal friend of Heinrich Himmler and was given a job with the Gestapo. It was not a prominent nor even a lucrative job, but he was given to understand that it was merely a steppingstone to the position earmarked for him—chief of police in one of the great German cities.

One of the more peculiar traits of the extremely peculiar reichsführer and chief of the S.S., Himmler, was that he kept the promises he made to his intimates. His promise to Bernard Kühn, however, he did not keep. Instead, on August 15th, 1935, the good doctor found himself stepping ashore in the Hawaiian Islands accompanied by his wife and two of their children, Hans Joachim, aged six, and Ruth, aged eighteen.

And Ruth was the cause of this curious translocation!

The Kühns' elder son, Leopold, was in a good position. He held the post of private secretary to Dr. Joseph Goebbels, minister for propaganda and public enlightenment.

Early in 1935 Leopold's chief, the little clubfooted doctor, gave a gala party at the ministry for his staff. As Leopold Kühn had no fiancée or particular female friend, he took with him, as his partner, his sister Ruth.

Ruth was a really beautiful girl. The freshness of unsullied, still-burgeoning maturity was upon her, like the bloom upon a fine ripe peach. There were members of the Nazi Party at this time who still directed their domestic lives after an acceptable code of morals. Dr. Kühn was one of them. He brought up his sons and his daughter along the narrow path of moral rectitude. Ruth, though brushed with innocence, knew exactly what she must do to keep that innocence untarnished and, until this party at the propaganda ministry, fully intended that her innocence should be the main item in the dowry she would take to her fortunate husband.

When she was presented to the minister for propaganda he held her hand just a little longer than was really necessary, and she was too untutored to read the signs— yet. From the beginning the engagement was unequal and unfair. The ugly, crippled, almost dwarflike Goebbels could exude great charm, and one of his main weapons was his voice.

The present writer, after a series of vicissitudes which he has recounted elsewhere, found himself in the beleaguered city of Berlin in March 1945 when the Russians were but forty miles from the gates in the east and the Allied mobile forces were dashing up from the west. During his stay he attended one evening a meeting of several thousand dispirited, war-weary, bewildered Berliners who had congregated in the hope of receiving some encouragement from the minister of propaganda and public enlightenment.

13

When Joseph Goebbels stepped to the rostrum to speak only his head could be seen above the rail through the bullet-proof glass shield protecting him. Had it been anywhere else in the world, and with an audience of any but Germans, there must have been a demonstration of unkind merriment. But from the moment that the fanatic eyes flashed above the rail of the rostrum and their owner began to speak, a fantastically mellifluous voice controlled everyone within hearing. It was not the words he used, not the promises he made, for he had only the threadbare clichés of Nazism on which to fall back. Nevertheless the vast crowd was hypnotically hushed within seconds, not merely by the actual sound of the voice, but by the mysterious charm which it held.

Later in the evening at that reception ten years earlier, this little man had invited Ruth Kühn to dance with him—and despite his clubfoot he danced well. At close quarters, with his arms around one and the prestige of his position and the flattery of his invitation to enhance it, this charm must have been even more potent.

To the rake, virginity is one of the main attractions for sexual prowess for it erases temporarily the boredom of overindulgence by its freshness and removes the necessity for perversion, which only too quickly jades the sexual palate. Against one so skilled the girl had no chance, and even if the charm and the art had had no effect there were few, even among moral Nazis, who would have dared to immolate themselves on the altar of chastity when the führer's staunchest friend wielded the sacrificial knife.

Within a short time Ruth Kühn, not yet seventeen, had become the deformed dwarf's mistress. She was only one of a number of the minister of public enlightenment's lights of love. He plucked them as they took his fancy and discarded them when the bloom began to fade, and under his blighting heat they faded soon. He was not discreet enough to prevent the particulars of his extensive amours from becoming public knowledge. The discussion of them provided diversion from the führer down to Gefreiter Schmitt. Frau Goebbels certainly knew of them, but the strange charm which bewitched the führer and Gefreiter

14

Schmitt must have bewitched her too, for she never caused her husband the embarrassment of divorcing him or apparently ever threatening to do so; and at the end was content, both for herself and her children, to accept poison from his hand and to die in his arms as he fell back dead.

What happened exactly in the case of Ruth Kühn is now likely to remain a mystery for all time unless the woman—she is still alive in Germany—should ever choose to speak. Quite suddenly Goebbels not only cast her off but decided that she must leave Germany.

The head of the geopolitical department of Berlin University was General Haushofer, and the general's son, Karl, was one of Goebbel's closest intimates. The majority of students who passed through the general's hands entered the foreign service, usually becoming members of Ribbentrop's espionage service.

General Haushofer had had close connections with the Japanese espionage authorities since 1914, and as good fortune would have it, at the very moment of Goebbels' *contretemps* with Ruth the Japanese had asked if they could be given some assistance in acquiring the services of Europeans for their espionage organization. One of the great difficulties with which the Japanese spy masters have always had to contend has been the color and other physical characteristics of their own people, which makes them conspicuous in any area outside their own theater.

The coincidence of Tokyo's request with the German minister of propaganda's predicament could not have been more fortunate. When Goebbels explained his problem to his friend Karl, Karl's father could say that he could use not only Ruth but Ruth's family. Nothing could have been more satisfactory for the Little Doctor because it removed the embarrassing girl literally to the other side of the world. And thus it was that the Kühn family, with the exception of Leopold, who remained at his post as Goebbels' private secretary until he met his death on the Russian front, arrived in the Pacific.

Their "cover" was Dr. Kühn's supposed interest in the Japanese language and the ancient history of the Hawaiian Islands. They gave every appearance of being a typically

15

united Teutonic family. Certainly they aroused no suspicions in the minds of anyone who ought to have been curious about a German family transplanting themselves so many miles from the fatherland. Not even the travels of Ruth and her father to the adjacent islands caused a single eyebrow to be raised. Indeed, it would seem that the Kühns had everything in their favor.

Friedel Kühn, the doctor's frau, was plump and bespectacled and treated her husband with the respect which has always been one of the good qualities of German women. But she had the pigeonhole type of mind which could sort and evaluate and store away even small details of military significance. While she gave every appearance of centering all her existence in the welfare of her family, she disarmed those who would have been on their guard had they ever thought what her true role really was. Even when she left Hawaii for two fairly protracted periods, her absence merely provoked expressions of commiseration for her family thus left without the prop of their domestic bliss. Yet, had the interested authorities only known, each time she was visiting Japan as a courier, carrying secrets of United States naval and military defenses in the Hawaiian Islands.

Despite her experiences at the hands of Joseph Goebbels, or perhaps because of them—for nothing enhances the beauty of maturity more than the awakening and satisfying of inherent sexuality—Ruth's appearance was more strikingly attractive than ever. She was fond of tennis and swimming and was an exquisite dancer, and these accomplishments, added to her natural grace, soon brought her invitations to every social event. The majority of these gave her contacts with American naval officers made hypersusceptible to female company by absence from home and the normal expression of those qualities inherited from the old Adam; and these contacts provided her with extremely useful information, all unwittingly disclosed by the aspirants for her favors.

Then, too, to observers the Kühns were clearly well provided with money. Since the source of their wealth was the Rotterdam Bank Association it was concluded—quite wrongly—that the doctor had made some very shrewd investments in the Netherlands. It is known now that in the six years 1935 to 1941 the Kühns received more than $100,000, and it is believed that this was by no means all their remuneration.

The Kühns were in the service of both the Germans and the Japanese, though the latter were unaware of their contact with the Nazis. Copies of all the information they supplied to the Japanese consuls in Hawaii, who were their contacts, they sent to Ribbentrop's intelligence via General Haushofer.

Early in 1939 the Kühns moved from Honolulu to the quieter Pearl Harbor. It is now generally accepted that there is no hotter bed of gossip than a woman's beauty parlor. Either the Kühns or their superiors made this discovery two decades ago.

As Ruth was very skillful at her own beautification, and as there was no amenity of this kind for the navy wives in Pearl Harbor, there was nothing strange to be seen in her opening up a beauty parlor. This new venture marked the intensification of Japanese espionage in the southern Pacific.

The success of the beauty parlor was as overwhelming as it was instantaneous. At a meeting with Otojiro Okudo, the consul at Honolulu, the specific requirements of the imperial spy masters were explained to the Kühns. Their chief assignment was to supply the exact numbers of the United States naval forces in the Pacific with their exact locations and exact dates of departure and arrival at any given spot, with particular reference to Pearl Harbor.

The innocence of little Hans, now eleven years old, was to prove a very useful adjunct to the beauty parlor. The boy was encouraged by his father to develop his natural curiosity about and interest in ships, particularly in naval ships belonging to the Americans. It was not long before kindly American sailors were inviting the boy aboard their vessels and pointing out to him all the mysteries of their equipment. What harm could there be in answering the spate of questions which Hans, like any normal little boy, asked, when he would not understand a word of what he was being told? But Hans was observant and had a retentive memory. When he got home he was able to give an exact account of what he had seen and heard.

The Kühns' next step was to work out a simple code and light signal system by which they could transmit their information from the attic window of a small house they rented above Pearl Harbor direct to a Japanese agent. The pace was now increasing at such a rate that personal contact with the Japanese as frequently as changes in the dispositions of United States naval units now made desirable was dangerous. The signal system eliminated the risk.

The system was tried out on December 2nd, 1941, and was a complete success. Otojiro Okudo now came himself to Pearl Harbor and was able to transmit by radio to Japanese naval intelligence, via his consul general, the exact location of all American warships in Hawaiian waters.

As the Kühns, father and daughter, watched the Pearl Harbor base filling up during the next few days, they had great difficulty in keeping their mounting excitement in check. And the excitement of their Japanese masters was commensurate with, even if it did not exceed, their own.

In position by December 6th, the Japanese naval commander could congratulate his masters on their great good fortune. The gods had given them a sure sign that they were on their side by persuading the enemy to concentrate the greater proportion of his naval forces in one spot so that, by a simple plan, he could be attacked with the full weight of Japanese aerial vengeance. The plan was to succeed, but the people who were largely instrumental in its success provided the sacrifice.

The Kühns were eventually brought to trial. The evidence was all against them. The suitcases were produced and among the other evidence were copies of their reports written in German and even a copy of the signal code, which had all been found in the house when it was searched.

The doctor, his wife and Ruth all attempted to claim the leadership of the little ring. The Americans accepted the

18

doctor's version and he was sentenced to death. Friedel and Ruth were imprisoned.

The doctor made a bid to save his life by telling all he knew about Axis espionage in the Pacific. The Americans must have found his information valuable, for on October 26th, 1942, his death sentence was commuted to fifty years' imprisonment.

But whatever the fate of the Kühns, Japanese espionage had scored a great victory. It was a victory for which espionage preparations had begun more than thirty years before the Kühns had arrived in Honolulu. In the library of congress, in Washington, D.C., there are two sets of Japanese Foreign Office documents titled *Honoruru Gumbi Chōsa, Investigation of the military preparations of Honolulu,* 1907 to 1926, and, *Hawai Rikugiu Jōhō-bu Shubō, Weekly Intelligence Reports from the Army Intelligence Bureau on Hawaii,* 1922 to 1923, totaling 2,318 pages of documents altogether.

It is passing strange how events resolve themselves. Had Leopold Kühn been a normal young German he would have had a girl friend to partner him at his chief's gala party in 1935 instead of his young sister; or that young sister might have been neither beautiful nor possessed of the untouched virginity which attracted the deformed satyr of a minister of propaganda; or she might have possessed those skills which might have permanently satisfied the jaded palate of Goebbels. Any of these things could have prevented the Kühns from being exiled to the Pacific and spying for Japan. Instead, everything conspired to send this German family to this place, to work for these masters. In fact, the presence of the Kühns in Honolulu and their spying for Japan has a very great significance.

First, it underlines the close affinity that Japanese espionage has always had with the German. When Japan abolished its "closed door" policy in the mid-nineteenth century and began to develop from a medieval feudal state into a highly organized modern nation and the policies which she adopted made an espionage system essential, it had been to the methods and organization of one of the greatest spy masters of all times to which she had turned.

The Prussian, Wilhelm Stieber, had produced what was then not only the most powerful espionage system in the world, an instrument with which Bismarck and his monarch had been able to forge the German empire, but also the most up-to-date system.

Second, Pearl Harbor was the brilliant culmination of more than half a century of spying in Honolulu and was one of the greatest coups of a truly fantastic system of espionage. It is fantastic not only in the vastness of its organization but in the physical area of the globe's surface which it covered.

In this story we shall hope to reveal not only the methods and the vast ramifications of Japanese espionage from its beginnings in the middle eighties of the last century down to Pearl Harbor, but to describe its activities in places as widely separated as St. Petersburg and New York, and in such tremendous areas as Siberia, Central Asia, China, Manchuria, the Pacific, the West Indies, Central America and the United States, linking these activities with the development of Japan's policy.

But to put the whole picture into proper perspective we must turn first to the model.

CHAPTER 2

The Model

One day in 1848 King Frederick William of Prussia found himself alone and unaccountably involved in one of those disturbances which, in those days, were becoming an all too frequent occurrence in Berlin. The disturbance had been spontaneous; someone had recognized the king and called out an insult. This had attracted the attention of others and soon the credulous, timorous Frederick found himself faced by a hostile mob. It seemed for a moment as if he would receive physical harm. He looked about him but could see no way of escape.

Like many timorous men, the king had a certain courage. He could not escape; he would not harangue these ill-mannered subjects; he would stand and wait for the blows which he was sure must come. All he hoped was that the end would be quick.

At that moment a man detached himself from the crowd, which even in its anger stood a little way off in deference to his royal person, and advanced toward him.

"Down with the tyrant!" the man shouted. "Death to the king! Let's end it now!"

So long had the tyranny of the secret police been at work that even now the leaderless crowd hung back, none of them willing to do anything which would make him a marked man.

The man continued to approach, still shouting his threats, his arm raised, though whether to strike a blow or to egg on the crowd the king could not be sure. Now he was within reach. His back was to the crowd. The king flinched a little but held his ground as his would-be assailant pushed his face close to his and shouted a last threat. "Don't be afraid, your majesty!" the man then whispered quickly. "I'm a police agent. My men are in the crowd. They will see that nothing happens to you."

"Thank God!" murmured the king.

"Death to the tyrant!" shouted the man, and seizing the king by the arm began to bustle him along the pavement.

Struck mute by the handling of the king's person, the crowd on the pavement made way for them. As they came level with a door a few yards down, the man made a sudden movement toward it, threw it open and pushed the king inside, quickly following himself. When the door was locked and bolted the man leaned against it, let out his breath in a sudden rush and passed his hand across his damp forehead.

"Sire!" he exclaimed to the trembling king. "That was a narrow shave! But I must beg your majesty's indulgence. I am not a police agent, but I had to say something. It would have been fatal had your majesty's courage failed you at the last moment."

The king forgot his trembling and smiled at the man.

"You certainly saved my life," he said softly, "and I am grateful to you. May I know the name of my gallant, quick-witted rescuer?"

"Wilhelm Stieber, sire. At your majesty's command, always."

"Wilhelm Stieber!" replied the king. "I shall not forget."

Wilhelm Stieber was born on May 3rd, 1818. His father was a minor official in Merseburg, Saxony.

Wilhelm had not yet reached his teens when Herr Stieber was transferred to Berlin. There he educated his son with a view to ultimate ordination in the Lutheran ministry.

Before he had completed his education, however, Wilhelm had decided that he had no vocation for the ministry and turned his attention to the study of law. In the law he found at last the best use for his intellectual powers, qualified without difficulty and within a short time had become one of the most sought-after criminal lawyers in Berlin.

His clients were the riffraff of the criminal world, petty thieves, petty forgers, confidence men, rapists. They were the little, maladjusted men who took to crime as the only mode of expression they had—so far as they could see—of kicking against authority, cruel, unjust authority which was ceaselessly vigilant in harrying them, the underdogs.

Stieber's personality was such that he was able to get inside the minds of these little men, and when he assumed the title of champion of the underdogs they were willing to accord it to him. They did not know—for years they were never to discover—that their champion, in circles more influential in the realms of authority, was one of the most ardent monarchists.

Stieber never acted as attorney for the prosecution. He was always attorney for the defense. And his success in this role was phenomenal. Between 1845 and 1850 he success-fully defended 3,000 clients.

What was the secret of his success as a lawyer? Was it

his brilliance of intellect and oratory? Was it his superior knowledge of the law? It was certainly knowledge. But it was not knowledge of the law, extensive though this was.

When Stieber told the king that he was not a police agent he was not speaking the strict truth. He was not, admittedly, the normal kind of police agent, but he was in the pay of the police. He was, in fact, an *agent provocateur,* employed to smell out proscribed radicals, the enemies of the monarchy and the monarchists.

Besides this, he was editor of the *Police Journal.* Thus he had constant dealings with the police, and from these contacts and from the material supplied to his journal he was able to gain information in advance regarding the evidence which the police intended to bring against his clients. So he went into court fully prepared to meet with rebuttal and legal argument the facts and arguments put forward by the prosecutors. And, surprisingly, it never appeared to occur to the police that they were supplying the material for his success.

He used his role as champion of the underdog as a cover for his role as *agent provocateur*. He was not, he never would be, a man who acted from altruistic motives. A lawyer who consorted with the scum of the underworld, a shady "mouthpiece," would never be expected to be a monarchist. If he were, why should he devote his efforts and skill to defend, and only defend, those who were "agin the government."

But as well as being a cover, his association with his petty criminals was a source of information for his activities as *agent provocateur*. The proscribed radicals, even though they might be honest, decent men, and men of substance who had never stolen a penny from their grandmothers or even momentarily been tempted to do so, were, nevertheless, criminals. What they were doing, what they were saying, where they were to be found, all circulated along the grapevine of the underworld and came to Stieber's knowledge. So he smelled them out and was as successful in that as he was in the courts.

But Stieber was an ambitious man. It was not his intention always to be an *agent provocateur* and defender

23

of petty thieves. He had his attention fixed on high places, and one or more of those high places he intended to fill.

His brilliant, quick-moving intellect also made him an opportunist. But quick to seize every opportunity, even he must have been overpowered by the prospects which suddenly opened up before him, so it seemed, on that day in 1848—he was then only thirty—as he stood in the crowd, looking at the lonely, frightened king.

On that day Stieber put his foot on the first rung of a tall ladder of success the moment he whispered in the king's ear. Frederick William was grateful to his gallant protector and did not, like some infamous princes, forget him as soon as he was safe once more within the protecting walls of his palace at Potsdam. Until the king went quite mad in 1857 and had to be put away, he heaped reward upon reward on Stieber.

In 1850 Stieber was appointed a commissioner of police. In the following year he visited England, ostensibly for the prince consort's Great Exhibition in the Crystal Palace in Hyde Park, but in reality to check up on the activities of Karl Marx and other German radical exiles then living in London. In 1852 he went to Paris where, posing as a liberal, and in his old role of *agent provocateur,* he obtained a list of radicals still living "underground" in Germany. His return was marked in Germany by the wholesale arrests of these men and women.

During the years which followed he became such an ardent supporter of autocracy that he almost outrivaled the autocrat himself. This ardor he translated into action against the radicals, thereby strengthening the king's position and so keeping green the king's sense of gratitude toward him.

But an autocratic policeman tends to make as many enemies as an autocratic monarch, and when Frederick William's brother became regent on the king's retirement, Stieber quickly discovered that the regent was not among his admirers. He was dismissed from his post and was fortunate that the support he had received from the now mad king could still save him from even worse revenge.

Deciding that it might be wiser for his physical well-being to leave his ungrateful country for a time, Stieber went to St. Petersburg. There, between 1858 and 1863, he assisted in the reorganization of the Russian secret service. He chose St. Petersburg because it was the one place where he could legitimately expect to be helped. A few years before he had been able to hush up a scandal involving the wife of a Russian attaché in Berlin.

There is one aspect of this phase of Stieber's career which at first sight appears extraordinary. But when we come to know him better we shall see that it fits snugly into the jigsaw of the man's genius. While in disgrace and helping the Russians in St. Petersburg, he collected all the military information on which he could lay hands and sent it to Berlin, where it was found to be of great value. Optimist and always superb opportunist, he believed that he had encountered only a temporary setback and that the time would undoubtedly come when he would be restored to his rightful place. When this happened what he was doing now would be remembered to his advantage.

Nor had he too long to wait. In 1863 Stieber returned to Prussia and almost at once was recommended and introduced to Prince Otto von Bismarck by the proprietor of the *Nord-deutsche Allegemeine Zeitung*.

At this time Bismarck was busy laying his plans for the aggrandizement of Prussian power and role on the European stage. He had reached that point in his planning where he had decided upon the elimination of Austria as a first step in the right direction.

A careful man and, of his kind, wise, Bismarck began to put his preparations in train. A first requirement of any action against the Austrians was the acquisition of the knowledge of their country's state of preparedness and military potential to resist attack. He suggested that Stieber might care to organize this intelligence for him.

It was exactly the opportunity for which Stieber had been waiting and hoping. He was certain that if he could bring off a brilliant *coup* he must be reinstated in his former position. Confident in his own capabilities and believing that the more he did personally the greater his success would be seen to be, he decided that he, and he alone, would conduct the operation, unless he found himself compelled by the enormity of the undertaking to have assistance.

So it happened that on a June day in 1863 the little Austrian village of Brunsbruck ran to the doors of its cottages, shops and workshops attracted by the cries of excited children who were running beside a small, horse-drawn cart as it slowly made its way down the village street.

The smiling, forty-five-year-old driver was a stranger. The good people of Brunsbruck had never seen him before, and this fact alone was sufficient to bring them to the street. But when he drew up his cart before the village inn and announced that he had sacred statuettes for sale, they left their doors and came crowding around him as the children had done.

The peddler was a good salesman. He was persuasive in his talk, he was witty, he cracked jokes that were new—at least to them—and which appealed to their country sense of humor, and before they knew where they were, they were buying one of the Sacred Hearts, or a Madonna, or a Holy Child which he was displaying for their inspection. He did not seem to be greedy, either. His charges were less than half those normally charged by door-to-door hawkers for sacred statuettes "blessed by the Holy Father himself."

When everyone was satisfied for the moment, he drove his cart round to the back of the inn, where he took the horse from between the shafts, tied her up and adjusted, for her convenience, a nose bag of sweet-smelling fresh hay. Then, having seen that her wants were satisfied, he went into the inn to attend to his own.

The taproom was practically empty. Only two or three men were sitting with steins in their hands, talking a little and drinking more quickly than usual because there was more work to be done. The peddler picked up the stein which the landlord had drawn for him and walked over with it to a table at which two men were sitting.

"Good day," he greeted them. "It's a pleasant village and pleasant people you have here."

The men grunted their appreciation of his appraisal and approval. He was a friendly man for a stranger. As soon as he spoke to them their country shyness and awkwardness with city-dwellers—they were always so damned superior —disappeared. Within a few minutes they felt that they had known the man for years.

"Any news?" one of the men asked.

"Not much," the peddler answered. "In the capital the army struts about as usual. Countess von Weber has been brought to bed of a boy, though the count has not been in Vienna for 372 days and she has never left the city. . . . Oh, it's the same old story!"

"What do they think about Prussia in the capital? Do they think Bismarck has got his eye on us?"

The peddler shrugged his shoulders.

"Why, yes. They believe he's bound to want to annex us, but they're confident our army is better than any Prussian army."

"Then they're expecting war?"

"Some time or other, they say it's bound to come; but not yet. And the longer we have, the better our defenses will be. Have you ever seen anything like this?" Suddenly he changed the subject. He drew from his pocket two or three cards on one side of which were drawings. He handed one to each of the men. For a moment or two there was silence, and then both men began to chuckle. And the chuckles grew into loud guffaws.

"Are these from the city?" one asked.

"Of course," the peddler answered. "The latest thing. There's scarcely a man of quality, or who can afford the price, that hasn't one, or two, or three."

"Who draws them?"

"A young artist I know."

"Does he have models, or does he do it out of his head?"

"His aunt keeps a brothel. He has made small spy holes in the walls of some of the rooms. He draws from life."

"Great heavens! And you really mean people . . ."

The peddler nodded. "Like to have one?" he asked.

"I could never afford it. How much?"

The peddler named the price—a few pence. The men handed back the cards. "When do you leave here?" one asked.

"Oh, not until tomorrow, if the landlord can give me a room."

"We have no money with us now. But we'll be here tonight. Save us one or two."

"I have plenty. I'll get them out and you can take your choice."

That evening the landlord of the inn did a roaring trade in beer as every man in the village and from the countryside around, it seemed, crowded into his taproom; and the peddler did a roaring trade in his pornographic drawings.

As he sold the drawings he drew the men into conversation. They answered him willingly. With their minds' eyes gloating on the new acquisitions, now secure in secret pockets, and their minds far away, they answered his questions, unconscious of the fact that they were telling this stranger how many soldiers were billeted in the neighborhood, which regiments they belonged to, how they were armed, what strong points there were round about, exactly where they were situated. And when bed called them at last they were equally unconscious of the peddler noting in a book, in a personal code, all the information he had gathered during the evening.

As, next morning, he drove away, his customers, both those who had bought his sacred statuettes and those who had purchased his pornography, waved him farewell as he passed them on the road to the next village, calling to him to return soon with newer wares; for his visit had been a red-letter day in their quiet lives.

So he went on his way with his sacred statuettes and his pornography. It is not such an outrageous mixture of wares as would at first sight appear. Mankind is divided into two sorts—the pure and the impure. His Sacred Hearts brought him into the kitchens, his drawings into the taprooms. In both he was popular. In both he learned much.

For two years the peddler traveled the roads and

28

byroads of Austria, questioning the unsuspecting, noting in his small black book, received everywhere as a friend by reason of his personal charm. Then, at the end of two years, his task completed, he returned to Berlin and to his master, Prince Otto von Bismarck, the Prussian king's Iron Chancellor, and laid before him a full and detailed account of Austria's armed strength and the disposition of her forces. It was as complete a picture of Austria's military preparedness as it was possible to gain without direct access to general staff blueprints.

By 1866, which was judged the opportune moment, the Prussian military leaders had devised a timetable which they were able to follow rigidly, based upon the peddler's information. The result was the Seven Weeks' War, terminating in the complete defeat at Sadowa of Austria's military might, and strewing upon the battlefields many of those who had bought the peddler's pictures.

Between police work and military espionage there is fixed a great gulf. Allan Pinkerton, the famous American detective, failed miserably when asked by President Lincoln to organize a system of military intelligence. The great spy—and great spies are a very small, select band—can combine the two sets of qualities required for success in both branches. Stieber very soon proved that he belonged to this select band.

In the Seven Weeks' War against Austria, which was fought strictly on the basis of the intelligence supplied by him, Stieber himself played an important and active role. In the months of preparation he organized an entirely new section of the secret police and went into the field with it as its commander. We recognize this new force to be the forerunner of the intelligence corps; and it is preserved still in the German military organization as the *Geheimefeldpolizei,* the secret field police.

Though primarily organized to protect the persons of the king, his ministers and generals, Stieber's secret police were also to prevent foreign spies from obtaining Prussian military secrets. It was, in fact, counterespionage; and counterespionage in those days was a new concept. This was the first of Stieber's contributions to modern spycraft. It was a contribution which was to appeal most strongly to the Japanese.

The originality of Stieber's mind *vis-à-vis* espionage is demonstrated by other innovations and introduced by him. They are commonplaces today, but the measure of Stieber's greatness as a spy and a spy master is the fact that those innovations sprang from his mind.

There was, for example, military censorship, under which no dispatch, letter or telegram might be sent from the front unless it had first been censored by Stieber's staff. Alexander the Great had first used censorship of mail when his armies, thousands of miles from home, were threatening to revolt in the deserts of Persia. But he used censorship so that he might discover who the disaffected were and remove them.

Always aware of the necessity for secrecy concerning his movements and plans, Alexander had consistently forbidden his soldiers to write home to their families. Now, faced with wholesale mutiny, he directed that all officers and men might write one letter home and promised that they should be carried to Greece by special couriers. The men were delighted and poured out their hearts to wives and sweethearts.

The couriers set off, but twenty miles or so on their way they were met by trusted soldiers of the general. These took and read every letter and noted the names of all those who complained. They returned with their lists to Alexander and in a few days all the dissidents had been removed.

But this was not Stieber's motive. The motive was tied with yet another of his innovations. This was false propaganda, in which he was excelled only by his notorious successor, Dr. Joseph Goebbels, Hitler's minister of propaganda and public enlightenment.

Stieber argued, and the validity of his argument cannot be denied except on moral grounds, that the judicious manipulation of unpleasant facts may be used to boost the morale of one's own people and to weaken the morale of the enemy. The uneasiness which was caused in certain sections of the British public between 1939 and 1942 by

Lord Haw-haw's (William Joyce's) broadcasts from Hamburg to England serve as an excellent illustration of the insidiousness and danger of this kind of attack.

In Stieber's day there was honor among high commands and they were honest in describing losses and defeats in their communiqués. Now, when the communiqués had to be submitted to Stieber, he played down the losses and suggested victories, if need be. It was ridiculous, he argued, to let the enemy know how many men he had killed because he was sure to know your strength when you began, and by a simple arithmetical calculation could gauge your strength or weakness after engagement. It was equally ridiculous to depress the people at home by telling them how many of their husbands and sons had been killed or were missing or wounded. Such news only distracted them from their essential duty of providing supplies.

As a result of the great success of the Seven Weeks' War Stieber was restored to favor, and appointed a privy councilor. Napoleon I had held the view that an agent was fortunate if he received financial rewards for his labors. Steadfastly he refused to award the Légion d'Honneur to his spy master, Schulmeister, also one of the select band of great spies. The Légion d'Honneur was the only award and reward Schulmeister coveted, and again and again throughout his career he urged his friends to persuade the emperor to bestow it on him. King William, however, was of quite another opinion. He believed that an agent should be awarded the decorations granted to combatant soldiers if his work merited such honors.

Since the removal of Napoleon I from the European scene the fortunes of France had been in a state of flux. After making himself dictator by a *coup d'état* in 1851, President Napoleon had had himself elected emperor by a plebiscite in the following year.

Napoleon III's ineffectual rule, accompanied by many undemocratic restrictions, had set the French seething with restlessness once more. Like other dictators we know of, he decided to embark upon a program of conquests in the hope of deflecting thereby the attention of his subjects from difficulties at home. In this he was encouraged by his ambitious Empress Eugenie, a former Spanish countess.

After allying himself to England in the Crimea between 1854 and 1856, he later won Savoy and Nice by taking sides with Piedmont against Austria. He followed this by adding Algeria, Senegal and Indochina to France's overseas possessions. Encouraged, and ambitious himself, he then announced his intention to push the eastern frontiers of France to the Rhine.

For the next few years he began to prepare the way with a propaganda barrage which did not deceive Bismarck so much as it deceived himself. The Iron Chancellor used the time to make his own preparations.

Soon, however, it looked as if Napoleon, *vis-à-vis* his boastings of what he intended to annex from Prussia, was *vox et praeteria nihil*. Bismarck, who had been planning to give the French the lesson of their lives, felt himself constrained to take action, in which he was helped by Stieber.

By this time the Spanish throne had fallen vacant. Napoleon nominated a candidate; so did King William of Prussia. The Prussian candidate was elected.

Napoleon feared a Prussian-controlled Spain on his southwestern frontier because it raised the ancient and modern bogey of encirclement. He therefore demanded that the Hohenzollern prince should be removed. But when this was not done, still he only blustered. Determined, however, that Napoleon should have his war, Bismarck called on Stieber for aid.

The Prussian king was asked to put the Prussian views to the French ambassador. In those days diplomats did not always use codes, and when the ambassador's telegram to his government was received, as it had to be, by Stieber's censorship department, Stieber withheld a certain portion of it. The resulting message entirely distorted what the king had said. When the telegram was published in France every Frenchman was roused by it to truly Gallic wrath. Pressed by public opinion and assured by his generals that his army was "ready to the last gaiter button" when actually it was badly trained and only partly mobilized,

Napoleon declared war on Prussia. If Napoleon had had half the information about his armed forces that Stieber had, he must have held his hand even then—unless he had been quite crazy.

For the two previous years Stieber had been infiltrating his spies into France until literally every nook and cranny was known to him. He had personally made a thorough tour of the future enemy's terrain, noting all kinds of information likely to be useful to Prussia's military leaders.

No spy master or chief of intelligence had ever gone into a similar task so exhaustively as Stieber. In the invasion zones his agents listed the stock of every single farm, so that when Prussian billeting and mess officers went about their tasks they would know exactly how many cattle, how many sheep, how many chickens and how many eggs Farmer Lebrun could supply for their needs. Stieber kept his lists up-to-date, and if Farmer Lebrun produced five heifers where the list said eight a fortnight before, he was called upon to explain what had happened to the missing three.

Stieber also knew the exact amount of the savings of the leaders of urban and rural communities. The state and dimensions of roads and byroads, the size and capacity of bridges, the sites of stores of arms and ammunition and the type and quantity held in them, numbers and types of transport, sites and strength of strong points—all were listed. Nothing appeared to have escaped him.

He claimed that his agents in France alone numbered forty thousand! The claim cannot be allowed, for such a number would have required a headquarters staff and organization far greater than Stieber maintained at any time. Nevertheless, his army of spies must have exceeded by three or four times, or even more, the number of spies ever employed by any other spy master anywhere in the world at any time up to then. It was a new concept of espionage. As his modern successors were to invent a new type of war—total war—Stieber, a half century earlier, invented what very nearly approached total espionage.

His personal qualities were a blend of tireless application to the task in hand, cunning, subtlety and utter, even

33

ferocious, ruthlessness. He demanded similar qualities in every single one of his agents. He insisted that everyone who was even suspected of having a knowledge of Prussian military strength should be liquidated. He decreed that when a company of Prussian soldiers passed through a village they should be preceded by outriders who were to warn all the inhabitants to get indoors and close their shutters. Any peasant who peeped from behind his shutters while the company passed by was to be seized, tortured and hanged.

But while he demanded such excessive security, Stieber did not complain if sometimes his agents were caught, tortured and hanged. It served them right for being careless.

Stieber was in the closest contact with and deep in the confidence of Bismarck. The Junkers, however, hated him and never missed an opportunity for snubbing him. But no insult seemed to affect him and he compensated his ego by treating the conquered with arrogance, striking terror into them by dire threats which he would have had no compunction in implementing had his victims not capitulated.

The French suffered a defeat at the hands of the Prussians in 1871 which still eats more deeply into the hearts and national pride of Frenchmen than the *débâcle* of 1940.

The Prussians established their headquarters in the Palace of Versailles. Thither the French leader, Jules Favre, was summoned when he expressed the desire, on behalf of his colleagues, to treat for the capitulation of Paris. The Prussians stipulated that Favre must come to Versailles alone, unaccompanied even by a personal servant. He was expected to have discussed the French side of the matter with his colleagues so fully that there would be no necessity for him to refer the Prussian terms to them. It was accepted that he was to be their envoy extraordinary and plenipotentiary, with the emphasis on plenipotentiary.

There is no record of what Favre may have felt about this invitation. But the propaganda of the day had attributed to the brutal and licentious Prussian soldiery the same sort of bestial atrocities which were laid at the door of German soldiers in Belgium in World War I—girls not yet in their teens raped by a score or more at one session, months-old babies impaled on pitchforks or bayonets and held, while still alive, in the flames of the burning thatch of what would have been their homes. But Favre must have wondered what particular brutalities the Prussians at Versailles had in store for him.

His surprise may be judged, therefore, when on arrival at Versailles he was welcomed courteously, if stiffly, by a Prussian colonel and conducted to a pleasant suite of rooms. When the surprise had worn off he doubtless imagined that this was part of the technique. They would lull him with politeness, fair words and creature comforts and then suddenly blast him sky-high when he was least expecting it. But even these thoughts were dispelled when the servant allocated to him to be his valet during his stay at Versailles was brought to him. He saw Gustav Olendorf to be a quiet, graying man in his early fifties whose eyes smiled at him even if his countenance was servant-solemn, who moved quietly about his duties and proved so efficient in his service that Favre would have liked to have engaged him to serve him always.

Favre had brought with him a portfolio which he insisted upon carrying up to his suite himself when the servant who was attending to his baggage would have taken it from him. When the colonel had withdrawn, having impressed upon him that if any of his needs had been overlooked a word to the valet would repair the omission, Favre walked over to the escritoire on the far side of the room between the two great windows and deposited his precious portfolio in it.

"I have prepared a bath for monsieur in the bedroom," the valet informed him in excellent French. "I thought that after the dusty journey from Paris monsieur would find it refreshing."

He followed Favre into the bedroom and helped him off with his clothes and before the Frenchman stepped into the large hip-bath tested the temperature of the water and added a little more cold.

"I understand, monsieur, that tonight monsieur is to be permitted to compose himself," the valet said as he unpacked Favre's valise. "I shall serve dinner in the sitting room. Perhaps monsieur would find it more comfortable if I put out his *robe de chambre* for him?"

"Yes, by all means," replied Favre, thankful that he was to be given the opportunity of sleeping before his meeting with the Iron Chancellor.

Presently the valet excused himself. "I have towels warming," he explained. "I will go and fetch them."

While he was gone Favre wallowed, as far as the dimensions of the bath would allow him, in the pleasant warmth of the water. He chuckled to himself as he remembered his past fears. Perhaps these Prussians were not so bad after all; perhaps they would not be too excessive in their demands? That valet was the devil of a time gone! Surely he wasn't warming the towels at the other end of the palace? Ah, there he was!

The valet returned, deftly soaped and rinsed the envoy extrordinary and plenipotentiary and held up a towel as large as a sheet, which he wrapped round him as he stepped from the bath. When the Frenchman was dry the valet held out his *robe de chambre* for him, placed his slippers conveniently and put ready his tasseled nightcap.

Dinner was excellent. The bottle of Château Neuf du Pape could not have been better chosen. As the valet hovered discreetly at his side, anticipating his wants, he chatted goodnaturedly with the man. Where did he live? Was he married? How many children had he? Any grandchildren? He, Favre, had five. Where had he learned to speak French so well? Was he glad that his country had defeated France? But that was not a fair question. He had no wish to embarrass the good fellow.

After dinner Favre seated himself in an armchair by the fire and the valet placed a bottle of cognac and a glass by his side.

"Has monsieur any orders?"

"Bring me my portfolio from the escritoire, if you please, and then I have nothing more," Favre told him. "Try to find out what time the conference is tomorrow and wake me in good time."

"Certainly, monsieur. And if monsieur has any need of

anything now or later, if monsieur rings I will come at once. My room is *à côté*."

"Thank you. But I'm sure there will be nothing. Good night."

"Good night, monsieur."

When he was alone, Favre poured himself a glass of brandy, took a sip and then opened his portfolio. From it he took a sheaf of papers. They were minutes of the fateful meetings with his colleagues, and *aides-memoires,* and the proposed French terms, the progressive phases through which he was to negotiate until the limit was reached. For the dozenth time he went over them, refreshing his memory, almost learning them off by heart.

At eleven o'clock he put them away in the portfolio, yawned and stretched, placed the portfolio in the escritoire, locked it and pocketed the key. Then he went to bed.

It was almost midday when he awoke next morning as the valet pulled back the curtains and let in the high-noon sun. He sat up in bed, slightly alarmed.

"What time is the conference?" he demanded.

"His excellency sends his compliments, monsieur, but pressing affairs prevent his excellency from meeting monsieur today. The conference is postponed until tomorrow."

"Pressing affairs?" Favre began. "But what is more pressing . . . Oh, well!" He resigned himself to the twenty-four hours of idleness; and after the tiring regime of the last weeks he was not sorry.

The valet attended him as impeccably as ever. The fellow had dark shadows under his eyes as though he had not slept. But if he had not slept, lack of sleep did not seem to impair his service.

Next morning the valet awakened him at nine.

"His excellency asks you to meet him at eleven o'clock," he said, looking even more drawn and haggard.

Precisely at eleven the envoy extraordinary and plenipotentiary entered the conference room and found himself face to face with his country's greatest enemy.

"Pray be seated, Monsieur Favre," Prince Otto von Bismarck invited him.

Favre sat down, put his portfolio on the table before him and opened it. Before he had had time to withdraw the papers the Prussian chancellor began to speak. As Favre listened, with every minute that passed he found himself growing more and more amazed and bewildered. It was a miracle! Bismarck apparently knew everything that had passed between him and his colleagues.

There was no argument, no negotiation. How could there be, when all his bargaining power had been vitiated by the foreknowledge of this stern man? He signed, and returned to Paris bewildered; so bewildered that he overtipped the valet.

In Paris Favre reported to his colleagues, who shared his amazement at his revelations. But neither Favre nor his colleagues nor anyone else except the "valet" and Bismarck would ever know what had happened until, many years later, the "valet" wrote his *Reminiscences*.

In recounting this episode, Stieber says: "I often wonder what Favre's reactions would have been had he known that the valet who helped him with his bath and served him his dinner was none other than I, Wilhelm Stieber, minister of police and chief of espionage.

"When I went to fetch the towels which I had warming, I went to the escritoire where I had seen Favre put his portfolio. It was not then locked. I took a quick glimpse at the papers, sufficient to show me what they were. Then when Favre had gone to bed I opened the escritoire with a duplicate key and sat down to copy out all the papers which were in the porfolio.

"But as the new day broke I had finished only two-thirds of my task. I hurried to the chancellor, taking what I had, and explaining the rest. Prince Bismarck said that he must have the rest and to put off the meeting until tomorrow, which would give me the opportunity of finishing the work that night.

"So throughout the second night I worked until half past four. By the time for the meeting, the chancellor had read and mastered the documents.

"I remember standing at the top of the steps watching the carriage taking Favre back to Paris disappear in the distance, and though almost overcome with weariness from lacking two nights' sleep, I could not help but smile as I yawned and clinked the coins which he had given me in my hand."

Among the prisoners taken by the Prussians was a certain General de Cissy. Though a bad general, de Cissy had been an active man and he found the restrictions of his confinement exceptionally irksome. Like the majority of regular soldiers, he had no secular resources. But as a Frenchman, he had a liking for one diversion above all others, in common with his compatriots.

Under the existing code of treatment for prisoners of war, and particularly for prisoners so elevated as General de Cissy, the conditions of confinement were much more refined than they are under the Geneva Convention today.

Then it was not held against a prisoner if he gave his parole not to escape in return for certain privileges. Parole, once given, was accepted at its face value by the detaining power and was regarded as binding on the honor of the prisoner.

Having given his parole, therefore, General de Cissy was permitted a certain freedom of movement in the city of Hamburg, which was the place of his imprisonment. Looking round for an object of diversion, his choice fell upon a very beautiful young German aristocrat, the Baroness de Kaulla.

Despite his advanced years, or perhaps because of the long experience those advanced years had bestowed on him, the general was an ardent wooer and a skillful lover. The baroness, not entirely inexperienced herself, knew a good lover when she met one, and the liaison settled down into a *modus vivendi* which both participants found entirely satisfactory.

In the course of time the general was released from captivity and returned to France, though there were occasions, after he had been informed that he was to be released and before his actual departure for the motherland, when it had seemed that he would never be able to part from the consolation which he found to be so devoutly to be desired. However, patriotism prevailed even over love despite Chaucer's prioress' pronouncement, *Amor vincit omnia*; and patriotism was rewarded. The general was appointed minister for war.

By 1875 the French were harboring thoughts of revenge on the Prussians. The armed forces were being reorganized; the chiefs of staff were planning the campaign to come.

As his excellency left the war ministry one evening at the close of a long day's devotion to preparations for revenge, an urchin ran up to him and, thrusting a note into his hand, after making certain that he was General de Cissy, ran off into the dimness of the street.

Puzzled, General de Cissy returned to the lobby of the ministry where there was a light by which he might read. He slit open the envelope clumsily and withdrew a sheet of paper and scarcely comprehending what it meant read that the Baroness de Kaulla had come to Paris and was waiting for him at the Hôtel des Étoiles, now alas no more.

In the weeks and months that followed, the frantic idyl of Hamburg was renewed. Madame de Kaulla moved into an apartment of her own and engaged servants. Like most regular soldiers the general had little money besides his not very princely salary. She waved his regrets aside. She had money to spare and was prepared to spend the last *sou* for the consolation of his love.

As soon as his work was done he hurried to her apartment. Often he was weary with grappling with the plans which must be prepared; often perplexed by the problems which confronted him without any visible solution. His mistress received him with an embrace, drew off his coat, drew off his boots, drew him gently down to the sofa, put up his feet and brought him a glass of champagne. Then, sitting on a footstool beside him, she would soothe his hot brow with her cool hands while he discussed his problems with her. It was even more banal than these words!

But among the reorganized units of the French armed forces special attention was being paid to secret service. French espionage and counterespionage had once been among the most successful secret services in Europe. But after the great heights to which Napoleon I's spy master, Schulmeister, had brought it, it had fallen into decay, like many other institutions of the empire. Now it had been decided that Stieber must be fought with his own weapon.

So, before many months had passed, the general's and the baroness' idyl was brought to a rude termination by the intervention of the deadly prosaic *deuxième bureau*. The bureau had discovered that Stieber had become aware of the Hamburg liaison and when the general had returned to France and been appointed to high office he had threatened the baroness with the promise of awful consequences to her family if she would not agree to go to Paris and renew her *affaire* with her admirably situated lover.

This was perhaps the one occasion on which Stieber's flair for reading character let him down. There was no need for threats. The basis of the baroness' relationship with the general was purely sensual. On that account she could even overlook the little matter of his being French. She was quite prepared to do as Stieber asked so long as he made it worth her while. Delighted with such sweet reasonableness, Stieber, who was never stingy with his agents, excelled himself in the allowance he gave her.

So she had come to Paris, and before she was deported at the instance of the *deuxième bureau* she had supplied Stieber with such full information regarding French plans and intentions that the French never recovered the lost ground and revenge had to be forgotten.

Stieber employed many women among his agents: barmaids, waitresses, domestic servants and prostitutes. The Baroness de Kaulla was not the only women of aristocratic antecedents, if no less doubtful morals, whose name figured on his payroll, though she is, perhaps, the most famous of them.

After the Franco-Prussian War had terminated, Stieber set about organizing a system of permanent resident spies abroad on a scale never before conceived.

Waiters in foreign hotels, workers in factories, hairdressers, itinerant German bands, prostitutes of particular skills which made them attractive to the jaded sexual palates of high-ranking naval and military personnel and civil servants, all had their place in his organization. Money was poured into the project on a scale comparable—when the results achieved by both in their effect on world activities in their own day and age are taken into account—with the vast sums being spent by the American government on atomic research. All Europe was aware of the existence of Stieber's secret army, impressed and frightened by it; and, for the most part, did little to counteract it.

Within Prussia itself Stieber's secret police were almost as numerous, and certainly as ubiquitous. There were many citizens who were discontented with the doctrine known as the "Prussian Idea." This doctrine aimed at suppressing completely and utterly the liberty of the individual. (Had the Nazis any really new ideas and practices at all?)

Many victims of the "Idea" could visualize only one way of restoring individual freedom—the permanent removal of its chief exponents: the emperor and his chancellor. In his later years Stieber, as minister of police, was constantly being called on to protect his masters from assassination. To deal with this situation Stieber introduced yet another of his innovations, a diabolical plan but one which illustrates how clearly he understood the characters and weaknesses of his enemies.

In Berlin Stieber set up an establishment to which he gave the name, The Green House. To say that it was a brothel owned by the minister of police and therefore enjoying complete police protection may be startling enough. But Stieber's Green House was much worse, much more evil than a brothel.

Selecting his permanent staff with great care, he chose women skillful in pandering to all known male sexual aberrations and capable of responding with equal skill to any that might be conjured up by a particularly abnormal imagination or craving. Besides such women, he enlisted the services of boys and men, and those knowledgeable in the use of drugs such as opium and hashish.

Then choosing his clientéle with equal care, he introduced to The Green House men in high positions, judges, front-rank civil servants, leaders of society, including at least one royal prince, and men whom his underworld grapevine had informed him either were or were suspected of being anti-monarchist conspirators or opponents of the "Prussian Idea." No man could visit this establishment without an introduction from Stieber.

He did not necessarily give the introduction himself, but selected his victim and had the existence of The Green House brought to his notice; in the case of a man whom he knew to have unusual appetites by one of his lesser minions approaching him in a quiet, dark street and, after a brief muttered conversation, thrusting a card of introduction into his hand; or by one of his own high officers, who would strike up an acquaintance with the man and at the close of a convivial evening suggest a visit to a new brothel he knew of.

These latter victims were generally normal men. If they refused the invitation once, a kind of pressure was put on them until they did accept. But Stieber has said that very few did not take up the first invitation.

The madame of The Green House had already been primed as to the guest's special proclivities. If he was already indulging in any depraved behavior he was matched with a partner skilled in that special behavior, and who could intensify his appetites by allied but more advanced wantonness.

Men of normal appetites were allowed to satisfy themselves normally and then, little by little, they would be introduced to variations from the normal until eventually, scarcely conscious of what was happening to them, they would suddenly discover that without the ministrations of The Green House they could not be satisfied. The same pattern was followed with those who were drug addicts already, while those who were not were transformed into addicts.

Briefly, Stieber took the depraved and thrust them ever deeper into depravity; while he took the normal and turned them into depraved beasts. Once the transformation had been achieved he began to turn the screw.

There was nowhere else in Berlin, nowhere else in

43

Germany, perhaps nowhere else in Europe, where the habitués of The Green House could obtain the relief they could get there. When this point was reached, Stieber suddenly confronted them and threatened both to cut off supplies and facilities and to let their families and friends know what they were doing, unless—

The "unless" in the case of civil servants meant revealing all the secrets of their departments, knowledge of which would place Stieber in a position of power in Prussia second only to, if not on a par with, Bismarck himself. In the case of antimonarchists and those opposed to the "Prussian Idea," it meant identifying their fellows and their conspiracies.

There were a few who preferred to commit suicide rather than to betray, but these, compared with those who told Stieber all they knew, and acquired information for him, were an infinitesimal number. Though Stieber has admitted in his *Reminiscences* that he could have acquired the information by normal espionage, the success of The Green House exceeded all his hopes. He maintains that The Green House was quicker and surer than normal methods, and that he could never have obtained the power over the individuals that he did acquire in any other way.

The Green House was one of Stieber's later innovations. He outlived William I and remained in office after Bismarck had been dismissed.

Some time before he retired and settled down to write his *Reminiscences,* after fifty years' service as a spy, he received in 1876 a visit from some strange little men with almond shaped eyes who had come from the other side of the world.

They had come to him, they said, because they had been told by Prussian officers who were helping to organize and train their army, that Prussia had the finest espionage system in the world. Where they lived, they also had enemies, and they realized that their main protection against those enemies would be to know their intentions and secrets. This they might achieve only by espionage. But they had no espionage system; and if they were to organize such a system, naturally it would be foolish not to have the best. Would he advise them, and perhaps teach them his system?

Stieber, though a Saxon by birth, was a Prussian by environment and inclination. He had all the Prussian arrogance and pride, and a weakness for flattery. His *Reminiscences* are most revealing of traits. But his pride in his espionage system was not without justification, and the Japanese had not erred in going to him. Stieber would advise the Japanese; he would explain to them his espionage system in all its ramifications, even The Green House.

He found them apt pupils, and before he died in 1892 he had seen them introduce his system, with modifications and even some innovations, into their sphere of influence as effectively as he had battened down Europe with his own spies and counterspies.

CHAPTER 3

Background to Espionage

While Wilhelm Stieber was defending his underdogs in the petty courts of Berlin and saving his king from the violence of the Berlin mob, while he rode through Austria peddling his sacred statuettes and his pornographic drawings and was counting the chickens of Farmer Lebrun in France, while he was learning the secrets of General de Cissy and trapping his opponents in the depravities of The Green House, on the other side of the world in an archipelago of islands known as Nippon, or the Land of the Rising Sun, a phenomenon was emerging.

Nippon, or Japan, as it was soon to become universally known, had been a secret land for many centuries. It had kept itself cut off from the rest of the world except for a few

Dutch traders and some Buddhist monks who brought their religion from Korea.

It had an emperor who was considered by his people to be a god, and people who considered themselves to be children of the sun goddess. They believed that their country was the fairest on the earth, since it had been created by the gods, and themselves to be the chosen people of the gods, since they had been put there to inhabit it.

In the middle of the nineteenth century they were still a feudal state. But though the emperor was their grand seigneur, they were ruled by self-appointed tenants-in-chief, called shoguns. Below the shoguns were the lesser orders of tenants, the daimio, or barons, and the samurai, or knights, the hereditary bearers of arms. Below them came the serfs, the farmers, the merchants and the peasants. Their economy was tied to the rice production.

They were not an inspired people. They had taken their language, their form of writing, their philosophy, even one of their religions, from the ancient civilized Chinese. They had been torn by civil wars for more than four hundred and fifty years until, in 1600, the power was seized by a family called the Tokugawa, who, at the end of fifteen years of ridding themselves of their enemies, brought real peace at last to their country.

With peace, the Tokugawa shoguns reorganized the basis of their power, not on armed force, but by controlling the economy, by making the emperor even more of a recluse than he had ever been before, holding him completely incommunicado from all the daimio, and by clipping the power of the daimio by various means.

Peace brought inevitable changes to the social structure of the country, for it had a direct effect on the role of the samurai, the fighting men. Since the samurai were allowed to follow no other profession but arms, and since there was no longer any opportunity for practicing their profession because of the restrictions laid upon the daimio, their employers, they found themselves with nothing to do. The shoguns, therefore, encouraged them to turn to scholarship, and this in turn gave rise to an intellectual class, destined to produce a highly refined and artistic civilization.

Under the Tokugawa the merchants began to flourish as never before. Soon the wealth of the country began to flow into their hands and strict sumptuary laws had to be introduced to control them. But these laws they managed to evade, even as they evaded paying their taxes.

These new developments could very easily have undermined the authority of the shogunate. The Tokugawa shoguns realized this. Fearing most of all the conjunction of the internal changes with the few outside contacts they had, in 1639 the shogun closed Japan to all foreigners except the Chinese and the Dutch.

Now while the peace which the Tokugawa shoguns brought to the country provided suitable conditions for the development of a national culture, the strict closure of Japan to all foreigners had a restricting influence on the general development of the nation. For at this time Western culture was bursting into full flower, and the exclusion of those European merchants who had just begun to take an interest in this strange country denied to Japan the inevitable influences which they would have brought with them.

Eventually the country ran into financial difficulties. Forced loans were levied on the merchants and the coinage was debased, thereby creating inflation. The economy was soon completely undermined and the sufferings this brought with it led to agrarian uprisings.

In fact, everything was against the shoguns, and gradually a movement was created to end the exclusion of Western merchants, which was seen to be the cause not only of the economic disasters now falling on the nation, but of the general retarding of the nation's medical, scientific, artistic and military resources. But even without this internal movement, outside factors and influences would ultimately have broken down the barriers.

In the late eighteenth century the Russians were becoming more and more active on their Pacific seaboard and in Kamchatka, Sakhalin and the Kurile Islands. Then

Western trade with this part of the world began to expand, accentuating Japan's position, which was further accentuated by the appearance of the steamship in the middle of the nineteenth century, with its need for bunkering facilities. But it was the Chinese defeat in the First British-Sino War which inserted the thin end of the wedge.

The shoguns were impressed, and though still determined to keep their country closed, in 1842 they did at least open up specific ports to foreign ships for taking on water and supplies.

The necessity for opening up Japan had been in the minds of the Americans ever since 1815, but it was not until 1846 that Commodore Biddle arrived in Edo Bay to attempt negotiations. The commodore's politeness the Japanese construed as weakness, and his mission failed.

Then on July 8th, 1853, Commodore Perry sailed into Edo Bay with a strong squadron. Going ashore with an impressive guard, he presented a letter from President Fillmore demanding trading rights, bunkering stations and protection for shipwrecked American sailors. Remaining with his squadron in the bay for a week so that the Japanese should have no mistaken ideas of American strength, he then sailed away, announcing that he would return in the spring of 1854 for an answer.

The American letter caused considerable consternation at the shogunate. So perturbed were the authorities that they took the unheard-of step of sending a translation of it to each daimio, asking for opinions. The daimio advice was that the demands should be resisted to the last degree, short of war. But when Perry returned in 1854 and made it quite clear that it was either a treaty or war, the Japanese yielded and on March 31st the Treaty of Kanagawa was signed.

Once opened to trade, it could only be a matter of time before foreign cultural influences made themselves felt. This process was hastened by the willingness of young samurai to risk death for a chance of acquiring knowledge, for an edict of 1636, forbidding all Japanese to leave Japan, was still in force.

Within a short time the Americans, English and French

had insisted on wider treaties. These, signed in 1858, granted to the United States, France and England the right to establish supply bases for their navies at Yokohama, Hakodate and Nagasaki.

Their signature was the sign for outbursts of antishogun and antiforeign feelings which were soon translated into actions. Those daimio who secretly had long been opposed to the Tokugawa shogunate defied the shogun's orders and went direct to the immured emperor. Foreigners were attacked and British and American officials assassinated. In 1863 the United States Legation at Edo was burned down.

In June of that year the shogun, who had been summoned to Kyoto by the emperor, was compelled to issue an imperial order to drive all the foreigners out of the country. One daimio, the lord of Choshu, attempted to obey the order and fired on ships passing through the Straits of Shimonoseki, which were in his demesne.

The British retaliated immediately by bombarding the capital of Satsuma. The following month, September, an Allied fleet destroyed the Choshu forts. Impressed by this, the Satsuma and Choshu daimio began to press for a policy of Westernization.

Under the pressure of these events the shogun was deprived of much of his authority. The process was continued until, in November 1867, the governing shogun, who had not long succeeded to the shogunate on the death of his father, handed his resignation to the young Emperor Meiji.

Early in January 1868 direct imperial rule was re-established and the former shogun was ordered to surrender all his demesnes. The new regime spent the first few years in making numerous changes in the administrative structure. The senior posts were divided among the court nobles and daimio, but the actual exercise of power came into the hands of a very capable and ambitious group of samurai. Thus, from the very beginning of her modern history, we see that the military clique were a great power in Japan.

On April 6th, 1868, the emperor, in an ancient ritual,

announced a charter oath to the nation's ancestral gods and goddesses. This oath was entirely revolutionary in its concepts and paved the way for the reforms which were rapidly effected. Its fifth clause, by implication, forbade antiforeign feeling and activity and directly foreshadowed a policy of Westernization.

Important among the first reforms were those reorganizing the social structure, those permitting freedom of movement throughout the country to all, the right of farmers to plant any crops they wished, the right of every man to choose his own profession, the withdrawal of the right of vendetta from the samurai and the guarantee to all men, of whatever class, of equality before the law.

The social reforms abolished the military caste system, and this made it necessary for new armed forces to be developed. It was in this sphere that Western ideas were first adopted.

In our understanding of the Japanese character as we shall see it at work, we must take note very carefully of another tool forged in this period.

The religion which the Japanese had invented to meet the requirements of their beliefs about themselves, and which was peculiar to Japan, was known as Shintoism. We have referred briefly to the Japanese claim to be of direct divine descent. This cult was started by Jimmu, who made himself first emperor in 660 B.C. Jimmu claimed to be the great-great-great-grandson of the sun goddess, who was herself the daughter of the creators of heaven and earth.

When the earth was created out of chaos, the sun goddess's grandson was sent down, with a suitable retinue, to govern it, and made landfall on Mount Takachiho, in Japan, which was the first country to be formed. At the foot of this mountain Jimmu was born, and passed his youth and early manhood.

The emperors of Japan, including the present emperor, Hirohito, have all, therefore, sprung from divine parentage; and despite the repudiation of divinity by Hirohito under orders from General MacArthur, vast numbers of his subjects still refuse, in 1956, to surrender what has been for them, for twenty-five centuries, one of the basic dogmas of their religion.

Since Japan was the first country to be created, this automatically made it the most beautiful country on earth, the country chosen by the gods before all others and, therefore, together with the person of the emperor, to be revered by its inhabitants.

The people themselves were also of divine descent, though in lesser degrees, since they were the descendants of the retinue of the grandson of the sun goddess when he came down to Mount Takachiho. This, of course, was as it should be, for only those of divine descent could be worthy inhabitants of the country chosen by the gods.

These ideas, as with the Hebrew concept of the chosen people, were kept flourishing by the national religion which sprang from them. Shintoism, which means The Way of the Gods, was accepted with unquestioning faith by all classes and ranks of Japanese. Its basic principles were ancestor worship and nature worship.

At the head of the deities—gods and goddesses who numbered many hundreds of thousands—was the sun goddess. After her, since they were her direct descendants, were all the past emperors and the present occupant of the imperial throne. Then came deified spirits of dead warriors and scholars who, by their deeds and works, had added glory to the country and people. After them came a man's own ancestors.

Mountains and rivers, earthquakes and storms, winds and seas, fire and floods—all that was beautiful and terrible in nature—were given their places in the divine hierarchy. They were worshiped with no less devotion and awe because they could be seen, touched and experienced.

So deeply ingrained in the national character did Shintoism become that when Korean missionaries brought Buddhism to Japan in the sixth century A.D., in order to impress the benefits of their religion on the Japanese people they decided to assimilate Shintoism rather than attempt to replace it. This was a brilliant move, for it made possible, two centuries later, what was the most wholesale, and most amazing, conversion in the religious history of mankind. The Japanese court, and the people *en masse,* accepted Buddhism—and at the same time continued to practice Shintoism.

From the late eighteenth century it had been a revival of Shintoism which had been one of the chief factors working for the overthrow of the shogunate. To concentrate the loyalty of the people on the emperor and government, there could clearly be no better device than a religion which was as ancient as the race and in its dogmas so ready-made to achieve this object. But to be most useful to the regime Shintoism had to be lopped of its Buddhist outgrowths, and an attempt was made to do this. It was soon discovered, however, that the two religions were so interlocked in the average Japanese mind that the attempt was dropped lest Shintoism should be harmed.

Instead, the authorities began attempts to establish a new state religion in which emphasis was placed on the divinity of the emperor. The attempts were extremely successful. By 1930 the new religion, known as State Shintoism, had more than 15,000 priests and more than 100,000 shrines, the chief of which was the Grand Shrine at Ise, dedicated to the sun goddess.

No matter to what religion he belonged, attendance at these shrines was the yardstick by which the loyalty of every Japanese to his emperor and country was measured. The educational system—originally modeled on the French, and subsequently on the German systems—and propaganda were employed to disseminate the state religion.

It had three basic tenets, and it is these which must be constantly borne in mind in any consideration of Japan's activities from the Meiji Reformation in 1868 down to 1945. The tenets were:

1. The emperor is divine and derives his divinity from his great divine ancestors, possessing particularly the physical and spiritual attributes of the sun goddess.
2. The gods have Japan under their special protection. Therefore, its people and its very soil and every institution pertaining to it are superior to all others.

3. These attributes place upon Japan a divine mission to bring the whole world under one roof, so that all humanity may share the advantages of being ruled by the divine emperor.

In (3), in a nutshell, is Japan's foreign policy, for the fulfillment of which her domestic policy was fashioned and geared from the moment of awakening.

When Commodore Perry presented his ultimatum in 1853, Japan was 250 years behind the Western civilizations in almost every facet of national existence, and particularly so in her economic and industrial structure. The Meiji leaders realized the importance of having a modern economic structure, and realized too that this could only be based upon a modern industrial structure.

In the last years of its existence, the shogunate had arrived at something like the same point of view and before 1860 a shipbuilding yard and an arsenal had been established. By 1866 English cotton spinning machinery and technical instructors had been imported and a beginning had been made of the famous Yokusuka Naval Yard.

These establishments the Meiji leaders took over and added developments of their own—silk reeling, tiles, cement, woolens and bleaching powder, all of which were intended to be guides for future private enterprise. Postal and telegraph services were set up in 1871, and by 1893 2,000 miles of railway tracks had been laid. The Bank of Japan was founded in 1882, and within twenty-five years an extensive modern banking system was in full operation.

Almost it seems at the wave of a wand such an amazing advance had been made in the textile industry, due to cheap machinery and cheap female labor, that Japan was supplying one-quarter of the world's cotton yarn. An almost comparable advance was made in the heavy industries and the manufacture of machine tools. The merchant marine also expanded steadily and the shipbuilding industry was capable of building warships before the outbreak of World War I.

Side by side with these industrial and economic developments the army, under the expert tuition of

German officers, and the navy, under no less expert guidance, had been transformed into fighting services almost equal to those of any Western power. The institution of these services rounded off the Japanese picture, so that we see the amazing phenomenon of a medieval state emerging completely as an industrial and military power within the space of a single generation.

Her new condition naturally produced for Japan a number of serious considerations. Overriding all, of course, was the injunction laid upon them by the third tenet of State Shintoism, to "bring the whole world under one roof"—the Japanese roof. No time limit had been set for the achievement of this by divine ordinance, but she now found that being a modern power placed cheek by jowl with the ancient conditions on the mainland of China presented her with responsibilities toward herself.

China had once been the great Asiatic power in the Pacific. Though now on her last legs, there were indications that she was not going to surrender her position to upstart Japan without a struggle, however ineffective that struggle might be.

A much more serious threat, however, came from the Russians in Siberia. Naturally, they saw in Japan a rival to the power which they themselves hoped to achieve, and had to a certain extent already achieved, in the northern Pacific. They were even now regarding the confusion in Manchuria and Korea with conspiratorial eyes. An expansion of their influence in these countries would greatly weaken Japan's own position.

It was not only a weakening in her political position which Japan saw in the challenge of both China and Russia. If the influence of both or either, and particuarly Russia, expanded, this would constitute a direct and serious threat to her economic position and strength. The Asian mainland was the obvious market near at hand for her products. If Russia should at any time exclude her from this market she would be dealt a blow that would stunt her growth, with very serious consequences.

So, both from the point of view of divine command and from the more realistic view of economic security, China and Russia were the obvious enemies. Not until the threat of both was removed would Japan be able to breathe freely in the direction of the Asiatic mainland. To remove the threat would require recourse to physical measures; in other words, there would have to be war. She had the army and the navy for this very purpose.

But while they were teaching her to organize and administer a modern army, her German helpers were also impressing on her the need for preparation before waging war; and a particular instrument of this preparation, as the Germans knew very well from personal experience, was espionage.

Japan was not entirely ignorant of espionage. Under the autocratic shogunate it had been absolutely necessary to employ agents to keep an eye on would-be rebels. Though she had cut herself off from the outside world, she had not been so foolish as to keep herself in ignorance of what was happening in China and had sent a few agents there. But this espionage was something quite different from the form and scope which the German military instructors were advising. There was soundness in their arguments, too. If Bismarck could build an empire using espionage as one of his chief agents, if Napoleon I had won his victories by careful espionage preparation, then Japan must have such an instrument to pave the way for her own future, inevitable warlike activities in Asia.

Since she would be beginning from scratch and had all the world to choose from, she could choose the best. And the best at this time in the field of espionage was Wilhelm Stieber's system. So, as we have seen, in the middle seventies they sent pupils to Stieber, and he and his assistants taught them all they knew about espionage.

The Japanese in every other aspect of their development had been copyists entirely, though copyists *par excellence*. Wilhelm Stieber had been an inventor and innovator in the realm of espionage, up to this time without peer. Yet, curiously enough, the Japanese were to introduce innovations into the art of spying which were to outclass some of Stieber's; and one of the most important of these innovations was the patriotic societies.

CHAPTER 4

Accent on Patriotism

Fuzzo Hattori was fifteen years old. He was a child of the New Japan, having been born in 1878.

His father was an artisan employed in the Yokusuka Naval Yard, skilled with his hands but not overintelligent.

His mother was the daughter of a small shopkeeper and still bore the traces of her young beauty, though she was long past the age when Japanese women surrender themselves to the care of their families rather than to the pleasures of their husbands. She was an obedient wife. She had been brought up to be that. She was content if she could feed and clothe her children. That was the sum total of her ambitions for, like her husband, her intellect was not sharp.

As often happens in the union of a not wildly intelligent couple, one member of the family, the fourth son, the young Hattori, was quick-witted, keen-minded, deep-thinking. Though only in his early teens, he had for some time been displaying these surprising qualities.

One spring day in 1893—the retired Wilhelm Stieber was at this time coming to the end of his *Reminiscences* and of his life—Fuzzo Hattori, in a brief period of leisure, took his new kite to the park for its maiden trials. It was not good weather to give the kite a fair test, for the breeze was light, and he had not properly gauged his toy's balance. As he struggled with it with growing annoyance, attempting to correct its erratic sideways oscillation, suddenly a voice behind him said: "Let me try, young man."

Turning, Hattori saw a little plump gentleman smiling at him and holding out his hand for the string.

"If you wish, sir," the boy answered, and gave the little

gentleman the string. But the little gentleman was no more successful than he had been.

"Did you make it yourself?" the stranger asked presently.

"Yes, sir."

"You've got the thing top-heavy. You must shave the support at the top. I used to be an expert maker of kites when I was a boy. Come home with me and I'll show you how to do it."

The boy hesitated. He had heard of boys being picked up in parks by middle-aged gentlemen. He wasn't like that. He already had his eye on his neighbor's thirteen-year-old third daughter, who visited him in his sleep and did unrelatable things to him.

"Oh, come!" the stranger said, as if reading his thoughts. "You have nothing to fear from me. I have six sons of my own." And he smiled his smile and the boy was reassured, and a few minutes later he was taking his first ricksha ride, sitting beside the little gentleman.

"What is your name?" the man asked.

"Fuzzo Hattori, sir."

"Mine is Mitsuri Toyama."

Toyama watched the boy to see if his name meant anything to him and saw that it did not.

At the house, Toyama took the boy into his study, and for the next hour they worked together on the kite; and as they worked, the man questioned the boy about his parents and his home, his work and his interests, and made the discovery which the older Hattoris had made—that for the son of a poor family the boy was a freak, that he had brains.

When at last the boy had to go, Toyama invited him to come to his house again, and there was something in the man which unconsciously attracted the boy. He promised to return. In a short time the visits became weekly occurrences, and later, twice or thrice weekly. On these visits Toyama would offer the boy tea and he would talk. As he talked, the boy listened attentively. Toyama spoke of the new Japan, and of the third tenet of State Shintoism, and of the future that lay ahead.

"We must bring the benefits of our divine emperor's rule and our own superior way of life to all the other people of the world," Toyama said. "It is the will of the gods. It will take a long time and will be a hard struggle, for our enemies will resist with all their might. So we must make a start now and use every effort to prepare ourselves for joining battle."

The boy nodded, and the man went on: "First we must make ourselves strong and rich and powerful. This we shall do by building up our industries and our army and navy. But while we are doing this we must also be finding out all we can about our enemies."

And on another occasion: "Every Japanese man and woman must dedicate himself and herself to this task. Every woman by bearing and rearing all the children which her husband can beget upon her. In this way we shall have the people for our factories and our armies."

Toyama's precept was so heeded by the people that between 1874 and 1913, that is, in a generation and a half, the population of the Japanese archipelago rose from 27,000,000 to 51,000,000, or nearly double. In the old days Japanese women had been the most successful and entensive practitioners of birth control at a time when the women of the West, even the prostitutes, were for the most part ignorant and innocent of any feminine method of contraception, and the men only knew *coitus interruptus,* which the majority of them refused to practice.

Toyama went on: "Every man must devote all his talents and his energies to the help of the fatherland. He must do so not in any spirit of seeking rewards for himself. His reward will be when he holds, subject to his will and to his favors, all the other peoples of the world."

The picture he painted was an inspiring one, and with all that he said the boy found himself in full agreement and was prepared to dedicate himself to his country.

"First," said Toyama, "we must control those enemies nearest to us. China is decadent and weak and will cause no trouble. But Russia is another matter. She recognizes the weakness and decadence of China and intends to expand her own influence over that foolish country. It is

Russia whom we must first subdue, and to do this it is now that we must begin to discover her weaknesses."

Then one day the boy made a discovery. He could not get to Toyama's house quickly enough, and when he arrived he burst into his friend's study and threw himself at his feet.

"Honorable sir! Why did you not tell me?" he asked.

Toyama put out his hand and, cupping the boy's chin, lifted up his face.

"What should I have told you?" he asked in his turn, smiling.

"That you are the founder of *Genoysha*," the boy said.

He beckoned the boy to the cushions beside him.

"Yes," he said. "I am the founder of *Genoysha*."

Half a dozen years before, in the late 1880's, Mitsuri Toyama had hit upon the means of putting into practice his theories of discovering the weaknesses of the Russians. Calling together a number of his rich and influential friends, to whom he expounded his ideas, he invited them to join in the founding of a patriotic society which would put his thoughts into deeds.

Without a single dissentient, his friends agreed, and there came into being the first example of one aspect of Japanese espionage organization, though it has a near relationship with the revolutionary societies which flourished in Russia under the later tsars. As time passed these patriotic societies, as they were called, were to become one of the most important features of Japanese espionage activities.

Toyama and his friends gave their society the name of *Genoysha,* which means The Black Ocean Society. They took the name from the strip of water which separates Kiyushu from the mainland and is called *Genkainada,* the Black Sea. The patriotic societies were secret only insofar as their specific activities were concerned. They were known to the public and their general objects were proclaimed, but their methods and their results were jealously guarded from the public eye and ear.

"Tell me about *Genoysha*," Hattori said.

"*Genoysha*," replied its founder, "has an eight-pronged

59

program which is aimed at discovering and exploiting the weaknesses of our enemies the Russians. If I tell you more, you must swear by the sun goddess herself that you will never divulge what I say to another living soul."

"I swear by the sun goddess, our divine emperor and by all my ancestors!" Hattori assured him solemnly.

"In Sinkiang and Russian Central Asia, we have been told," Toyama went on, "the people are in great distress because of the financial and taxation policies of the administration. The people are unsettled and have many grievances. We have sent men, whom we have trained, into these areas to discover the true facts and how, if they prove to be true, we may use them for setting the people against their masters.

"Other men we have sent to study the agricultural system of that region and how it may be improved. When the society is satisfied that this, too, can be used as a weapon against the Russians, we shall contribute money which will be used to ensure a progressive development there. As soon as the people see what we can do for them they will turn to Japan for guidance and forsake the Russians. Naturally, the Russians will resist, but with the people on our side Japan's task will be easier.

"Yet other men we have sent to explore the defenses of Russia, Tibet, Burma and India in Central Asia. At the same time they are to study and report on the conditions of the roads.

"All our agents, as we call them, on whatever work they are engaged, are to seek out and make friends with the Moslem and Buddhist priests in those areas. Through them, when the time comes for Japan to begin her struggle, we shall have the support of their followers. They are also to make contact with the local and Chinese nomadic groups for the same purpose, and with important personages who may be useful to us."

He paused and looked at the boy, who was regarding him in wonder.

"It is a great work," Hattori said. "I should like to be an agent of *Genoysha*."

So the day had come at last, the day for which Toyama

had been working ever since that afternoon when, while helping the boy with his kite, he discovered him to be intelligent, quick-witted and serious.

"And so you shall," he said simply. "How old are you now?"

"I am sixteen and one month, sir."

"When you are seventeen you can begin."

And for the rest of Hattori's visit they laid plans.

Within a month Hattori had married the third daughter of his neighbor, and Toyama, who gave as his wedding gift a sum of money such as Hattori's father had never dreamed of and a promise of a monthly payment should Hattori ever have to go "on a journey" for him, was present at the festivities.

"She is made for childbearing," Toyama whispered to the young husband when he had seen the fourteen-year-old bride prepared for the bridal bed.

She was fertile, too. Within nine months she gave to Japan her first son. As she lay in her husband's arms on his seventeenth birthday, she confessed to her lord in a whisper that though she was suckling her one-month-old son she was pregnant again.

Three days later her husband "went on a journey," and they were not to see each other again for five long years.

When he left his wife, Hattori went to the house of Mitsuri Toyama, and from there they went together to the headquarters of the Black Ocean Society. Waiting for them were half a dozen men whom Hattori had never seen before, solemn men who greeted them silently with bows.

"I present to you Fuzzo Hattori," Toyama said, "who has expressed the wish to work for our society to the greater glory of Japan and our divine emperor. If it is your pleasure, I will administer the oath to him."

"Does he know our rules and what is expected of him, and does he believe himself to be strong enough in body and in spirit to carry out the tasks we shall set him?"

The speaker was a little, bent man, whose kimono was worn and as old-looking as himself.

"I have instructed him myself, honorable sir," Toyama replied.

"Then if you are satisfied, we are satisfied," the old man exclaimed to a chorus of grunts of approval.

Toyama turned to the boy, his face solemn, his voice quivering slightly with emotion which one would normally have believed him to lack, and said: "Fuzzo Hattori, you face now the most solemn moment of your life. I have spoken to you about all that will be required of you. I have treated nothing as a triviality. If you should have doubts about your desire to undertake all that we shall ask, now is the time to say so. We shall think no worse of you if you withdraw now; but if you decide to go on and then find that your vocation is not a true one, for our protection death may be the only solution."

Without hesitation, the young man answered: "I have no doubt, honorable sir, that my vocation is a true one. But if it should happen not to be, then I should wish for death, which would be preferable to loss of face."

Toyama held out his hand and took Hattori's.

"Very well," he said. "Repeat after me, in the presence of these witnesses, this solemn oath."

And firmly, without faltering, giving the impression that he was transfixed with the sense of his mission, Hattori repeated the oath.

"I swear by the sun goddess, by our divine emperor who is the high priest of the Grand Shrine of Ise, by my ancestors, by Mount Fujiyama the sacred, by all the rivers and seas, by all the storms and floods, that I here and now dedicate myself to the service of the emperor and my country, without seeking personal reward except the merit I shall lay up for myself in heaven. And I solemnly swear that I will never divulge to any living man except those who are set in authority over me, whom I will obey though they may order me to kill myself, anything that the society may teach or show me, or anything which I shall learn or discover in any place where I may be sent or find myself. If I break this oath, may my ancestors disown me and may I pass eternity in hell."

When Toyama unclasped his hand Hattori bowed to the assembled men. They returned his bow in silence. No one wished him good fortune; no one sent him on his way with a kindly word of encouragement. He bowed again to Toyama, turned and left the room.

The first stage of his journey brought him to Sappiro, in Hokkaido, the northernmost island of the archipelago. Here he reported at a school which the Black Ocean Society had established for the training of agents.

On the Asiatic mainland, the society had founded a headquarters at Hankow and another establishment on Russian territory, an ostensible jujitsu school at Vladivostok. In 1893 a member of the headquarters staff had been transferred from Hankow to Sappiro, as it was thought that with a central school of this nature, situated on the security of their native soil, the agents under training would make more rapid progress than they did under conditions which restricted their leisure moments.

At the Sappiro school Hattori concentrated upon learning Chinese and the dialect of the area to which he was to be sent. Besides this there were courses in jujitsu, in the art of deception, in security and in the Japanese equivalent of intelligence.

At the end of eighteen months he was regarded as sufficiently trained to be sent out on his mission. But before he went into the "field" he must report to headquarters in Hankow for his final briefing—and a special course of conditioning.

Attached to the headquarters at Hankow was what was called The Hall of Pleasurable Delights. It was a much more attractive name than Stieber's Green House in Berlin, and it had a multipurpose character.

Within The Hall, every oriental version of all the vices could be experienced. Set up originally for the purpose for which Stieber had founded The Green House—the obtaining of intelligence by blackmail from decadent Chinese notables—its second function was to serve as a meeting place for agents operating in Sinkiang and Russian Central Asia.

Once he had entered the field, the agent was never again to contact any of his superiors directly except on their instructions. Any agent who had a report to make was to go to The Hall of Pleasurable Delights, engage the services of a prostitute and hand to her his report. She would know what to do with it, and there is no more secret place for handing over a report than a bed.

But The Hall of Pleasurable Delights had a third purpose. In the West, in these modern times, it is the fashion to discount sex as a weapon of espionage. Gone, they say, are the days of Delilah and Mata Hari. Men, they say, are now more conditioned to sex and are unlikely to reveal their secrets under its influence. Then in the next breath they contradict themselves and forbid their agents to indulge in promiscuity while engaged on a mission, since there is no greater danger to, no more certain undermining influence of, security.

The Japanese, on the other hand, have never been so muddleheaded. They knew that if they laid upon their agents an injunction to refrain from dalliance they would be obeyed, so deep-rooted was the discipline, the devotion to duty, with which their men were imbued. But they knew, too, that enforced celibacy of this kind can be harmful to a man's morale, particularly when the opportunity is to hand. So, in The Hall of Pleasurable Delights they prepared their agents for every variation from the norm of conventional sexual behavior he might be likely to meet, and taught him special skills by which he might acquire the confidence—here synonymous with *love*—of women able to aid him in his mission.

With agents who were to have the "cover" which Hattori was to have, there was yet a further reason why a course in The Hall of Pleasurable Delights was essential. Any man who is to peddle pornographic literature and drawings will be all the more successful if he had been conditioned to pornographic activities in the flesh.

For this had been chosen as Hattori's "cover." He was to emulate Stieber. He was to go into the towns and villages, the cottages and tents of Sinkiang as a Chinese peddler of pornographic drawings and—no, not sacred statuettes, but something even more efficacious for the health of the body than the soul—bottles of Black Ocean Panacea, guaranteed to cure all ills from ingrowing toenails to epilepsy.

For five years the boy whose kite had started it all sold his filthy pictures and his nasty medicine, talked with Moslem qadis and Buddhist monks, made love to the daughters of local headmen, talked of defense works and roads and the grievous burden of taxation and oiled the palms of men whom he believed would be useful to his masters. Once he returned to The Hall of Pleasurable Delights to report, once to the jujitsu school at Vladivostok.

The latter he found to be an even greater success than The Hall of Pleasurable Delights. Those who were responsible for it knew that they would never attract the stupid Russians unless a course of twenty lessons in jujitsu included, free of charge, twenty hours of dalliance with the most practiced female dispensers of delight in the Orient, and the most cunning wheedlers of information in the pay of the Black Ocean Society.

But in addition to being a machine for acquiring intelligence, the jujitsu school was the base for Black Ocean agents in eastern and central Siberia, especially those deployed along the route of the Trans-Siberian Railway, which was then in the process of being built. In this aspect of its work, it was far more successful than the Hankow school. Its personnel were now supplied exclusively by the Sappiro training school which, in its *métier*, was so successful that from its foundation it never lost a single agent except from natural causes.

When he arrived in Vladivostok in 1898 Hattori found congregating there and almost ready to set out, a photographic expedition—disguised, naturally—whose destination was Khabarovsk, the most important Russian center after Vladivostok. It had been trained and sent by the Sappiro school and was the second such expedition, the first having successfully completed its mission in the previous year. Hattori would have liked to accompany them, but his new assignment called for his return to Russian Central Asia. When he returned from this mission in 1900 he found his recall to Japan waiting for him.

Back in the fatherland he became private secretary to Toyama and begat on his nineteen-year-old wife nine more children before she prematurely reached the change of life at thirty-five. Then, so that his patriotism should never be in doubt, he took a concubine, a young girl of thirteen, by whom he produced six more children for the emperor before his own powers began to fail, when he handed her over to his second son.

The case of Hattori is by no means a special one. In the same way that Toyama had sought him out and influenced him, so the other members of the Black Ocean sought out suitable "agent material," played upon their patriotic feelings with great skill and eventually inveigled them into the service of the society.

Thus, like Hattori, every agent of the society was hand picked, and though none perhaps had quite the same advantage as Hattori in becoming the favorite of Toyama, they worked with a selflessness which to our Western eyes is almost unbelievable. Probably no other espionage organization in the world has had such loyalty, such devotion or such patriotism in its agents, or such material to work upon.

Hattori sets the stamp; all the others were molded in his likeness, as he was molded in the likeness of those who had preceded him.

2

The founding of the Black Ocean Society set the fashion for other patriotic societies with diversified objects but one main aim—to discover and work upon the weaknesses of the Chinese and the Russians.

Two smaller societies which were founded shortly after the Black Ocean amalgamated in 1898 to form the East Asia One-Culture Society. As its name implies, it operated ostensibly in the cultural field. Its pronounced aim was to formulate and spread a common system of writing, and on this a Sino-Japanese *rapprochement* was to be formed. Its activities, however, were not confined to China.

A school was founded in Shanghai known as the Tung Wen College, which was to train members for work in East Asia. By 1908 the college had no fewer than 272 graduates working in China, Burma, India, Annam, the Philippines and Mongolia. In 1937 it was still functioning. By then it was occupying buildings of Chiaotung University and was supported by army funds. Its real activities were widely known and the Chinese openly referred to it as the Japanese spy college. In 1939 it had four thousand members and was still extremely active at the time of the capitulation in 1945.

One of the outstanding members of its staff was reputed to be a certain Qurban Ali. Qurban Ali had come to Japan in 1924 at the invitation of Ki Inukai, one of the founders of the college. He had already a long record of subversive activity against the Soviet Union and had been prominent in Manchuria. He was an expert in Turki, and became an instructor in Turki languages at the Tokyo Military College. Later he transferred to the Tun Wen College where, besides languages, he also gave instruction in the technique of subversive tactics.

But the most important of all patriotic societies was the Black Dragon Society, founded in 1901 by Ryohei Uchida. It derived its name from the Amur or Black Dragon River, which forms the boundary between Manchuria and the Soviet Union. Again the name gives the hint of its chief aim—to drive all the Russians back across the Amur River, out of Manchuria and Korea, and wherever else they might be in the Pacific, outside Siberia. In other words, its activities were to be directed toward waging war with Russia; and its aim was the success of Japanese arms in that war.

All its charter members were already experienced in espionage in continental Asia. Uchida had organized the Black Ocean's jujitsu school at Vladivostok; Sugiyama had been director of The Hall of Pleasurable Delights in Hankow; until he died at a ripe old age in 1944, Mitsuri Toyama, the archpatriot, founder of the Black Ocean, was for many years adviser to the Black Dragon besides being the director of the Imperial Rule Assistance Association, Japan's official, unified political organization.

In 1944 the Black Dragon had an estimated membership in excess of ten thousand and had a long record of activity which spanned such widely separated points of the globe as the United States and Latin America to Ethiopia and North Africa. Among its members, up to its dissolution, it had an unknown number of high government officials including at least one prime minister, Koki Hirota.

The last president of the Black Dragon was Yoshihisu Kurusu, who was also a director of the Imperial Rule Assistance Association. It was Kurusu, and not an official of the government, who on June 3rd, 1943, broadcast to President Roosevelt and Mr. Churchill the threat of the dire consequences which would overtake the Allied forces if they did not surrender unconditionally to Japan. This was an indication of the tremendous power which the society exerted throughout its career.

The Black Dragon, like the other patriotic societies, maintained its own establishments. In Tokyo it had two schools which catered to all aspects of espionage under the cover of innocuous sounding names: the Nationalists' Training Academy, at whose head in 1944 was Giichi Fukushima; and the Tokyo and Osaka Foreign Language School.

Among the lesser but still important societies was *Dai-A-Gi Kai,* The Reawakening of Greater Asia Society. Founded in 1908, it had a fourfold program which included the study of economic, geographical, educational, colonial and religious conditions and organizations in China and Central Asia; the sending out of agents; the founding of branch societies and the dissemination of oral and printed propaganda. At the beginning of its existence its headquarters were in Mukden, but after the Chinese revolution of 1911 it moved to Manchuria. It had branches throughout China, in Siam, Afghanistan, Turkey, Persia and India.

Of later patriotic societies the White Wolf and the Turan Societies are important. The former was founded in 1924 and seems to have evolved from the arrival in Japan, three years earlier, of a representative of the Pan-Turan Society of Budapest. The Turan Society was the offspring, born in 1933, of the union of certain elements of the Black Ocean and Black Dragon Societies. The White Wolf and the

Turan Societies were both probably affiliated with the Gray Wolf Society of Turkey and the Pan-Turan Society of Budapest, both of which were composed predominantly of Moslem refugees from Russia, particularly Russian Turkestan.

There is an ancient belief that the Turkic and Mongol peoples had a common ancestor in the White and Gray She Wolf. The stress of these two societies was, therefore, racial rather than religious, and the ultimate aim of their subversive activities against Soviet Russia was the establishment of an independent Pan-Turkic and Pan-Islamic state in Central Asia. They had a dual interest for Japan. Any trouble they could cause Russia was worthy of being encouraged, and control of them would ensure Japan's complete authority on the Asian continent, when the day came.

3

Though the patriotic societies were private and independent of each other they were, nevertheless, related to one another and to the Japanese government by various ties. We have seen, for example, that Mitsuri Toyama, who was the hero of every Japanese expansionist both inside and outside the government, was the founder of the Black Ocean and adviser to the Black Dragon. There were also Chinashi Hirayama and Choichi Kaji, who, while being charter members of the Black Dragon, also helped to organize and subsequently advise the East Asia One-Culture Society. Though not actually members, two very prominent party leaders, Shigenobu Okuma and Ki Inukai, collaborated in many of the undertakings both of the Black Ocean and Black Dragon.

All the societies—and there were many others to which reference has not been made, since their influence tended to be local and their activities more restricted—placed the emphasis on patriotism. Nevertheless, they shared a common, predatory purpose—the control of Asia (and eventually the world) and the bestowal of Japanese cultural, economic and administrative benefits on all those unfortunates who were not descended from the sun goddess and her retinue.

They permeated the political life of the entire nation and exerted a continuous and extremely powerful pressure on the exponents of Japanese aggression. They did this in a variety of ways. They helped those sympathetic with their aims to high government or army posts; they eliminated those who opposed them. It is notorious and true that almost every political assassination in Japan during the thirties and forties—and there were many—could all be linked with our friend Mitsuri Toyama, though the links might be such that had he ever been arraigned before the courts the evidence against him would never have secured a conviction.

The societies recruited their members from every walk of life. They demanded, first and foremost, extreme zeal for the ideas and ideals which they represented. Should such zeal be lacking, no matter how outstanding the other qualities and qualifications of the applicant might be, he was rejected. It was this extreme zeal which made the societies both important and dangerous beyond the boundaries of Japan.

Those members chosen for the more important work were trained in languages and subversive tactics. These represented the cream of the rank and file. The milk, however, was also regarded as an equally essential ingredient. To it was assigned the role of collecting information, and it was composed of shopkeepers, tourists, salesmen of literature and pornographic drawings and medicine, wrestling instructors, fishermen, businessmen, students of Islam and of the English language, professors, priests and archeologists.

The whole approach to espionage was based firmly on patriotism. No reward was offered to the agent and none was expected, except the merit which his activities would lay up for him with the gods. Thus, the records of the societies are packed with the biographies of "little" men who earned a place of honor by their unspectacular, unobtrusive lifetime of devotion to their particular brand of patriotism. What they learned and passed on to their leaders was by their leaders passed on to the government or to the military forces, into whoever's jigsaw the "piece" most snugly fitted.

In a country such as Japan which has an age-old military tradition and which, in modern times, indulged in peacetime conscription, it is never possible to draw a clear line of distinction between civilian and fighting man. In the same way, it is not always possible to separate the activities and functions of the patriotic societies from those of military intelligence. Throughout the whole of this period of Japan's history there was a close cooperation between the work of the societies and formal intelligence; and their activities were more often than not complementary.

In 1932 the patriotic societies—note, *not* the government—decided that the Moslem policy must be more vigorously implemented than hitherto and that it must be applied to a much more extensive field in the Near and Middle East.

Wakabayashi and Tanaka, who were protégés of Mitsuri Toyama and Ryohei Uchida and, following in Araki's footsteps, ostensible converts to Islam, were given the task of making the new policy effective. They enlisted the official support of General Araki and General Isogai. This was immediately forthcoming, with the result that groups of officers were taught the various languages of the Moslem groups and instructed in Islam. A number of the apparent converts subsequently made annual pilgrimages to Mecca. There they set up their tents among those pilgrims whose languages they spoke, and it was the easiest thing in the world to give and receive hospitality under cover of which they made useful contacts, spread propaganda and obtained useful intelligence with great success.

It would be wrong to suppose that all the agents of the patriotic societies were army officers. Admittedly, a high proportion of them were drawn from the armed services, though this was incidental to the soldiers being members of the societies. Reciprocally, the societies supplied military intelligence with many of its best agents.

Nor were the societies supported only by the military.

71

The foreign office also closely, though with the maximum of discretion, identified itself with the policy of infiltrating the Moslem communities by propaganda and by cultural means.

The diplomatic missions to Moslem countries became the training ground for Moslem experts. In 1944 secretaries at the Japanese embassies in Kabul and Ankara were nominees of patriotic societies.

The projects supported by the foreign office funds were many and various. Among them were the East Asia One-Culture Society's school, and the foreign language schools in Osaka and Tokyo. Agents were directly supplied with money either by the foreign office itself or by embassies, legations and consulates in the Moslem countries.

The patriotic societies were early in the field. The role they played in paving the way for the first great success of Japan's trial of strength with Russia was an outstanding one.

The Japanese could not tell when the moment would come when it would be either necessary or profitable to go against the Russians. For their own part, they were ready to wait until they had completed their preparations, and the longer the time given them for this the better chances they would have of success.

Fortunately the Russians, while encroaching little by little into Manchuria, were not anxious, it seemed, to force a quick decision. They had realized, as much as Japan had realized, that there would have to be a combat between them before an ultimate decision could be reached.

Like Japan, they also needed to make preparations. Their preparations were of quite a different nature from Japan's. They were separated from their base by many thousands of miles, so they must build up their strength in Siberia in order to become independent of European Russia once the war had started.

They were now bending their efforts to this achievement. To make movement of material and men more rapid, they were building the Trans-Siberian Railway and planning railways south of the Amur River, both of which projects they began to speed up in the nineties.

Such a railway, stretching across what to the eye appeared to be limitless country for the most part uninhabited, and where it was inhabited only sparsely so, would be vulnerable to attack. Further, not only would it be vulnerable to attack, but would obviously be one of the primary objectives of a potential enemy. So while they were constructing the railway they were also building fortifications, erecting forts, strengthening the few already existing and setting up a fortified line in some depth. In addition, they were reorganizing and strengthening their naval bases at Port Arthur and all the main centers such as Vladivostok and Khabarovsk. They were locating stores, ammunition and weapons depots. They were constructing new electrical powerhouses.

The Russians, however, had not learned the value of espionage in preparation for war and sent very few agents to discover what the Japanese were doing. The Japanese, on the other hand, while building up their war industries at home and getting a foothold on the Asian mainland—in Korea and parts of Manchuria—had large numbers of agents watching and reporting on all that the Russians were doing. There was nothing that escaped them in Asia, all the way across Asia, and into European Russia itself.

CHAPTER 5

Preparations for the First Trial

One of the Siberian towns which had had its importance enhanced by the coming of the Trans-Siberian Railway was Iman. By the end of the 1890's the Russians had converted it into a military center and had set up and maintained there a garrison whose task was not only to protect the railway but to build up the fortifications in the surrounding area.

For some reason which is not made clear, Iman had not yet, in 1897, received the attention of Japanese spies which its position and opportunities for obtaining vital information about Russian activities and intentions here warranted; warranted, that is to say, in the opinions of several perspicacious Japanese patriots, among whom was Ryohei Uchida.

In 1897 Uchida was still a member of the Black Ocean Society. To his way of thinking, the society was not paying nearly enough attention to that part of Siberia in which Iman was situated. He was pondering this problem one evening as he was riding home from a meeting of the society. At the meeting he had put a proposal before his fellow members that a resident agent should be sent there without delay, and he had been disappointed and angry at the cool reception it had received.

He had pointed out that besides its importance as a Russian garrison town, Iman also lay across the lines of communication of at least five itinerant agents working in more distant regions, each of whom had to present his report periodically in person at the jujitsu school in Vladivostok. This not only took time but removed the agent from his area of activity temporarily; but while he was gone important things might happen and he would miss them.

If they put a resident agent in Iman, besides gathering information about the Russians' doings in the area he could also collect the reports of the itinerant agents and send them by special courier to Vladivostok. It seemed a logical thing to do and yet his proposal had met with a strange lack of interest and the argument that at the moment the society had no suitable agent to send there; and besides, there were places more important than Iman.

Like his superior and friend, Mitsuri Toyama, Uchida was constantly on the watch for men who might serve their country under Black Ocean's direction. As his ricksha boy strode out, silently and easily, making no sound, Uchida reflected what he would do if only he could find such a man now. Even while he was muttering silently to himself, the ricksha stopped before his house. He paid the boy off and strode down the path leading to the entrance. As he did so, he heard the boy's quiet voice calling after him.

At any other time Uchida would have dismissed the boy impatiently, convinced that he would only be begging. But he did not do that now. On an impulse he stopped and turned round and asked the boy what he wanted.

The boy moved toward him and he saw that the eyes, creased slightly in a respectful smile, were bright with intelligence, so bright as to be strange in a ricksha boy.

In a few words the boy explained that he had heard about the Black Ocean Society and knew that Uchida was an important member. He wished he could be a member of the society and serve his country in some special way.

Uchida regarded him closely as he spoke and saw that he was not the youth he had thought him to be but a young man perhaps in his middle twenties. He asked him into the house and questioned him. He learned that the young man's name was Choichi Hirayama, that he was twenty-six and that though he had been married for three years, fatherhood up to now had eluded him.

"What would you do to help your country?" Uchida asked him.

"Anything that might be required of me, sir."

"Would you leave Japan and go into far places and among strange people?"

"If it were asked, sir, willingly."

Uchida grunted and looked at the young man in silence for a moment or two and then, abruptly, told him to strip. Without question, Hirayama loosened the cord about his waist and pulled off his jacket and let his drawers fall about his feet.

Uchida looked at the strong arms and shoulders, the flat belly, the powerful thighs and calves, the almost sculptured muscles of the back and arms, and saw not just the lithe figure of a ricksha runner but the smooth strength of the wrestler. In every movement that he made there was the alertness of the wrestler, too.

For the moment Uchida was content to go no further,

but asked Hirayama to return the following evening. In the meantime he was to tell no one, not even his wife, that he had spoken to him.

The next evening the young man returned, and for most of the time it was Uchida who talked. It was so on many following evenings. But each time a little more of the plan was laid, and soon it was the turn of Choichi Hirayama to take the oath which Mitsuri Toyama had administered to his protégé, the boy with the kite, Fuzo Hattori, less than a year ago.

Before this happened, however, Hirayama had begun his training. He had sold his ricksha on Uchida's instruction and with Uchida's financial aid had become the assistant of Nakamura, the owner of a small general store. From the aging storekeeper he learned quickly the secrets of buying and selling, and no one was ever more sorry to lose so apt a pupil and so hard-working an assistant as Nakamura when Hirayama announced that the next week he must leave him.

At the same time, Uchida had insisted that Hirayama's weak wife should leave her bobbins in the Motomura Cotton Mills. As soon as she had only to attend to the wants of her husband, the seventeen-year-old overworked girl began to put on the flesh her still-growing body so sorely needed, and before her husband took the oath to the Black Ocean and went to the training school at Sappiro, he was the father of twin sons.

Since in Iman Hirayama was to set himself up as a Japanese storekeeper, his stay at Sappiro was not prolonged. When he had mastered enough spoken Russian to eliminate any initial language difficulties and had acquired the rudiments of appreciating any information which might come his way and had grasped the intricacies of operating what is known in espionage jargon as a "letter-box," a reception center for the reports of and special instructions to agents, he returned to Tokyo.

With money given him by Uchida from his private purse, he laid in a stock of goods which the experts had advised him would find favor with the inhabitants of Iman. These he crated and labeled, and when at last all was ready he went to say farewell to his "benefactor."

And Uchida was pleased with him. "You have done well, Choichi Hirayama," Uchida said. "I expect, and know, I shall receive great rewards from you. But this last warning I must give you. From now on, you must expect no further help from me. If you fail as a storekeeper you fail as an agent. And no matter how well you may succeed, you will receive no reward from your country but its gratitude, for the merit you will acquire with the gods would make even the greatest earthly reward seem paltry."

With that last warning, but with great contentment and a still greater determination to succeed, Hirayama set sail for Port Arthur accompanied by his twin sons and his wife and the third child just moving in her womb.

The transformation which had taken charge of Hirayama's life since the night he had had the great honor and greater good fortune of taking Ryochei Uchida to his home had done nothing to dim the flash of his dark eyes and the warmth of his quick smile.

When he opened his store in Iman the inhabitants eyed both him and his shop with curiosity. They stopped and peered in, but only the more bold entered and made trial purchases. In their remoteness they were suspicious of anything new, and especially new, strange people who came and settled among them.

For a time Hirayama saw himself stalked by the shadow of failure, and doubts began to assail him as to the ability he believed himself to have, under Uchida's coaching and old Nakamura's cunning tuition, of attracting customers and then winning their friendship.

He was pondering his problem one morning in his empty store as he broke open a crate of goods which had newly arrived. It was warm, and as he paused in his hammering he took off his jacket. As he struggled with the fastenings of the chest sweat broke out on his body and lit up the muscles of his back and shoulders and arms until they looked like polished stone.

With his back to the door of his shop, he did not see or

hear the entrance of Madame Gregorieva, the wife of Captain Gregoriev of the Iman garrison, until, as he straightened up to rest a while, he became aware of her sibilant breathing.

Captain Gregoriev was forty-three, slim to the point of skinniness, though the military tailor in St. Petersburg cleverly managed to disguise his lack of manly appearance. But the tailor could not deceive Madame Gregorieva who, at twenty-one, after two years of marriage, wished she had chosen a man instead of a uniform for a husband.

In contrast to his wife, the captain was a very busy man. His work at the garrison placed such a strain on his mental and physical strength that more often than not he fell asleep over his dinner and retired immediately the meal was over to his bed, where he recuperated his vitality with ten hours' solid sleep.

Madame Gregorieva, on the other hand, had nothing to do all day after she had given her orders to the servants but to wander bored from room to room or gossip over teacups with the wives of other officers.

As she stared at the little Japanese, with his wrestler's body, bending over his crates, the impact of her loss struck her with a new and disturbing force. When he turned and faced her she was almost overcome by her confusion.

"Madame, I am sorry, please excuse me," the Japanese was saying, bowing in that exaggerated way they had. "I did not hear madame come into the shop. What can I have the honor of showing madame?"

With a vast effort she controlled herself. "I would like to see your silks," she said.

She had entered the shop attracted by a bale of printed cotton he had on display. But her eye had caught the silks stacked high on shelves near the ceiling.

She made him get every bale down. She made him carry each bale to the door so that she might see the true shade in the daylight—and see, too, more clearly, his wrestler's litheness and his wrestler's strength.

At last, with Russian imperiousness, she ordered him to cut her twelve yards of olive green, though she needed only six for a gown. He would have delivered it to her house, but

78

she made him wrap it, and with it in her arms she fled into the street.

She had gone less than a hundred yards when she met Madame Prohkorova, the wife of Lieutenant Prohkorov, her husband's adjutant. They exchanged greetings and she told her friend what she had bought. She dropped her voice to a whisper and there was something in her voice which made Madame Prohkorova curious to see the little Japanese.

It was not until the fourth Russia lady had made purchases that morning that the truth began to reveal itself to Choichi Hirayama. Then he smiled to himself and laid his plan.

He used great subtlety. Only occasionally did he work in his shop clad only in his drawers, and they came more often than they would otherwise have done in the hope that they would this time be able to admire his fine physique.

When the other inhabitants of Iman saw that the Japanese received the patronage of the garrison ladies, then they knew that they might safely give him theirs. In a short time Hirayama's store was flourishing. It did not produce great wealth, but he was successful. Within two years he had opened a branch in Nikolsk, where he put in a Russian manager.

But before he did that, many things had happened. Peddlers and travelers of his own race called at the shop when they saw the sign above the door. He received them hospitably, for he could talk to them in his own language and they could give him news; and when they pressed small pellets of rice paper secretly into his hand he gave no sign. He knew what to do with them.

He became fluent in the dialect of the region, too, and the men of Iman took a liking to the quiet, smiling little foreigner. One of his particular friends was a schoolmaster who came to ask questions about his country and its customs. He suggested that he should teach the Russian's pupils wrestling, and it was not long before he was also teaching their fathers.

He was always ready to contribute a few kopeks to their charities, or give his services, or join in their activities. He

79

was a man of ideas, too, they found; and they would have elected him to the city council had he not been a foreigner.

His wife, now plump and quietly happy, bore him a child each year. He loved her even more than he had loved her when he had asked his cousin to go to her father and ask if he might marry her.

And he allowed himself to be seduced by the wife of Captain Gregoriev.

The first time it had happened he had gone to her house to leave some paper chrysanthemums for her. She had admired some he had decorating his shop. She had wanted those, but he had told her that they were poor quality and he would order some from Tokyo especially for her.

He was not entirely innocent in his motives. Since the day she had bought the silk she had made her wishes quite plain. She received him in her sitting room and as he explained to her how the flowers were made, she touched him.

Ten days later she came into the shop, and when they were alone she asked him why he had not visited her again.

"It is too dangerous, and unwise," he had said, turning away.

"My husband is away for five days," she said, commanding him. "I wish to make curtains of brocade. You will please bring what you have to my house this evening so that I may decide which goes best with my furnishings." She gave him no time to answer, but turned on her heel and left the shop. That evening, when it was dark, he got down the bales of brocade and carried them to her house.

At first he would not yield to her, and she berated him in her necessity.

"Where is the captain?" he asked.

"I told you—he is away for five days."

"Where?"

"At Kobolsk."

When he had first come to Iman, Kobolsk, some twenty miles away, had been a small village. With the coming of the railway it had changed to an important center. What, he wondered, was the significance of the captain's visit there? When he left the captain's house that night he knew that the Russians were building a new fort at Kobolsk large enough to accommodate a garrison of two hundred men and a score of cannon.

In the coming months Captain Gregoriev's absences became more and more frequent and more prolonged. Whether Madame Gregorieva realized the significance of the price demanded of her or not, she did not seem to care. If she thought about it at all she would probably have blamed it on her husband. But there were none of her husband's activities at Kobolsk and other places round about which for long remained unknown to Hirayama.

Madame Gregorieva was not the storekeeper's only source of information. The wives of the other officers now met constantly at his shop and gossiped as they fingered the rolls of brocades and gave his fans a trial flutter, and their gossip was nearly all concerned with their husbands' work, the arrival of reinforcements, the postings to other strong points of this unit and that, the problems of getting enough ammunition for the small arms and artillery.

Such information Hirayama checked by skillful questioning of his friends the townspeople, who worked for the Russian Army. They gave him not only confirmation but fresh information; and all of it he sent down to Vladivostok with the reports of the peddlers and the medicine men who visited him after dark.

Soon there was not anything which the Russians in Iman and the surrounding region were doing and planning which did not reach Japanese intelligence. On the basis of this information the Japanese Army laid its plans for dealing with Iman when the time came, as we shall see.

What Hirayama was doing in Iman other Japanese spies were doing, though not perhaps with the same weapons or using the same methods, at almost every other place where the Russians were making their preparations. In the important Russian base at Port Arthur, the porters and stevedores and other dock laborers were for the most part Japanese agents. They were disguised as Chinese or Manchurians, and the Russians, even when they could recognize them as being Japanese, were not perturbed. The main thing was that they worked well, for next to nothing.

It has been estimated that one in ten of every coolie working for the Russians in Manchuria was a Japanese agent. Not all of them were Japanese. It was found that poor Chinese were quite ready to supplement the starvation wages paid them by the Russians by giving the Japanese snippets of information in return for one or two roubles; and these snippets rapidly built up into a vast mosaic picture of Russian activity.

Once the war had begun, and the Japanese found that espionage paid such handsome dividends, they employed more and more Chinese to spy for them. They took these men mainly from the Chinese who, in peacetime, had served the Russians as interpreters, clerks and couriers, but who had not fled when the Russians had retreated because they owned a parcel of land or had their families settled in the district. With their source of livelihood gone with the Russian armies back across the Black Dragon River, these people were very content to serve a new master. They had to live. The Japanese would give them fifteen dollars a month, which was better than having no rice.

The Russian high command had put two crack regiments to garrison Port Arthur, the 1st Tomsk Regiment and the 25th/26th Siberian Rifles. They had done so because they were not entirely misjudging the situation, and Port Arthur was a pivot of Russian strength.

Yet the 1st Tomsk Regiment and the 25th/26th Siberian Rifles were served entirely by Japanese agents. They cleaned the rooms of the officers, where they could read any notes a careless young lieutenant might leave lying around. They cleaned the offices, where files were not always kept under lock and key at night, and where much that was interesting could be gleaned from wastepaper baskets. They waited at table in the officers' messes, where subjects of strategic importance were discussed despite the ban on talking "shop" in the mess. They performed chores for the N.C.O.s and private soldiers who, as in most armies, often knew more than officers of field rank.

Captain Gregoriev—and there were many Captain Gregorievs in Siberia at this time—employed a small army of coolies to dig and build and carry earth and stones as he built new fortifications and strengthened existing ones. Of course, he did not know that as soon as Hirayama had reported what was happening one in seven of all the coolies working for him and all his colleagues was a Japanese agent trained to study fortifications, estimate strength, draw plans and discover their weaknesses.

Like Iman, Na-Shao was an important strategic center for the Russians, who went to great lengths in fortifying it. As a first line of defense they sowed a field of electrical mines. They believed themselves to be very clever in using these mines instead of self-detonating mines which would blow up as soon as anyone trod on them or otherwise disturbed them. By using electrical mines, which they wired in several series so that not all of them should explode at once, they would be able to wait until the whole field was covered with Japanese attackers and then, by pressing buttons, they could wipe out the enemy at will.

At Japanese headquarters there was a map on which was marked the exact positions of all the detonating wire junctions with the main leads. When the time came, the commander sent out a party of men under cover of darkness who cut every single lead and rendered every single mine harmless. Also on the map was marked the exact position of the artillery batteries in the fort itself, with a note beside each indicating the type of gun and the amount of ammunition with which it was supplied.

The information had been supplied by Japanese agents who, under Russian instruction, had planted the mines and helped join up the wires; who had placed the guns in position and hauled up to each emplacement the supplies of ammunition. And when the time came, Na-Shao fell within the hour.

One in ten of the coolies who were working on the new chain of electrical power stations was a Japanese agent. By skillful subversive activity they were able to delay the completion of the program for a considerable time. They also prepared plans of every one, marking on each plan the vulnerable points of the plant. Armed with these plans when the war started, small parties of trained saboteurs rendered many of the power stations ineffective and caused great confusion among the Russians by the subsequent dislocation of the power and light supply.

The vast scope of Japanese espionage in Manchuria and Russia in this preparatory period is almost inconceivable. Even if Stieber's claim that he employed 40,000 agents could be allowed, his claim would pale into insignificance beside the vast secret force which the Japanese were employing in this area alone; and this was only one section of their effort. Almost equal numbers were being used in China, Burma, India, all across Asia and, in connection with the effort against Russia, in European Russia itself.

In the autumn of 1900 the Japanese War Office appointed Colonel Motojiro Akashi to be military attaché in France, Switzerland, Sweden and Russia. His appointment, which had been resisted by the war office at first, had been made at the insistence of Ryohei Uchida, now a prominent member of the Black Dragon Society, who had threatened that unless Akashi were appointed, the society might find it necessary to withhold the reports of its agents from the military.

A short time before he left Japan for Europe, Akashi was summoned to a meeting with Uchida and another leading executive of the Black Dragon, Sugiyama, who had once been director of The Hall of Pleasurable Delights in Hankow. From these two members of the Black Dragon Akashi received his orders.

He was to visit France, Switzerland and Sweden just for long enough to make himself acquainted with the situation there. He was then to go to St. Petersburg, which he was to make his headquarters.

"Very soon now," Uchida said, "we shall find ourselves striking a blow against our enemies in Siberia. European Russia is very far distant from us, but it is there that policies are made and instructions are given concerning Asiatic Russia. We believe that we could acquire important information if we could have agents there."

Colonel Akashi bowed his agreement.

"There are, of course, many difficulties in the way of our

achieving this, colonel." It was Sugiyama speaking now. "But we believe there is a way in which we could not only acquire information but cause difficulties for the Russian government.

"As you are probably aware, colonel, there is much dissatisfaction with the regime in Russia. For many years now, revolutionary societies have been formed and have operated in secret to bring about the overthrow of the tsar and the elimination of his government.

"If we could make contact with some of these revolutionaries we could, I think, in return for offers of money and materials with which they could be helped to carry out their activities, obtain from them information regarding policies and military strength in East and Central Asia. For these revolutionaries have their agents in high places."

Again the colonel accepted the validity of these views.

"There are two leading revolutionaries," Uchida informed him, "whose identity and capabilities have been revealed to us. One is a priest of the Russian Orthodox Church, a certain Father Gapon. The other is an electrical engineer called Eugene Azeff. If you can make contact with either of these men, or better still, with both, we are sure you could achieve a high measure of success, colonel."

Once more the colonel assured them that he would devote himself faithfully to this end, and for the next hour or so the three men discussed details of what Akashi could offer the secret revolutionaries of Russia, how he should report to the Black Dragon the information he acquired, what he should do to encourage the revolutionaries to intensify their pressure on the Russian government.

So, on the morning of the second day, the military attaché set off to take up his appointment, and some months later arrived in St. Petersburg. There he lost no time in making contact with the two revolutionaries, and in a few weeks could regard himself—if a little cynically—as their friend.

Akashi pressed forward with his plans and had a notable success and won for himself the reputation of being one of the outstanding agents of the Black Dragon.

The peak of the early success he achieved on February 4th, 1904. On this day, two days before their formal declaration of war, the Japanese attacked the Russian fleet at Port Arthur.

At the moment of the attack Akashi was addressing the Russian Socialist (Revolutionary) Congress which was being held secretly in Stockholm, and to which he had been invited through the good offices of Azeff. As the guns of both fleets fired salvos at one another, Akashi was telling the congress: "I am authorized by my superiors to inform you that Japan is prepared to supply arms for revolutionary uprisings in St. Petersburg, Odessa and Kiev."

It was the most successful speech of the congress.

Had Colonel Akashi known the characters of the two men who were to make his success possible he might have hesitated before getting in touch with them, for they were two strange men indeed.

In the year after the Stockholm congress, on a Sunday in October, 1905, Gapon came out into the open and marched at the head of a large crowd to the Winter Palace of St. Petersburg, where the tsar was in residence, to present a petition to the tsar on behalf of the people. Troops opened fire on the demonstration and thousands were killed, but Gapon escaped abroad and lived for some time in London. Unfortunately, he fell victim to comfortable living and the revolutionaries lost confidence in him, and so did Akashi.

He returned to Russian secretly in 1906 but, finding that he was no longer acceptable to the revolutionaries, he turned traitor to the cause and offered his services to the police. This, naturally, upset the revolutionaries—and Akashi—and placed the priest at once in great jeopardy, and on March 28th, 1906, he was lured, by a trick, into an empty house in St. Petersburg and hanged.

The man who had most to lose by Gapon's defection was Colonel Akashi's other friend, Eugene Azeff, who, while working with the revolutionaries, was at the same time one of the most trusted and successful agents of the Ochrana, the secret police. In this role, he stands at the pinnacle of double-dealing as recorded in the annals of revolutionary, secret police and espionage history, of all times, throughout the entire world.

He had begun by working for the police as a student by informing on fellow students engaged in revolutionary activities, for which treachery he was paid the princely salary of fifteen dollars a month. From that he was promoted to Ochrana headquarters in St. Petersburg. At the same time he gained the confidence of the revolutionary leaders to such an extent that he reached a position of great trust among them. He planned and organized some of the most spectacular assassinations, even making bombs with his own hands. Not even when the assassins were arrested—on his information—before they could throw their bombs, did any suspicion fall on him! Equally, the Ochrana was blissfully ignorant of his association with the revolutionaries. He took money from both sides.

But Nemesis, though she may play a waiting game with such men, eventually strikes—and strikes hard. In 1908 both the Ochrana and the revolutionaries discovered him for what he was. Yet he escaped the vengeance of both sides, spent the rest of his life as a wandering fugitive and died in a German internment camp in 1919. It was Azeff who discovered Gapon's approach to the Ochrana. It was Azeff who planned and witnessed his execution.

Perhaps even more significant than his friendship with these two men was another Akashi made in St. Petersburg.

There was at this time in the Russian capital a noted Tartar Moslem, Abdur Rashid Ibrahim, who, besides publishing a Tartar newspaper called *Ulfet,* was adviser to the government on Moslem affairs. He and Akashi understood one another very well, and when the Russo-Japanese War eventually broke out they worked together in organizing Moslem resistance in the Russian rear.

As a recompense for the aid he had received from Ibrahim, when Akashi returned to Japan he arranged for the Tartar's son to be educated in Tokyo at the Black Dragon's expense. In 1906 and 1909 Ibrahim himself visited Japan and entered into even closer collaboration with the Japanese.

Aakshi went from success to success, surprising even

Uchida and Sugiyama, who, on the night of their meeting on the eve of the colonel's departure for Europe, had found Akashi competent, but not outstandingly so.

In World War I, Akashi was appointed assistant chief of the general staff. With the collaboration of General Sadao Araki, he encouraged Baron Ungern von Sternberg's project for establishing an autonomous Mongol empire. As a part of this plan, Akashi and Araki organized and directed the Japanese occupation of Siberia. He died in 1919, however, before the full fruits of all his schemes could be harvested.

Akashi was not the only Japanese working to discover all he could about the enemy's strength and intentions in metropolitan Russia. The Japanese Navy, working independently of the patriotic societies and military intelligence, had placed their agents at strategic points.

In the kitchens of imperial navy headquarters at Odessa, the great Russian Black Sea naval base, Alexander Alexandrovitch plunged his arms up to their elbows in dough. He had been making bread for the Russian Navy for many years now, afloat and ashore, and could carry out the operation with his eyes shut.

As he worked he looked about him and thought what a good place Odessa was to be in. He could not imagine what it would be like to live, for example, in Moscow, where there was, so he was told, no sea, no beach and very often no sun. But then, he had been reared on the western seaboard of the Crimean Peninsular. The gentle sounds of the sea had been the first sounds he had heard, and they were the sounds he liked most of any. That was why he had chosen the imperial navy when the urge had come upon him as a boy to see what he could see of the world.

But of all the places he had visited, of all the oceans he had sailed, of all the men he had seen, none was like Odessa, the Black Sea and his own countrymen. He could not understand a man leaving his own country, cutting himself off from his own people for years and years on end, when there was no really good reason for it. Like that little Jap, for instance, at the table next to his kneading trough, cutting up cabbage for soup.

Without pausing in his pummeling of the mobile, almost living substance under his fists, he turned to Yasunosuke Yamamoto and said: "Suke, how long is it since you were home?"

The plump little man, not more than five foot one, looked at him with his face creased in a smile which was almost perpetual, his dark eyes gleaming from their up-tilted almond-shaped slits.

"Six years, Alexander Alexandrovitch," he said.

"Don't you ever want to go home?" the young Russian asked.

"No!"

"I can't make you out. When I was afloat I liked seeing all the sights and people, and how they lived, and I hope when my time here is up to see more, if only I can get aboard a battleship; but I'm glad to be home here in Russia for a spell, among my own people. There's no one like your own people for friendship, Suke. It's understandable really, because you know what to expect from them and they know what to expect from you. You can't have friendship without tranquillity. Don't you miss your friends?"

"No. But then I never had any friends."

"Not even in your own town?"

"Not even in my own town. You may think it is strange, but I don't admire my own countrymen."

"But why?" The surprise in Alexander Alexandrovitch's voice was the measure of his incredulity.

"They are narrowminded. They believe that no people are like them. That they are the chosen of the gods. That no one can do things like they do them."

"Well, that's natural. I think there are no people on earth like the Russians, though I wouldn't go so far as to say we're the chosen people. And I think that the Russian way of doing things is a pretty good one."

"But you don't say it's the only way."

"No. Different people have different ways of doing things; what suits me doesn't necessarily suit you."

"There you are, you see. But it isn't just that. I don't like the way things are going in Japan."

"How are they going?"

"Well, we've got a state religion."

"But so have we."

"But ours is not like yours. Every man in Japan must accept the state religion, and do you know what that religion says? It says that the divine mission of Japan is 'to bring the whole world under one roof'—the Japanese roof, naturally—'so that all humanity may share the advantages of being ruled by the divine emperor.'"

"You mean that the Japanese emperor is one day going to rule Russia?"

"Just that."

"But . . . but . . ."

"I know it sounds mad, but it is more than mad, it is dangerous."

"You mean they really mean to conquer all the world?"

"Just that. They are planning for it now, and soon you will see, they will start trouble, and they won't stop until they have done what they want to do, or someone stronger than they are defeats them. Now perhaps you can understand why I don't like what they are doing in my country, Alexander Alexandrovitch."

"Well, I'm not very clever, but even I can see that it will mean war. Do you really mean that they intend to fight the whole world?"

"In the end, yes. But they will attack the countries one by one."

"Then there is no need to worry. Because everyone will see what they are doing, and . . . well . . . the tsar will stop them for one."

"Don't be so sure. Madness gives a person great strength. It gives to a nation the added strength of fanaticism."

"Ah, now you're taking me out of my depth. What are you doing this afternoon?"

Alexander Alexandrovitch knew that he would never talk like that about Russia, whatever the Little Father did. But he felt sorry for the little man who had no friends. Alexander Alexandrovitch was almost the only man in the kitchens who would have anything to do with the Japanese. The others said that a man who talked like that about his own country was a traitor. But there were two sides to that. If you could see that the rulers of your country were doing bad things, why then . . . you could stop them!

He was on the point of saying so to Yamamoto when another thought struck him: hadn't the people been trying to get the tsar to change his government for years, and still couldn't make him? Perhaps the ordinary man had no power against those in power.

"What did you say?" he asked.

"I said I thought I might take a walk along the sea front this afternoon," the Japanese repeated.

"May I come with you?"

"I shall be honored, Alexander Alexandrovitch."

So when they were free the Russian naval cook and the Japanese cook went for a walk, the Russian in his uniform, the Japanese, who was a civilian employee of the Russian Admiralty, in a smart European suit.

But somehow they did not walk along the sea front but found themselves strolling along the jetties of the naval harbor. There were one battleship, three destroyers and several corvettes tied up there. They represented perhaps a few per cent of Russia's naval forces.

"Does Japan have any ships like those?" Alexander Alexandrovitch asked.

"Many, and all of them the very latest types," Yamamoto answered.

"But none as new as the light cruiser *Grand Duke Dimitrov,* I'll bet."

"I don't know how new she is."

"She's just completed her trials. A friend of mine is in her. He says there's no other ship in the whole fleet can touch her. Do you know she can do twenty-five knots?"

"That's a high speed, but to get that speed they must have sacrificed most of her armament."

"Don't you believe it!" And the young Russian reeled off all the details of the tsar's proudest addition to his fleet.

The little Japanese listened, putting in a question here and there. His face was impassive, belying the excitement growing within him with every sentence the young man spoke.

91

"Let's walk along the shore," he suggested presently, "and then perhaps you will do me the honor of taking a glass of vodka with me?"

"I was going to suggest the same thing," Alexander Alexandrovitch replied, and in his sentimental Russian way he thought he might be able to supply some of the friendship which the Japanese wanted—you could tell he wanted it—but never seemed to get. In time, perhaps he might be able to tell his friend that he would get along much better if he was not always running down his country and his countrymen however much he was against what they hoped to do, intended to do.

The following morning Yamamoto came late to his vegetables.

"Sleep too long?" Alexander Alexandrovitch asked.

"No," the Japanese smiled. "I had some leave due and I thought I would take some of it. I'm going off tonight."

"Where do you plan to go?"

"I thought I might take a trip to Istanbul. I've never been there."

"You certainly ought to see the Golden Gate," Alexander Alexandrovitch assured him.

So that evening Yasunosuke Yamamoto took the train and three days later disembarked at—St. Petersburg.

Hailing a *droshky* he ordered the driver to take him to the Imperial Japanese Embassy.

The servant who opened the door to him bowed low.

"Will you tell Commander Yoshiro that I wish to speak to him urgently?" he said.

"What name shall I tell the commander, sir?"

"Lieutenant Commander Yasunosuke Yamamoto."

Within three minutes the naval attaché was receiving him as deferentially as the servant below.

"I came in person," Lieutenant Commander Yasunosuke Yamamoto said, "because I have full particulars of the speed and armament of the *Grand Duke Dimitrov*. She has just completed her trials, as you no doubt know, but did you know that she leaves for Port Arthur on the twelfth of February?"

For some reason, instead of making the attaché look

serious, as he had supposed it would, Commander Yoshiro smiled.

"In that case she will be too late," he said.

"Too late?"

"Yes, Lieutenant Commander Yamamoto. By then the war will have started with Russia, and might be almost over by the time the *Grand Duke Dimitrov* reaches the China Sea. Nevertheless, your information is very valuable."

"I knew it was valuable; that is why I came with it in person. I did not dare to risk it to the post. So we are ready at last!"

"Yes, we are ready."

Commander Yoshiro was right. By 1904 Japan believed herself to be in the position from which she might attack Russia with every hope of success. Fifteen to twenty years of preparation had not only brought Japanese industrial and military development to a high pitch, but a vast army of secret servants, more vast than that in the service of any other nation in the world, had uncovered Russia's military secrets and intentions in that area in which she could best be attacked. She was now to discover for herself what the old Prussian spy master, Wilhelm Stieber, had insisted was infallible truth—that well-made, extensive and patiently insistent espionage preparations can achieve half the victory before the first blow is even struck in battle.

CHAPTER 6.

The First Great Victory

On February 4th, 1904, at the very moment that Colonel Akashi, the Japanese military attaché in St. Petersburg, was making the most successful speech before the secret congress of the Russian revolutionaries in Stockholm, telling them that his government was willing to provide them with arms for uprisings in certain specified centers, the Japanese fleet opened fire, without any declaration of hostilities, on the Russian base at Port Arthur. Formal declaration of war was not to be made until two days later.

The naval commander of Port Arthur was not taken entirely by surprise. Reading the signs, he had become convinced that it would not be long before the Japanese began the conflict and that the importance of the base would make it an early object of their attention.

The naval commander was Admiral Baron Fersen, a member of the German Balt nobility, one of the 272 great feudal landlords who divided up the Russian province of Estonia between them. The baron's family owned about 100,000 acres of good arable land and forest land, centered on a small village about thirty miles northeast of Revel—now Tallin—the capital of the province.

The administration of an estate of this size, one would have imagined, would have filled most of the baron's waking hours. But he had an urge to go to sea which could not be denied; so appointing a regent to control his affairs, he went off and joined the tsar's navy.

Partly because he was a first-class naval officer, but chiefly because he was a Fersen, his promotion was rapid, and at the incredibly early age of forty he was appointed to flag rank, and shortly before the war broke out he was advanced to vice-admiral in command of Port Arthur.

As the baron pondered how he might best foil the attempt he was certain Admiral Tojo of the Japanese fleet would make to render Port Arthur useless as a naval base, he hit upon a novel and brilliant idea.

He had searchlights taken off ships and rustled up any others that were available and had them placed at strategic points around Port Arthur, pointing out to sea. If Tojo then succeeded in getting through the mine field into the harbor—and on two previous small-scale raids he had shown himself capable of that; "You'd think he had a plot of the mine field!" Fersen grumbled, quite unaware that Tojo had just that—suddenly all the searchlights would be switched on. This would have the dual effect of picking out the Japanese ships for the Russian gunners, which was good; and it would so dazzle the Japanese gunners that they would not be able to find the range and so would be rendered completely ineffectual, which was even better.

Admiral Fersen's prediction of Tojo's attempt proved right. But that was all!

When the Japanese admiral chose a particularly dark night for his assault and Fersen received news of the enemy fleet's approach, he rubbed his hands together with delight. The darker the night the more effectively would the Japanese be dazzled by the searchlights.

Fersen gave the order that the Russian fire was to be withheld until the Japanese fleet was well within the harbor defenses.

At a signal from the admiral baron, all the searchlights were switched on, and there was the Japanese fleet all lit up, a sitting target for the Russian gunners! It was a magnificent sight!

Unfortunately, it did not last for long! Before the Russian gunners could find their range the Japanese gunners, instead of being dazzled, opened up with such perfect shooting that within three minutes the whole of Port Arthur was plunged in darkness as every single searchlight was put out by a Japanese direct hit.

Tojo had been supplied, days before he made his attack, with the exact position of every single searchlight, and his gunnery commanders had been able to draw up a plan which gave their gunners the absolute range for the searchlights allotted to each of them.

Even Tojo was surprised by the success he achieved. He had not expected the Russians to let him get so near before they opened their attack. By doing so they had made the success of the Japanese gunners all the more certain.

As for Admiral Baron Fersen, he continued to be puzzled by the failure of his plan until those more cognizant with Japanese ways of spying explained to him that those very coolies who had helped to place the searchlights in position were most likely Japanese agents, as in fact they had been.

The assault on Port Arthur was by way of being a trial

run. When the news of Tojo's success was reported, those in authority in Tokyo gave the order to advance to their forces in north Manchuria, and formally advised St. Petersburg that Japan was in a state of war with Russia.

There was scarcely a single point all along the line which the Japanese had taken up that did not fall to their first assault. The Russians fell back steadily until they reached their second series of fortifications. But here again, the Japanese knew exactly their strength and weakness, and exploited their knowledge to the full.

Early in April the inhabitants of Iman and Nikolsk were surprised to see displayed in the windows of Hirayama's shops these notices: SALE: ALL STOCK OFFERED AT ONE QUARTER USUAL PRICES.

Both Hirayama in Iman and his manager in Nikolsk were at once besieged, if not with customers, at least by the curious.

"This war between your country and mine," he explained, "is not good."

"We know that," one man shouted. "But what has that got to do with you or us? Who makes war? It is not you or us, but those who govern us."

Hirayama held up a scrap of paper.

"Look what I found under my door two days ago. It says: 'Go home, little foreigner. We don't want you here!' So I go."

"We'll find the fool who wrote that," another exclaimed. "And when we do . . ."

The crowd made plain what the speaker left unsaid. For a moment Hirayama was afraid. Supposing they did find out who had written the paper. He screwed it up and dropped it surreptitiously on a heap of rubbish behind him and shook his head.

"No, it is better that I go. War changes men. You will see."

What he could not sell he gave away; and two days later, with the wife he loved and the seven children she had given to Japan, he left Iman.

The uniform the Japanese Army gave him changed his

appearance, but there was always the fear in his mind, as he pointed the way to the forts which Captain Gregoriev had built so carefully, and interpreted to his superiors the language the people of Iman had taught him, there was always the fear that someone he knew would recognize him.

But nobody did, and when the war was over and Russia defeated, he returned to Iman and opened up his store again. And the people of Iman were glad he had returned and determined to make up to him the losses he had suffered through a war for which he was responsible no more than they.

So once more Choichi Hirayama flourished, and when the new war came his people were the allies of Russia, so he stayed where he was; and the war passed him over, as it passed over his neighbors.

Until one day in 1917, when there arrived at his house stealthily a certain Captain Kalmykov.

"But why do you come to me, captain?" Hirayama asked. "Of course you are welcome, but these people are your people. Won't they think it is strange you should take refuge with me?"

"They won't when they see what I am going to do," the captain answered. "The people here are not Bolsheviks. I shall lead them in their support of the government of the good Admiral Kolchak."

"But I still do not understand why they will not be offended that you live with me rather than with one of them."

"Have you opened the crates that came this morning?" the captain asked.

"Not yet."

"Then open them."

Still puzzled, Hirayama did as he was bid, and his bewilderment changed to speechless surprise. For the crates contained, instead of cloth and fans and embroidery, rifles and ammunition and gold.

"A gift from your government," Kalmykov smiled.

But for all Kalmykov's efforts, the government of the

good Admiral Kolchak gave ground under every assault, both physical and ideological, of the Bolsheviks. The situation became so confused that the Japanese Army felt constrained to intervene to restore order, and Hirayama's shop became their headquarters in Iman.

Then, when order was at last restored, the people of Iman received another shock. The government which the Japanese put in power was not that of Admiral Kolchak, but of the Bolsheviks, and high in office was Captain Kalmykov. The people realized then that all the time the captain had been pretending to lead them against the Bolsheviks, he had been working to overthrow the government of the admiral. But they realized, too, that in this wicked work the captain's chief aide had been Choichi Hirayama.

This time they had no sympathy for the little Japanese, and he knew in 1921 that he must leave Siberia for good. But Ryohei Uchida had need of him still and sent him to open up another store on the Chinese Eastern Railway in Manchuria.

But by now a germ had attacked him far more viciously than his neighbors in Iman had done, and advancing age helped it. The flesh sloughed from his body, the muscles went flabby and held no strength any more, and his mind was no longer alert.

Two years later he was appealing to Uchida for permission to retire. The permission was granted and he returned to the fatherland, where he settled in a village north of Lake Biwa. There he died on December 10th, 1924.

He was fifty-five years old. Twenty-seven of those years he had been an agent. What he left was scarcely enough to support his widow. He had certainly not worked for money, but from the deep conviction of the rightness of his people's divinely bestowed role as rulers of the world.

Wherever the battle moved there were resident spies, like Hirayama, and the itinerant spies who knew the by-ways and unmarked tracks, the forts and the depots and the inclinations of the inhabitants, who put on the uniform of the advancing armies and interpreted and guided, making the way plain where otherwise it might have confused. But these peacetime spies were not the only Japanese agents to prove their worth.

By now Japanese military espionage had thoroughly organized a branch to move slightly ahead of the main body, and had set up a highly systematic scheme for relaying the intelligence gained by these agents and any others to those officers for whom the information was of vital importance.

Along the whole front bureaus were established under the command of officers whose business it was to control the intelligence in their sectors, sift the information that came through to them and pass it on to the general staff.

In the Russian lines there were secret bureaus corresponding to these bureaus. They were managed by agents, Chinese for the most part, but thoroughly loyal, whose business was to arrange the sending of spies into towns behind the Russian lines and to all Russian troop concentrations.

Each individual spy who worked in this way had attached to him three or four runners by whom he sent to the Chinese-controlled bureaus the information he had managed to acquire. As the Russian lines never exceeded fifty to sixty *versts* in depth, a spy assisted by three runners could answer an inquiry put to him by the Japanese in three or four days and maintain an almost uninterrupted flow of intelligence.

When the information was received by the Chinese-controlled bureaus they had to arrange for sending it through the Russian outposts to the Japanese lines. The couriers used for this purpose were mostly Chinese peddlers or poor coolies of the lowest class, indistinguishable from the beggars who swarmed all over Manchuria. Their intellectual capacity was such that they did not properly realize what they were doing. They knew that they must go to certain Japanese officers in the Japanese lines; and they knew that they must not be caught or lose the minute scraps of rice paper with the strange marks on them. But that was about all. They received the equivalent of one dollar a message at today's rates and considered the risk they took well covered by that microscopic sum.

But the system had a surprising flexibility, too; surprising because the Stieber model had had everything systematized and cut and dried. Local commanders were encouraged to use their initiative to procure information that was vital to their plans, and often we find commanders prepared to organize their own small cells in order to discover exactly what the Russian commander facing them was planning. One such was Colonel Yamaguchi, who, in June 1904, was in command of the key town of Inkou, in northern Manchuria.

Inkou was important not only as a strategic base but because it was a junction for several branches of the Manchurian railway system. Sooner or later, Colonel Yamaguchi was sure, General Mishchenko, who was commanding the Russians on this sector of the front, would attack him.

"It is so important to them," he remarked to his second-in-command, "that Mishchenko will throw in every man he can lay hold of. Now, while I have every confidence in my men and know that each will fight until he is killed, that is no good if we are going to be defeated in the end. To compensate for our being inferior to the Russians in numbers, I intend to try to find out when Mishchenko plans to attack us, and if possible the details of his plan. So I, too, have worked out my little plan."

He clapped his hands.

"Bring in Fang and Ching," he instructed the orderly who answered his summons.

Fang and Ching entered and bowed. They were small men, though slightly taller than the colonel, and their faces were narrower, their cheekbones higher set and more pronounced. Fang carried a tray before him supported by a string that went around his neck. On the tray was an assortment of small gaily colored articles. Some of the articles were arrayed in an orderly fashion on one side of the tray while the rest were jumbled in a disorderly heap on the other side.

"Well, Ching," the colonel said, "what information has Fang for you this morning?"

Ching looked at the tray.

"General Mishchenko has called up two cavalry battalions and two infantry regiments from the rear. He has added two more artillery companies, one heavy, the other light, to the three he already had the day before yesterday."

The colonel had also been studying the tray.

"Right," he said, and smiled at the astonishment he saw on his second-in-command's face.

"But how does he know that?" the major exclaimed.

"Of course, this is only hypothetical information," the colonel answered. "However, if he can do it here, he can do it there. How does he do it? Simple. The green bundles of ribbon each represent a cavalry battalion. The red ribbons are infantry battalions, and each of those little boxes are infantry regiments. Every article on Fang's tray represents some formation or type of weapons in certain quantities. The way Fang set them out tells Ching when they have been added or withdrawn. Now, Fang, what are you to do?"

"I am to peddle my wares among the clerks of General Mishchenko's headquarters. I am to keep my eyes and my ears open. I am to make friends with the general's clerks. They are mostly my countrymen who, fools that they are, decided to go with the Russians, so it should not be too difficult. Each morning I shall go to the south corner of the main square an hour before noon."

The colonel turned to Ching.

"I shall go each morning to Fang to buy from him a ribbon or a box, and as I do so I will read what his ribbons say. I shall then send one of my runners with the information to you."

"Excellent!" exclaimed the colonel. "Go now."

Over the next ten days a runner arrived daily in Inkou, and from the information he brought Colonel Yamaguchi made his tally of his enemy's strength and discussed with his second-in-command what his plan would be if he were Mishchenko and had these forces under his orders for an attack on Inkou.

Then came the day when the first of the matchboxes arrived. It came in the morning by runner, and in the evening another came.

Despite his outward calm, the major could sense his commanding officer's inward excitement when he received the first matchbox.

"He has done it!" he exclaimed, his eyes flashing. "I never thought he would. But somehow he has managed it."

"What has he managed?" the major asked a little shortly, irritated by the colonel's mystery.

"When I have five more of these matchboxes I will tell you," the colonel answered, grinning provocatively, so that for the first time the major saw how bad the colonel's teeth were.

"He's like a child playing a silly game," the major complained to the colonel's adjutant, who was his wife's brother.

"When you become a colonel you enter your second childhood," his wife's brother replied. "So mind you don't get promotion, brother-in-law."

But when three matchboxes arrived the next day it was the major who displayed most impatience for the arrival of the sixth and last.

That evening at dinner the colonel announced to his officers that he wished them to hold themselves in readiness all next day to attend a conference with him immediately he summoned them. He did not know when this might be, but they must come at once.

They looked at one another with slightly raised eyebrows. None of them could supply a possible or even likely solution to the colonel's mystery.

The summons reached them in the mid-afternoon of the next day.

When they were assembled and seated in the colonel's office they saw that he had arranged before him six matchboxes.

He rose, and picking up one matchbox and peering at it, he began: "Gentlemen, General Mishchenko intends to attack Inkou and the railway at six A.M. on June 27th. That's exactly a fortnight from now. He will attack the

102

railway at the following points and with the following forces, and Inkou with . . ." And for the next half hour he outlined Mishchenko's complete plan, always referring to the matchboxes and to a few notes he had scribbled on a piece of paper.

"I have not yet worked out our plan of defense, but I shall do that now, with your assistance," he said when he had completed his exposition.

When the conference was over his second-in-command stayed behind and, picking up the matchboxes from the desk, looked at them carefully. There were a number of small ideographs on each, but none made any sense to him.

"A good idea, wasn't it?" the colonel smiled. "Fang is a clever man. One of these matchboxes on its own tells nothing to anyone. But the six put together reveal General Mishchenko's plan in detail."

At six A.M. on June 27th General Mishchenko launched his assault on Inkou and the railway; and no one was more surprised than he to find the Japanese in strength at every point of attack. There could not have been a leakage of information. He had not told his subordinate commanders of his plan until two days ago; and that would not have given the Japanese commander, if he had heard of the plan then, the necessary time to deploy his troops. Until he had told his subordinates of his plan, only he, his adjutant and his confidential clerk had known of it and all were to be trusted implicitly—he thought. But of course he did not know of the clerk's friendship with the peddler, who sold many interesting things besides ribbons and boxes. He was still puzzled when he found himself the next day pushed well behind the line from which he had started.

But besides the intelligence bureaus and the *ad hoc* activities of army commanders, there was yet another kind of organization. This consisted of a number of completely independent groups of three or four spies operating from a particular base. They were entrusted with the solution of some accurately defined problem, such as reconnoitering one specified section of the Russian Army, or the observation of troop movements.

These groups were always provided with considerable

means which enabled them to set up a kind of "jam pot" center which would attract to it people of every class, who would gossip freely. The most frequently used "jam pot" was a baker's shop, for here soldiers of all ranks would call, since army rations were always inadequate and bread, besides being a staple food, was cheap.

Soldiers rank next in the line of gossips after maiden ladies and wives with too much time on their hands. From the conversations of their customers, and by means of casual, unsuspicious questions, the trained agent could pick up invaluable information.

It must not be thought, however, that the Russians put up no resistance to the espionage assault made upon them by the Japanese. It was not very long before the significance of what was happening at places like Inkou and Na-Shao dawned even on the Russians.

Shortly after the war began General Harting, who up to then had been chief of the political police, had been appointed by the Russian Army G.H.Q. to take over the supervision of Russian intelligence in the field. He was given a special grant of about 25,000 dollars for this work, which was a widow's mite compared with the vast sums with which the Japanese provided their espionage, and the result was not very satisfactory.

Local Russian commanders then set up their own private counterespionage echelons, which were much more effective. They became so effective, in fact, that they caused the Japanese to invent new devices for the communication of their information and for their couriers to conceal their messages. These would be buried deep in pigtails or hidden in the soles of shoes or sewn into the seams of clothing. These methods have now been so extensively used that they are no longer safe. In those days, they had never been attempted before. Information of very great importance had to be committed to memory and repeated orally to the officer in charge of a Japanese bureau, and this called for the necessity of employing a more intelligent class of agent.

But the greatest damage had been done before the war

began and before the Russians decided to tighten up their counterespionage.

The Japanese introduced several innovations into their clandestine activity during their fight with the Russians. They were the first ever to use groups of saboteurs behind the enemy lines on an organized scale. Small groups of two or three agents, well-trained in the use of explosives, were sent to blow up the railways, electrical power stations and other installations of strategic importance. But perhaps the most striking innovation was their attitude toward spies and spying.

In the West it was not until the First World War that spies were freed a little of the contempt in which they were always held by *soi-disant* "decent" people.

As the pathetic German spy, Carl Lody, was standing on the scaffold in the Tower of London, he remarked to the governor of the Tower, who had visited him often during his confinement and who was now required to witness his execution: "I don't suppose, sir, that you would care to shake hands with a spy?"

To which the governor replied: "I will shake hands not with a spy, sir, but with a very brave gentleman."

And it was King George V himself who was the first to have the courage to declare publicly: "A spy is the bravest man I know," and who later conferred the first knighthood ever to be bestowed on a British agent on Sir Paul Dukes, who operated in Russia during the Bolshevik revolution and the first months of the Soviet regime.

The Japanese, however, from the beginning of their espionage activity had brought espionage within the scope of *bushido,* their extremely strict and elevated code of morals and conduct. Espionage, they declared, practiced in the service of one's country, was both honorable and fair; for did it not demand courage and daring, two of the virtues most highly prized by the samurai?

This code they extended to their enemies. A young Russian soldier, disguised as a Chinese, was captured, convicted of spying and executed. The Japanese were so impressed by his bravery and his ideal of devotion to his country that when he was dead they sent a letter to Russian headquarters in which they lavishly praised his behavior, courage and devotion.

The Russians reciprocated. When a Russian patrol on the East China Railway captured two Japanese officers disguised as Manchurians in the act of attempting to blow up the railway, they were court-martialed at Harbin and condemned to hanging. But when General Kuropatkin, the Russian commander-in-chief, heard that they were officers he modified the order, in deference to their rank, to death before the firing squad.

This approach to espionage was, of course, all of a piece with their general approach to service for their country and the ideal of patriotism. It encouraged many who might have hesitated to accept the risks of spying, anywhere, at any time, and it made them doubly dangerous. One of the best examples of *bushido* at work is provided by the *kamikazes,* the suicide pilots of the Second World War.

Nor was it only on the battlefield itself that Japanese espionage was so effective in all its manifestations.

When Admiral Fersen's ships had had their effectiveness whittled away to almost nothing by the first attack and when the armies in Manchuria and Siberia were falling back under the amazing pressure of the little yellow men, St. Petersburg decided that they must do something to relieve that pressure. An effective fleet in the Black Ocean should, it was argued, be able to intercept reinforcements both of men and materials being sent from the home islands to the Asian mainland.

Orders were, therefore, given to Admiral Rozhdestvenski to move his Baltic Fleet to the Orient. But before he could do this there were certain preparations which the admiral had to make.

While he was making his preparations one day in September 1904, Kenzo Kamakura and Seiko Akiyoshi, two clerks in the Potemkin Shipping Company's St. Petersburg offices, were taking special trouble with their dressing. Both had joined the Russian Orthodox Church some months previously and today Kenzo Kamakura was marrying a Russian girl, and Seiko Akiyoshi was to support

106

him. As they giggled and twittered to one another, there was a knock on the door.

"It will be the florist with the boutonnieres," said Kamakura and, as he was still without his trousers, went on: "You're more presentable than I am; open the door, Seiko."

So Seiko, with his suspenders dangling behind him and his white tie half-knotted, went to the door to admit, not the florist's messenger, but two men.

"Kenzo Kamakura?" one of the men asked.

"No, I am Seiko Akiyoshi. My friend Kamakura is in the next room. You wish to see him?"

"Yes."

Kamakura answered Akiyoshi's call.

"You wish to see me, gentlemen? I am in a great hurry. I am to be married in one hour."

"I'm afraid you'll have to postpone your wedding," the spokesman said.

"But I can't do that!"

"Kenzo Kamakura and Seiko Akiyoshi, we are agents of the Ochrana, and we are arresting you on suspicion of being Japanese spies."

"On what evidence?"

"You will learn that at headquarters," he was told.

As a matter of fact, the Ochrana had little evidence, but a search of the men's rooms revealed that they were supplying the Japanese Embassy with information about Admiral Rozhdestvenski's Baltic Fleet. It was also revealed that both men were lieutenant commanders in the Imperial Japanese Navy.

As the embassy in St. Petersburg received the information from the two spies they passed it on both to Tokyo and the embassy in Berlin. The embassy in Berlin, in turn, conveyed it to another lieutenant commander, who was touring Europe, and at this moment was at the Skaw, the northernmost point of Denmark.

It was only when Rozhdestvenski's fleet passed the Skaw that the Danes discovered the tourist to be sending code messages to the embassy in Berlin. It was too late then, but they arrested him on suspicion of spying.

All around the coasts of Europe and Asia at points where the Russian Baltic Fleet must call for bunkering the Japanese had placed spies, who immediately informed Tokyo of the arrival and departure of the Russian ships from each point. When the fleet sailed into the Sea of Japan, Japanese fishermen in speedier boats than the warships went ahead of them and warned the Japanese high command of their progress.

It was a fantastic chain of spying, but it was espionage on this scale, based on really firm and sure foundations, which played a very large part in the successful outcome of the war for Japan.

For a little over a year the Russians kept up the unequal struggle, but at last were compelled to sue for peace. They could not deal with the military reverses in Siberia and the Japanese-fostered unrest in their Moslem provinces and the ever-increasing revolutionary activity nearer home, also helped by Japanese money and arms.

Though they must have been expecting it secretly, the other nations of the world, and especially the Western world, were dumfounded when Russia threw in the towel. From now on they regarded the almond-eyed men of Nippon with a new respect.

As for the Japanese, they bowed to one another with great satisfaction. They had driven the Russians back across the Black Dragon River and weakened their power in Manchuria and in China. No longer would they have to worry about a Russian threat either to the edifice which they were continuing to build at home or to their own position on the Asiatic mainland. In this one sharp blow Japan had made herself the dominant power in this sphere of her influence. Never again would she have to fear the interference of the Russian bear. The rest of the world had believed that she was taking a gambler's chance when she attacked Russia. She knew that the element of chance was not excessive. She had laid her plan and worked to it, and it proved to have been well laid. She had proved by practice the theory that had been taught her by the now dead Wilhelm Stieber. As she began to plot the next phase of her plan, which would ultimately bring "the whole world under one roof" if she made sure that industrially and economically she would be in a position to give effect to her plots, she also made certain that her espionage preparations would be as effective, when the next battle was joined, as they had been in knocking out Russia.

CHAPTER 7

The Final Touches to the Plan

It is necessary for us to go back a little way from the first great victory of Japanese arms and espionage to consider briefly what had happened in the political sphere. For it was against this somewhat peculiar background that she contrived to implement her "divinely" inspired policy of world domination.

The samurai, the hereditary fighting men, had been the thorn in the flesh of the reformers since the birth of the new Japan. It must be admitted that the rulers did not handle them very well.

In August 1876 they had been compelled to accept a lump sum payment in the form of interest-bearing bonds in lieu of their pensions, which were placing too great a strain on the nation's economy. The following year there was a general uprising of samurai which was easily quelled by the new conscript army, but those in authority realized that they must do something to keep them permanently quiet. They therefore acceded to the samurai demands that there should be some form of representative assembly. This led in its turn to the formation of political parties, and in 1890 the emperor and government instituted a parliament.

A Diet was established consisting of two houses, a House of Peers and a House of Representatives. A peerage, on English lines, was introduced, but not all peers *ipso facto* sat in the upper house, a number of them being elected by their fellow peers for a seven-year term, while the princes and marquises sat for life. The representatives were elected by popular suffrage. Under the original constitution, property qualifications were set so high that the suffrage was by no means universal.

The emperor's position was reduced to that of a constitutional monarch. Theoretically, he combined in his person all the legislative, executive and judicial powers, but he did not exercise these powers except by advice. Compared with the English monarch's constitutional powers, the emperor's were even more restricted, for no political document signed by him was valid unless countersigned by all the members of the cabinet.

In this way, the emperor was identified with all the measures decided upon by the government of the day. Aligned with the state religion, the main tenet of which was the divinity of the emperor, this identification gave unusual power to the government. In practice, it gave the cabinet all the emperor's political powers while, in turn, the emperor's inability to do wrong by reason of his divinity was transferred, by implication, to the acts of government.

Though outwardly the system had all the apparatus of two-chamber democratic government under a constitutional monarch, in practice it was merely a sham. The limitations set upon the powers of the Diet hamstrung any effective government by them should their proposals not be in accord with the intentions of the government. The Diet met only once a year for a three-month session, and the government had the power to convoke, prorogue or dissolve it.

There was one check upon the government in its exercise of the vast powers theoretically assigned to the emperor. This was the privy council, which, consisting of a president and vice-president, twenty-four members and the cabinet, had to approve constitutional amendments, laws and supplementary constitutional decrees, as well as all emergency decrees, including emergency financial decrees, treaties, international agreements and the institution, when required, of martial law.

110

One power was confined to the emperor and remained outside the competence of the government. In his role as supreme commander of the armed forces, the emperor was advised in all military matters by the chiefs of the army and naval general staffs, and the army and navy ministers. By ancient custom the two latter offices were restricted to officers on the active list.

It was under this constitutional setup that the war with Russia, and all Japan's subsequent warlike activity, was undertaken, and it is necessary to have an understanding of this very brief outline in order to appreciate the background to the events of the next thirty years.

With the success that came to Japanese arms in the Russian war came the even firmer establishment of the conviction that the gods favored the expansionist policy. With this success in mind, in 1910 Japan formally annexed Korea without any opposition whatsoever from outside.

World War I was to prove a great blessing to Japan. Her development program had by this time put such a strain on her economy that she was on the verge of bankruptcy. She aligned herself with the Western Allies, who were only too ready to buy her cheap products, and this not only saved her from economic collapse but enabled her to press forward with her development program even more vigorously.

It also strengthened her position in East Asia. Here she had been aided by the Chinese revolution of 1911, which had weakened China so considerably that she had never recovered, nor was likely ever to recover. Japan took over the German leased territories in Shantung and in 1915 presented her Twenty-one Demands to the Chinese government, which accepted them. These gave Japan extensive rights, particularly in Manchuria and northern China.

With Japanese connivance Marshal Chang Tso-lin made himself the virtual ruler of Manchuria, and that country remained separated from China until 1928. In that year Chang was assassinated, and his successor proclaimed his adherence to the policy of Chinese nationalism, in so doing rejecting the advice of Japan. The outcome was the Japanese attack on Manchuria in 1931 and the setting up of a puppet state under Henry Pu-yi, the last Chinese emperor.

Two years later Japan attempted to set up a second puppet state by detaching the Five Northern Provinces. Here she met with her first failure and withdrew to lick her wounds, determined never again to fail.

In the events that led up to the seizure of Manchuria and in the actual seizure itself, Japan had the services of one of the strangest figures not only in her espionage history but in espionage history anywhere. His name was Kenji Doihara, often called, though with more than a tinge of facetiousness, the Lawrence of Manchuria.

CHAPTER 8

The Lawrence of Manchuria

One evening Kenji Doihara sat with his father and two of his brothers talking over the course of the war in Europe, which was not going well for the Allies, with whom Japan had aligned herself.

He was twenty-one, plumply round, not with puppy fat—he was too old for that—but with an incipient coarse grossness which was to clothe his bones more permanently as the years passed. Twenty years from now, had you sliced him neatly horizontally through the middle you would have probably expected to find him ringed like a tree, and counting the number of rings of fat you might have gauged his age. The innermost ring would have represented his first year of maturity, this year, of which this evening was a part.

Presently a servant came in and spoke to his father. "A

112

message has come from the imperial prince," he said, "requesting that Kenji San shall call on him at once."

The father turned to his son. "You must go," he said. "Acquaintance with the imperial family can bring great honor to us."

As Kenji bowed to his father he stored these words in his memory. He hoped that he would soon have need to remind the old man that he had spoken them.

At the prince's palace he found his imperial highness alone except for his chamberlain.

"I have received your package," the prince said at once, after their greetings were finished.

It was a superfluous remark, for set out before the prince were the half dozen photographs of a very beautiful naked girl, which he had sent to the palace that morning.

Looking down at the photographs, Kenji Doihara felt no shame. He remembered only that they had cost him his most prized possession, a little jade fawn that he had won from the son of a Manchu merchant. It was an exquisite piece of almost priceless value. He thought much more of it than he did of his fine German Zeiss camera, which made possible the pursuit of his main hobby.

He had tried every wile, every argument his cunning could devise, had run past the limit of his patience without losing it in anger. Then when these had been of no avail, he had thought of the jade fawn. Only when she was sure that he was not teasing her, but that he meant it when he said she might have it for her own if only she would take off her gown and let him photograph her, had she seen reason. Even then she had made him repeat his earlier promise that he would never show the photographs he took to any living soul.

Naturally he had repeated the promise. Just as naturally, as soon as he had developed and printed the photographs he had sent them by messenger to his imperial highness.

That had been his object all along. That was why he had sacrificed his jade fawn—to win the consent of a fifteen-year-old girl.

"And what is your imperial highness' decision?" he asked.

It needed all his courage to control his apprehension as he waited for the prince's answer. Supposing he had sacrificed the little jade fawn for nothing?

"You are right, Doihara," the prince said. "She is the most beautiful woman in Japan. I would like to know her."

Inwardly, Doihara's heart sang, but he pulled his features into a frown.

"Your imperial highness," he began, and his voice was sharp with resentment, "our family has been one of the leading samurai families for more than a hundred generations."

"What a touchy fellow you are!" the prince smiled soothingly. "I have a proposition to make. An honorable one. I wish your sister to enter my household as my first concubine."

"But my sister is already betrothed, your imperial highness," Doihara began.

The prince snapped back at him. "The offer I am making could be excelled only if the son of heaven himself made her his first concubine or if one of my unmarried brothers were to make her his wife, which the difference in rank prohibits anyhow."

"I am not my sister's father," he said quietly.

"I have asked you here to know if you will support my proposal, both to your father and to the girl," the prince said.

"Yes," said Doihara quietly, though how he could control his excitement he did not himself know. "Yes, I will do that, your imperial highness."

But it was not easy, either with the girl or with his father, and he might not have succeeded had not his brothers joined him, seeing in such an alliance the opportunities he himself saw. It was they who reminded his father that he had said: "Acquaintance with the imperial family can bring our family great honor." Here was an offer of much more than acquaintance. How could he think of rejecting it?

As for the girl, she would do as her father commanded. But she, silly child, would be a wife of a samurai rather than the concubine of a prince, even an imperial prince. She wished to beget warrior sons, not royal bastards. And she had done nothing wrong to deserve such punishment. It was Kenji who should be punished for persuading her to let him photograph her naked. He had promised . . .

His brothers looked at their brother. He stared back at them defiantly. They smiled at him, and he knew he had won.

A few weeks later Doihara called at the prince's palace, not to see the prince but the prince's first concubine.

"Well?" he asked cautiously.

"Oh, brother!" the radiant girl exclaimed. "I shall never be able to thank you."

"You are happy?"

"I cannot tell you how happy. The prince smothers me with kindness and showers me with presents. When he is here he never leaves my side."

Doihara moved closer to his sister and dropped his voice to a whisper. "Beware of the fickleness of princes," he warned her. "A year from now, when childbirth has distorted your beauty, he may look about him. . . ."

"You are wrong, brother," the girl cried. "He loves me. He will do everything I ask. Even my smallest whim. I never dreamed that life could be so wonderful. I shall never be able to repay you, brother."

Doihara did not reply immediately, but presently he said, slowly, watching her carefully to judge her reaction, "Sister, there is something you could do for me."

"Anything you ask, I promise you."

"Tell the prince that I speak nine European languages and four Chinese dialects without a trace of accent. Tell him that there is much I could do for the divine emperor and for the fatherland if only I could be sent to China in a responsible position. The prince has great influence with the government. He could arrange it if only he knew what I am capable of."

"Is that all you want, brother?" his sister laughed. "This very night the prince shall be told what a brilliant brother I have. He will have to promise to send my brother to China. . . . Have no fear, brother."

When they had drunk tea, Doihara left the first concubine happy and confident. As he made his way to the teahouse of the Great Swords, he mused that it had not been easy, but he would never have given up his plan until he had succeeded. He smiled to himself. The most difficult part of all was to persuade his sister to pose for him naked. If that beginning of his plan had misfired . . . ? But he did not allow things to misfire. And now he only had to wait until the summons came!

The summons was not long in coming.

Within a few months General Honjo, of the high command, was sent to Peking as military attaché and Kenji Doihara, promoted to the rank of major, was posted as his assistant.

There was very little to choose between the characters of Honjo and Doihara. Both were entirely ruthless, utterly without any moral values or scruples and relentless, if daring, plotters.

Now that Doihara had achieved his ambition of getting to China, it was not long before he was putting the second part of his plan into effect. His basic scheme was to create a kind of moral desert on the Asian mainland. His slogan would be, "Asia for the Asiatics," though for "Asiatics" one should read "Japanese." He would accomplish his plan by undercover means, undermining by plots, sabotage, assassinations, the promotion of vice of every kind, by bribery and corruption the influence of the Chinese republican government both in China and Manchuria.

As a beginning he would use the contacts which his position as assistant military attaché gave him. Before long one of the high-ranking Chinese officials, who was not one of his "men" but who saw what was happening, was able to say; "Doihara probably has more Chinese acquaintances than any living Chinese engaged in the most intense political activity."

The Honjo-Doihara combination was soon making its nefarious influence felt in Chinese affairs. It was during this early period that Doihara made the only great mistake of his career, though he managed to emerge safely even from that.

There was in China at this time, the early 1920's, a powerful movement called Anfu, meaning "Peace and

Joy." It was so powerful that for a time it controlled the Chinese government. Honjo and Doihara supported the movement strongly.

How it happened is not clear, but presently it came to the knowledge of the better elements of the Chinese government that certain important members of Anfu had sold concessions in Manchuria to the Japanese, who already had many concessions there, without the official approval of the government and had pocketed the proceeds. Though this was not known, Doihara had been the prime mover in the business.

The matter became public knowledge and the nation rose against the government in a solid, angry body. There were demonstrations and riots and demands that the government should resign. A number of patriotic students stormed the Presidential Palace, their intention being to seize the person of President Hsu and compel him to dissolve the government. Hsu, however, believed that their real intentions were more violent and was panic-stricken. As he paced the palace, a frightened, trembling man waiting with oriental fatalism for the noisy students to break in and kill him, Doihara suddenly appeared before him.

"You are in great danger, Mr. President," Doihara said. "You should not be here."

"I know I am in great danger," the distracted Hsu cried. "But what can I do? Where can I go? There is nowhere in the palace where I could hide and they would not find me!"

Anfu had proved a broken reed. After this it would no longer be of any use to Doihara. But he might still pluck the chestnuts—the Chinese government, and more particularly the president—out of the fire, and, who knew? Perhaps have those that mattered even more tightly in his hands. The first thing to be done was to rescue the president from his present dangerous predicament.

"Stay here, excellency," Doihara said firmly. "And do not move from here until I return."

The firm voice and the lack of fear steadied Hsu. He was a strange one, this fat little Japanese officer. He was a cunning one, too! But what could he do? He, Hsu, was

117

trapped here in the palace. To judge from the noise, the mob had got into the grounds.

Within a few moments Doihara returned. Accompanying him were two servants carrying between them a large wicker basket with a lid.

"It will be a little cramped, excellency," Doihara smiled, "but it will be better than being torn apart alive by these young hooligans."

"Do you mean I am to get in that basket?" Hsu exclaimed.

"Exactly, your excellency. It is a clean laundry basket, though the little laundry in it is somewhat soiled. Quickly, excellency!"

He almost picked Hsu up and bundled him into the basket, covered him with soiled linen and tied down the lid.

"Follow me," he said to the servants.

They picked up the basket and followed Doihara as he went to meet the mobbing students. Facing them, he held up his hand for silence, and such was his personality that the young men stopped their yelling.

"If you are looking for President Hsu," he shouted so that they could all hear, "I'm afraid you are going to be unlucky. I have just searched the whole palace for him and cannot find him. Oh, just let those men pass through, will you, like good fellows? There's no reason, because you're enjoying a riot, why the laundry should not be done as usual."

His own smile, and the inappropriateness of the laundry basket on this scene, had their effect on the crowd. Laughing, the students opened their ranks and let the servants pass through unimpeded with the laundry basket —and President Hsu.

When the basket was safely out of the palace grounds, Doihara addressed the crowd again.

"I would suggest that you appoint leaders and let them come with me and we will search the palace again," he said. "The rest of you stay outside here. If you all come in, the palace wouldn't be fit to live in again. There would be no sense in that, either."

So representatives were appointed, and for two hours

they scoured the palace with Doihara. When they returned to their fellows the impetus of their patriotic emotions had lost its thrust and they dispersed quietly, if disappointed.

Meanwhile, President Hsu was in the safety of the Japanese Embassy. When the danger was past he would emerge to continue his efforts to fashion some order out of chaos. But his task would be no easier now than it had been in the past, despite the help and guidance of self-appointed Japanese advisers. Internal factions, corruption, the ambitions of war lords and the obstreperousness of the Five Northern Provinces and of Manchuria were powerful obstacles in the way of anyone trying to draw China into a cohesive whole which would have unity and a degree of power. In the turmoil that distracted him, Hsu did not realize that the Japanese, represented by Honjo and Doihara, were doing all they could to weaken China with their advice, and that as for Manchuria and the Five Northern Provinces, the more they could be encouraged in their recalcitrance, the better would Japan's own ends be served.

The importance of Manchuria for the Japanese lay in the fact that it lay nearest to the home islands in a place which would facilitate the execution of a later phase of their master plan, the domination of southern China; that by the control of it they could build up forces of men and materials there and use it as a springboard for the next step, the conquest of the Five Northern Provinces; and that in its present state of internal insecurity it should fall an easy prey to outside, meaning Japanese, influence.

As time went by, Doihara realized that he was wasting his time in China, for he now believed that he was tackling the problem from the wrong end. He must first work for the annexation of Manchuria. When Manchuria was in Japanese hands, the Five Northern Provinces would not present a great problem.

Even so, he realized that Manchuria could never be absorbed as easily as Korea had been annexed. In spite of its inherent weakness there was an army which was not too badly equipped and supplied; and just as important, it had a bold and determined leader in Marshal Chang Tso-lin.

Manchuria had always been a kind of buffer state. The Tsarists had cast longing eyes on it and had, in fact, laid predatory hands on it, for they saw that it could blanket any land attack the Japanese might make on them in Asia.

During the Russo-Japanese War Marshal Chang Tso-lin had ranged himself and his forces on the side of the Japanese, and he had helped them considerably by harassing the Russian lines of communication.

When the war was over, the Japanese rewarded their ally by obtaining for him, from the Peking government, a pardon in respect of his previous acts of banditry and the appointment of governor of his native province of Fengtien, in Manchuria.

But Chang was a war lord born and could not be satisfied with the governorship of a province. So in 1922 he left Manchuria with his army and joined in one of those strange and, to Western perception, almost incredible local wars which happened to be raging about Peking at this time.

Unfortunately for whatever he had in mind, he backed the wrong side and his army was defeated by the forces of the war lord Wu Pei-fu. Thereupon Chang retreated to Manchuria to lick his wounds and, declaring the independence of the three eastern provinces, which we now know as Manchukuo, set himself up as a ruler.

He quickly revealed himself as a most admirable administrator though, at the same time, he emerged as a ruthless, pitiless autocrat, destroying everything and everybody who opposed him. Nevertheless, under his rule Manchukuo flourished and was rapidly becoming a very rich prize. To the chagrin of the Japanese, however, Chang now found that he could get along very well without them; and if they were going to be foolish enough to intervene, then he would not hesitate in opposing these former allies.

Doihara had the measure of Chang at once and sought permission from Tokyo to go into action in his own particular way. Before he began, however, it must be clearly understood that he must have *carte blanche* and be sure of the necessary funds.

By this time, Doihara's activities in China had commended him highly in the right Tokyo quarters. Almost automatically Doihara had his way in everything; and it was from this moment on that he began the most amazing phase of his career.

Like Schulmeister, Napoleon's master spy, like Wilhelm Stieber, the founder of Prussian espionage, Colonel Kenji Doihara was a natural spy and spy master. He had the peculiar vision, the tortuous mind, the relentless hardness, the pitilessness, that the successful spy master must have. Soon he was demonstrating to what degree he possessed these qualities.

He formed his own service, or rather, services. The largest was known as the combatant secret service, which was composed of 5,000 criminals who had fled from Russia after the revolution. Other forces were composed of White Russians, and there was a vast army of 80,000 Chinese renegades, called ch'ang mao tao, the long-haired sect, who were willing to carry out Doihara's orders in return for his support. For, while concentrating upon Manchuria, he did not neglect China, and particularly the Five Northern Provinces, which were scheduled next after Manchuria for Japanese tutelage.

Besides these hordes of operatives, who were used more for sabotage, assassination and the stirring up of strife than for purely intelligence purposes, Doihara employed many other nefarious, and in some cases unmentionable, devices.

To his way of thinking, addiction to opium was a virtue, abstention a vice. He converted the Chinese so-called clubs into combinations of saloon, gambling house, brothel and opium den, with the accent on the latter. He employed traffickers in opium who wandered throughout Manchuria and China, visiting every village fair, where they set up booths from which they advertised the sale of a guaranteed cure for tuberculosis. The medicine was either opium or an opium derivative. Once the unfortunate victims had become the slaves of the drug, it was but half a step to becoming the slaves and informers of Doihara, who controlled the supplies of the drug.

Many of those in his pay themselves employed labor. By his directions, these laborers were first paid half in cash and half in opium; and then entirely in opium.

At his request, Japanese cigarette manufacturers began to make a new brand of cigarettes, known as Golden Bat. The sale of Golden Bats was prohibited in the mother country; they were for export only. Doihara controlled their distribution in Manchuria and China. In the mouth-pieces were concealed small doses of opium or heroin, and many unsuspecting purchases were thus gathered into Doihara's evergrowing army of addicts.

The more vicious of Oriental gentlemen attain, so they believe, the greatest orgastic release in sexual intercourse with Occidental women. Doihara accepted this imagined perversion as a ready-made weapon with which to weaken further the peoples against whom he was striving.

In Mukden and Harbin and other satisfactory locations he set up brothels in which the prostitutes were all White Russians. The source of supply was a plentiful one, for no fewer than 100,000 White Russians had fled from Siberia into Manchuria and China after the Bolshevik Revolution. They came with nothing; they remained with nothing. Such was their nature that they could not raise themselves out of the depression of mind and spirit into which their fate had plunged them; that they lived, literally, from today to the day after next. In a brothel they were at least sure of their food, and the happy oblivion of opium when they were not on duty. For, for every six pipes of opium they sold to clients they were given one pipe for themselves.

It was a terrible thing that Doihara was doing here. He set about deliberately to destroy half a continent with drugs and depravity of every kind. The success he had was even more terrible.

In 1926, in order to remove Marshal Chang Tso-lin from the Manchurian scene so that they might prepare for their own ends with greater speed, unhindered, the Japanese, through Doihara, persuaded the war lord to have his revenge on Peking. Supported by equipment supplied by them, Chang arrived before Peking and sat himself down there for two years.

But during these two years Kuomintang armies swept over the whole of China. Under the able direction first of the Communists and then of General Chiang Kai-shek, by 1928 they had reached Tsinanfu. By now the Japanese had put a considerable army into China, under their concessions, and were in control of the Tsingatao-Tsinan Railway, and at Tsinanfu they offered considerable resistance to the Kuomintang forces.

Realizing what was happening, Marshal Chang's oldest and best friend, General Wu Shu-chen, whom he had left as regent in Manchuria, begged Chang to return there urgently if he did not wish the Japanese to control his country.

Chang's return was the last thing the Japanese wished to happen, and hearing of General Wu's urgent appeal, on May 19th, 1928, they instructed their ambassador in Peking to warn Chang that he must not return to Manchuria. This opposition removed Chang's hesitation and he made preparations for his journey home.

Now Chang had an agent in Tokyo, an Englishman called Swineheart, and on May 31st he received a message from Swineheart urging him on no account to travel by train to Mukden, as he had it from the most reliable source that Doihara had given an undertaking to the Japanese government that Chang would never reach Manchuria.

Chang, who for some strange reason was completely blind to Doihara's activities in his own country and even looked on him as a friend, was sure that Swineheart was mistaken. He did, however, mention the warning to a Japanese colonel, who at once said that, to set the marshal's mind at rest, he would travel with him, in the same compartment, all the way to Mukden.

On June 4th, General Wu Shu-chen received a message to meet his friend and overlord, Marshal Chang Tso-lin, at a station some twelve miles south of Mukden two days later. He believed that the marshal had made the request while, for his part, Chang was delighted by the courtesy of his friend.

"You were kind to come to meet me, Shu-chen," he said.

"I was happy to come to meet my old friend after so long a time," Wu replied.

And both of them continued to believe, the one in the

123

courtesy, the other in the friendship of old acquaintances.

The marshal and the general talked in general terms only before the barbarian colonel who was keeping his promise to Chang to ride in his compartment with him. Chang was regretting now that he had ever accepted this offer of "protection." Of course, Swineheart had picked one of the myriad rumors with which Tokyo has always swarmed, and always will. In ten minutes the train would be in Mukden and it would all be over. Nothing could happen now.

"In that case, Marshal Chang," said the Japanese colonel, "perhaps you will excuse me while I get my cap and sword from the next compartment."

"Please do," said Chang.

When the colonel had gone along the corridor, Chang said to his friend: "Tell me quickly, how are things?"

"Bad! Bad!" said Wu. "The Japanese are becoming more and more powerful. If we do not join with the Kuomintang they will have us under their rule. Thank the gods you have returned, my . . ."

Wu did not complete his sentence. The compartment in which the two men were sitting was at that moment passing under a bridge. Suddenly a tremendous explosion lifted the carriage from the tracks and simultaneously the collapsing bridge crushed it like match wood. When the debris was removed, Wu and seventeen of Chang's officers traveling in the carriage were dead. Chang died some hours later without regaining consciousness.

Doihara had carried out his promise.

Among the would-be rescuers was the Japanese colonel, who had gone, not to the next compartment, but right to the rear of the train where he had escaped unhurt.

The removal of Marshal Chang and General Wu did not, however, bring the results that the Japanese were sure the assassinations must have. An obscure general rose up in Chang's place, and with the courage of the obscure he refused to give way one pace before the increasing pressure of the Japanese but encouraged his people more and more firmly in the notions and ideals of nationalism.

For the next three years Doihara and his hordes plotted, assassinated, roused riots, dug deeper and wider their wells of depravity in vain.

At last the Japanese government saw that it would achieve its ends only by the direct use of force, and in September 1931 startled the world by their full-scale invasion of Manchuria, which they attempted to cry down by referring to it as the Manchurian Incident.

On September 19th, 1931, they captured Mukden; on February 5th, 1932, Harbin fell to them. A fortnight later they declared the "independence" of Manchuria.

Unfortunately for Japan, what they had done in Manchuria did not look legitimate in the light of international law. It was essential at this stage, for the success of their wider plan, that the rest of the world should not become suspicious of their intentions and be roused to intervene.

Doihara cast about him for a solution and hit upon a possibility. Indeed, it was to turn out to be the only solution. The Japanese should set up a puppet state at whose head, to give it a semblance of independence, should be none other than the unhappy, timid, weak young man, the last emperor of China, Henry Pu-yi.

But here again there were difficulties! The stupid young man, weak and timid though he might be, steadfastly refused to accept the Manchu throne.

And there was no one else!

Doihara was pondering his problem one evening as he paced his room. Convinced now that threats would not move Henry Pu-yi to accept the honor they were offering him, he was at his wits' end to know what to do. A knock on the door interrupted his pacing.

"Come in!" he snapped, pausing in his walking and facing the door.

A servant entered, his eyes fixed on the floor, his whole body trembling a little.

"Well, what is it?" the colonel demanded.

"There is a stranger below, sir," the servant answered. "For two hours he has been here now, demanding to see

125

you. We have told him it is impossible, but at last—" The wretched man shrugged his shoulders and waited for the rage to burst on him.

Instead Doihara asked: "What is his name?"

"He will not give his name, sir."

"What sort of man is he?"

"He is a strange man, sir. A Manchu."

"There is nothing strange in that. There are thirty million Manchus."

"But it's his voice, sir. He speaks like a gentleman, but his voice is high, sir. As though . . . as though . . . he were a eunuch."

"There would be nothing so very strange in that, either. Is he armed?"

"No, sir. He has left his pistols and his dagger on the table."

"Does he give a hint of what he wants?"

"No, sir."

Intrigued, Doihara made up his mind. Whatever the fellow wanted, it would divert his thoughts for a few moments from the stupidity of Henry Pu-yi.

"I'll see him," he said. "Bring him up."

While the servant was gone, he drew his sword from its scabbard and placed it on the table, ready to hand, and put the table between himself and the door. He had many enemies, he knew. It was as well to be prepared. He disliked using his pistols; he had never really mastered the weapon whereas with the sword there was scarcely his equal.

The servant came into the room and stood to one side to allow a small Manchu to enter.

"What do you want?" Colonel Doihara asked.

"To speak with you alone."

The colonel nodded to the servant and the man went out shutting the door behind him.

"Well, what is your name?" Doihara said.

"That does not matter for the moment."

"Very well, then what do you want?"

The servant was right; the voice was peculiar. But eunuchs ran rapidly to fat and this young man did not seem to have an ounce of fat on him. Admittedly he was young; too young, in fact, to have been made a eunuch at birth. Those days were too long past.

"I have heard much about you, colonel, and I want to work for you."

"How have you heard?"

"I have my sources."

"The Chinese have sent you!"

The suspicion suddenly came down on Doihara. With a quick movement he had seized his sword and had its point within an inch of his visitor's heart.

"If you make the slightest move, you will be dead before you know what has happened," he threatened. "Now, tell me who sent you."

Whoever the fellow was, he was certainly a brave one. He even had the impertinence to chuckle.

"Your nerves are all on edge, colonel," he said. He was even mocking.

"Who sent you?" Doihara repeated.

"Nobody sent me."

The rage suddenly exploded in the colonel. He would teach the fool a lesson. With a flick of his wrist so quick that his victim did not see it, he ripped up the front of the silk gown, yet left the flesh beneath unscratched.

"Perhaps that will convince you . . ." he began and stopped, his mouth falling open, the point of his sword dropping with a thud to the ground. For the same flick of the sword point that had ripped up the gown ripped up something else besides. The gown gaped open, and slowly, as it did so, a linen band bound tightly round the man's chest was pushed aside and fell apart, revealing the firm, full breasts of a woman.

Doihara passed his hand across his face.

"A woman?" he muttered.

"There is no point now in withholding my name any longer," she said. "I am Princess Yoshiko Kamajama. My father was Prince Su, of the late imperial court."

So Kenji Doihara met this strange woman whose one delight was to go about in men's clothing seeking adventures which normally a woman would shun. He had heard stories about her but had not believed them they were so fantastic.

"I have come to offer my services to you," she said. "But you are weary. If the servants had let me up sooner . . . I will come back tomorrow."

"No . . . stay!" he said.

Next morning he spoke to her of Henry Pu-yi as soon as she awoke.

"Let me persuade him," she suggested. "If what I hear about him is true, it should not be difficult."

If she failed, she could do no harm.

"Very well," he said. "You shall try."

So the Beauty in Male Costume, as she thereafter came to be known among the Chinese opponents of Doihara and his gangs, went to Henry Pu-yi. She was patient, but soon it was apparent that she alone would never persuade him to ascend the Manchu throne. Nor did the bomb she planted in his bed. But the snakes did. After the snakes Henry Pu-yi decided that he might as well die an emperor as a commoner.

His acceptance was Doihara's greatest success to date, and his grateful masters rewarded him with the rank of lieutenant general.

After Henry Pu-yi was settled on the Manchu throne, Princess Yoshiko Kamajama continued to work for Doihara. At the same time she found the opportunity to marry and divorce in quick succession three "princely persons" in the Five Northern Provinces of China.

On the eve of her fourth marriage she was attacked by unknown assailants and stabbed. From the wounds she received any other woman—or man—would have died.

But it was not until November 11th, 1945, that a message carried by a news agency, under the date line Peiping, announced: "Long-sought-for Beauty in Male Costume arrested today in Peiping by Chinese counterintelligence officers."

With the Manchurian Incident closed, Doihara turned his attention fully to the next phase of the plan. This was to detach the Five Northern Provinces of China from Peking and turn them into a second puppet state which would act as a base for the main project of seizing the whole of China.

He himself went to work on men of high rank. Some of them resisted his bribes and his promises; but some fell for him. Among the latter was Huang-sen, an official of the Central Bank of China.

Doihara operated in Peiping—as Peking was now called—as Ito Soma, a Japanese financier, esthete and patron of the arts. In this role he made friends with Mei Lang-fan, the star of the Chinese theater, who introduced him to Huang-sen.

Ito Soma, Mai Lang-fan and Huang-sen met on nights of the full moon on the steps of the Altar of Heaven to discuss poetry, painting, philosophy and Huang-sen's hobby— goldfish. Ito Soma knew the names and habits of six hundred different kinds of goldfish, and Huang-sen was charmed by him.

Presently, in a conversation about the mating habits of one species of fish, Huang-sen confessed to having another hobby—women. Unfortunately, he was now so acutely embarrassed financially that he could not pursue this hobby as enthusiastically as he would wish. A day or two later he was amazed to receive a gift of 200,000 Chinese dollars. At first he refused the money, but Soma soothed him and the temptation was really too great.

Not very long afterward Huang-sen became the secretary of General Chiang Kai-shek. When the Japanese threats became more violent, Chiang called a council of war, at which were present only General Feng Yu-hsiang, General Pai Tsung-chi and his trusted secretary, Huang-sen.

The generals planned to trap a large flotilla which the Japanese had anchored in the Yangtse River at Hankow. In some way the Japanese got wind of what was going to happen, and when the Chinese forces arrived they found no ships.

Chiang immediately ordered an investigation, and this revealed that his secretary had confided the plan to Ito Soma, alias Kenji Doihara, and he paid the supreme penalty.

It was only by executions and ruthless counterespionage that Chiang was able to resist to any degree the espionage of Doihara. In 1938, after the next phase of the plan had begun to operate, Chiang had to execute eight divisional commanders who were known to be Doihara's agents. It is said by reliable sources that more high-ranking Chinese officers were executed in the first six years of the war for dealings with Doihara than for any other military offense of extreme gravity.

The confusion which this one man spread among the enemies of Japan and the assistance which his own government and armies received from his activities will never be entirely evaluated, since he spread his nets so wide that they could never be pulled in altogether.

Though to call Doihara the Lawrence of Manchuria may be a libel on Lawrence's memory, his achievements exceed in scope and outweigh in importance and results the activities of five Lawrences.

CHAPTER 9

Everyone *Can* Spy: Everyone *Must* Spy

With the successful termination of the Manchurian Incident, Japan completed her first half-century of espionage on the Stieber model. Her development in this aspect of her growth toward a modern power on Western lines had been as remarkable and presented as fascinating a phenomenon as in any other sphere; perhaps even more so.

While Kenji Doihara was exercising his evil genius in Manchuria and China, a West European had already been attempting to make an assessment of this Japanese phenomenon. He was a young German at a loose end. Now not so young, he is still, in 1957, at a loose end, though in a very confined sense, and looks like remaining so for the rest of his natural term unless the mood of the free countries changes and the prisoners of Spandau are debouched upon the cruel world.

His name was Rudolf Hess, who was to rise to a position of great prominence as a particular friend of Adolf Hitler's and was destined to achieve a world reputation, first as a mystery man, and then as a madman, by flying to England from Germany fairly early in World War II in an effort, so he said, to bring hostilities to an end.

In 1925 Hess had enrolled as a student at the School of Geopolitics in Munich. The School of Geopolitics was one of those strange manifestations of elaborately confused thinking which from time to time take seed, sprout and burgeon in Germany.

In the early days after the First World War there had come to Munich a former professional officer of the defeated German Army. He came to Munich in a mood of distinct relief, for conditions were so bad in the fatherland that it was difficult for millions of men trained in industry and the professions to find work, let alone a professional soldier.

Why the rector of Munich University should have offered him the post of lecturer in geography, Karl Haushofer—we have met him before at the beginning of our story as the man who solved Goebels' difficulties with Ruth Kühn—was himself slightly puzzled, when he came to consider all things quietly and dispassionately. But it was true, nevertheless, and here he was in the ancient and lovely Bavarian capital, determined to hold down the job even if it meant living poised over the precipice of bluff.

Admittedly, he knew enough about the subject to cope with first-year students. It was the more senior courses that he really feared. It is not possible to deceive adolescents for long—as so many teachers have discovered to their cost—and it would take even less time for his colleagues on the faculty to get his true measure.

But Karl Haushofer was not entirely devoid of brains and he brought to the situation in which he now found himself as a civilian the courage that had marked his career in the Kaiser's army. If he could not long survive as a

131

geographer, he would create his own subject, inventing its theory and its terminology, and then sell it for all he was worth.

Casting about for such a subject, in a sudden flash of inspiration he hit upon a very simple, though at that time new, concept of the relation between geography and politics. Explained very briefly, his contention was this: a country's foreign policy does not determine its history; but rather, a country's history is determined by its geographical position and configuration, since it is these which predetermine its foreign policy.

Now this idea, particularly as developed and expounded by Haushofer, had the great merit that there could be something in it, even if, at first sight, it was difficult to say categorically what that "something" might be. Haushofer was also extremely fortunate in being in the best place for launching his subject, for of all professional agglomerations, those of the German universities have always been Athenian in their enthusiasm for setting up altars to this -ism and that -ism. Not entirely to his utter surprise, in a very short time Haushofer discovered that he had many disciples. Indeed, so rapidly did his following increase, and so wholeheartedly was his theory embraced, that in a very little while Haushofer left the staff of Munich University and with a chosen band of his most enthusiastic supporters he founded the School of Geopolitics.

Rudolf Hess was greatly taken with the theories of geopolitics and the founder of geopolitics was greatly taken with him, and they became close friends. As his field of study, Haushofer assigned Japan to Hess; and besides keeping the young man quiet in assigning this particular country to Hess, Haushofer was bestowing upon him a special mark of his favor. For many years Haushofer had been a persistent advocate of an alliance between Germany and Japan. He based his advocacy on the belief that eventually Japan must expand into and control East Asia.

Hess spent two years gathering his material and another two years in writing his paper. But when at last he placed his manuscript of 132 typewritten pages containing some 40,000 words in his master's hands, Haushofer found, to his surprise and initial irritation, that his pupil had limited his studies to Japanese espionage.

Hess set out his thesis under three main headings—the history of Japanese espionage; espionage on a mass basis; the objects of Japanese espionage.

According to Hess, Japanese espionage had had its origins in about 1860. When Commodore Perry had compelled the Japanese to open up their ports to foreign trade, the Japanese had opened their minds to Western civilization. For fifty years the Japanese government sent countless diplomatic, trade and naval missions to gather precious information in Europe and America.

They also sent men who pretended to be in search of training and who were, therefore, admitted to the great engineering works and arsenals of the Old and New Worlds. Manufacturers had to agree to hiring Japanese labor as the price for trading with Japan. But in reality, these laborers were trained engineers who came to discover the industrial secrets of the West. In like manner, economic and industrial espionage was carried on by delegates, students and tourists. Hess then continued with a review of the development of Japan as a world power and her formulation and implementation of her expansionist policy, and then stated objects of her espionage.

These objects, Hess wrote, were to discover not only industrial and military secrets but to pry into the political and cultural affairs of foreign nations. He proceeded to show that nothing, literally nothing, was outside the scope of Japanese espionage activity, quoting as examples of their thoroughness that the personal habits and weaknesses of responsible officers in the armed forces and of important persons in the industrial defense effort were discovered and listed; that agents would not only study the output of an airplane plant but seek to determine which plants supplied the airplane plant with spare parts, over what routes these spares were shipped and whether there were alternative routes, such information being necessary in order to know exactly where to place a bomb with most effect.

In the diplomatic field they were always looking for

secret agreements and confidential consular reports. They had long suspected that the United States and Great Britain had entered into secret undertakings with regard to the use of bases in the Far East against Japan.

Under his second heading, espionage on a mass basis, Hess observed that espionage was second nature to the Japanese. For generations they had had what amounted to an internal system of mass espionage in the operation of which neighbor spied upon neighbor.

Japanese leaders had always treated their people like children. Since the time of the shogunate, plain-clothes agents and voluntary or impressed informers had been widely employed, and this had developed in the Japanese as a nation a penchant for spying that was so ingrained that they pursued it whenever the opportunity offered, particularly when traveling abroad. This was not to say that every Japanese found outside the boundaries of his own country was a trained spy or an agent of the Japanese intelligence service. Nor did the Japanese travel so that they might have opportunities of spying which in their intense patriotism they believed would acquire merit for them. Nevertheless, whenever a Japanese saw a chance of spying, he spied, and passed on whatever information he gathered either to a Japanese consul or to the police when he returned home.

The sight of a Japanese tourist without a camera was a very rare one. By and large he was a keen observer, though he suffered from a deplorable lack of judgment, with the result that he collected a great mass of useless information and misinformation which he noted down carefully in travel diaries and which eventually found its way into the files of the intelligence.

In Hess's opinion, the most efficient of Japanese amateur spies were the expatriates. They were not averse to criticizing their country in the presence of foreigners in order to gain a confidence if they believed they could acquire information only by a show of false friendship. In fact, the number of Japanese who really thought ill of their country was so small as to be entirely without significance.

It has long been the tradition of espionage services

throughout the world to disclaim any knowledge of a captured agent. The Japanese have never followed this practice and diplomatic and consular representatives have always made forceful attempts to protect their agents. The arrest of an agent invariably drew indignant protests and bail was always immediately forthcoming, though these actions were tantamount to an admission of complicity in the activities of the agents.

The reports of both professional and amateur agents were conveyed to intelligence headquarters in Tokyo generally by one of three methods: through consulates, who passed them on by couriers to the embassies, who in turn sent them to Japan, more often than not in diplomatic bags; or they would be handed to special agent-couriers who were ostensibly on tours of inspection; or they would be handed to the captains of Japanese merchant and passenger ships at the last minute before sailing to Japan.

The Japanese agent had the advantage over the agents of almost every other power in that the difficulty of his language, which prevented all but a few foreigners from learning it, protected him against eavesdroppers. Similarly, the difficulties of the written language permitted him to make notes without having to resort to the use of codes.

The great mass of information that was supplied by all these sources was collected by the army, navy and foreign office intelligence bureaus in Tokyo. It was carefully studied, classified and cross-indexed, and then submitted to staff officers. The latter, as well as the intelligence chiefs, also sent instructions to agents abroad when any specific project was under consideration.

Hess made one serious miscalculation in his assessment of the system. He saw the patriotic societies as jingoistic arrogant secret societies whose belief in Japan's divine mission as the ruler of the world was as irrational as it was fanatic. Nevertheless, he recognized that they were the mainspring of Japan's aggressiveness and that they had an influence on Japanese foreign affairs as great as that of the politicians.

Hess had some forthright remarks to make about the Black Dragon Society, some of which were penetrating and

135

some very wide of the mark. Its recruits, he said, came mainly from among those samurai, the fighting men, who found themselves lordless under the reconstruction of the social order and thus without employment. These samurai were known as ronin, or wave men.

The ronin collaborated fairly closely with army intelligence and were supported, in part, by army funds. The extremist elements of the younger cliques, whose aims coincided with those of the societies, were members of one or another of them. There may have been a certain number of ronin in the ranks of the patriotic societies' agents, but, as we have seen, the agents were picked from every walk of life provided they had outstanding patriotic zeal and were otherwise good "agent material." It is strange to note, as Hess noted, that there is no evidence to be found of any collaboration between the societies and navy intelligence. Indeed, a coolness existed between them which, in the general circumstances, was remarkable.

It is true, as Hess remarked, that many of the patriotic societies' agents on the Asian mainland were seen as the lowest scum, strong-arm thugs, hired assassins, blackmailers and adventurers who lived on compulsory "patriotic" contributions or protection money. Such men were employed however, because the societies operated in every sphere, and conceited and brazen though they may appear, they were nevertheless courageous. Their role was to provoke brawls and street fights and other incidents which any other power would have been very anxious to conceal. But the Japanese used such incidents as excuses to present demands, exact apologies which inflicted loss of face on those who made them, or pigeonholed them for use in the future as pretexts for opening hostilities.

Hess's study of his subject was a very exhaustive one. The intricate workings of the Japanese system of espionage based on Wilhelm Stieber's pattern, which was the child of a typical German mind and on which the German espionage system had always been, still was and still is firmly founded, was entirely comprehensive and of extreme interest to his own typical German mind.

He recognized, too, how much farther the Japanese had

taken their model, expanded it and improved upon it to meet their own specific needs. These needs, as we have seen, were dictated first, by their expansionist policy as laid down in the third tenet of State Shintoism, and second, by the need to make themselves secure in Asia so that their development should neither be impeded nor seized by a foreign nation to enhance its own power.

It was the latter which threatened them in this early period. They recognized Russia to be the first great enemy, and it was against Russia that they directed their main espionage effort until the enemy was rendered ineffective and the immediate threat thereby removed.

But while they were subjecting Russia, not only in Asia but in Europe as well, to invasion by the largest secret army ever put into the field up to this time, they were not unmindful of what may be termed "the follow-up."

Even with Russia no longer a direct threat, the Japanese could never feel themselves entirely secure while China was in a turmoil of decadent disorganization. Such a condition was simply inviting some other power to step in and put China to rights. There were several Western Powers, and most notably the British, who had tremendous interests, industrial and financial, in China.

The British had established a colony at Hong Kong into which many millions of pounds sterling had been poured. They had, also, strong interests in Shanghai and other Chinese ports. China was a good customer for their products. Japan's cotton industry was already threatening the interests of the great Lancashire cotton industry. If Britain saw her position in the Orient undermined by the chaos in China, her previous record made it very plain that she would not hesitate to gain control of China in some form or other. (The fact that she was, in the event, too slow off the mark was not to be foreseen by the Japanese at this time.)

This Japan must avoid at all costs; and it was their early realization of it that prompted, even compelled, the Japanese, at the same time that they were concentrating on removing the threat of Russia, to take preparatory steps to bring China under her own control.

In China, then, in the first fifty years, she built up an espionage organization which, even in its very beginnings, was greater than the organization of any other country altogether, and which was capable of tremendous expansion all the time.

She brought to this section of her secret services all the cunning, the devilishness and the unremitting care which she devoted to all her espionage activities. As an example of this tremendous care, we have notes on the case of an agent called Kotai Kozumi. Kozumi was selected to work in the Moslem provinces of west Asiatic Russia. He first of all spent four years at the Tokyo School of Foreign Languages and at the Military Academy.

When he was considered fit by these two institutions, he was sent to Qurban Ali, president of the Tokyo Islamic Order, who before he came to Japan had had many years of most successful subversive activity to his credit. Qurban Ali was to teach Kozumi not only an impeccable accent but also the right mannerisms. Five more years went by before the teacher was sufficiently satisfied with his pupil to allow him to be sent into the field.

It was this boundless patience, which only the Oriental with his very different conception of time can exert, which is one of the outstanding aspects of Japanese espionage. The care which was taken with the preparation of their agents produced a large proportion of the danger they presented.

By the time that Manchuria had been secured to Japan as a mainland base, the chaos of China had been rendered even more chaotic by the machinations of Japanese agents. By means of bribery, threats, violence and particularly drugs, scarcely a Chinese of any note was not under Japanese influence. With covert support they set the war lords one against the other, and by manipulation made it impossible for any one or combination of war lords to achieve a position in which power to bring China to order might have been achieved. They worked ceaselessly, and with equal cunning, in undermining the morale of the masses by forcing them into dope addiction, and destroyed one of the strongest sets of man's ethical values by the extension of brothels in which they encouraged sexual depravity, on the main principle of Stieber's Green House, but on a scale which makes the mind boggle. At the same time they stirred up unrest by bringing constantly to the surface of the normally fatalistic Chinese mind the extremity of his economic lot.

China alone is a vast area, and they covered it all. But while they were making their preparations there, they were not neglecting an even wider field.

Japanese agents were active in Burma, Siam, India, Indochina, Afghanistan and Malaya. Realizing as early as the eighties that to be masters of the Pacific—and also because they had an old score to pay off: Commodore Perry's actions in 1853—they would sooner or later have to join battle with America, long before the close of the nineteenth century they had agents in Honolulu who were sending weekly reports to Tokyo on American defenses and activities there. This organization operating against the Americans was maintained unremittingly right down to Pearl Harbor. The Philippines, also, were subjected to the same kind of attention.

It is safe to say that by the end of the first fifty years of its existence, starting from scratch, Japanese espionage covered half the physical surface of the globe and to such a degree that it is doubtful whether anyone could number exactly the vast army of the emperor's secret servants.

The other half of the world they had not neglected either. In all the countries of Europe, in Turkey, Egypt, Abyssinia and North Africa, and across the Atlantic, small cells of agents centered mainly on attachés at legations and embassies were probing, discovering and reporting.

And as yet Japan had not turned her serious attention to North and Central America, and to the rich preserves of the Dutch East Indies.

It was a fantastic program. As it developed during the twenties and thirties it was to become more fantastic still. Set beside the espionage efforts of the two greatest world powers, it reduces England to an homunculus and the United States to a disembodied wraith, entirely without substance.

America's espionage history is a strange one, and throws Japan's efforts into even more horrifying relief.

For the first hundred years after the Declaration of Independence, all efforts of the leaders of the American administration were devoted to internal, domestic development. This called for neither spies nor counterspies.

In 1898, however, Washington realized with something of a shock that the tyrannical rule of the Spaniards in Cuba had seeped into the knowledge of Americans and that popular feeling demanded an end to the former entirely introvert policies.

The war with Cuba lasted only four months and ended in a victory for American arms and consciences. But it also meant more. By the American annexation of Guam, Porto Rico and the Philippines, and later in the year, of the Hawaiian Islands, America became an "overseas power" —dare one say it?—imperialist.

At the time, Japan was building up all her efforts for a knockout blow at Russia, which she delivered successfully in 1905. This and her closed-door policy in Manchuria led to a definite deterioration in Japanese-American relations, which became so aggravated by precautionary American anti-Japanese measures on the Pacific coast that in 1907 there was a most serious threat of war.

President Theodore Roosevelt, however, met the situation by a combination of a show of force and appeasement, and two agreements were signed with Tokyo in 1907 and 1908. The Japanese, foolishly, read the appeasement to mean that their special position in Manchuria was recognized by the United States, and were rudely disabused when Washington proposed that the Manchurian railways should be internationalized. Nothing came of the idea, but in disappointed retaliation Japan signed a treaty with her late adversary, Russia, in which both parties undertook to help one another in defense of their interests.

The First World War, and Japan's alliance with the Western Powers, seemed to remove the threat of Japanese opposition, at least for the time being. But when Japanese militarism flared up in the twenties and thirties, one would have thought that America would have realized that she was "on the list." The antidote would have been espionage and counterespionage systems which would have kept Japanese at home and their activities abroad under constant and strict surveillance. But on the contrary, the American leaders appeared to spurn the aid of spies and counterspies.

Until the First World War, America had possessed no corps of intelligence police. Such a corps was formed on her entry into the war and developed rapidly. In January 1918 it was decided to increase its strength by degrees to 750, but the armistice and demobilization foiled this intention, and between the two wars the corps shrank to such ludicrous proportions that it can hardly be said to have existed at all.

This state of affairs lasted until June 1939, when, in view of continued reports that Japanese and Nazi spies were active in Panama, Hawaii and the Philippines, President F. D. Roosevelt issued a proclamation declaring that all matters of an espionage, counterespionage and sabotage nature would be in the hands of the Federal Bureau of Investigation, the Military Intelligence Division and the Office of Naval Intelligence.

The directors of these three agencies were to form a committee to coordinate their activities. In 1940 the directors drew up an agreement which defined the Jurisdiction of each agency, with particular emphasis on foreign operations, and renewed this agreement in 1942. The Corps of Intelligence Police was resuscitated in 1940 and rapidly expanded until its eventual total strength reached 4,431 noncommissioned officers.

It is true that during the inter-war years, the Military Intelligence Division, the Office of Naval Intelligence and the F.B.I. had been functioning, but they were so sparsely manned that they were quite unable to cope with espionage in America except to a pathetically meager extent.

Perhaps the best way to illustrate how pathetically meager American espionage and counterespionage effort was is to compare the secret service budgets for the middle thirties of Japan, Great Britain and America.

In 1934-35 the Japanese secret service was allowed an

appropriation of 13,814,000 yen, the equivalent at the then rate of exchange of 4,000,000 American dollars. At the same time Great Britain was spending 800,000 dollars and the United States 50,000 dollars.

The gap was to widen still farther, until in 1938-39, the Japanese allotted 25,000,000 dollars, while the whole of the British Empire was spending only 1,000,000 dollars and the United States government 240,000 dollars on their espionage and counterespionage services.

The Japanese began serious espionage activities in the United States in 1927. By that year she was also deeply involved underground with Russia. Incidents, shootings, betrayals, alarms and widespread bribery were the order of the day on the Amur River frontier, in Korea, Manchuria, Outer Mongolia and Inner Mongolia, and elsewhere.

In the American and British spheres of interest they were already expanding their activities in the Philippines and in Hong Kong, Singapore and Malaya, and in other parts affecting the Western Powers such as the Dutch East Indies, French Indochina and Siam. It will be noted that all these areas were to be occupied fifteen years later and that they had been the object of long-term preparatory espionage.

The Japanese were still working on the Stieber model, which had long since become outmoded, for it had been proved by the Western Powers to be too top-heavy. But if the model were outmoded it is still strange to the layman that the United States, in view of all the circumstances, should be at the other extreme.

Nor was this shown only in the virtual nonexistence of espionage and counterespionage organizations, but in the outlook of the administration on foreign espionage within the borders of America.

In 1939, for example, the maximum penalty for spying in the United States was the ridiculously light one of two years' hard labor; and when in the previous year a federal grand jury had indicted eighteen German agents, four of whom were in custody, and it was revealed that the Japanese and German secret services were collaborating in America, the State Department vetoed the disclosure of this information to the public for fear of the effect it might have on international relations.

Nevertheless, when specific Japanese activities in the United States come to be considered, it will be seen that providence favored America. For all their monstrous army of spies, the vast Japanese Goliath of espionage was routed by the minute American David of counterespionage. But with adequate forces much of the interim damage could have been avoided, as we shall see.

CHAPTER 10

Everyone in the Card Index

One of the things about Japanese espionage which had struck Rudolf Hess most forcibly was the intense interest which the ordinary man in the street took in it.

In his report Hess says: "Every Japanese when he goes abroad considers himself to be a spy; and when he is at home he takes upon himself the role of spy catcher. I suggest that this preoccupation with espionage is ingrained in the Japanese, since for very many years under the shogunate a system of secret police was extensively active whose main task was to secure the shoguns against plots on their lives and against their positions."

Hess was quite right in his first observation. Whether his suggestion that it was ingrained by long subjection to the activities of secret police is correct or not, the Japanese authorities worked upon and whipped the interest of the ordinary Japanese deliberately and continuously by well-planned assaults which increased in intensity as Pearl Harbor approached.

Behind Japanese espionage toward the end of its first half-century and well into its second fifty years were the ostensible directors of military and naval intelligence,

General Eiki Tojo and Admiral Kiyoshi Noda. In fact, the *eminence grise* of all undercover organizations was General Jiro Minami, a veteran in his middle sixties.

Minami, who was descended from a long line of samurai, was a patient, resourceful plotter. When the puppet state of Manchukuo was set up after the conquest of Manchuria, he asked for and received the appointment of Japanese ambassador to the court of Emperor Henry Pu-yi. About this time, he organized with that other veteran, Lieutenant General Kenji Doihara, the Great Asia Association, which had as its ultimate goal the conquest of all East Asia and the Pacific.

From Manchukuo, Minami moved into Korea which, it is said, he ruled "with an inflexible will, and all Japan by telephone."

Encouraged by Minami and his subordinates, the people of Japan were led to see espionage activity in every move made by any nation in the Pacific, particularly the United States. Thus, when Colonel Lindbergh and his wife made a flying tour of the Kurile Islands in 1931, the American air ace was denounced as a spy.

People like the retired Lieutenant General Kiokatsu Sato were applauded when they made pronouncements such as this one of Sato's; "It is our duty to detest and loathe the people of the United States." And Japanese approval was strengthened, if this were necessary, by the approval of Germany and Italy.

Not only were foreigners treated with suspicion, but Japanese who had social and commercial contacts with foreigners became the objects of intensified police attention. Any foreign tourist carrying a camera was inviting arrest, while the Tokyo personnel of the Soviet news agency, Tass, were the most intensely watched men in Japan.

Then there was the German, Dr. Walter Donath, whose life was made wretched in the interest which the *Kempei tai* took in him.

Dr. Donath was the chief of the German Cultural Institute in Japan, a body set up by the mutual interest of the two governments as a part of the deep and abiding friendship which they had for one another. This being so,

144

one would have thought that the doctor would have been immune from surveillance; but in fact he could not move about Tokyo, and certainly not farther afield, without a secret service "shadow."

One day Dr. Donath decided that he would pay a visit to a branch of the institute on the island of Shikoku, about sixty miles from Kobe, to see how it was faring and to dispense encouragement. As it was in the manner of being a business trip, Donath decided to take with him a Japanese student, whose expenses would be met by the institute, to help him over any language difficulties which might arise.

An overnight boat brought them from Kobe to Takamatsu, in Shikoku, very early in the morning. As they stepped onto the jetty, a plain-clothes policeman stopped them and questioned the doctor closely about his business and his plans for the day. The doctor gave him every detail.

From the jetty they went to the hotel where they had made reservations, and while they were at breakfast, yet another *Kempei tai* agent arrived and questioned Donath at great length about his antecedents, his occupation, his feelings toward and his opinions on the Japanese people, about war in general, and the chances that the Japanese might have in a war with America. Then he, too, had to be provided with the doctor's itinerary for the day.

After spending a useful morning in Takamatsu, Donath and the student took an early afternoon train to another town on the island in accordance with their plan. At the new station they were met by yet another plain-clothes man who escorted them to where they wished to go and waited for them while they did their business in order to take them back to the station.

The following morning at breakfast yet another agent disturbed them with a request for the new day's itinerary and asking the same questions with the express purpose of seeing if the answers would be the same today as they had been the day before. When the man had gone, Donath paid a visit to a factory. As he was sitting in a waiting room there until the man he had come to see could receive him, the police telephoned to warn him that on his return to

145

Kobe he would be passing through a fortified zone and that if he took photographs while traversing it he would be arrested.

The agent who had visited him at breakfast had already warned him about this. In any case, Donath knew that the police were aware that he had no camera; whoever had searched his room and his baggage at the hotel the previous evening had been very maladroit and left signs of his activities everywhere.

As Donath and the student left the factory for their hotel they were stopped by yet another agent, who told them which bus they must take. On another bus which took them from their hotel to their point of embarkation, on a motorboat which took them across the narrow strait to another island and on a second bus which transported them to the boat for Kobe, they were accompanied by yet another agent, who waited with them until the boat sailed.

During the two days that Donath had been away from his base he had rarely been out of sight of the police, who knew—and noted down on their card index, which was most rigorously kept—every move he had made, and had (seriously) kept a tally of the number of times he had performed his most intimate functions in public conveniences.

The extent to which the spy mania was carried is well illustrated by the action of the police in banning the sale of copies of the famous drawings of the Straits of Naruto—which were then being fortified—by the well-known Japanese wood-block etcher, Hiroshige. This appears to be quite a logical action, until it is known that the artist died in 1853.

In 1939 a new antiespionage law was passed by the Diet which provided for a much wider application of the death penalty. Simultaneously there was a tremendous expansion of the counterespionage services.

The public was educated to an even higher pitch of the awareness of the danger of spies by means of exhibitions which displayed what the Japanese believed to be the devious and criminal methods and activities of foreign spies. Hundreds of posters papered the streets, and antispy weeks and even antispy days were promoted. Antiespionage slogans were printed on matchboxes, and there was scarcely a shop window which did not exhibit either a slogan or a poster. The press, the radio and the speeches of officials constantly encouraged every Japanese man, woman and child to be on the lookout for foreign spies and to report the smallest suspicious incident. By these means the whole population was lashed into an unprecedented hatred of all foreigners. And behind it all was the *Kempei tai,* the secret military police, or counterespionage service.

The *Kempei tai,* like the Nazi Gestapo, had always been the most powerful, the most hated and the most feared of all Japanese institutions, both by the Japanese at home, and later by the peoples of the occupied territories. It derived its power, for the most part, from the semi-independent position which it held within the army.

Though it was organized as a combat arm of the army, it was commanded by a provost marshal general, who was directly responsible only to the minister of war. In Japan itself, though its authority ran directly from the minister of war to the commander, the ministries of the interior and Justice had occasional and not very serious supervisory powers. Of the rest of the authorities, the navy alone appeared able to keep a check on it, for we find the minister of the navy issuing instructions dealing with the *Kempei tai* control of navy personnel.

All the members of the *Kempei tai* were hand-picked volunteers from the army, and in peacetime were required to have six years' military service before they could be eligible to make application. The standards of intelligence, education, facility in the learning and speaking of languages and of health and physique were extraordinarily high. Since successful counterespionage requires an intimate knowledge of enemy countries, candidates were often drawn from foreign office, embassy and consulate staffs.

Those fortunate enough to be honored by membership in the *Kempei tai* were given one year's training at special schools. The instruction given in these schools was comprehensive, and among the courses provided were law, languages, espionage and counterespionage methods,

147

horsemanship, fencing and unarmed combat, invisible writing, shadowing and entering and leaving buildings.

There was also equally extensive field training. Students were sent to carry out exhaustive investigations of the organization and production methods of Japanese industries, from which they were expected to return undetected. As a further test of their skill, they were made to disguise themselves and to go to places where they were well known.

In 1945 it was estimated by American intelligence that the *Kempei tai,* including the occupied territories, was comprised of 70,000 men, of whom 24,000 were officers. These figures applied only to Japanese members, and if the numbers of native recruits in the occupied territories were added, the total would probably be doubled.

The *Kempei tai* were entitled to wear regular army uniform with special insignia, which consisted of a flowerlike star surrounded by leaves. When working in plainclothes, the agents frequently wore a button resembling a chrysanthemum on the underside of a coat lapel.

Besides its counterespionage functions, the *Kempei tai* was responsible for army discipline, and in this it had supreme power. A member of the force could arrest a member of the army up to three ranks higher than himself. He could decide and carry out punishment in the field. To demonstrate his superiority he might dress with a complete disregard of uniform regulations and refuse to salute; and to emphasize his special standing he was released from all routine duties.

Wherever the *Kempei tai* was, whether in the home islands or in the occupied territories, its most important function was counterespionage. To perform this function efficiently in their view, its members haunted all hotels, post offices, railway stations, piers and other public places. They supervised photographic supply shops, cafes, brothels, theaters and cinemas and, perhaps rather curiously, sweet shops.

They regulated the sale of electrical appliances, arms, drugs and explosives. They kept tab on canteen waiters, government contractors and the employees of all the important industrial undertakings. They kept a constant shadow on every foreigner who entered the country from the moment he stepped ashore to the moment he left, and they did this so thoroughly that they boasted that they could tell, if asked, how many times an individual went to the lavatory in one day. They exercised a censorship of press, radio, literature and the theater.

Bearing all these many and varied functions in mind, it can readily be understood why the membership of the *Kempei tai* had to be so vast. But for all its many thousands of agents, it could not function with anything like a hundred per cent efficiency without outside help.

As Rudolf Hess discovered, they used informers, who either volunteered or were pressed into service, and controlled them by threats or blackmail. Yet like the Gestapo's reputation when it was at its peak, the reputation of the *Kempei tai* seems to have been founded largely on the myth which it deliberately built up around itself of being omnipresent and omniscient.

Thus, then, stood Japanese espionage and counterespionage when they entered upon their second half-century of existence. Vast beyond the dreams of any spy master in the history of espionage anywhere in the world up to 1930, both arms of the service, and particularly the espionage arm, were to become even more vast as the tempo toward the final showdown in the Pacific, which would include the United States, Central America, the Dutch East Indies, Malaya and Burma as well as the American possessions in the Pacific, as the scene of military endeavor.

CHAPTER 11

The Plan Goes into the Last Phase

The plan to set up a puppet state in the Five Northern Provinces of China did not go according to plan, so Japan thereupon turned her attention to controlling the whole of the country. Hostilities broke out between the two countries in 1937.

Despite Japanese victories and the loss of almost the whole of her coastline, railways and river systems, China was still resisting when the local war merged into the Second World War.

While all this had been going on, the internal condition of Japan had been subjected to many vagaries, which included an economic slump, political, military and social unrest, and a series of incidents which had resulted in a new order being imposed on the country. This new order was a one-party political system based largely on the fascist model.

And through all this there began to emerge the real intentions of Japan. As early as January 1934 the foreign minister, Koki Hirota, had proclaimed that "Japan bore the entire burden of responsibility for peace in East Asia." Three months later, in April, what was to become known as the Annam Statement, warned foreign powers against giving China any sort of aid.

In 1935 she signed the Anti-Comintern Pact with Germany and Italy. She had left the League of Nations in 1933 as a result of the Manchurian Incident, and had become somewhat diplomatically isolated, and it was the appreciation of this which made her seek an ostensible friendship with the Anti-Comintern powers.

In December 1935 she abrogated the Washington Naval

Treaty, which had established a naval ratio for the United States, England and Japan of 5:5:3. Though in effect this pact was advantageous to Japan, and was accepted at the time as being so, in her new arrogance she found that the arrangement damaged her prestige, though her motives went much deeper. A month later, in January 1936, she walked out of the London naval conference.

The Anti-Comintern Pact brought Japan into conflict with the U.S.S.R. She was actually in the middle of a large-scale battle with Russian forces over Manchukuo's claim to Outer Mongolia when news arrived of Germany's signing of a non-aggression pact with Russia. Unwilling to bear the brunt of the whole weight of Russia, she settled the incident, and though by signing the pact Germany had proved false to her friends, nevertheless, in the following year Japan was content to become a full member of the Axis by joining the Tripartite Pact in September 1940.

There can be no doubt that Germany's resounding victories in Europe up to this time had convinced Japan that the time was now ripe for her to get rid of her enemies in the Pacific and East Asia.

To immunize Russia, a five-year pact of neutrality was signed in April 1941. This, coming after a year of preparations which had included pressure on the Netherlands to supply specific amounts of raw material, agreement by the Vichy government to allow Japanese troops to be stationed in Indochina to help in the war against China and the intervention in the French-Siamese War which broke out in the autumn of 1940, was more than a straw in the wind.

The Japanese plan, to which all indications pointed, was to seize China and all Southeast Asia and the Pacific. In China and the Pacific the main obstacle to the plan was the United States of America. America was giving material and moral aid to Chiang Kai-shek and encouraging the Dutch to resist Japanese demands in the Indies.

Since 1938 the policy of the State Department toward Japan had been growing increasingly tougher. In 1939 the twenty-eight-year-old commercial treaty had been terminated, and in its place had been introduced a licensing system for a variety of petroleum and metal products for export to Japan. The effect of this measure was to place Japan in an economic predicament and the Japanese government realized that unless they were to be thwarted altogether in their plans, some agreement must be reached with America.

A new ambassador was sent to Washington in the spring of 1941. As soon as Admiral Nomura arrived he entered into conversations with Secretary of State Cordell Hull. The negotiations dragged on inconclusively until July, for the United States government put forward plans designed to contain Japan and obstinately refused to give way one inch.

On July 2nd Japan decided to carry out her plans with regard to Indochina even if this meant war with America and England. The Americans had broken the Japanese diplomatic code and learned of this intention. They immediately froze all Japanese assets in the United States, and Canada and England did likewise, while the Netherlands introduced a licensing system. Thus Japan was cut off from all vital supplies of war material imports. Nevertheless, she went ahead with her plan and occupied Indochina.

Early in August Japan, still hoping to immunize America as she had immunized Russia, submitted new proposals, among which she guaranteed the safety of the Philippines, and asking in return that the United States should persuade Chiang Kai-shek to end his resistance in China, lift the embargo on war materials and stop her military preparations in the area. Naturally, these proposals were promptly rejected.

At another conference in September, the Japanese government decided that they would go so far and no farther, and that if the Americans still refused, they would go to war. America rejected these new proposals on October 2nd.

But still the Japanese did not give up hope that the State Department would weaken, and really final terms were put forward.

Admiral Nomura and a special envoy, Saburo Kurusu,

were warned, however, that the terms must be accepted by November 25th or "things are automatically going to happen."

The deadline was then changed to November 29th, but on November 26th Cordell Hull returned yet another no.

On December 2nd the Japanese issued orders to the naval forces, which had already been despatched to meet the contingency, should it arise, that Pearl Harbor was to be attacked.

Against this background of events had been imposed long-term policies of espionage in the Dutch East Indies beginning as far back as 1931, and in the United States for almost as long a period. We shall now see, first, how the Dutch were defeated before the first Japanese soldier landed in the Indies, and then America's own strange behavior during her spy invasion.

CHAPTER 12

The Ten-Year Plan in the Dutch East Indies

The chief of the Java police looked across his desk at his second-in-command and from him to the young detective sitting beside him.

"Well," he said, "I don't know what to think! If you had told me this about anyone else in the Indies, I might have believed you. But Tomegoro Yoshizumi . . . well . . . it's unbelievable!"

He stood up and began to pace about his office.

The young detective watched him for a moment or two, a slight uncertainty and unhappiness in his gaze. Then he turned and looked at the assistant chief at his side. The assistant chief's eye quickly opened and closed. Had he winked, or merely blinked?

"I know, sir," the assistant chief said. "It does seem

153

incredible. However, Peters here has produced the evidence."

"But I've known Yoshizumi for years!" the chief exclaimed. "He was here before I was."

"He came to the island in 1932, sir. He's been here for five years," the assistant chief said.

"And all that time he's built up his business and become a highly thought of member of the community. Why, I've dined at his house a dozen times! I like the little fellow."

"I like him, too, sir," the assistant chief remarked. "But all the same, while he's been taking us all in with his politeness and his dinners and his honesty in business, he's quietly been making a—a kind of inventory of all the raw materials and the commercial values and sending it off to Tokyo. And not just here in Java, sir, but throughout the whole of the Dutch East Indies. He's had his agents everywhere who have kept his information up-to-date for him."

"You really believe he's the head of this organization, Peters?"

The young man nodded.

"Yes, sir. There's no doubt about it. When I found this fellow with a knife in his back—three weeks ago it is now—he had a whole batch of reports on him and he kept muttering Yoshizumi's name."

The chief brightened.

"That's what makes me suspicious," he said. "A chap like that wouldn't tell the police his chief's name. It's a plant."

Peters answered quietly but firmly. "He didn't know I was a policeman, sir. He didn't know what he was saying. He was light-headed from loss of blood."

When the man had died and Peters had been trying to discover his identity, he had come upon the packet of papers in a belt strapped to his waist next to his skin. Luckily he had broken the seals of the packet carefully. The significance of the lists had not been obvious at once. It was only as he pondered them that he realized what they were. Then he had had them photographed and had made up the packet again as it had been.

Peters was fairly new to the Indies. He knew Yoshizumi by reputation as a leading Japanese merchant and had heard that he was highly thought of. But Peters was also young and had an eye on promotion.

He had gone to his chief and told him his theories, and his chief had laughed at him as though he were out of his mind. But when the young man had asked for permission to keep an eye on the Japanese merchant, he had agreed.

"It will be good practice for you, at all events, and keep you out of mischief," he had said.

The first thing Peters had done was to pay a visit to the merchant. Yoshizumi had agreed to view the body. The dead man was a stranger to him. On a table in the morgue the clothes and possessions of the corpse had been laid out. The package was prominently displayed among them.

"I'm sorry I cannot help you," the merchant had said politely.

The day after Yoshizumi's visit, when Peters had gone to the morgue to give the morgue keeper instructions about the disposal of the body, the man had said casually that on arriving that morning he had found the door unlocked, though he was sure he had locked it before going home the evening before.

"Missed anything?" Peters asked.

"Not a thing!"

Peters examined the lock.

"Have you ever forced this lock with the point of a sharp knife?" he asked.

"Why should I? If I mislay one key there's always another at police headquarters."

Around the interior of the keyhole the agent had observed some small scratches. They were bright, as if newly made.

Peters went back into the morgue and looked at the dead man's things still lying on the table. They were all there.

For some odd reason Peters picked up the package. The seals were intact, but as unaccountably as he had been prompted to pick it up, he now opened the package. His first glance told him that these innocent figures were not those on the lists he had first seen. Back at headquarters a comparison with the photographs settled the matter. There had been a secret visitor to the morgue in the night, and he had substituted this package for the one the dead man had carried.

Peters now put a shadow on Yoshizumi and a record was kept of all his movements and contacts. His house was also watched twenty-four hours a day, and within a week he had received two secret callers, men not unlike the dead man, men whom a prominent member of the community would not normally receive at his home, even secretly.

All Yoshizumi's private and commercial incoming and outgoing mail also received attention. It was a business letter addressed to a firm of instrument makers in Yokohama which revealed Yoshizumi's great secret. Instead of an inquiry or an order, the outer envelope enclosed an inner one, and in this was one of Yoshizumi's periodic reports, an up-to-the-minute census of the bulk and value of the Indies' raw materials.

The chief of police, compelled to action by the irrefutable evidence produced by Peters, took counsel with his superiors. They were as reluctant to believe the story as he had been, and though the evidence could not be denied they were quite firm that, because of Yoshizuma's reputation and position in the Indies, and especially in the commercial life of Java, there must be no scandal.

He was sent for and confronted with the evidence. Then he was told that he would be kept inconspicuously under house arrest and must board the next ship bound for Japan and never return to the Indies.

So, quietly, Yoshizumi withdrew from Java, and in time, if he was remembered at all, it was by elderly reminiscent gentlemen deploring the bad new days, hankering after the good old ones.

2

Japanese espionage in the Dutch East Indies provides an excellent example of foresight and planning.

The Indies are rich in those raw materials which Japan yearly found essential for her industries in ever increasing quantities. They lay within the Pacific and South Asian sphere of that phase of her expansionist plans designed to make her the master of the Orient.

Execution of the espionage plan for the Dutch East Indies was begun in 1932. It was a comprehensive plan, having for its objective the determining of the strengths and weaknesses of every single aspect of the life of the islands. In order to achieve this objective every espionage device known to the Japanese was brought into play. They were also to be two innovations introduced before the plan was complete and the Japanese armies landed to take over from the emperor's secret servants.

Among their devices for learning what they could of the military secrets of the Dutch, the Japanese opened brothels in which the prostitutes were trained in wheedling military information from their clients. They also set up throughout the Indies a chain of hotels managed by highly trained agents who were skilled in this kind of activity.

The majority of the Dutch forces stationed for tours of two or three years had left their families at home in Holland. When leave came round, there was neither the money nor the time to get home or to venture far afield outside the Indies themselves. It became a custom, therefore, for a large number of the men to visit a neighboring island, or a distant part of the island in which they were stationed, and to enjoy for a few days not only a change of scene but a change of environment in the luxuries of civilization to be found in hotels.

The Japanese hotels were cheap, clean, extremely comfortable after the hard bareness of barracks and provided good food and abundant drink. It was the cheapness which first attracted the attention of the Dutchman, brought initially to his notice by circular and advertisement. What attracted him to make his second, third or fourth visit was another amenity offered by the hotels at no extra charge.

Lieutenant van Joost, stationed in Java, decided to spend his first leave in Sumatra. He was pleased to be

157

getting away from the communal life of the barracks into quieter and more civilized surroundings, and remembering a card which he had received one day shortly after his arrival—and had fortunately put by for future reference—he reserved a room in the Lotus Hotel at Palembang.

When he arrived at the hotel he was surprised to find that it was much more comfortable and pleasant than he could ever have hoped for at the price.

His bag was carried up to his room by a silent, smiling, white-coated porter, while the assistant manager who showed him up hoped he would find everything he needed; but if anything had been overlooked, he had only to ask.

After an excellent dinner van Joost went to the lounge, attracted by the orchestra which had already begun to play for dancing. Thoughtfully, the management had provided partners for lonely young men like the lieutenant, and not partners who were continually pestering for drinks to be bought for them. The evening soon became a very pleasant one. The atmosphere was friendly and the quiet gaiety dispersed all memories of the barracks and the tedious round of military life in Java. At one point van Joost left the lounge and as he was returning he was met by the assistant manager who had shown him to his room.

"Have you everything you need, lieutenant?" he smiled.

"Thank you—yes."

"You are enjoying yourself?"

"Very much."

"You could not enjoy yourself more, if, for instance . . ." The assistant manager drew him to one side, and spoke to him in a low voice.

"But isn't it expensive?" van Joost asked presently.

"It is included in the daily charge. All you have to do . . ." And his voice sank to a whisper again.

When the orchestra put away its instruments at midnight, van Joost had one last drink at the bar and went up to his room. He was happy; he felt comfortable inside. But the smile on his face as he climbed the stairs was faintly sceptical. However, when he opened the door of his room his scepticism vanished.

Before the end of his leave it seemed to van Joost that he

had known his companion a long time. There was no doubt that she had put the final perfect touch to his leave. She was gay, always happy and intelligent. She seemed genuinely interested in him, too. She wanted to know what he did in the Dutch Army in Java. How long would he be in the Indies? Did he ever practice shooting his guns? Was it a good gun? What sort was it? Did they ever make him go out on exercises like they did the troops in Sumatra, poor things? What did he do when he went on an exercise? Were they going to send more soldiers to the Indies? The interest she took in him made him feel a person. It was good to be made to feel a person when one was so long time a soldier.

Was he young and innocent? Perhaps. But his companion had been very skillful. She had asked her questions one at a time, choosing the moment carefully, so that the memory of them was quickly blotted out by other memories.

Unfortunately there were few among the Dutch security forces, whether military or civilian, who possessed the awareness of the young Detective Peters. What was happening to officers and men going on leave appeared to escape the notice of the authorities altogether.

So did the activities of blackmailers and extortioners, who worked mainly upon the more prosperous Chinese expatriates who had relatives in China within the influence of the Japanese there. These agents, who became extremely active after the outbreak of the China Incident, used their weapons to get information regarding those Dutch with whom their victims came into contact.

The authorities could not remain unaware, however, of the results of the activities of another type of agent. These were the agitators who skillfully worked among the poor, urging them to throw off the yoke of the Dutch oppressors, who were draining the wealth of the Indies, which rightly belonged to the natives of the islands, into their own pockets. When demonstrations and riots broke out the Dutch administrators knew that the natives were being provoked, but they did not know that the *provocateurs* had been trained and sent by the Japanese. As a final outcome of these activities the Japanese scored an outstanding

159

victory, even in the darkest hour of their defeat, for it was their pupils who led the revolt against the Dutch when the war was over, though this had not been quite the way in which Tokyo had envisaged the end.

Had the Dutch known what yet another kind of agent was doing they might have been deeply concerned. But in this case the Dutch had an excuse, for the medical spy was a completely new adjunct to espionage. A number of specially trained medical officers of the Japanese Army Medical Corps were sent to the Indies. Working as laborers, waiters and clerks both in their work and particularly in their leisure they set themselves to study the sanitation and general health conditions of the islands, so that when the Japanese armies arrived they would know exactly what must be done to prevent the outbreak of epidemics.

The moving force in all this glut of espionage was a certain Dr. Tsubota. It was he who invented the second innovation which the Japanese introduced into the technique of spying in this period.

As the time drew near for the invasion of the Indies, it became more and more imperative for the Japanese to know more and more of Dutch military plans. But when the Japanese, after the start of the China war, in their great need for raw material, began arrogantly to threaten the Indies if they did not supply them, the Dutch unaccountably stiffened. Security was tightened and a new awareness of what was happening produced a serious threat to Japanese espionage. Dutch officers and men no longer patronized the Japanese hotels. Even the prostitute spies in the ordinary brothels found their clients to be extremely ignorant all of a sudden of what was going on.

It was at this time that Dr. Tsubota conceived his novel idea. Large numbers of the clerks in the employment of the Dutch military administration were Javanese. Always intelligent, often high-born, a prominent proportion of them were homosexuals, which has not the significance in that part of the world that it has in the West. These Javanese clerks, in whom the Dutch had great confidence, by the very nature of their work would be in possession of many of those secrets the Japanese wished to learn. Dr. Tsubota therefore groomed yet another entirely new type of agent to whom he gave the name of "male Mata Hari." Since the Japanese were in possession of the bulk of intelligence when they landed in the Indies, Tsubota's scheme could not have been so farfetched as it might seem to Occidental minds.

3

Seven months after the respected Japanese merchant Tomegoro Yoshizumi had been discreetly deported from Java, Detective Sergeant Peters burst unceremoniously into his chief's office.

"They've got him!" he shouted.

"Who are you talking about?" his chief demanded.

"Yoshizumi, naturally."

A smile spread over the chief's face.

"Where?" he asked.

"Here, in Batavia!"

On his arrival in Tokyo, to regain face Yoshizumi had volunteered to return to the Indies and his offer had been accepted.

This time he came to the islands not as a respected merchant but as a native; and as a native, he picked up almost where he had left off, though he changed his technique a little. Within a few weeks of his arrival the Dutch police had heard of his insolent return. A disgruntled contact had provided the information. But though the whole of the force had been alerted, their quarry had been able to elude them. Now at last they had found him. Faced with a fat wad of 57,000 guilders—the balance of the sum provided by Tokyo—he confirmed his identity. This time there was no discreet deportation, but trial and imprisonment.

It was one of the very few successes the weak Dutch counterespionage had. Perhaps the blame does not lie entirely at their door, for they were enveloped in a web of spying such as has rarely been spun by any nation.

And on the other side of the Pacific this same nation was simultaneously spinning another web, not so completely enveloping to be sure, but faced with an almost equally counterespionage-weak victim—the United States and Central America.

CHAPTER 13

The Assault on Central America

The assault on the North American continent would be a very different matter from the assault on the Asian mainland, if only by reason of the four thousand miles of ocean separating Japan from her objective. Even for her attack on both Russia and China, Japan had foreseen the wisdom of having a base where men and materials might be built up in sufficient quantities to assure success from the first moment of joining battle.

The securing of such a base presupposes certain conditions. If the country to be used is not so friendly that it will submit to an amicable arrangement being reached, then it must be so weak that it cannot argue effectively when you set about establishing yourself there without permission. It must also border on the country which is your ultimate objective. It must be supplied with communications of a sort which will facilitate your movement toward your objective should you have to make that move quickly because your enemy has interpreted your plan. It must have reasonable landing facilities so that you are not impeded by physical considerations in the difficult operation of speedily building up your strength. These are ideal conditions; sometimes the gods favor you and provide them. Since the gods not only favored the Japanese plan for "bringing the whole world under one roof" but had laid it upon the people with strict injunction, it would have been thoughtless of them not to provide such bases.

A SKETCH MAP
of MEXICO
Showing Centers of
Japanese Interest
Railway ++++++++
Road ━━━━━━

And indeed they had. For the assaults on the Asian mainland, there had been Korea and Manchuria, the former taken without a blow, the latter weak and amenable to cunning undermining. Not surprisingly, therefore, the base was to hand for the assault on the American continent.

A glance at the map will immediately reveal the physical suitability of Mexico.

The Gulf of California is an excellently sheltered inland sea, approximately eight hundred miles in length, with an average width of one hundred miles. Comparatively free of reefs and rocks, it has a central channel some fifty miles in breadth and seven hundred miles in length which is 6,000 feet deep.

It is, therefore, a ready-made, natural harborage capable of accommodating a vast fleet. It could be made as impregnable as any base might be by fortifying San Gabriel, at the southern tip of Lower California, and Mazatlan, on the Mexican mainland opposite San Gabriel.

Roughly halfway up the Mexican coast of the gulf is the port of Guaymas. As ports go, it is not a modern port, but equipment transported with the first waves of supplies could soon remedy that. Guaymas, however, has a strategic importance. The main west Mexican highway starts only a few miles away and runs up to the border of Arizona. Almost parallel with it runs the Southern Pacific Railway.

Parts of Mexico are flat, sufficiently so to provide airstrips as bases for assault aircraft. On the other side of the Central American isthmus is the Panama Canal, a waterway as vital to America, and especially an America at war in the Pacific, as the Suez Canal is to the Eastern Hemisphere. Control the Panama Canal and you take away at once half the enemy's sea strength.

If physically Central America had its attractions, its ethnological attractions were no less. The people of Central America are innately lackadaisical; the climate of their country and their heredity are too strong for them to be otherwise. True, they had some armed forces, but numerically they presented no problem and their equipment even less of one. Not only that, their leaders at this crucial time were susceptible to bribery and corruption, and there was constant internal friction in every one of them, which not only weakened their governments but their whole structure.

As a base for such reasons as the Japanese wanted it, it could not have been much improved. It was a pity, no doubt, that it was such a long way from the home base, but that aspect could be provided for.

So a major part of Japanese espionage preparations was directed toward Central America, and here we shall see the extraordinary adaptability which was one of the prominent features of their spying.

Certainly they had learned well the main principles of spying—that the spy must have a good ostensible reason for being where he is; that he must make himself inconspicuous and dissolve as much into his background as possible; and that neither by word nor deed must he attract the suspicions of the inhabitants toward himself.

So while you will find both in Central America and on the West Coast of the United States the full exploitation of sex which the Japanese used as one of their main weapons of espionage when most other nations shied away from it as they would from a case of bubonic plague, you will not find peddlers of pornographic pictures and literature, no dope peddling, no panaceac medicines, no priests or monks, no traveling salesmen of ribbons and laces, buckles and fans. Instead you will find small farmers, dentists, barbers, language students, shirt sellers, soda water bottlers, doctors and thousands upon thousands of fishermen.

In their espionage invasion of America the Japanese came up against their greatest handicap when spying in an Occidental country—their physical characteristics, which they cannot disguise and which mark them down, not only as foreigners, but as Japanese. Here they met the problem in all its force, for according to their ideas if their spying was to be effective they must use the same vast numbers here that they used elsewhere; and it was not possible for them to coerce sufficient numbers of natives to enter their service. So they had to choose roles for their agents which would allow them to operate without suspicion. As we shall see, they chose those roles well and with considerable ingenuity.

We have seen this ingenuity at work in the efforts of Dr. Tsubota in Java, who coped with a difficult situation by employing an entirely new type of agent, his male Mata Haris. But it is doubtful whether any nation except Japan would have opened an espionage campaign, even in Central America, by attempting to teach the Mexicans to fish *scientifically*.

One of the experts in the Japanese conception of scientific fishing was Dr. Yochuchi Matsui, who arrived in Mexico in 1935 by a special arrangement between the

Japanese and Mexican governments. Matsui may have intended to give the Mexican Pacific fishermen the benefit of his knowledge, but he had another and, for the Japanese, more important reason for coming to Mexico. When he had paved the way he was to attempt to persuade the Mexican government to give permission for the establishment of a colony of Japanese fishermen at San Gabriel Bay, on the southernmost tip of the peninsula of Lower California.

Not long after his arrival, Dr. Matsui made the acquaintance of Captain Manuel Camiro. Camiro was already aware of the doctor's chief assignment and undertook to act as his intermediary with the Mexican government.

Finding his first attempts at explaining scientific fishing met with little success with the Mexican fishermen, who had no fault to find with their own methods which their grandfathers and great-grandfathers had used for centuries before them, he decided to concentrate his efforts on achieving his primary assignment. So, with Camiro, he moved to Guaymas, the little fishing port about midway up the east coast of the Gulf of California.

At Guaymas, Matsui and Camiro began to entertain the local officials in a comparatively lavish style to prepare the ground for meeting more important and influential government officials. But when the latter were encountered they proved to be disappointingly uncooperative.

Their lack of cooperation had its springboard in the fact that in San Gabriel Bay a considerable number of Mexican pearl fishers were already engaged in a not unlucrative business. Not unnaturally, the pearl fishers themselves saw in the Japanese proposal a threat to their own livelihood, and the government divined that it would most certainly mean a loss of revenue for them. By an arrangement between the pearl fishers and the government, the pearl fishers made a most vigorous protest of which the government was bound to take notice officially.

But Camiro and Matsui were persistent and patient men, and for three years they entertained and bribed, but were

166

no nearer to reaching their goal than they had been at the beginning.

It was Camiro who lost interest first, and this loss of interest was prompted by a message conveyed to him by the San Gabriel Bay Pearl Fishers Association. A full meeting of this body was held on December 19th, 1938, and resolved unanimously that if Captain Camiro continued his efforts on behalf of Dr. Matsui he should be permanently removed, and that this decision should be immediately conveyed to the captain. Knowing his countrymen very well, Camiro at once left Guaymas and wisely never showed himself there again.

Matsui, however, stayed on, for Guaymas had for some years been the headquarters of Japanese espionage on the west coast of Central America.

At 323 Avenida XIV, Guaymas, in 1930, a Japanese called F. Matsumiya had set himself up as a bottler of soda water. His little factory soon became so popular that there was scarcely a master of all of the many Japanese fishing boats and other types of vessels that used the port who did not visit it as soon as they stepped ashore, even before they went to report to the shipping office.

Matsumiya was a self-sufficient man. He made no Mexican friends nor did he take part in the social life of other Japanese residents in Guaymas and nearby Empalme. But besides the masters of fishing boats he did receive other visitors, who came alone and departed almost as soon as they arrived.

One of the largest of Japanese fishing boat companies was the *Nippon Suisan Kaisha*. Approximately eighty per cent of the stock of this company, which was interlocked with the great Matsui arms combine, was owned by the Japanese government.

Nippon Suisan Kaisha had a branch office in Guaymas the assistant manager of which was a man named Edisioka. Anyone wishing to make contact with the captain of a fishing boat first approached Edisioka; but he was unable to give a definite answer until he had consulted the soda water bottler of Avenida XIV. If a matter required the cooperation of superiors, Matsumiya would telephone to S. Imamura, the manager of *Nippon Suisan Kaisha*'s head office in Mexico City. Imamura was known on several occasions to postpone appointments with high Mexican officials in order to attend to soda water bottler Matsumiya's requests without delay. Every Sunday afternoon Edisioka went to Empalme to visit a friend, José Gokoku.

Gokoku—which means "for the nation"—had first come to Empalme in 1935, where he had opened up a restaurant next door to the Roman Catholic Church. When his business was progressing he sent for his wife and son to join him.

Now, there were other considerations of importance to the Japanese in laying their plans besides the eminent suitability of the Gulf of California as a harborage. For example, any invasion force destined for the United States could be landed at Guaymas and march north toward Arizona along the main road connecting Mexico with the American southwest states, or, better still, be conveyed by the Southern Pacific Railway, which provided the only means of transport on the west coast of Mexico in the rainy season. The most important marshaling yard and repair shops of the S.P.R. were situated at Empalme.

Edisioka was not Gokoku's only visitor on Sunday afternoons. Working in the marshaling yard and repair shops at this time were at least a dozen Japanese mechanics who, with four or five compatriots from Guaymas, formed Gokoku's entire clientele.

At five o'clock on Sunday afternoons all of them would meet at the restaurant. Gokoku's son, a young man of about twenty, would squat outside the door and remain there until the first of his father's customers began to leave, which was usually around midnight.

Though Gokoku provided refreshment, eating was only a subsidiary function of the gathering. Seated on hard chairs facing Gokoku and Edisioka, each of those present would make his report for the week.

In the course of their duties as mechanics, the S.P.R.'s Japanese employees traversed every inch of the permanent

168

way. But besides carrying out repairs to the line, with magnificent Leica cameras fitted with tele-lenses they explored every road and trail between the railway and the coast and every mountain and desert track between the railway and the interior.

This group was also in contact with the Yaqui Indians. Early in April 1939, Urbalejo, chief of the Yaquis, and his second-in-command, Joe Mattus, held a secret meeting with Nazi agents at Yuma, Arizona, which was arranged by Edisioka's men.

At the Sunday afternoon gathering there would also be one or more Japanese who lived in the towns and cities of Sonora, the province of Mexico in which Empalme and Guaymas are situated. The most frequent of these visitors were L. Z. Okamura, from Cananea, up near the United States border, and Dr. Iwamoto. These two would arrive on Saturday at Edisioka's house, accompany him to Empalme on Sunday and return home on Monday.

Gokoku's restaurant was certainly not a financial success. Nevertheless, in November 1937 he became the owner of a Ford V-8 truck, which had been presented to him, as a matter of fact, by Edisioka. Thereafter, whenever a Japanese fishing boat put in at Guaymas for fueling or repairs, Gokoku and his truck would disappear for two or three days. He would explain to inquisitive neighbors that he was foraging for vegetables for his restaurant, but they noticed that he very rarely had any success.

On these journeys he most frequently took a northerly direction. Occasionally, however, he would go south to Mayo River Valley and would be away for at least a week. On January 9th, 1938, he traveled 150 miles to Navajoa to visit a compatriot called Imukahi, who owned an ice-making plant and 500 acres of level ground there; another called Morimoto, the owner of a small corn-milling business; a third, Tanada, a barkeeper; and a Japanese dentist, Ieda, from Topolobampo.

Gokoku was not the only Japanese around Guaymas to become the proud owner of a new Ford V-8 truck. Every farmer, fisherman and restaurant keeper in the area was also presented with one at the same time. Like Gokoku,

169

these men were transporting arms and ammunition from Japanese boats and caching them at such centers as Huatabampo, Topolobampo and Los Mochio.

Until February 11th, 1938, a small house in Calle 22, Guaymas, was used as a temporary depot for arms. On this day, however, a crate of fish which was being unloaded by a Japanese fisherman crashed to the ground and split open. True, a few score of fish scattered in all directions, but so did boxes of ammunition. When Mexican labor union officials visited the house the following day, having heard of what had happened from a member who saw the incident, it was empty.

Dr. Matsui never did get his scientific fishing colony at San Gabriel and he eventually turned his attention to Turtle Bay, on the west coast of Lower California. Turtle Bay was what might be called the headquarters of the largest invasion fleet ever to operate in peacetime, and it was here that a handsome young Japanese fisherman broke the heart of Carmencita.

There had put into Turtle Bay one day a Japanese fishing boat, called the *Taiyo Maru No. 3,* for repairs to her engine. Some part had had to be brought from Mexico City, so she had stayed nearly a fortnight.

On her very first evening in port several members of her crew had come into the tavern. Among them was a handsome dark bright-eyed young man. As Carmencita handed him the drink he had ordered, accidentally their hands had touched. They had looked at one another and then dropped their eyes.

When the tavern closed and Carmencita left to go home, she found him waiting for her. Shyly he asked if he might see her home. Almost as shyly she gave him permission.

By the end of ten days Carmencita was deeply in love, and on the night before the *Taiyo Maru No. 3* sailed, Shoichi clung to her as desperately as she clung to him and begged her to have no eyes for any other man. He would be back in two months. Would she wait for him? Impatiently.

And yesterday the *Taiyo Maru No. 3* had sailed back into Turtle Bay.

As soon as she heard the news, Carmencita ran down to the harbor.

"Is Shoichi there?" she had called up to a Japanese sailor swabbing the deck.

He smiled at her. "Shoichi who?" he asked.

"Shoichi Motomura."

He shook his head. "No, he's not here. He's not with the ship any longer."

She had not believed him. He was teasing her. She had stood by the gangplank for hours scanning the faces of every sailor who came ashore. It was dark before she was convinced that Shoichi was not on board. And not only Shoichi but any other member of the crew who had served the *Taiyo Maru No. 3* when she was last in Turtle Bay.

"Oh, well," one ignorant fisherman was laughing now. "Let it be a lesson to our girls not to fall in love with Japanese fishermen. The local boys are always here."

The *Taiyo Maru No. 3* was only one of five hundred Japanese fishing boats operating off the coasts of California and Central America. The Japanese had first started coming to these waters in the late twenties and had gone on increasing in numbers until in 1939, out of the 1,000 foreign-owned fishing boats working the American fishing grounds, fifty per cent were owned by Japanese masters or fishing companies.

In the early years of this invasion, a large number of the Japanese boats were British ex-coast guard vessels, bought cheaply and refitted in Japan. But when the refitting was carried out the three-inch gun and machine gun mountings were not removed. They were left *in situ,* and it would be only the work of a few minutes for the guns to be back in place should a fishing boat ever be required to turn raider.

When new fishing boats were constructed in Japan, gun mountings were also included. This was not due to the "slavish copying" of which the Japanese have always been guilty.

In size the boats ranged from a maximum of 2,000 tons down to eighty tons. The larger ones had a cruising range of 6,000 miles, and it was no uncommon occurrence for them to put into port after a trip lasting several months with their unusually large holds quite empty. The hulls of these larger vessels were often constructed of tempered steel. This is an unusual feature in any type of bona fide fishing boat. At a time when ship-to-shore telephones were the very latest word in nautical communications and many large passenger liners did not possess them, all the larger and a prominent number of the smaller Japanese fishing boats were equipped with them. They were also equipped with the most up-to-date diesel engines and with radios.

Under the pretense of fishing for bait, the fishermen were constantly taking soundings of the approaches to harbors, and of the harbors themselves. Practically all the members of the crews possessed expensive Leica cameras with which they photographed harbor installations and the coastline, even going so far as to use infra-red cameras at night.

Half the crews of fishing boats flying the American flag but under Japanese control were Nisei, or American-born Japanese. The other half were alien Japanese. The regulations governing the landing of alien seamen were strangely lax. No record of their landings and departures was ever made, and Japanese agents were quick to perceive the advantages of a state of affairs which would allow them to go ashore disguised as a fisherman, carry out their missions and return aboard without any note being made of their entrances and their exits. The majority of the alien Japanese seamen were officers in the imperial navy.

They were prone to strange actions. In November and December 1938, for example, there was a glut of tuna, and most of the fishing boats in Turtle Bay were laid up. The glut continued into January 1939, but when in that month the American Pacific fleet put into San Pedro and San Diego for maneuvers, there was not a single fishing boat that did not up anchor.

The majority of the boats in Turtle Bay were owned by the Southern Commercial Company, whose manager was a Japanese called T. Abbe. As soon as the fleet had finished its maneuvers, Abbe made for Japan on a flying visit—taking a consolidated report on all that the fleet had been engaged in doing.

172

The Mexican fishermen who made fun of Carmencita and her lover who did not return in the *Taiyo Maru No. 3* entirely missed the significance of the situation. The *Taiyo Maru No. 3* had not put in at any American port while she had been away from Turtle Bay; nor had she had time to go to Japan and back. Yet the whole of her crew had been changed!

The *Minato Maru* specialized in changing her master. On November 30th, 1935, flying the Tobata flag and carrying a crew of eight officers and twenty-eight men, she set out for San Diego commanded by Captain F. Fukino. But on December 20th she arrived at Balboa, at the entrance to the Panama Canal, thousands of miles off course and in the opposite direction from San Diego.

Two days later she left Balboa, giving her destination as San Pedro. On January 17th, 1936, she put in at Salina Cruz, in Mexico, having changed her Tobata flag for that of Tokyo. On March 14th she stopped at Guaymas, where Captain Fukino visited Matsumiyo, the soda water bottler. Eventually she did reach San Pedro, but now no longer flying the Tokyo flag but the Shimonoseki flag; and her master was no longer Captain Fukino, but Captain Suekichi Imamura.

After staying four days in San Pedro, the *Minato Maru* sailed to Mazatlan. Once every four months she was scheduled to call at San Pedro. When she arrived there on September 19th, Suekichi Imamura had been replaced by Captain Yukio Yamashita. On her next visit at the end of December, Yamashita in his turn had been replaced by Yukatsu Okomoto.

The *Minato Maru* was not alone subject to these strange happenings. The *Sendai Maru, Bansiu Maru* and *Taiyo Maru Nos. 1, 2, 4, 5* and 6 could all have reported similar experiences.

None of them put in at any port on their way to and from San Pedro; nor had they had time to go to Japan. The changes had, in fact, been made in midocean from Japanese warships; for all these masters were lieutenant commanders of the Japanese Navy, and leaders of groups of spies.

173

Japanese fishermen spies were by far the most numerous of all the various types of spies operating both in Central America and on the west coast of the United States. It is estimated that at peak they must have numbered almost ten thousand. The results achieved by them warranted only a small fraction of this number. But it was a Japanese idiosyncrasy to work with astronomical figures. They were doing exactly the same thing in the vital Panama Canal Zone, though there the agents were not fishermen or coolies or soda water bottlers.

In 1937, there were no less than forty-seven Japanese barbers in Panama City and eight in Colón. Panama City is at the Pacific entrance to the Panama Canal; Colón is at the Atlantic entrance. In Panama City they were concentrated round the highly select and exorbitantly expensive Avenida Central and the Calle Carlos A. Mendoza. There were so many of them that they formed a union, the Barbers' Association, to which no barber who was not Japanese was admitted, though Japanese fishermen were made welcome at the meetings! The meetings were held in a second-story room at 58 Calle Carlos A. Mendoza. The founder of the Barbers' Association was not even a shopowner, but a barber's assistant named A. Sonada.

The Japanese consul in Panama, Tetsuo Umemoto, attended the meetings regularly, and he and Sonada sat side by side, facing the rest of the members. Sonada's real position could be partially gauged from the fact that Umemoto never sat down until the barber's assistant was seated. But whenever another member was present, neither Umemoto nor Sonada would sit down until he was sitting, but would stand and bow very low until a sign indicated that they too might be seated. This man's name was T. Takano, and he owned a very small business in a less wealthy district, at 10 Avenida B.

Another important member of the association was Katarino Kabayama, a gentle-voiced, placid-countenanced businessman in late middle age who lived at 11 Calle Colón. Kabayama had not always been a businessman. In his younger days he had been a barefoot, tattered fisherman. But even then, when he had gone aboard a

174

Japanese warship visiting Panama, not bothering to change out of his tatters, he had been piped aboard, while the assembled crew had come to a smart salute. When he had left, after a two-hour interview with the commander, he had been piped over the side. Then he had rowed back to his fishing boat.

Kabayama was a close associate of the consul. Whenever Takano visited the captains of Japanese ships calling at Panama, Kabayama invariably accompanied him. If asked, he would say that he was doing business with the mess stewards.

But he was not the only businessman who found it worth his while to operate in the canal zone. One of the others was a certain T. Tahara, who came as the traveling representative of the newly formed Official Japanese Association of Importers and Exporters for Latin America. He rented a room in the offices of Boyd Brothers, the shipping agency, in Panama. For the big businessman he made himself out to be, his mail was curiously insignificant in bulk. This gave rise to speculation. His superiors felt that he had thus been compromised and recalled him to Tokyo.

Before he set up his experimental cotton station in Costa Rica, Takahiro Wakabayashi had also operated in Panama as the representative of the Federation of Japanese Importers and Exporters, which was really the O.J.A.I.E.-L.A., Tahara's organization, under a slightly changed name.

With disarming audacity, Wakabayashi established himself in the Tivoli Hotel, which was run by the United States government. Very soon he was extremely active negotiating for manganese. He saved time by traveling in a private charter aircraft. The amounts of manganese he bought were trifling, but he was very successful with the photographs of military installations throughout the Canal Zone which he took from his airplane.

Rather out of the usual run was a shirt shop which used to be on Calle Loa, between the Avenida Herrera and the Avenida Amador Guerrero. The owner was an attractive Oriental lady who called herself Lola Osawa.

Lola's real name was Chiyo Morasawa, and she had arrived at Balboa from Yokohama as long ago as May 24th, 1929, in the liner *Anyo Maru*. As soon as she landed she disappeared from the public view, and it was not until a year later that she reappeared at the other end of the canal, in her shirt shop.

Lola's husband lived with her in rooms over the shop. He had entered Panama illegally, for his passport contained no visa. He gave out that he was a merchant. In fact, he was a reserve officer in the Japanese Navy. He and Lola specialized in photographing all objects of military importance in the Canal Zone, and they operated without interruption for more than ten years.

When the Axis countries agreed to collaborate in espionage, the Canal Zone became one of their most vital points of interest. Control of the canal, which automatically entailed command of the zone, could cripple the movement of the United States fleet. So they set about wooing the republics on either side of the Republic of Panama, Italy serenading Costa Rica and Nicaragua, while Germany exerted all her charm on Colombia.

But the Japanese had their own ideas. At Corinto, in the Cauca Valley, thirty miles from Cali and two hours' flying time from the canal, they established a colony of several hundred of their countrymen on terrain that was long, level and flat and which could be transformed in a few hours to an airstrip capable of accommodating aircraft landed from carriers or assembled on the spot.

In 1934 the Japanese increased their efforts to obtain a base near the Pacific entrance to the canal. Permission was sought to set up a refrigeration plant on Taboga, a small island facing Panama, not to be confused with the British-owned island of Tobago, in the Lesser Antilles. Taboga would have been an excellent vantage point from which to observe the canal's Pacific defenses.

When permission was refused, and a rumor became current that the authorities were considering banning all foreign fishing in Panama waters, a Japanese store owner in Panama, Yoshitaro Amano, was so undismayed that he formed a new company called Amano Fisheries Ltd. The "flagship" of Amano Fisheries was the *Amano Maru*. Built in Japan in July 1937, it was the largest and most luxuriously appointed fishing boat in the world at that time. When in September 1937 it became known that the United States was contemplating excavating another canal through Nicaragua, and that some out-of-the-ordinary fortifications were being built in the military zone at Managua, Amano lost no time in going to investigate.

He arrived in the area at 8 A.M. on October 7th, 1937. At 8:30 A.M. he was under arrest, charged with suspected sabotage and taking photographs in a prohibited area. As happened when he went to visit Wakabayashi in Costa Rica and was arrested there on similar charges, and as happened when he repeated the experience in Colombia, he was acquitted. There are some who hint that the fact that he rated as a millionaire in Panama may have had some bearing on these verdicts.

The Japanese who arrived in Panama were well provided with passports, which enabled them to change their names from time to time. On June 7th, 1934, for example, the Japanese Foreign Office issued passport No. 255,875 to Masakazu Yokoi. Though he had permission to visit all the Central and South American countries, he applied only for a Panamanian visa. He arrived in Panama on September 28th, 1934, and did nothing but consort with fishermen and barbers. On July 11th, 1936, while on a return visit to Tokyo, he was issued with another passport, this time in the name of Shoichi Yokoi, and thereafter traveled on whichever of the two documents seemed to offer him the greater safety at the moment.

Since professional men are not expected to maintain regular office hours, the dental profession was a favorite "cover" for Japanese agents. In Panama City and Colón they were not so numerous as the barbers. In fact, Mexico, and especially its western provinces, was the particular hunting ground for dentists.

The strategic importance of the Southern Pacific Railway has already been noted. There was also an equally important highway leading to the United States, which began in Guaymas and passed through the border town of Nogales.

At 40 Calle Granja, Nogales, lived the dentist, Dr. Hoiyo Takaichi. Hoiyo was not an outstanding member of his profession, but no Japanese tourist or businessman entering the United States from Mexico would consider going on his way without having first visited him. Among his "patients" he counted at least thirty Japanese scattered at various points along the highway carrying on a variety of poorly paid occupations. Yet each was the owner of an expensive camera.

In the town of Hermosillo, placed strategically at the other end of the highway, was another dentist, Dr. L. M. Iwamoto, who had his consulting room and surgery at 81 Calle Serdan. Iwamoto had his own little band of twenty or so agents, who were employed in barbershops, ice cream parlors and restaurants in the town.

From the very rare attendances which he made at his surgery Iwamoto did not seem to have his heart in his professional work. He preferred making visits to Guaymas, where he never failed to call on Matsumiyo, the soda water bottler.

The liner *Tyoko Maru* called at Guaymas on a monthly schedule. Each month, a few days before the departure of the *Tyoko Maru* on her return to Japan, Iwamoto would drive to the Japanese farming colony in the Mayo River Valley. He would inspect there, not the colonists' teeth, but the progress they were making on the long, level acres they were "cultivating." He would then return to the soda water factory, and when the captain of the *Tyoko Maru* called to say farewell to the soda water bottler, he would be handed the latest report of the Mayo River Valley project.

So the barbers, dentists, farmers, traveling salesmen, shirt sellers, consular officials and fishermen watched over the defenses of the Panama Canal and prepared Central America for the day when the fleet of Japanese transports and supply vessels would sail into the Gulf of California and set up in Mexico and Costa Rica and Nicaragua the

178

bases from which they would humble the great United States of America.

In the meantime, in those same United States, other secret servants of the divine emperor were spinning their webs in preparation for the day when the earthly armies of the sun goddess would march over the border of Mexico into Arizona.

CHAPTER 14

The Student of English at Stanford

On August 13th, 1936, a Japanese fishing boat, one of the *Taiyo Marus,* tied up at a dock in San Francisco. Presently down the gangway came a dapper little Japanese, well-dressed and carrying an expensive piece of baggage. He was directed at once to the United States immigration officers who took his passport and looked through it.

"Ever been in the United States before, Mr. Ohtani?" the official asked.

The passport had been recently issued, and except for the one visa and the particulars of the holder, it was in its pristine state. But Mr. Ohtani might have had another passport before this one, and that passport might have run out.

Mr. Ohtani shook his head.

"No, sir," he told the official. "I have never been in the United States before."

"What is the object of your visit, Mr. Ohtani?"

"I am coming to study English at Stanford University."

"You seem to talk English all right to me," the official smiled.

"I wish to speak English perfectly."

179

"A good many of your compatriots come here to learn English."

"So I believe."

"Well good luck, Mr. Ohtani. Enjoy your visit to the States."

The little Japanese picked up his suitcase, pocketed his passport and moved toward the pier entrance.

The immigration official looked after him and remarked to a colleague: "Funny people those little Japs."

"I know," replied his friend. "But what makes you pass that judicially considered judgment at this moment?"

"Well," said the official, "look at his clothes and look at that bag he's carrying, and he's coming to Stanford to learn English. He could obviously afford to come first class on a luxury liner, and yet he's come the 4,000 odd miles from Tokyo in a stinking fishing boat."

To which his friend replied, since he was of Scots descent: "And very commendable too. He'll have saved at least half the fare of a luxury liner."

"I didn't know the Japs were so thrifty."

"I couldn't say whether they are as a nation. Not all Scotsmen, not even all Aberdonians, are thrifty. But there's a leaven of good in all nations, and that little man belongs to the leaven."

"Yeah, I suppose you're right."

What the official did not know was that Mr. Ohtani had traveled in the *Taiyo Maru* for sentimental reasons—he had once been a member of her crew, despite the fact that he was actually a lieutenant commander in the Imperial Navy of Japan, and the *Taiyo Maru* was a fishing boat. Nor did he know that when Mr. Ohtani had said that he had never been in the United States before he was lying; nor that he never intended to enroll as a language student at Stanford University or any other academic institution.

Mr. Ohtani went from the docks straight to the railway terminus and took the first express to Los Angeles. On arrival at Los Angeles he was driven to the Tia Juana, the Japanese quarter, to a brothel called the Molino Rojo, the Red Mill. Mr. Ohtani stayed in the Red Mill only ten minutes, and when he emerged he hailed another cab and told the driver to take him to the Olympic Hotel.

Within a day or two of settling in, Mr. Ohtani realized that his stay in Los Angeles would be protracted and that he might as well make himself as comfortable as possible. So dressing carefully, he went out to the Japanese quarter, to a restaurant called the Kawafuku Tei, one of the best-known Japanese restaurants in Los Angeles.

He had not been in the bar for half an hour when he had already made the acquaintance of a young compatriot as charming as she was beautiful. Inao Ohtani was alone; Chieko Nagai was alone. What could be more natural than that the dapper little gentleman with his deeply penetrating eyes which turned on a smile whenever he looked at you should ask a very attractive young lady to dine with him, and that she should accept the invitation?

After dinner he suggested that they should go to a night club to dance. Long before midnight they could have believed themselves to be old friends. Before they parted they had become more than old friends.

Ohtani was charmed by his little mistress, and when any woman charmed him, he could prove himself generous. If the immigration officials could have seen the couple as they made the rounds of the Los Angeles night spots and could have appraised the jewelry which adorned Chieko Nagai's slender throat and tapering fingers and the silken sheaths in which she was swathed from throat to toe, they would have changed their minds about the thrift of a language student who saved money by traveling 4,000 miles from Japan to San Francisco in a stinking fishing vessel.

With his private life satisfactorily arranged, Inao Ohtani could apply himself to the task which had brought him to the United States. If he conducted his leisure moments with Chieko Nagai with a certain ostentation, he went about his other activities with such circumspection that there was no one on the west coast of California, even at the United States naval bases at nearby San Pedro and San Diego, who could have told you what those activities were.

No one who knew the couple even saw anything strange
181

in Ohtani's twice or thrice weekly visits to the Red Mill, sometimes immediately after he had come from his mistress. They certainly did not seem to worry or hurt her.

But when Inao Ohtani visited the Red Mill he did not pass the two hours he spent there in upstairs dalliance. Every moment he was in serious discussion in the bolted and sound proof office of the proprietor, So Yasahura.

One day in June 1937 Ohtani suddenly announced casually to Chieko Nagai that he was going to take a vacation. He thought he ought to see New York. He did not ask her to accompany him and she did not suggest it. Once he had told her, she was not even surprised that he planned to travel to San Francisco on the midday plane.

His decision had not been so sudden as it might have seemed to Chieko. The night before he had visited the Red Mill and there So Yasahura had handed him a sealed envelope in which was a brief note signed by the Japanese naval attaché in Washington.

So he came to New York, but his stay there was brief. After a rapid glance at the Empire State Building and the Rockefeller Plaza, he returned to the Pennsylvania Station, and four and a half hours later was entering a cab outside the Union Station in Washington, D.C.

"The Alban Towers," he told the driver.

The Alban Towers is a magnificent block of modern apartments, one of which, at this time, was rented permanently by the Japanese Embassy to house the naval attaché, who was the Japanese chief of naval intelligence in the United States.

When he left the Alban Towers in the early hours of the morning, Ohtani carried with him a small bag which he had not had when he arrived. At his hotel he undressed wearily and getting into bed he took the bag with him under the covers.

Two days later he was back in Los Angeles. In the train and in the aircraft he nursed the small bag on his knees all the time. Now he drove straight to the Red Mill. As So Yasahura transferred the bundles of American dollars from the bag to the safe, Ohtani talked, and three hours passed before he left for the Olympic Hotel and Chieko Nagai.

For almost another year Ohtani took exercise in San Pedro and San Diego and danced in the night clubs of Los Angeles and Hollywood. From all points of view they were a gratifying eleven months.

On May 3rd, 1938, another summons came for him from Washington. This time he did not tell Chieko Nagai to her face, but left a note for her saying briefly that he had had to go on a journey.

When at last he returned, at six o'clock on the evening of May 27th, he was driving a 1937 Chevrolet carrying a District of Columbia license plate, number 57-512.

In the lounge of the hotel Chieko ran to meet him, all her Japanese restraint forsaking her.

"You're leaving me," the porter heard her say.

Ohtani hushed her and hurried her to the lift. In his apartment, he had to confess that she was right. Yes, he had to go back to Japan, but he would not be leaving for some weeks.

At eleven o'clock in the morning of May 30th, three days after his return from Washington, Ohtani stood by the reception desk of the Olympic Hotel. From time to time he looked at his watch and from his watch to the clock which was on the wall above the desk. Presently through the doors into the lobby came another Japanese, slightly taller than Ohtani, and bespectacled. Ohtani hurried forward to meet him.

"Ko Nagasawa?" he asked.

"Yes."

"I am Ohtani—Inao Ohtani."

The little men bowed gravely to one another.

When Nagasawa had registered and Ohtani was accompanying him to his apartment, he suggested that if Nagasawa were not too tired from his journey they might play a game of golf after luncheon. Nagasawa replied that nothing would give him greater pleasure.

So at half past two, the two Japanese gentlemen, looking slightly ridiculous in plus-fours and white cloth caps—the *costume de rigeur* of the American golfer—with bags of golf clubs almost as tall as themselves slung over shoulders, passed through the lobby to Ohtani's 1937 Chevrolet.

Their play was not good. The professional undoubtedly would have told them not to talk so much and to concentrate more on the game. And they took an unconscionable time to go around. Again and again they stood aside to let following towsomes and foursomes through; and then they stood silent, impassive and polite. But as soon as they were sure the other players were out of earshot they broke into conversation even more voluble than before.

Had you understood Japanese and been near enough to overhear what the little men were saying, you would no longer have been surprised by the length of their conversation, for Chieko Nagai's lover was none other than the chief of Japanese naval espionage for southern California, which included the farmers and the fishermen operating in Mexico. Naturally, it took a long time to brief his successor in that post, Lieutenant Commander Ko Nagasawa.

On the next and following days, Inao Ohtani introduced the new chief to his principal operatives. They were an odd assortment.

First among them was a photographer, N. Kamakura, with no visible means of support but whose purse was always well lined. Then there was a striking Japanese woman with the unlikely name of Beby O'Hara. Beby had been dismissed from her situation as stewardess in the *Tabuta Maru,* a Japanese luxury liner, for an indiscreet love affair with a passenger. She had settled—on her savings, she said—at the Miyako Hotel and had invested in a course of beauty culture. She was acquainted, but only acquainted, with another Japanese guest at the Miyako. He was K. Yamakashi, a more intimate friend of his chief's, whose photographs he developed with his own in his hotel bedroom.

At this precise moment there had occurred a most unfortunate rift between Yamakashi and his current mistress. The wretched woman had been unwise enough to call on her lover unannounced, while he was using his bedroom as a darkroom. When she let herself in with the key he had provided for her, she also let in the light and ruined all the films which were being processed. The next thing she knew was that she was sprawling on the floor of the corridor outside the room, where she had been placed with unnecessary violence by an enraged and outraged K. Yamakashi.

It says something for the discipline of K. Yamakashi that at this time, when he might have sought a more intimate acquaintance with Beby O'Hara, he should introduce her to Ko Nagasawa, and thereafter had to watch the new and beautiful friendship which developed rapidly between the newcomer and the slant-eyed woman with the Irish name.

On June 16th, 1938, Ko Nagasawa was sitting in the lounge of the Olympic reading the Japanese language newspaper published in America, the *Rafo Shimpo*. This was his first task as soon as he came down in the morning. He was not attracted by the banner headlines on the first page but would turn at once to the market lists. If he was satisfied with what he found in the lists, then he would come back to the front page.

This morning he found something which made him hurry at once to the telephone and ring up Beby O'Hara to cancel their date for the evening. He gave no explanation and allowed her no opportunity to question him. Putting down the receiver, he hurried up to Ohtani's apartment. Within the hour the two lieutenant commanders were on their way to Washington, summoned there by the price of green peppers. They were away from Los Angeles for a fortnight. The greater part of this time was accounted for by the round-about route by which they returned. This took them via Yosemite, Yellowstone and Mount Rainier, where they visited groups of Japanese laborers.

Arrived in Los Angeles, they drove directly to the Red Mill, where they remained closeted with the proprietor for several hours. The immediate outcome of these discussions was the decision of the Nippon Suisan Kaisha, a Japanese shipping firm, to open a branch office in Los Angeles.

A gentlemen called Y. Takimitsu was appointed manager of this branch office. Anyone with any real knowledge of that kind of business in Los Angeles could have told them before they opened up that they would be wasting money and time. But lack of business did not worry Takimitsu. He was a keen fisherman and was delighted with the opportunities his new job gave him of indulging his hobby, which he always made sure of doing in waters close to places of strategic naval interest.

At the beginning of July, Inao Ohtani said farewell to Chieko Nagai. It was not such a tearful parting as he had supposed it might be. He did not know that since he had introduced her to Y. Takimitsu a fortnight earlier she and the manager of the Los Angeles branch of the Nippon Suisan Kaisha had arrived at an understanding.

In San Francisco, Ohtani went down to the docks and after he had cleared with the immigration officials and his passport had been stamped he boarded the *Taiyo Maru* which had brought him two years all but a few weeks earlier through the Golden Gate. Back in Tokyo he became one of the outstanding officers at headquarters of Japanese Navy Intelligence.

Ko Nagasawa remained at his post in Los Angeles until shortly before Pearl Harbor, carrying on the work so ably performed by his predecessor.

Ohtani, Nagasawa and Yamakashi were not the only Japanese agents who posed as language students. Had you scratched ten per cent of the Japanese language students in America you would have found a lieutenant commander.

Nor were Yamakashi, Nagasawa and Ohtani the first language students to be sent to the west coast of America. In 1932, four years before Ohtani had arrived, a language student called Torii had been killed while crossing a Los Angeles street.

His death revealed three things: that he was really Lieutenant Commander Torii "on active service"; that the Japanese were using language students as spies, though this meant little, since there were not enough American counterespionage agents to watch them effectively, and that some very strange things were happening at 117½ Weller Street, Los Angeles.

CHAPTER 15

117½ Weller Street, Los Angeles

As he waited for the ambulance to arrive, the patrolman knew that the little Japanese over whom he was bending was dead. But he said nothing to the crowd except to ask them to stand back. Nearby the pale and trembling driver of the car stood looking down at the still body, muttering to himself that there had been nothing he could do. The little man had stepped right out in front of him, almost as if he meant to get knocked down.

From the distance came the crescendoing duet of ambulance and police car sirens. They blared with a sudden strength and stopped, and the crowd gave way before the stretcher-bearers and doctor and the headquarters' men. The doctor knelt beside the body, listening with his stethoscope. Presently he put the instrument away and stood up, nodded at the policeman and made a sign to the stretcher-bearers.

"Take down the particulars," the police lieutenant said to the patrolman, "and report to me." He stooped and picked up a slim leather brief case lying in the road. "Was this his?"

A man in the crowd said he had noticed the Japanese carrying it under his arm just before he stepped off the pavement. The lieutenant carried it with him to the car.

Within a quarter of an hour the spot was cleared and the Los Angeles street returned to normal. Another inhabitant had been killed in a traffic accident. It happened in some street almost every day of the year. It was just another tragedy of this fast-moving age of machines we live in.

On the surface it may have seemed that, but it was not long before the police discovered that though there might be nothing out of the ordinary about the manner of death, there was something strange about the victim. Documents found on the body showed that the Japanese was a language student called Torii. Another document, however, disclosed that besides being a language student Torii was also a lieutenant commander in the Japanese Navy. Even the words "on active service" might not have raised suspicions unduly, because there were a number of legitimate reasons why a Japanese lieutenant commander should be posted to America to perfect his English. It was the contents of the brief case which revealed the dead man to be what he did not appear to be.

The brief case was locked. The police had the identity of the victim and where he lived. There was no necessity for them to examine the contents of the brief case. All that remained to be done was to inform the Japanese consul, arrange the formalities with regard to handing over the body and regiment the evidence for the coroner's inquest. But before any of these things could be done the police received a telephone call from a compatriot of Torii, a Dr. Furusawa, the proprietor of a private nursing home situated at 117½ Weller Street.

There were two things about this call which made the police suspicious. The afternoon editions in which the accident would be reported were not yet on the streets; so how had Dr. Furusawa learned of the accident? The second thing was the anxiety expressed by the doctor, not on account of Torii's death, but for the safety of the brief case.

He was assured that the brief case was safe and that it would be handed in due course to the Japanese consul. It did not require a psychologist to recognize the relief in the doctor's voice when he thanked the police for the news.

But the attention of the police was now focused on the brief case. Why did the doctor regard it as far more important than the life of the unfortunate Torii?

The case was opened, and after a cursory glance through its contents, the Federal Bureau of Investigation was called.

In themselves, the contents of the case did not present a serious threat to the security of the United States.

Certainly, to learn that Lieutenant Commander Torii in his role of language student was a spy contained the elements of shock; but it was decided, however, that no action should be taken at this point purely on the basis of the contents of the case. Instead, a little watchfulness might produce more important results. So the contents were photographed, the case relocked and handed over intact to the Japanese consul.

But what was Dr. Furusawa's role? If Torii was a spy, where did the doctor fit in? The investigations of the F.B.I. were to plow up some curious facts.

2

Dr. Takashi Furusawa had lived in the United States for several years. He had, in fact, graduated at Stanford University. While still a student he had met his wife, Sachiko. She was a beautiful woman with an outstanding personality and a lively mind. They had met when she was working as a waitress in a Japanese restaurant in Little Tokyo, the Japanese quarter of San Francisco. How she had come there was part of a pathetic story.

At the age of fifteen, she had married a commander in the Japanese Navy. He was very much older than she, and consequently had a very different outlook on many things which his child bride, perhaps mistakenly, considered important. But besides being beautiful and intellectually alert, Sachiko was a girl of determination and action. After five years of what were to her dullness and frustration, she left him and took passage to San Francisco. There she worked first as a chambermaid in a hotel and then became a waitress in the restaurant where Furusawa saw her and fell in love with her. When she had obtained a divorce from the commander and Furusawa had qualified, they married.

The doctor's early years in his profession were not easy. Gradually, however, his outstanding ability, both as a physician and a surgeon, became more and more widely appreciated. He was eventually elected president of the Southern California Japanese Physicians Association and, not long afterward, president of the South California Fishing Club, an honor bestowed in recognition of his prowess as a fisherman, which only slightly exceeded his prowess at golf. He was, therefore, a man of high professional reputation, respected and popular. Just the sort of man to attract a spy master looking for a local cell leader in Los Angeles.

Coming to Los Angeles in 1930, he rented 117½ Weller Street, which thereafter also became known as the Medical Building. His establishment was a private nursing home to which, theoretically, any patient might apply for treatment. It was perhaps a little strange, therefore, that no resident of Los Angeles, either American or Japanese, ever became a bed patient there. .

The Medical Building was frequented solely by Japanese, who arrived from more distant parts of America, stayed at the nursing home for two or three days only— during which time they never ventured outside its doors— and when they did leave, were taken either to Los Angeles or to the San Francisco docks, where they arrived just in time to board a Japanese liner sailing for Japan.

Yet, apart from his duties as president of the Japanese Physicians Association and of the Fishing Club, his rounds of golf and his angling expeditions, Dr. Furusawa's duties at the Medical Building seemed to preclude his taking a very prominent part in the public and social life of Los Angeles.

Mrs. Furusawa, on the other hand, devoted much time to public works. She was a very active member of the South California Federation of Women's Societies. She was appointed an officer of and an adviser to the Koysan Buddhist Temple Women's Society. She was one of the founders of the Los Angeles Branch of the Women's Patriotic Society of Japan, whose headquarters were at 7425 Franklin Avenue, the official residence of the Japanese consul.

For the time being there were no facts, beyond Furusawa's anxious interest in the spy Torii's brief case, to connect him and his nursing home with Japanese espionage. The F.B.I. was not in a position to devote num-

190

bers of personnel to keeping 117½ Weller Street, its inmates and its visitors under constant surveillance. They did, however, set a comparatively tight watch on the place and were to discover a good deal that was as serious as it was important.

It must be remembered that though they made these discoveries and could build up a fair picture of what happened, their field of vision was restricted. This arose from the official attitude toward both espionage and particularly counterespionage, which denied them the necessary facilities for full investigation; and also from the fact that there was no coordination between the F.B.I. and other counterespionage agencies such as, for example, the Office of Naval Intelligence. This agency was working on its own, like the F.B.I. Like the F.B.I., the O.N.I. also made disquieting discoveries and was instrumental in frustrating some Japanese plots, as we shall see. Not only did this situation allow the Japanese to carry on their undercover work almost unmolested, it often acutely embarrassed the respective agents of the F.B.I. and the O.N.I.

Nevertheless, the death of Lieutenant Commander Torii and the cynical anxiety of Dr. Furusawa, by bringing 117½ Weller Street to the notice of one counterespionage agency, at all events, had, within limitations, important results. One of these results was to disclose a link between German and Japanese agents, and between the east and west coasts.

3

About the time of Torii's death, a certain German count, Hermann von Keitel, was behaving rather peculiarly in New York.

Von Keitel employed a German butler, called Manfred, whom he would invite into his study to drink with him. This seemed to indicate either that the count was an eccentric or that the true relationship between the two men was not that of master and servant.

What was quite clear, however, was the count's interest

in Japanese affairs. Certain suave, silent oriental gentlemen were frequent visitors to his apartment; and from time to time he himself made the journey by train to Washington, where he visited Commander Josiuki Itimiya, the Japanese naval attaché, at his home in the Alban Towers.

Near the Hudson Terminal, in the financial district of New York, there was at this time a small stationer's shop, a one-man business which just, but only just, provided a living for its proprietor.

One day the count walked into this shop bent, it seemed, on enhancing his reputation as an eccentric. He announced to the delighted but somewhat surprised proprietor that he would be prepared to place quite a large order for some embossed stationery on the somewhat singular condition that a sample of it should be displayed in the shop window in a certain position, with the surrounding stationery arranged in a certain way.

For the sake of the order the proprietor was prepared to humor his client. He embossed the note paper and arranged a sample in the window in the way stipulated. He did not, however, notice that during the days following Japanese would come to his window, pause, glance in quickly and move away.

The subsequent behavior of the count convinced him that his client was perhaps rather more than eccentric. No normal man would change his address so often or have note paper embossed with the new address each time. But if it meant a pleasant increase in his takings, who was he to object?

Quite suddenly and without warning, however, in the middle of March 1933, the stationer lost his client. But it turned out to be only a temporary loss, for in the following September the count called and announced that he was going to the Pacific coast. He wished some visiting cards to be prepared for him—with a sample displayed as usual— omitting the title, and bearing simply: Hermann von Keitel, 117½ Weller Street, Los Angeles.

It was his arrival at the Medical Building shortly after this which brought the count into the orbit of the F.B.I. But it did not take them long to discover that besides being a count he was also a high-ranking German naval officer.

This discovery aroused sufficient interest for his progress to be followed by F.B.I. agents wherever he went from now on, and it was through him that they discovered the identities of other spies, both German and Japanese.

They looked in on, though from a distance, the party which Dr. and Mrs. Furusawa gave for their guest two days after his arrival at the Kawafuku Tei, that well-known Japanese restaurant in Los Angeles; and they noted that among the other guests were certain Japanese attachés.

Indeed, Japanese attachés appeared to have a particular liking for the count, for during his stay at 117½ Weller Street attachés in Los Angeles, San Francisco, Seattle and Portland—all of which places were important in the life of the United States Navy—visited the Medical Building.

The Furusawas must have felt very secure, because on the eve of von Keitel's departure they gave him another party at which, besides the attachés, was Momotu Okura, commandant of the South California Imperial Veterans Association, a body which was controlled by the Japanese government. Okura was now a citizen of the United States and his son, Kiyoshi P. Okura, was an examiner for the Los Angeles Civil Service Commission.

Von Keitel stayed in Los Angeles, off and on, for about a year before returning permanently to New York. Here, naturally, the F.B.I. continued to watch him. The first thing they discovered was that he was on intimate terms with Roy Akagi, manager of the New York office of the Southern Manchurian Railway. So Akagi was added to the list of those under surveillance, and this uncovered the fact that he was frequently in the company of George Gyssling, the German vice-consul in New York. Gyssling, who was only twenty-eight and a typical Nazi, had made himself extremely unpopular in America for his outspoken criticisms of conditions during the depression.

One evening toward the end of December 1933 Akagi, with the F.B.I. on his tail, went to the Foreign Press Association offices at 110 West 57th Street. He did not go into the building but waited in the entrance where he was presently joined by Chuzo Hagiwara, the New York chief of *Domei,* the official Japanese news agency.

Now, there was nothing extraordinary in two Japanese meeting and spending the evening together. But they did not do this. They went straight to East 66th Street where they entered number 5, which was a very exclusive German club. The watching F.B.I. agents noted that they were admitted without difficulty and concluded that they had been expected. Shortly afterward, Gyssling, accompanied by two other Japanese, entered the club, and close on their heels came Count von Keitel.

So the F.B.I. were now able to add to their list of suspects Gyssling, Akagi and Hagiwara. With von Keitel providing the link, it was also clear that there was close collaboration between the east and west coasts.

On the west coast, the Furusawas of Weller Street were being very busy, Mrs. Furusawa particularly so. Whenever a Japanese liner arrived at Los Angeles she would hurry to the pier to welcome, in person, certain Japanese officers, whom she would entertain lavishly at the Kawafuku Tei. Shortly before the liner was due to leave she would hurry down to the pier again and go aboard. Each time she would be carrying a brief case when she went on board, and each time she came ashore she would be empty-handed.

In the early days of his prosperity the famous film star, Charlie Chaplin, had employed a Japanese valet and handyman named Torzichi Kono. In 1933, Kono was no longer in Chaplin's employ; in fact, several years had passed since he had worked for the comedian. But in the intervening years he certainly seemed to have found for himself a much more lucrative source of income.

He was now ensconced in a sumptuous apartment in Bronson Street, Hollywood, and owned two cars, in one or the other of which he would drive up to 117½ Weller Street and have it wait while he was inside. When the American Embassy in Tokyo was asked if they could supply any information about him, they were able to say that he owned a very fine estate on the outskirts of the capital, which he visited for a few months every year.

In May 1934 Kono was one day seen to be in a great hurry; so great, in fact, that he drove through several sets of traffic lights. He did not stop until he had reached the Medical Building.

He stayed with Dr. Furusawa about a quarter of an hour, then at midnight took the express to San Francisco. Next morning he went by taxi to Stanford University and was seen to enter one of the men students' hostels. It was assumed, since he could not be followed inside, that he was visiting a Japanese language student, one of the few who did actually attend a place of learning.

From the university he returned to the station, where he took the day express back to Los Angeles. He drove straight to 117½ Weller Street and stayed the night there. Next day he took a transcontinental limited—an express that makes a limited number of stops—to Chicago. In Chicago he boarded an express for New York and there went at once to the apartment of Count von Keitel.

Von Keitel and Kono emerged from the apartment in time to catch the midnight train to Washington. There they visited Commander Yoshiaki Ichimiya, the naval attaché, with whom they stayed for several hours, and then returned to New York on an overnight train.

On the following day Kono began his journey back to Los Angeles. Von Keitel accompanied him to the station and when the train had left went straight to the offices of the Southern Manchurian Railway, where he stayed some time with Akagi.

When he left, Akagi visited Hagiwara at *Domei,* and he in turn went to see Vice-Consul Gyssling. Together Gyssling and Hagiwara went to the German Club, where they were presently joined by von Keitel, Akagi and two Japanese attachés.

And the F.B.I. was hamstrung by those two strange factors—the attitude of the State Department and the lack of coordination between the various intelligence and counterespionage agencies.

Fortunately, the F.B.I. was not missing very much. All this frantic activity was partly a general attempt by the Japanese to keep abreast of United States Navy development, partly to find out whether American reaction to the Annam Statement, which warned foreign powers against giving aid of any sort to China, was likely to include secret naval preparations which might threaten to defy the warning, but mostly it was a kind of friendly get-together between the Japanese and their new friends the Germans, in which the Japanese were doing their best to impress their friends with their methods and achievements in the United States.

In 1933 Colonel Eugene Ott, who was an intimate friend and close associate of one of the chiefs of German intelligence, Colonel Walther Nicolai, had been sent to Tokyo, a visit which appears to have been a natural offshoot of a desire in fascist-minded Japanese to make friends with German fascists. This desire had been manifested by a visit of delegates of the Japanese Fascist National Youth Movement to Berlin and by a visit by one of the most important *eminences grises* of Japanese affairs, Prince Tohigawa, to Alfred Rosenberg, the Nazi racial philosopher.

In actual fact Colonel Nicolai, who was later to become director of German military intelligence, had had contact with Sazo Nakamo, one of Japan's leading espionage experts. Nakamo had suggested that there should be cooperation on a world-wide scale between German and Japanese civil and military espionage. So the fiat had gone forth, and Count von Keitel had made the acquaintance of Akagi and Hagiwara and the Furusawas as well as the various Japanese attachés, including the naval attaché in Washington, who was always the chief of Japanese naval espionage in the United States.

The idea behind the suggestion, of course, was the difficulty which the Japanese had in establishing their own agents in Occidental countries on account of their undisguisable facial characteristics. The settlement of many innocent Japanese in America naturally helped them there, and it was there that they had established their most successful and numerous espionage system in any Western country, which they naturally wished to exhibit to their friends.

At the same time, it was mooted that the Japanese should reinforce Germany's espionage in the Far East and Asiatic Russia as a *quid pro quo* for Germany's reinforcement of Japanese espionage in the Western countries.

Despite the great friendliness of the "ring" in America with von Keitel and Gyssling and others, the Germans were not willing to accept such an arrangement out of hand, and Colonel Ott's mission was to study Japanese espionage methods and results and to report by the summer of 1934. He met with great kindness from Japanese officers, and within a few weeks of his arrival was invited to enter the Japanese Army as an observer. He also made the acquaintance of Admiral Nobumasa Suetsugu, a self-confessed admirer of Hitler, and of the Lawrence of Manchuria, General Kenji Doihara.

With the latter he developed a close friendship. Doihara seemed to take to him as he rarely ever took to anyone, even among his own countrymen, and when he went on his journeys he invited Ott to accompany him. Ott also became on very friendly terms with Colonel Hiroshi Oshima, who, at Doihara's request, expounded to him the organization of Japanese military espionage.

It was mainly on the basis of what he learned from Oshima that Ott made his report, the outcome of which was his own return to Tokyo later in 1934 as military attaché and Oshima's posting to Berlin early in 1935 in a similar capacity.

Though the suggestion for collaboration had emanated from the Japanese, it was with the mental reservation that they would impart to the Germans as little information of any consequence as was possible without raising German suspicions. The Germans, on the other hand, were prepared to treat the matter with unwonted honesty. For example, from 1934 onward the Japanese consul in Los Angeles was again and again invited to meet the captains of German vessels, who handed over to him the latest information to come their way.

The closest collaboration between the Germans and the Japanese was in Central and South America. Outstanding among the Japanese agents in these areas were J. Yamashito and Y. Matsui, who reached Mexico in fishing boats and operated in Guaymas, the port on the Gulf of California.

For a time the Germans seemed oblivious of the fact that they were receiving very little information from the Japanese, but eventually the realization emerged. Subordinate German agents in Mexico brought the matter to a head by entering a most vigorous protest. The Japanese bowed and were polite, made promises, but carried on as usual.

But if the Japanese were polite, the Germans were persistent, and on October 5th, 1937, the German minister in Mexico City, Rüdt von Collenberg, called a conference of his Italian and Japanese colleagues. Von Collenberg was a diplomat of the old school and looked askance at becoming involved in espionage, even that of his own country. He went to the meeting scarcely knowing what it was all about. But he had been well briefed by his civilian attaché, Dr. Heinrich Northe, and the arguments he put forward must have been impressive, for the Japanese thenceforward fully collaborated.

This collaboration was particularly successful in Costa Rica, where the chief operators were Takahiro Wakabayashi for Japan, Gerhard Henschke for Germany and Giuseppe Sotanis for Italy, which was now included in the agreement after the signing of the Anti-Comintern Pact.

Sotanis lived at the Grand Hotel in San José, Costa Rica, and was known as an ardent stamp collector. What was not known was that he was an even more ardent collector of arms and ammunition.

To carry forward their plans in this area, the Japanese proposed preparing an airfield which would be camouflaged as a cotton plantation. Wakabayashi was able to purchase an ideal site and Sotanis, who had a certain influence, though a shady one, with the Costa Rican government, obtained a concession for him to plant his cotton. Wakabayashi then brought twenty-one laborers from Chimbota, in Peru, where there was a Japanese colony numbering 20,000.[1] The laborers arrived, bringing with them one bag of cotton seed, and lodged themselves in one of the best hotels. The bag of seed never left the hotel.

Not long after the conference of diplomats, Yoshitaro Amano, who was the owner of the *Amano Maru,* then the largest fishing boat in the world, came to Costa Rica and made an attempt to contact Wakabayashi's experimental cotton station. Unfortunately, he bungled and was immediately arrested. Gerhard Henschke appears to have heard about Amano's misfortune first, and he at once got in touch with Sotanis, who, in turn, approached his "friend" the president of the republic and obtained Amano's immediate release.

The collaboration did not entirely solve the problem of the Japanese in America and they were constantly on the lookout for disaffected or corruptible Americans whom they could bribe to work for them. Unfortunately they were able to find two, and it was with their discovery that the administration allowed the O.N.I. and F.B.I. to enjoy the fruits of their labors and to bring the traitors to justice.

[1] *Note.* Other extensive Japanese colonies in South America were in Colombia, 25,000, Brazil, 40,000 and Paraguay, 15,000.

CHAPTER 16

The Ex-Naval Traitors

"Got a light, pal?"

The young man shook his head. "I don't even have a drag," he said.

The man who had accosted him—he might have been three or four years older—looked at him with intense closeness. "Down on your luck?" he asked. "Wait a minute!"

He turned to ask another passer-by for a light, and when he was drawing on his cigarette he held out a packet of Camels. "Have one," he said.

The young man took a cigarette and lit it from the glowing end held up to him. He took a deep pull, and the unaccustomed bite of smoke in his lungs made his head reel. He swayed, a hand to his eyes.

"Say, what's up?"

"This is my first drag for four days."

"When did you last eat?"

"The day before last—I think."

"Jesus! Here, you'd better come home with me. Hi! Taxi!"

The young man made no protest. He still could not focus his eyes. He allowed himself to be half-helped, half-pushed into the cab.

"Linden Street, Long Beach," he said to the driver.

At his apartment, where he lived by himself, he made coffee and put a loaf of bread, some butter and a hunk of cheese before the pale boy.

"Don't eat too quick," he warned. As the color came creeping back into the boy's cheeks slowly and faintly, he said: "What's your name? I'm Harry Thompson."

"I'm Willard Turntine, from St. Louis."

"Where are you living?"

"On the beach."

"Got any money?"

"One darned solitary nickel."

"You seem a nice enough kid. You'd better stay here with me until we can get something worked out. What are you doing here, anyway?"

"Looking for work."

"Huh!"

The sound was no criticism of the boy, but rather of the times in which they lived.

"Like looking for a needle in a haystack here in Long Beach," he said. "How old are you?"

"Eighteen."

"Well, let's forget it for now. Come on, we'll go some place and get you a decent meal. Then you can stick around."

"Thanks," the boy said, his embarrassment holding him back from saying more.

And that was how Willard Turntine met Harry Thomas Thompson—and thought he had made a friend.

3

Harry Thomas Thompson was in his early twenties. He had been a yeoman in the United States Navy but now, like Turntine, he was unemployed. Unlike Turntine, however, he was not short of money.

There has never been any proof, nor even a suggestion, that Thompson had any motive other than kindness for a penniless boy when he invited Turntine to come and live with him. Turntine never at any time subsequently hinted that the older man made any physical approach.

Turntine liked Thompson more as he came to know him better, but after a time his curiosity began to be roused by the fact that although Thompson had no work he always had plenty of money, some of which he was pleased to give to the younger man.

Plucking up courage one day, Turntine asked Thompson where his money came from and was given the vague but even more curiosity-rousing answer that he would know some day—perhaps. For it seems that Thompson had by this time developed ideas about Turntine, now that he really knew him.

Though no longer in the navy, Thompson seemed to hanker after his former life aboard the *Colorado,* the *Mississippi* and the *Texas,* the United States battleships in which he had served. For whenever these vessels, and the radio controlled ship *Utah,* in which some of his naval friends now served, put into San Diego and San Pedro, he always went to meet and have a drink with his old associates.

Thompson took Turntine with him on some of these trips and the boy was surprised to hear his friend asking very searching questions about ship movements, developments in equipment and changes in orders.

There is no doubt that of the two Thompson was the dominant character. On the other hand Turntine was no fool, and he was observant. He also possessed courage.

He asked Thompson why, since he had left the service because he did not like it, he made these visits to naval vessels, and received the reply: "I just like to keep in touch with what's going on."

But Turntine was not satisfied. He kept his suspicions to himself, but as each day passed he read more and more sinister implications into his friend's behavior and watched him more and more closely. And so he discovered Thompson's association with a little Japanese.

Choosing his time, he asked Thompson who the Japanese was and what the relationship was between them. As a result of what Thompson said, he knew then that his friend was deep in treachery. Indeed Thompson made no attempt to deny it. "The world owes me a living. O.K.?" he said. "If my country won't give me a living, another country will."

Now that Turntine knew the truth, Thompson saw that for his own safety the boy must also be compromised. He spoke to his Japanese master, and he agreed to see Turntine. The name of the Japanese was Tanni, and a meeting was arranged in Los Angeles. Tanni, however, could not make up his mind.

His secret no longer a secret, Thompson became careless about concealing communications which he received from Tanni from time to time. By Christmas 1934 Turntine's conscience had become so uneasy that he decided that he must go to the authorities.

A suitable opportunity did not occur, however, until the end of January 1935, when Thompson announced that he was going away for a few days. Turntine knew that the flagship, the U.S.S. *Pennsylvania,* was anchored at San Diego. He went to San Diego and by sheer persistence was at last taken before Admiral Joseph M. Reeves. He told Admiral Reeves his story and Reeves was impressed. He told the boy to go back to Long Beach and carry on as usual, taking care not to let Thompson know what he had done.

Admiral Reeves immediately passed Turntine's story to the Office of Naval Intelligence. O.N.I. agents, moving quickly, went to Long Beach and closely interrogated Turntine. They had already checked on the boy and found that he had a clean record.

They were as impressed as the admiral had been, especially when they saw one of the letters from Tanni, which Turntine had been able to cache, and which Thompson in his carelessness had not missed. Giving him the same instructions to carry on as before, they told him that he might hear from them later. They then went away to try to discover the identity of Tanni.

Tanni presented a problem, but eventually he was traced to Palo Alto. This suggested that he might be a language student at Stanford University; and so it turned out to be. By comparing the handwriting of the Tanni letter with the handwriting of the one or two Japanese studying at Stanford, they discovered that Tanni's real name was Toshio Miyazaki.

Miyazaki had entered the United States on August 24th,

1933, and almost immediately had enrolled at Stanford. Though only thirty, he was already a lieutenant commander in the Japanese Navy.

Miyazaki was now permanently shadowed by the O.N.I., who, a day or two after he had been identified, followed him to San Francisco. There he dined well and spent an hour or two in a brothel, leaving just in time to catch the train for Los Angeles, where he took a taxi to 117½ Weller Street. He was Dr. Furusawa's guest until Sunday evening, when he took a taxi to Long Beach and visited Thompson, now returned from his trip, at his apartment on Linden Street.

Thompson was aware of the impending visit. Earlier in the evening he had tossed Turntine a five-dollar bill saying: "Go out and lose yourself for an hour or so, will you? I've got a doll coming."

O.N.I. agents had also installed themselves in the building opposite the apartment building and were able to see into Thompson's room. As soon as Miyazaki arrived he handed Thompson a wad of dollar bills and then took from his brief case a large sheet of paper. The two men bent low over the paper for a quarter of an hour or so and then Thompson went into the bedroom, returning with a sheaf of papers which he handed to Miyazaki one at a time. Each paper was fully discussed, it seemed.

It was after ten o'clock when the Japanese eventually left, taking Thompson's notes with him. He drove straight back to Los Angeles by taxi, which took him to the Red Mill brothel. He was in the brothel for three-quarters of an hour, and then he caught the night train for San Francisco. On Monday morning he was attending his lectures at Stanford University.

The counteragents next discovered that Miyazaki banked at the Yokohama Specie Bank in San Francisco. His account revealed that he had been paying Thompson 200 dollars a month. He was meticulous in meeting his financial commitments with Thompson. Later the following letter from him to Thompson was to be made public:

. . . I am very glad to know you are doing very good. Don't hurry. Go slow and steady.

Since now your monthly salary will be sent not later than the first of each month, and tomorrow 300 dollars will be sent. . . . I shall have a very long trip next month, and may return in January, but not sure. I will send your January salary before I leave here.

Will you send me the schedule of the force tactics which will commence from 5th December? If you can get it before that time, send me from 3rd December.

(It is said that several phrases in this letter made Miyazaki's tutors wince.)

The day following Miyazaki's visit to his apartment Thompson told Turntine that he was rejoining the navy and bought himself a petty officer's uniform.

Turntine, who was now cooperating fully with the O.N.I. asked Thompson bluntly whether he, himself, was going to be given a chance of working for the Japanese. Thompson told him that Tanni could not find work for him at the moment, and for the first time uttered a threat.

"If you ever tell anyone about what's going on, or that you met Tanni, you won't live long!"

Dressed in his uniform Thompson went to San Pedro, where he spent most of his time in the bars, buying drinks for sailors and skillfully questioning them about the fleet's future activities.

The O.N.I. was now fully convinced that Thompson was a dangerous menace. They approached the State Department with the request that both he and Miyazaki should be arrested.

But the State Department was falling over itself at this time not to antagonize Japan in any way, and refused pointblank to authorize Miyazaki's apprehension. All that the O.N.I. could do was to warn sailors not to talk to Thompson.

Thompson masqueraded in his petty officer's uniform for several months. During this time he met Miyazaki frequently either at his own apartment in Linden Street or at the St. Francis Hotel in San Francisco.

When the sailors would no longer talk to him, Thompson had to confess to Miyazaki that he believed there had been a leak and that he suspected Turntine. Miyazaki did not directly order Thompson to remove Turntine permanently, but suggested that this would be the best solution. To protect Turntine, the O.N.I. secured work for him in San Francisco, so that he need no longer live with Thompson.

When Turntine told Thompson that he had got a job as a salesman in a San Francisco department store, Thompson was at once more suspicious than ever. But when Turntine was able to produce letters on headed stationery, Thompson appeared satisfied.

After Turntine left Thompson began to crack up. He took to drinking heavily, his bouts sometimes lasting for several days at a time. His behavior perturbed Miyazaki, who visited him at Linden Street. O.N.I. agents watching from the building opposite surmised from Thompson's demeanor and Miyazaki's gestures that the Japanese was soundly rating his agent. When Miyazaki left Thompson sat down at his table and spent an hour or two trying to compose a letter. It gave him great difficulty. He made several false starts, screwing up the sheets and tossing them into the wastepaper basket. The O.N.I. could not legally enter Thompson's apartment, but they arranged for the contents of the wastepaper basket to be handed to them. Among the screwed up sheets was found a rough copy of the final draft of the letter he had at last managed.

My dear Mr. Tanni, I respectfully request that this letter be treated as my resignation from the service of your country and the country of which I have been serving. It is with great reluctance and regret that I tender this resignation to the Japanese government as I can only state that I have enjoyed every moment I have spent in the service of your country, and hope that all information that has come to you through me has amply repaid for the salary paid me.

This resignation is to take effect as of the date of our last meeting. This is my own doing and free will and for the safeguard of my own person and has nothing whatever to do with anything you or your country has done or should do.

In saying goodbye I extend to you my heartiest congratulations and hope that anything you may undertake will prove of a successful nature.

Harry Thomas Thompson.

Miyazaki, realizing that Thompson's usefulness was finished, accepted the resignation. His superiors, anxious lest he might be compromised by the demoralized American, ordered his return to Japan.

The evidence against Thompson was so conclusive that now the Japanese had flown there could be no excuse for postponing his arrest. A brief announcement was made to the public in the press on March 5, 1936. At his subsequent trial, Turntine was the prosecution's star witness, but others showed that Thompson had been in the service of the Japanese since 1933. In July 1936 he was sentenced to fifteen years in the federal penitentiary on McNeil Island.

3

On March 5th, 1936, John S. Farnsworth picked up a copy of the *Washington Post* and quickly scanned its columns. The announcement of Harry Thompson's arrest on charges of spying caught his eye and he read it through carefully.

He shrugged his shoulders, emptied his glass, and pushed it across the counter to the barman. "Same again, Joe!" he said.

He drank his second drink slowly, still looking through the newspaper, and when he had finished, got off the stool and went up to his apartment. He glanced at his watch, got his hat and coat and went out. A short time later, he was in the room of the Japanese naval attaché at the Alban Towers and was regarding the little man, Commander Akira Yamaki, with utter incomprehension.

The commander was pacing the room like a caged

animal, his face distorted with a variety of emotions. "It's terrible, terrible!" he repeated over and over again. Then he turned on Farnsworth. "You should not have come here. Go away. See that no one notices you leaving. Drop everything you are doing and do nothing until you hear from me!"

"But, commander," Farnsworth protested, "just because they've caught this dolt it doesn't mean that they've got anything on me. I must say it surprises me that you ever used an uneducated yeoman who had no training and no sense, obviously."

"The risk is too great," the commander insisted. "This is one of the greatest blows Japan has ever suffered."

"Oh, come, commander!" Farnsworth smiled.

"It is true. Now go please, and remember—you are to do nothing until you hear from me."

"Commander, I have no money."

The commander went to his safe and counted out 300 dollars. Farnsworth took the money. But he did not know that it represented the last of a long series of payments he had received from the Japanese over the last three years.

4

John S. Farnsworth was born in Cincinnati and had graduated from high school at the top of his class. During his last years at school he had developed an ambition to enter the navy, and on leaving school he obtained an interview with his congressman, who was impressed by the boy and secured a place for him at the Naval Academy at Annapolis. While at Annapolis, though he seemed to concentrate more on women and drink than he did on his studies, nevertheless he passed out in 1915 with a brilliant mark.

Farnsworth served in destroyers in World War I, but in 1922 his interest turned to flying and he went back to Annapolis to study nautical aviation. From Annapolis, he continued these studies, in 1923, at the Massachusetts Institute of Technology, and when he left there he was promoted to lieutenant commander and posted to a teaching appointment at the Navy Air School at Pensacola, Florida. After a time there, he commanded the squadron base at Norfolk, Virginia.

Farnsworth's charm made him not only very attractive to women but he was popular with a wide circle of people. He married a society girl, well above him in social station, and his attempts to keep her in the style to which she had been accustomed, and to repay the hospitality they received, ran him into debt, and he began to borrow. Getting deeper and deeper into financial difficulties, he eventually borrowed from a naval rating, and when pressed to repay, refused. The result was a court-martial; the verdict—dismissed from the service.

It is one of the unfortunate consequences of cases like this that such an entry in a man's record is indelible. Farnsworth's attempt to obtain civilian employment failed always as soon as he had to confess that he had been dismissed from the navy. It can perhaps be understood that after repeated failures to procure a means of livelihood he felt he was being hounded by the authorities. In desperation, he offered his expert knowledge of aviation to Peru, China, Brazil and Russia. None was interested. Then he turned to Japan. The Japanese were interested, but not in a technical adviser. Perhaps he would consider other employment in which his knowledge and his background would be of great use?

Farnsworth first came to the notice of Captain William Puleston, chief of the Office of Naval Intelligence, early in 1934.

A few days previously Farnsworth had paid a call on a former navy friend, Lieutenant Commander Leslie Gehres, of the Navy Examining Board. For some time now it had been known in navy circles that Farnsworth had been haunting old navy friends hoping, it seemed, that his past might be forgotten and that he might be re-employed.

While Farnsworth was with him Gehres was called from his office for a few moments and when he returned he asked his visitor to excuse him, as he had some urgent work to deal with. Farnsworth took his leave.

Within a short time Gehres found that a copy of *The Service of Information and Security,* a highly confidential document printed especially for a very limited number of high-ranking navy officers, was missing from his desk. Perturbed at not being able to find it, as a last resort, after questioning his staff, he telephoned Farnsworth and asked him if he had by any chance picked up the book by mistake. Farnsworth replied that he had, and would return it the following morning, which he did. Being a good officer, Gehres made out a report of what had happened. It was this report which found its way to the O.N.I.

Captain Puleston called for the Farnsworth dossier and found that since he had left the service he had been divorced, had remarried and that the second marriage was now running into difficulties. But more significant, he also discovered that Farnsworth was no longer short of money but almost any day could be found flashing hundred-dollar bills.

This was strange, because he had confessed to Gehres and other naval friends that he had no employment. How then could he live in the New Willard, a luxury hotel in Washington, for days never getting any farther than the bar? Where did his money come from? His bank account revealed nothing.

O.N.I.'s experience with Harry Thompson caused Captain Puleston to wonder whether Farnsworth might not be getting his money from a similar source. So, when he began to look around for the ex-lieutenant commander's "Tanni," his attention was attracted to the naval attaché, Commander Ichimiya.

From the maids at the Alban Towers he learned that they were never allowed to go into two rooms in the commander's apartment. They also spoke of a strange acrid smell seeping under the doors of these rooms from time to time, which suggested photographic activity.

But Farnsworth and Ichimiya never seemed to meet. Yet, when Ichimiya's bank account was studied it was found that he regularly received large sums of money over and above his normal salary, and whenever he paid in one of these checks he also withdrew the greater part of it in new hundred-dollar bills.

Since the O.N.I. was very much understaffed, Puleston decided to ask the F.B.I. for assistance. The F.B.I. put a twenty-four-hour watch on Farnsworth, but for a time they gathered no evidence that he was in any way connected with the Japanese. But presently they got their break. Farnsworth paid a visit to Annapolis and there called on Lieutenant Commander James E. Mather at his home, staying for more than an hour. When he left F.B.I. agents visited Mather and asked what Farnsworth had wanted.

Both the lieutenant commander and his wife were above reproach. They told the F.B.I. that Farnsworth called on them from time to time, and believing his protests because they were loyal navy people themselves and could understand that the navy was in his blood, they had tried to make him happy by talking about navy affairs. When, however, the F.B.I. agents suggested that Farnsworth might be involved in espionage, though it came as a great shock, the Mathers were able to read sinister implications into his visits to them.

On several occasions, for example, while Mather had been out of the room, Farnsworth had questioned Mrs. Mather closely on various matters affecting the navy which a non-naval, even an ex-naval man, would not have asked. In fact, this had happened on this very visit.

Almost as soon as Farnsworth had arrived he had begun to ask questions about a new destroyer, the U.S.S. *Baddlitt*, very recently commissioned and purported to be the very latest in destroyer construction and equipment. Noticing the deterioration in Farnsworth's physical appearance since the last time he had called, and reading the all too obvious signs of too much drinking, Mather evaded answering the questions. But when, presently, he left his wife alone with Farnsworth for a few minutes, Farnsworth had said to Mrs. Mather: "Please tell me about the *Baddlitt!* I've just got to know!"

Since registering in Annapolis at the Carvell Hall Hotel, Farnsworth had made a telephone call to an unlisted Washington number. This was suspicious; but more suspicious still, he had given the operator a false name. The man who had answered had angrily said that he had the wrong number; but the man had spoken with an unmistakable Japanese accent. When the number was traced, it was found to be that of Commander Ichimiya.

211

But Ichimiya had been recalled to Japan and his apartment in the Alban Towers had been taken over by his successor as naval attaché, Commander Akira Yamaki. And so the F.B.I. learned for the first time definitely of Farnsworth's connection with the Japanese.

Now, the recall of Ichimiya and his replacement by Yamaki had been done with such secrecy that no one in American government circles was aware of the change until Yamaki had installed himself in the Alban Towers. The reason for the secrecy could only be surmised.

Farnsworth's action in telephoning the unlisted Washington number led the F.B.I. to check on his other visits to Annapolis, where he always stayed at the Carvell Hall Hotel. He had been to Annapolis seven times in the last two years, they discovered, and each time he had telephoned this same number at least once a day. On one occasion he had made three calls in four hours. The F.B.I. investigations were now extended, with the result that a picture of Farnsworth's movements over the past three years was built up. He had been to Boston, Philadelphia, Baltimore, Norfolk and New York. In every instance he had called Ichimiya in Washington.

In Boston, early in 1933, he had telephoned a second number, that of a Japanese called Sato, who was officially described as correspondent of *Domei,* the Japanese news agency. He lived in Morrison Street in Washington, and since he was seen only in the highest official circles, he was looked upon as a semi-official representative of the Japanese government. One of Sato's closest companions was Yamaki, it was now discovered. They dined together frequently in the leading restaurants of Washington, but when they parted each went to his own home. Nor were they ever known to meet again the same evening.

Then an F.B.I. agent made one of those chance discoveries which are always appearing in the pages of espionage history and which are almost invariably instrumental in bringing about the downfall of a spy. The agent learned from a maid at the Alban Towers that Sato often called on Yamaki at four o'clock in the morning, using the rear entrance and staying until dawn. Thinking that perhaps Farnsworth might also be using the back door to visit

Yamaki, a permanent watch was set on it. But there was no result until the day of Thompson's arrest.

Slowly but inexorably the F.B.I. ground on, and presently they had milled a fine flour of evidence which would be capable of suffocating Farnsworth as a spy. Among the information which came to them was that during the last three years Farnsworth had constantly visited commercial photostating firms in Washington. When employees of these firms were questioned they were unable to recall details of the material which they had processed for him, though they could say definitely that the work was always connected with naval matters. He had always waited while the photostating was being done, had paid on the spot and had taken away with him all the copies and the originals. Extending this line of inquiry to other cities, photostat operators in Norfolk and Baltimore recognized Farnsworth's photograph. They, too, recalled that he described himself as a naval officer who needed immediate copies of certain official documents.

Remembering the testimony of the maids at the Alban Towers concerning Ichimiya's ban on their entering two rooms in his apartment and of the odors which sometimes seeped under the doors, the F.B.I. began to wonder whether he might not also have been engaged in such work. With increasing satisfaction they found that within a month of Ichimiya's arrival in Washington in 1933, two photostating machines had been delivered to him at the Alban Towers.

By this time enough evidence against Farnsworth had been collected to justify his arrest, for besides the obvious contact there was between him and certain Japanese, interrogation of naval ratings and officers who had been approached by him revealed that unwittingly he had been supplied with a great deal of information. He had been told, for example, the effectiveness of almost every gun in the navy and the vital performance records of the aircraft carriers *Ranger* and *Saratoga*.

But as in the case of Harry Thompson, the F.B.I. was held back by the authorities. Eventually, when Farnsworth had to be arrested to avoid a scandal, he had ceased to be active as a spy, Commander Yamaki was safely back in

Tokyo and Sato was working innocently in New York.

Commander Yamaki's decision that Farnsworth was no longer to engage in any espionage activities on behalf of the Japanese, and even more so his withholding of money from Farnsworth, were about the biggest blunders the Japanese secret service ever made in America.

The publication in July of the fifteen-year sentence on Harry Thompson had an effect on Farnsworth that his arrest had not had. That night he went out and got very drunk indeed—on money he had had to borrow.

The following morning he went to the National Press Building on Fourteenth Street N.W., where he took the lift to the offices of the Universal News Service, a Hearst subsidiary. There he was interviewed by John Lambert, chief of the Washington office, and was passed on by him to Fulton Lewis Jr.

The entirely impecunious Farnsworth besides being in search of money was now bent on establishing justification for his collaboration with the Japanese. It had at last struck him that he, too, might have been watched by counterespionage agents.

His story was an ingenious one, and had the F.B.I. been unaware at this time of the true damage he had done, they might have been deceived by it. He told Fulton Lewis Jr. that he had been pretending to spy for the Japanese in an attempt to find out the extent of their espionage activities. He had not told the authorities what he was doing because he hoped that if he did a good job it might lead to his reinstatement in the navy. He offered Fulton Lewis Jr. the story for 20,000 dollars. Wisely, Lewis refrained from asking him why he had come to him instead of going to the O.N.I., and playing for time he said that he could not himself authorize the payment of so large a sum as 20,000 dollars but would have to consult his chief. Perhaps Farnsworth would call back the following day?

As soon as Farnsworth had gone Lewis informed the police, and the F.B.I., arguing that it would be dangerous to the security of the nation to leave him at liberty any longer, obtained the consent of the authorities to his arrest. He was taken into custody a few hours after he had left the National Press Building.

It was February 1937 before the United States attorney had his case against Farnsworth ready. The indictment included specific charges of having visited the Navy Department in August 1934 and January 1935 and the Naval Academy at Annapolis in April 1935 for the purpose of obtaining code and signal books, sketches, photographs, blueprints, maps and models.

To his defending attorney and to all who came into contact with him, Farnsworth protested his innocence, as he had done to Fulton Lewis Jr. and the F.B.I. But at the last moment he changed his mind and entered a plea of *nolo contendere*.

On February 23rd, 1937, he was sentenced to four to twenty years in a federal penitentiary.

Fortunately for the people of the United States, there were more patriots like Willard Turntine among them than traitors. Such a one was Kilsoo Haan, a Korean.

CHAPTER 17

The Night Club Owner on the West Coast

Not only did the imprisonment of Thompson and Farnsworth badly frighten the chiefs of Japanese espionage, but it led to a certain reorganization of American counterespionage. More F.B.I. agents, though still a totally insufficient number to cope with the worm in the damask cheek of the American rose, were detailed for counterspy duties.

Thus the movements of Count von Keitel were noted when he changed his domicile once more from New York to Los Angeles, though still continuing to function as liaison officer between the Japanese and German espionage systems on the east and west coasts. They knew, too, every time Countess von Keitel and the so-called butler Manfred made their frequent trips to New York and Hamburg as couriers. They searched the baggage of these two carefully every time, but the Germans were well versed in security and nothing was found to incriminate them. Manfred led them to other Japanese. These in turn were trailed and it was found that their common contact was Akagi, who, with Vice-Consul Gyssling, now appeared to be in charge of the New York organizations. But it was Kilsoo Haan, a Korean who spoke fluent Chinese and Japanese, who put them on the trail of Yamamoto.

By this time Yamamoto had reached a certain prominence on the west coast. Ostensibly he managed, and owned, a chain of night clubs and brothels. He was a typical gangster type, maintaining a bodyguard without whom he seldom moved, and he had as a very lucrative side line a dope racket, which chiefly peddled opium.

Kilsoo Haan had organized a secret anti-Japanese society called the Sino-Korean Peoples' League. In an attempt to worm his way into the secrets of the Japanese, Haan had approached the Japanese consul at Honolulu with the suggestion that he should be allowed to try to win over the Koreans in Hawaii to the Japanese side. He made his case so convincing that the Japanese agreed to his proposal and arranged a job for him as bellboy in a Honolulu hotel as "cover." Thus strategically placed for overhearing conversations, he concentrated chiefly on what passed between Japanese.

Not long after Farnsworth's conviction, Haan had gathered information from his eavesdropping which enabled him to send the following telegram to the Sino-Korean Peoples' League in Washington:

Have definitely learned through a conversation just overheard in the Japanese Consulate here [Honolulu] that Yamamoto and his organization are about to begin an intensive course of study for the purpose of sabotage in California Oregon and Washington when war comes stop The night clubs operated by Yamamoto are to be the HQ for this training which will include the construction and study of specially built scale models of bridges electric power plants water supply systems railroad yards and other such strategic points stop An NYK liner due

216

San Francisco next Thursday is bringing two men whose names I have been unable to discover with instructions for Y stop

The Sino-Korean Peoples' League passed this information to the F.B.I., and when the liner docked all Japanese disembarking were shadowed. All but two remained in San Francisco. These two, having visited the Japanese consul, went by train to Seattle. In Seattle Yamamoto met them and took them to his hotel suite where they stayed for three days, during which time they did not once emerge. At the end of this time they returned to San Francisco on a train which connected with a Dollar Line ship leaving for Japan. Immediately his guests had departed Yamamoto called a meeting of all his associates in Seattle at his club there and after an all-night session went to Portland, Oregon, where he called another meeting. After this meeting he visited the Japanese consul in Portland before going on to San Francisco, where he repeated the procedure.

Haan's intelligence was certainly reliable. Whatever Yamamoto's men were engaged upon, they dropped it immediately and began to deploy themselves in and around all the strategic naval and military positions along the whole of the west coast. Armed with the indispensable camera, they took photographs of all strategic installations from every conceivable angle. Yamamoto himself had never been so active or covered and recovered so much ground as he did during this period. He was so engaged in his new activities that his addicts and his exchequer suffered from lack of dope.

So many Japanese were engaged on the project that neither the F.B.I. nor the O.N.I. had the resources to keep track of every individual. They were extremely anxious, however, to identify the men who would make the models, so, hoping that these men would sooner or later be attracted by the magnet of Dr. Furusawa's Medical Building at 117½ Weller Street, they put a constant watch on it.

Nor were they disappointed. In April two Japanese arrived at the clinic who had not been there before. The following day Yamamoto flew in from Seattle and went directly to Weller Street where he stayed until evening, when he emerged with the two new arrivals. The three stayed the night at the Japanese Consulate, and in the morning Yamamoto returned to Seattle by air while his companions were trailed to an office in the business section of Los Angeles. This identified them at once as being two of the most prominent Japanese engineers on the whole of the Pacific coast. Whereas previously they had carried on a legitimate business, keeping regular office hours, now they closed their doors, admitting no one and refusing all commissions. A week or so later they began to receive visitors, among whom were the Japanese consul, Dr. Furusawa and various Japanese attachés.

At the end of the first week in May, the engineers began the unusual practice of leaving their office at some hour between 11 P.M. and 3 A.M. On these outings they carried large suitcases and went either to 117½ Weller Street, Yamamoto's well-known Little Tokyo Club or the Japanese Consulate.

One point exercising the minds of the F.B.I. was whether other Japanese were doing similar work in other strategic places like Portland and San Diego and Seattle. When attempts were made to find out they were not successful, but as the F.B.I. was beginning to get very anxious the Los Angeles engineers started to go farther afield.

The activities of Yamamoto's henchmen were of direct importance to the F.B.I. if they were to be able to check any outbreak of hostile behavior, but it was impossible for Americans to break into the gang without raising suspicions. To overcome this difficulty, the F.B.I. approached six American-born Japanese on whose loyalty they could depend and asked for their help. These Nisei undertook the role of F.B.I. agents, and though amateurs, within a few weeks were able to supply the general outline of the Japanese government's plans for sabotage on the Pacific coast when war started.

All Yamamoto's men were receiving an intensive course of instruction in the blowing up of bridges, electric power stations, port installations and all other strategic points the destruction of which would throw American defense on the whole west coast into complete chaos.

Sometimes Yamamoto himself was their instructor. At others, it was the engineers who were the teachers with the aid of their perfect scale models, which they carried about in their suitcases. Whereas Yamamoto dealt with small groups of two or three, there were always large gatherings when the engineers visited the clubs in Portland, Seattle, San Francisco and Los Angeles.

Presently the F.B.I. ran into difficulties. One day Yamamoto was observed leaving hurriedly for the airport in Los Angeles to board an aircraft for San Francisco. At San Francisco he was met by a chauffeur who handed him a note. As soon as Yamamoto read it he lost all his Oriental composure, and in an obvious rage took the next flight back to Los Angeles. His behavior at the Los Angeles airport made the F.B.I. fear the worst. Waving aside his waiting chauffeur he took a taxi, and for the next two hours was involved in the most elaborate evading action, which told the agents that he knew he was being trailed. The F.B.I. immediately warned their Nisei agents, but only four of the six received the warning. The following morning the other two men were found murdered.

For a time Yamamoto and his men lay low, but it was not long before their activities were once more in full swing.

Still the State Department refused to consider taking action until at last, without reference to the State Department, the F.B.I. arrested and jailed Yamamoto—for evasion of income tax.

While all this had been going on, Mrs. Furusawa of 117½ Weller Street, Los Angeles, was becoming busier than she had ever been. She was now head of the Japanese Navy Assistance League, which gave her "cover" to entertain Japanese sailors and naval officers when they visited Los Angeles and to whom she passed information and from whom she received instructions from Tokyo. Through Count von Keitel she was also a link with the new German consul general in San Francisco. This was Captain Fritz Wiedemann, an intimate friend of Hitler from the

219

earliest days and his personal aide-de-camp. He had held no consular or diplomatic post before he came to San Francisco in 1938, at the same time that General Eugene Ott was appointed to succeed von Dirksen as ambassador in Tokyo.

Taken by itself, Wiedemann's appointment would have been significant. Taken in conjunction with Eugene Ott's appointment to Tokyo and Gyssling's promotion from vice-consul in New York to consul in Los Angeles, it should have prompted the State Department to take really serious countermeasures.

Indeed, Axis and particularly Japanese espionage in America was now being stepped up, with the emphasis on activity on the west coast. But here again the Japanese were destined to meet yet another American patriot who was to foil several important plans.

CHAPTER 18

It Began with Nude Girls

There are few aspects of the American scene and of American thought and behavior more puzzling to the foreigner than the seeming inconsistency in connection with the display of the naked human figure. This is not the place to expatiate on this point, and one Englishman, at all events, seriously wonders whether any pattern of logic could be found however long and however deep he probed. But there was, at the San Francisco World's Fair in 1940, a side show which could have been put on exhibition in very few other countries, if any. It was called *The Candid Camera Artists' Model Studio*. For a small fee an amateur photographer might enter and take photographs of the attractive nude girls provided for this purpose.

The man who had conceived the idea and who was employed to be personally in charge of it at the fair was a well-known American entertainer named Al Blake. Blake had a most remarkable muscle control and would often pose in the windows of tailors' shops alongside the dummies and the public would be asked, with a prize as bait, to identify the living model. His ability to control his movements in this way had earned him the title of King of the Robots.

One afternoon in 1940 there came into *The Candid Camera Artists' Model Studio* a thickset, fiftyish Japanese with the inevitable camera slung round his neck. He took his quota of photographs and then walked over to Blake and reminded him that they had met in 1917, when Blake was appearing in Charlie Chaplin's film, *Shoulder Arms*. Without this reminder Blake would not have recognized Chaplin's former valet, Torzichi Kono, whom we already know through his connection with Dr. Furusawa's Medical Building and Count Hermann von Keitel.

The two men exchanged personal histories for a few moments and as Kono was on the point of leaving he said: "It's a pity you're not in the navy now, Mr. Blake. You could make a lot of money." Before Blake could ask him what he meant, the little man had gone.

Puzzled by Kono's remark, Blake tried to find out where the Japanese was living but had no success. Then one day in March 1941 they ran into one another accidentally on Santa Monica Boulevard, in Hollywood. They walked along together for a short distance and Blake, carefully watching Kono for any reaction, casually remarked that conditions on the American stage being what they were, he was seriously thinking of rejoining the navy, particularly as it seemed that the United States must sooner or later be drawn into the war. Kono showed considerable interest in Blake's proposal and asked him if he had friends in the navy who would help him to get back. On the spur of the moment Blake invented a very good friend aboard the flagship U.S.S. *Pennsylvania,* at that time stationed at Hawaii. After a little more conversation Kono invited Blake to dine with him that evening at his apartment on Bronson Street. Not wishing to overplay his eagerness, Blake pleaded a pretended prior engagement and eventually agreed to lunch with Kono two days later at the now familiar Kawafuku

Tei. At luncheon Kono probed Blake more deeply on his intention of rejoining the navy and Blake, who was shrewd as well as being a good actor, played up, commenting how much he admired the Japanese for their characteristic good qualities. Kono then asked Blake the name of his friend in the *Pennsylvania,* and after a show of reluctance Blake said: "Jimmie Campbell," and under continued pressure described Campbell's smartness, shrewdness and his service.

That same evening Kono telephoned Blake and asked him to meet him in a furniture store the next morning. Puzzled still, but now excited, Blake agreed to do so, and at that meeting, after a good deal of spy-fiction precautions, Kono told him to be without fail at Sunset Boulevard and Wilton Street at noon, where "a very important man would speak to him."

When Blake arrived at the rendezvous he found Kono already there, but he studiously avoided making any sign of recognition. Presently a large sedan drew up to the curb on which they were standing and at the faintest sign from the Japanese Blake got into the rear seat followed by the ex-valet. At the wheel was another Japanese who introduced himself, as he drove them out to the Hollywood hills, as Yamamoto. He said he was interested in Blake's proposal to return to the navy and asked Blake to tell him as much as he could about Jimmie Campbell.

At first Blake refused to answer. Who was Yamamoto anyway? Why should he answer questions put to him by a complete stranger? Calmly Kono soothed and reassured him, and appearing to be satisfied, Blake insisted that if he agreed to join forces with the Japanese there must be definite arrangements, particularly with regard to money.

The driver was silent for a few moments after Blake's outburst, then asked if he would be prepared to go to Hawaii. Blake replied that he was ready to go anywhere provided there was satisfactory money in it. Yamamoto said that Kono would arrange the financial details, but that all he would have to do would be to go to Hawaii and persuade Campbell to give him certain information. They then drove back to Hollywood. "You'll be hearing from me shortly, Al," Kono remarked as they parted.

During the next few days Blake became aware that the Japanese were being serious. Everywhere he went he was being tailed by them. With the realization of this, it also came to him with some force that he had got himself into quite a difficult position. For an amateur and a civilian to get himself embroiled in what was undoubtedly foreign espionage was not very clever unless he intended to be a traitor, which Blake did not.

He was now faced with the problem of getting in touch with the Office of Naval Intelligence without letting the Japanese know. His followers were persistent, and he was unable to shake them off by any means that his amateur imagination could devise. He thought of the telephone, until he discovered that a dictaphone had been planted in an armchair in the sitting room of his apartment. So while the telephone was out of the question, he became more resolved than ever to contact the O.N.I.

Before he could shake off his "shadows," Kono telephoned to arrange a second meeting and suggested that if he were prepared to leave for Honolulu within the week he should receive 2,500 dollars and all expenses. A further 5,000 dollars would be paid to him when he had delivered the information Yamamoto wished him to obtain from Campbell.

These proposals made contact with the O.N.I. more imperative than ever. But as soon as he got into the street he saw that the Japanese were still there, ready to fall in behind him.

But his pondering of his problem had not been in vain and now he had a sudden flash of inspiration. He went to a movie, and making sure from the foyer that the Japanese did not intend to follow him inside, he asked to see the manager, to whom he briefly told what was happening, and asked him to let him out by a side door.

At the Office of Naval Intelligence Blake told Lieutenant Leo P. Stanley all that had happened. Stanley, who had been impressed from the beginning by Blake's sincerity, asked if he were prepared to cooperate with the O.N.I. by doing whatever the Japanese asked him to do. Blake agreed, and Stanley said that the O.N.I. would at once put an agent aboard the *Pennsylvania* to impersonate the nonexistent Campbell. When they had laid such further plans as were possible at that point, Blake returned to the theater by the side door, remained for the rest of the performance and when he came again into the street saw that the patient Japanese were still sitting in their car waiting for him.

Later the same evening Kono telephoned and instructed him to make a reservation in the Clipper flying next day to Honolulu. The O.N.I., who were now tapping Blake's line, needing more time to install their agent in the flagship, intervened with the airline and Blake was told that there was no seat available. When Blake immediately telephoned Kono and told him of this, Kono arranged for him to meet Yamamoto again at once. At the meeting Yamamoto varied Blake's instructions. He was now to leave for Honolulu by the *Matsonia*, due out of San Francisco two days later.

By this time the O.N.I. had been able to identify Yamamoto. His real name was Commander Itaru Tachibaka of the Japanese Navy. He had been educated at the Japanese Naval Academy and the Naval War College in Tokyo, had been commissioned as a lieutenant commander and rapidly promoted to commander. He had arrived in the United States in 1930 and had enrolled at the University of Pennsylvania, where he had studied American history and American foreign relations. When he had completed these courses he transferred to the University of Southern California in Los Angeles. For several years now he had been traveling constantly up and down the Pacific coast meeting prominent Japanese.

When Blake arrived in San Francisco and called at the shipping office he was told that the *Matsonia* was full and that the next liner sailing for Honolulu would not be leaving for another week. Blake was not particularly worried, believing that this was another delaying tactic of the O.N.I. But as he left the office a Japanese fell in beside him for a few paces and whispered to him to follow him. He led Blake to a restaurant, where he surreptitiously handed him an envelope which contained a ticket for a passage on the *President Garfield*, of the Dollar Line.

Two days before Blake was due to sail, back in Los

Angeles Yamamoto had met Kono, again under fictional circumstances in a hat shop, and while they had tried on hats they had held a whispered conversation. Leaving the shop separately, Yamamoto returned to the Japanese Consulate, from which he had come, while Kono had gone to 117½ Weller Street, where he remained until it was dark and then emerged accompanied by two other Japanese. The three men had then gone straight to the Red Mill brothel, which they left just in time to catch the overnight train for San Francisco. In San Francisco Kono's companions had met two Germans, and with them had boarded the *President Garfield* shortly before she sailed with Blake aboard.

Now deeply involved in something for which he had had no training, Blake had become somewhat apprehensive. Lieutenant Stanley had promised to get in touch with him to tell him what to do when he got to Honolulu. But because of the dictaphone in Blake's apartment the O.N.I. had not been able to telephone him and the Japanese had kept such a close watch on him that personal contact had been out of the question.

On the *President Garfield,* it did not take Blake long to realize that he was being carefully surveilled by the two Germans and the two Japanese. If he sat or strolled on deck, the Japanese were not far away; if he went down to the bar, the Germans were already there drinking.

There was also on board a hardware dealer from the Middle West who was making a cruise for health reasons. He and his wife were listed as Mr. and Mrs. Horner. Mr. Horner, it would seem, was well on the way to becoming a chronic alcoholic, for he rarely moved from the bar. He was not a pleasant alcoholic. He spent most of the time when he was not holding a glass to his lips in truculently provoking people to speak to him and then, when they did, even more truculently disagreeing with them.

The day before the *President Garfield* was due to dock at Honolulu Mr. Horner turned his unpleasant attentions to the now very worried Blake, who had no idea how he was to get in touch with "Campbell." Horner was more than usually disagreeable, and when Blake said something to which he took particular exception, he attempted to attack

225

him physically. But before he could get near enough to the actor he slipped and fell and lay still on the floor. His wife began to fuss over him and implored Blake to help her get him to their stateroom. In the stateroom, while Mrs. Horner was fetching the ship's doctor, Horner miraculously regained consciousness.

"When you get to Honolulu," he whispered rapidly, "call the *Pennsylvania* from your hotel and ask to speak to Campbell. Arrange for him to meet you at the hotel. You'll be able to identify him by a tear in the left breast of his uniform tunic. Beware of dictaphones!"

As Mrs. Horner and the doctor came into the stateroom Mr. Horner relapsed easily into unconsciousness, but Blake thought he could detect a reassuring smile on the hardware dealer's lips.

Arrived at the hotel, Blake telephoned the flagship and arranged for Campbell to come to his room as soon as he came off duty that evening. When the time for Campbell's visit Blake had located a microphone carefully concealed near the table on which the telephone stood.

The two men greeted one another as old friends and Blake maneuvered Campbell close to the microphone, which he revealed silently. Then lowering his voice, but speaking close to the microphone, he made his proposals. At first Campbell appeared shocked by the suggestions, but gradually allowed himself to be persuaded. He left arranging to meet Blake again the next evening, saying that he would give a definite answer then. But an hour before he was due he telephoned to say that he could not come; and for the next week he played these delaying tactics.

Blake had not been to Honolulu before and spent much of the daytime sightseeing. He noticed that whenever he left the hotel the two Germans were not far behind. Both they and the two Japanese had registered at the same hotel as Blake, and by a further "coincidence" the Germans had been given a room on one side of Blake's while the Japanese were in the room on the other side.

The first thing the two Japanese had done after unpacking had been to call at the beauty parlor run by the German, Ruth Kühn.

When at last Blake and Campbell did meet, Campbell

flatly refused to hand over any information until he saw "the color of your money." Blake, playing his part with equal skill, refused to buy "a pig in a poke."

"How do I know what the information is worth until I've seen it?" he demanded.

But Campbell would not change his mind, and the men parted not on the best of terms.

As Blake was preparing to go to bed an envelope was pushed under his door. Inside it was a thousand-dollar bill and a message which read: "You are doing very well. Give to your friend this as a down payment. Act quickly."

Blake knew that Campbell always called at a certain bar for a last drink on his way back to the *Pennsylvania.* He at once telephoned the bar and was able to reach Campbell and ask him to return to the hotel. When Campbell saw the thousand-dollar bill he exclaimed: "For money like this I'll turn over the whole goddamned fleet!"

From then on the negotiations went smoothly and by degrees Campbell handed over an amazing collection of "information," which had been concocted, not without some difficulty, by the O.N.I. They knew that it would be assessed by Japanese naval experts, so it had to have the appearance of being genuine while being sufficiently wide of the truth to make it quite useless when it came to be used. The skill with which it was done may be judged by the fact that the Japanese accepted every word of it.

Inevitably the time came when Campbell, as a source of information, dried up. The Japanese then instructed Blake to return with it to the United States. While he was on this journey all the O.N.I.'s work was almost ruined by the F.B.I. in circumstances which threw into the arc light of incomprehension the fact that there was no coordination between the O.N.I. and the F.B.I. at this time, which was only a few months before Pearl Harbor!

Having negotiated the customs at San Francisco successfully, Blake made for the airport, where he was to take the plane for Los Angeles to hand over his information to Kono and Yamamoto. On the way to the airport Blake realized that he was being followed by a young American. At Santa Barbara the young man approached Blake, identified himself as an F.B.I. agent and asked him

227

to accompany him to the airport security office. Blake was, of course, cleared as soon as the F.B.I. had contacted the O.N.I., but he was worried lest the incident should have been seen by a Japanese agent, for in Japanese eyes this would at once have compromised him. However, Yamamoto's excitement when he saw Campbell's "information" seemed to indicate that all was well.

Yamamoto asked Blake to return to Honolulu at once, explaining that he would receive instructions when he got there through the Japanese Consulate. His suspicions were slightly roused, however, when Yamamoto began to haggle about payment; but he did agree to return.

By means of a dark movie and a double, Blake was able to contact Lieutenant Stanley personally, to be told by him that the O.N.I. had discovered that now his usefulness to them was finished, the Japanese proposed to liquidate him in Honolulu. It was necessary for Blake to return there, however, so that the Japanese should not yet become suspicious of the "information."

When he arrived back in Honolulu, Blake found that the two Germans were still at the hotel, but that whereas before they had taken only a passing interest in him after he had contacted "Campbell," now they were never far away whenever he went out.

Yamamoto had told him that he would receive his new instructions in Honolulu. It had occurred to him that in order to lull him into a sense of false security some chore would be given to him. But the days went by without any word at all from the Japanese; and everywhere he went he was dogged by the Germans!

As the days passed he began to feel intuitively that it was to the Germans that the task of liquidating him had been allotted. He believed that as soon as they caught him in some secluded spot they would attack. They made no attempt to lure him to such a place; they were content to bide their time.

When the days of waiting became weeks the strain of his situation began to tell on Blake. But he was anxious to do nothing which would be contrary to the wishes of the O.N.I., who desired that the Japanese should remain unsuspicious of the genuineness of the material he had passed them for as long as possible. Soon, however, he was to reach the point where he could no longer support the strain. He pondered how he might escape and still not betray the true nature of his information and, with a resourcefulness extraordinary in a man completely untrained in espionage, eventually worked out a plan.

One morning he went down to the hotel vestibule and, making sure that one of the ever-present Germans could overhear what he was saying, he asked the clerk at the desk to arrange for a taxi to take him that afternoon to a spot outside the town which, while noted for its beauty, was unfrequented.

At the time arranged he came down into the hall and noted, as he had hoped he would be able to do, that the Germans were nowhere to be seen. They had gone on ahead to the place, which by its nature was eminently suited for what they had to do.

Now Blake had chosen his time carefully. Shortly before there was a customary delivery of mail. Within half an hour of the time he was due to leave the hotel a plane for the United States was scheduled to take off. Because of the microphone in his bedroom he had not dared to make a reservation on the flight, but he hoped that he would have no difficulty in obtaining one at the last moment.

Coming down to the hall with his bag, he explained to the clerk that he had just received a letter from home informing him that his mother was very ill, so he was going to try to get a reservation on the afternoon plane. Might he, therefore, have his bill?

While the clerk commiserated and made out the bill Blake kept up a flow of worried conversation. His mother was all he had; if anything happened to her he did not know what he would do. He hoped he would be able to get a seat on the plane. Were they often fully booked? When would be the next plane out if he were unsuccessful? His object in all this was to impress the reason for his going on the clerk, so that if the Japanese should make any inquiries about him they would be sure to learn the reason. At the airport, where he arrived fifteen minutes before the plane was timed to take off, he made his inquiries and gave his reasons for leaving in equally emphatic terms, with the same object in mind.

He had no difficulty in getting a reservation and was soon high above the Pacific heading for safety; and the Japanese were not to learn of the tricks he had played on them for some time to come.

Now, the Japanese had sent Blake all the way to Honolulu for one specific purpose—to obtain information about the speed, equipment, armament and performance of one battleship of the United States Navy. On the face of it, it appears to be a tremendous expenditure of time and effort compared with the results that could possibly accrue from it, even supposing he were entirely successful. Yet this episode is indicative of all Japanese espionage effort in the United States. Their language students, night club owners, Thompsons, Farnsworths, doctors, brothel keepers—all were engaged in exactly the same kind of activity. They had been planted there, in their hundreds, not to find out any closely guarded top secret of the United States Army, Navy or Air Force. Were something of this order to be achieved, so much the better, but the main object of Japanese espionage in the United States was to gather a mass of information about every conceivable facet of American naval and military accomplishment and intention. No matter how trivial it might be, it must be collected, reported, classified and filed for future reference.

Collecting, reporting, classifying and filing are, of course, a feature of all intelligence work. It is the small, probably unimportant-seeming pieces on their own which, when collected together, form the essential, all important completed mosaic. But the individual agent must be trained to recognize until it becomes an instinct the correct interpretation of isolated minutiae.

The Japanese failed to do this. They collected, apparently being more interested in bulk than quality, vast mountains of trivia which, however they might be put together, could never amount to anything of importance. A large proportion of their material was not only unimportant but based upon misinformation. This led often to really vital items being lost in an ocean of uselessness.

But they kept at it in the United States, fondly believing that because Russia and Manchuria had proved to be successes arising out of intensive espionage preparations, the same success would be gained in America. It was not so much the times that had changed—their success in the Dutch East Indies was soon to prove that it was not that—but that the Americans are not an Oriental or a Slav people, and were therefore not fully understood by the Japanese. It was this which was to save America from any great harm in the long run. And yet, despite all this, the Japanese were to achieve one of the really great espionage successes of all time on the very site of Blake's success—Pearl Harbor.

Everything was now gathering a momentum which would increase daily and hourly right up to 7:55 A.M. on the morning of December 7th, 1941. And only a few brief weeks before this date, in a naval base as important to the British as Pearl Harbor was to the Americans, another Japanese spy was on the eve of being rendered ineffective, though only after he had done great damage.

CHAPTER 19

The Steward of Singapore

As the summer of 1941 dissolved into autumn the tension in the great British naval base of Singapore mounted with daily impetus. To those who could read the signs at all it would not be long before the Japanese made yet another move in the Pacific; and this would involve Singapore in catastrophe, for whatever the politicians at home might say about the impregnability of the defenses of the base, those on the spot knew just how weak those defenses were.

With the future looming thus alarmingly and ominously, one would have thought that there would have been a strict tightening up of security and that the most severe penalties would have been meted out for any breach of it. Yet those who ought best to have known better—the British officers —were among the worst offenders, and the place where they committed their crime most was the British officers' club.

One day in October a young American guest, Captain Anderson, was discussing this very point with a British colleague, Major Ross. Ross had first mentioned his anxiety, and the American had agreed with him. "You know," Ross had said. "If I were the big boy of Japanese espionage I would plant one good spy in this club, and be sure that he would be able to supply me with news of everything of military and naval importance happening in the colony."

Anderson looked round at the silent and efficient servants and nodded his agreement. Not one of them was white. All of them had the pronounced facial features of Malays and Chinese.

"Do you know the man I'd go for first?" Anderson asked. "That steward, Shawan."

But Ross did not agree. "Oh, good lord no!" he said pleasantly but firmly. "Shawan has been here for years. If he weren't here the club would cease to function. He's more pro-British than I am. Damned useful too! Engages all the servants, sees that we aren't cheated over the price of food and makes it his most sacred point of honor to see that we never run out of Scotch."

Anderson said no more about Shawan, but he was not convinced.

Suddenly Ross said: "Let's conduct a little experiment. I'll give a dinner party for a few of my pals. I'll choose them well, and I'll tell them that while we're feeding they are to discuss all those things which security conscious officers should not discuss, but they're to invent them. Then we'll keep a sharp eye on the waiters and see if any of them act suspiciously. Mind you, it'll only be a game, but it'll relieve the tedium of these exciting days."

So Ross announced that he had a birthday coming up and that he intended to give a small dinner party to a select few of his particular friends. He consulted with Shawan about the food and the wines and emphasized that he wanted the party to be one which his guests would remember affectionately for many years to come. Shawan bowed and smiled his very distant smile and replied that if they did not, it would be through no fault of his.

Before the dinner Major Ross entertained his guests in the bar, and he entertained them so well that when they went to the private room which Shawan had suggested as being more agreeable than a table under the vulgar gaze in the dining room, they were all happy and more than ordinarily loquacious. The conversation at dinner might have induced Major Ross's death from shock had he not known that all that was being said was invention.

"I must say," said one of his guests loudly, "that those forty Free French companies will be jolly welcome reinforcements. They left Trincomalee four days ago, so we can expect them any time now."

"My dear chap," exclaimed a fellow guest, "I shall be much happier when those twenty-nine Free French mechanized units get here. I'm told they'll arrive by the end of the month."

At the other end of the table another guest was saying: "Well, speaking as a loyal Scot, you can keep your Free French, I shall not sleep peacefully in my bed until we've built up our Scottish forces."

"Then that will be very soon," said his neighbor. "Old Archie Macfarlane told me today that they're sending us another six or seven battalions of your countrymen. I don't know what regiments, but they'll be here by the second week of November for certain."

In the middle of the table two other guests were uninhibitedly discussing the strength of the antiaircraft units.

"If only we had more Boforses," said one. "Out of the dozen and a half we've got, only twelve will function properly."

As this very indiscreet conversation was bandied back and forth, Captain Anderson wrote two words on a scrap of paper which he tore from a used envelope, and asked a waiter to give the folded message to his host.

Ross unfolded the paper and read: "Watch Shawan."

The steward was standing by a table on which he had

arrayed the wine. As Ross looked he saw Shawan tear the corner off a wine list and fumble for a few minutes with what looked like his suspenders. But not only that, he was doing something with a stub of pencil on the wine list itself.

For the time being Major Ross did nothing, but when at last the port was circulating he sent a message to the staff security officer asking him to join the party. He had seen the major in the bar with a guest before dinner. He worded his message so that the major could not refuse.

When the major arrived Ross behaved in a surprising manner. "Shawan," he said, "tell the waiters to get out. You can serve us if we need anything."

When the last waiter had gone, Ross said: "Shawan, come here!"

The steward approached him. "Sir?"

But instead of giving him an order, Ross seized his suspenders. On the under side of one, he found a small, specially made pocket, and from it he took the torn off corner of the wine list. On it was written: "P.W. end Nov." which being interpreted meant: "The *Prince of Wales* (England's most invulnerable warship) due to arrive Singapore at the end of November."

Meanwhile Captain Anderson had gone to the wine table and picked up the wine list which Shawan had been using. Against the cognac were lightly penciled 40 and 29, the numbers respectively of the Free French infantry and mechanized companies which had been mentioned in conversation. Against the Scotch was 6 or 7, the numbers of Highland battalions said to be on their way as reinforcements. Against the akvavit were the figures 12:18; twelve of a dozen and a half Bofors A-A guns serviceable.

When Shawan was investigated it was discovered that his real name was Colonel Tsugunori Kadomatsu of the Japanese Army, who, in 1930, had paid a visit to West Point to study American training organization. But instead of being stationed in the United States he had been sent by Japanese army intelligence to Singapore, from where he had kept his headquarters in Tokyo fully conversant with British military strength in the all-important base for the past half dozen years.

Of all those amazed by the revelation, perhaps Major

Ross was the most surprised. But he echoed the general view when he said: "I'd always thought the blighter was Chinese!"

It was views like these, carelessness like this, which had made it possible for Colonel Kadomatsu to make his contribution to Japanese espionage efforts which were to be crowned at Pearl Harbor. The colonel himself might not be aware yet of the significance of Pearl Harbor; neither the British, the Dutch nor the Americans themselves might be aware of it, until it happened. But an ally of the British and the Dutch was to know about it seven full weeks before it happened. How they learned of it is as fantastic a story of espionage economy as the whole history of Japanese espionage is a story of prodigality *in excelsis.*

Ironically, it was the first enemy of the Japanese, the Russians, who acquired the information; and even more ironically, it was one of Wilhelm Stieber's countrymen who obtained it for them.

CHAPTER 20

Colonel Osaki's Defeat in Success

One evening toward the end of September 1941 Colonel Osaki, the chief of Japanese counterespionage, sat in a Tokyo night club with an acquaintance. Presently the acquaintance remarked: "Here he is!" and called out: "Hello, Richard, come and have a drink!"

Richard Sorge, a German foreign correspondent who had lived in Tokyo for the past seven years, came over to the table and, having been introduced to Colonel Osaki, sat down gratefully.

Now, Colonel Osaki had engineered this meeting because he had devised a plan by which he was certain he would be able to confirm or eliminate certain suspicions he harbored against Sorge. It had all begun two years previously, toward the end of 1939, when the colonel's radio experts had begun to intercept radio transmissions in a code they were unable to identify or break; and his direction-finding apparatus was equally unable to give even an approximate pinpoint for the transmitter, though they could say definitely, from the strength of the signal, that it was in Tokyo.

The problem had remained with Colonel Osaki throughout the next two years; and the transmitter had remained in Tokyo. Driven almost out of his wits by frustration, pride and the proddings of his superiors, Osaki had eventually hit upon an idea. He asked the Foreign Intelligence Department to instruct their agents abroad to indicate if the countries in which they worked gave the impression of being aware of Japanese policies in advance of those policies being announced. When the consolidated report was placed before him, he had his first clue.

With a great deal of painstaking Osaki drew up a list of all those who might for some reason or other have had either official or unofficial access to advance information regarding Japan's expansionist plans over the last four years. His first list of suspects, as he called it, besides including officers, civil servants, officials and certain foreign correspondents: a Japanese called Ozaki (not to be confused with the colonel), a German, Richard Sorge and a Yugoslav working for the French, called Voukelitch.

Though these last three names were "possibles" only, he submitted them to the same tests as the others. To his surprise, when the rest were eliminated these three remained. But he had no evidence against any of them. He had arranged this meeting with Sorge in the hope that he would, in time, get the evidence he sought, or be assured of Sorge's innocence.

With consummate skill he brought the conversation around to women. Sorge had a Tokyo-wide reputation on account of his sexual activities.

"Have you seen the new dancer here, Herr Sorge?" the colonel asked.

Sorge shook his head.

Osaki went on: "She's one of the most beautiful women
236

I've ever seen; and I'm told quite one of the most unapproachable."

He was watching Sorge closely and saw the quick glance he shot at him as he said the last words.

"No woman is unapproachable," Sorge growled. "The more beautiful they are, the easier they fall. But women don't interest me any more."

"Oh, come, Herr Sorge," the colonel laughed. "Wait until you see Kiyomi."

They had not long to wait. Presently the lights in the room were dimmed and there appeared in a spotlight a young Japanese woman who went through all the movements of the traditional Rice Dance.

Within a few moments Osaki knew that Sorge's interest in women had been revived. "It's a pity she is so unapproachable," he whispered in Sorge's ear.

On the evening of October 3rd Sorge sat in the night club alone at his table watching his latest mistress dance the traditional Rice Dance. But his mind was not on either the woman or her dancing. He was worried. He had not seen one of his friends, an artist called Miyagi, for more than a week and did not know what he was doing or where he was. Another friend, Voukelitch, the foreign correspondent, had shut himself up in the French Embassy and refused to move out of the protection of its extra-territorial rights. He himself was now almost certain that Colonel Osaki had discovered what he was really doing and was only waiting to pounce.

Presently he called for his bill. When the waiter brought it he brought also another scrap of paper folded in such a way that he knew it came from Miyagi. It was a message saying that he, Miyagi, and some of their other friends were being watched.

Through her mask Kiyomi saw Sorge read the paper, and as soon as her dance was finished she telephoned to her chief and told him what she had seen. A quick check by Colonel Osaki revealed that the waiter, who was a known Communist, had on several occasions been seen visiting the offices of the journalist Ozaki. Colonel Osaki was well satisfied.

For his part, Sorge had decided that the time had come

for him and his friends to stop their private—and secret—work. But there was one last coup he must pull off before this happened: he must find out, if possible, the date on which the Japanese intended to attack Pearl Harbor.

On the evening of October 14th Sorge was again sitting at his table in the Fuji night club. Kiyomi was again dancing the traditional Rice Dance. She saw a man pass in front of Sorge's table and drop a small pellet of paper on it. Sorge looked up to see who it was and recognized Miyagi.

Sorge had arranged to call for his mistress after her dance, but she hoped that before he came to her dressing room she would be able to telephone Colonel Osaki. But Sorge was too quick for her.

As Sorge drove out into the country on his way to a small seaside chalet which he rented, he stopped the car and began to make love to her. After a time he drew from his pocket two cigarettes. But his lighter refused to light and he threw the cigarettes out of the car. He then produced the scrap of paper, tore it into fragments and threw them after the cigarettes, and then drove on. At the first public telephone booth Kiyomi asked him to stop so that she might telephone her family that she would not be home until next day. Sorge stayed in the car, apparently quite unsuspicious, while Kiyomi telephoned Colonel Osaki.

When she was sitting by his side again, they drove on to the chalet. There he told her to prepare something to eat while he went out to look at the fishing boat which he kept moored in the bay. On board he found another friend, a German called Max Klausen, whom he had warned previously to be there. Within a few moments Klausen had tapped out a message in Morse on the transmitter which was hidden in a secret compartment on the boat, and intelligence headquarters in Moscow was acknowledging the message which read:

"Japanese carrier force attacking United States Navy at Pearl Harbor probably dawn 6 December source reliable."

When they had locked the secret compartment Sorge shook hands with Klausen. "That's the last message," he said. "You must get out of Japan as quickly as you can."

Sorge returned to the chalet, ate the food Kiyomi had

238

prepared, and as if he had some premonition that this would be the last time that he would ever make love to a woman, his appetite that night seemed insatiable. Dawn was breaking before at last he fell asleep.

But his sleep was shallow and toward eight o'clock he got up and mixed himself a drink. Before he could raise the glass to his lips there was a knock on the door. He opened it to admit Colonel Osaki. Osaki said nothing, but held out to him the scraps of paper which Sorge had thrown out by the roadside. They were neatly pasted together, and the words on them read:

"Japanese carrier air force attacking United States Navy at Pearl Harbor probably dawn 6 December source reliable Joe." Joe was Miyagi's pseudonym.

At noon, the German ambassador received a courteous note from the Japanese minister of war, General Tojo. It informed him that two Germans had been arrested as spies. Their names were Dr. Richard Sorge and Max Klausen. The French ambassador received a similar note naming Voukelitch, who had left the embassy to pack his belongings on the previous evening. The prime minister was informed of the arrests of Ozaki, the journalist, and Miyagi, the artist.

It was Colonel Osaki's proudest day!

Richard Sorge was the grandson of Alexander Sorge, who was at one time the private secretary of Karl Marx. In 1914, at the age of nineteen, Richard joined the kaiser's army and was three times wounded. His experiences in the army and conditions in postwar Germany made him turn to communism in his disillusionment.

Having graduated as a doctor of political science, a sequence of experiences brought him to Moscow, where he met Dimitri Manuilsky. Through Manuilsky he was led to take up an occupation which he was to follow with outstanding success for the rest of his life—spying for Russia.

He was a remarkable linguist and became fluent in Russian, English, French and in certain of the Chinese and Japanese dialects. He studied carefully the historical and cultural backgrounds of the countries to which he was assigned, and since he regarded all other men as his

239

enemies he exercised the same care in getting to know as thoroughly all those with whom his work brought him into contact.

By 1933 Sorge had become such an outstanding agent that the Russians had complete confidence in him, and when they decided that they must have a first-class spy in Tokyo it was Sorge they sent, giving him—which was very rare in Russian espionage history—*carte blanche* as to choice of agents and an almost unlimited budget.

Before he came to Tokyo he had paid a return visit to Germany, and there had completely hoodwinked many of the highest in the Nazi Hierarchy into believing him to be a loyal National Socialist. He came to Japan with the full confidence of the German leaders, which automatically made him *persona grata* with the German embassy officials from the ambassador down.

He was not a stranger to the Orient. He had already organizèd Russia's so-called "China Unit" on the mainland of Asia, and it was one of his agents in this unit whom he transferred with him to Tokyo. Ozaki Hozumi, a young Japanese journalist, was to become, after Sorge, the most valuable member of the Tokyo cell.

Sorge's other colleagues, whom he had himself selected, were Max Klausen, another German, and the finest radio operator in the Russian secret service; Branko de Voukelitch, a former officer in the Yugoslav Army; and Yotoku Miyagi, a Japanese artist, whom Sorge had found in the Little Tokyo quarter of San Francisco.

As cover, Sorge was the accredited Japanese correspondent of no less than three leading German newspapers; Klausen was the representative of two or three German industrial undertakings, though none of them was very prominent; Voukelitch was the accredited Japanese correspondent of a French review and a Yugoslav newspaper; Ozaki was political correspondent of the Japanese *Asah Shimbun;* while Miyagi followed his profession as an artist.

The fact that Sorge, Voukelitch and Ozaki were bona fide correspondents made it possible for the three men to meet naturally in Tokyo and for their intercourse to raise no suspicions. Sorge did not rush the initial operation of his ring, but by meetings in cafes, restaurants and bars, at first casual and then arranged, he allowed it to appear that the relationship which ultimately developed had done so gradually.

Sorge's occupation also took him to the German Embassy, where he made it appear that he was meeting Max Klausen for the first time. It seemed to onlookers, too, quite natural that the eccentric correspondent should take pity on the lonely German salesman and invite him to join his circle.

Miyagi was brought in in much the same way. Sorge and Voukelitch were in the Uneo Art Museum one day when Voukelitch recognized a Japanese artist friend. He introduced him to Sorge and a discussion between the two men developed concerning the merits of Eastern and Western art, and Miyagi was invited to continue it at a cafe frequented by artists and journalists.

A base from which to operate is essential to any spy ring, and it must be a base to which all members may go openly, with ostensibly legitimate reasons for their visits and yet safe and secure from eavesdroppers. Sorge chose as his base a ramshackle house, the rent of which was well within his salary as a foreign correspondent.

Installed in his house, Sorge gave a party which shocked both his respectable neighbors and the members of the diplomatic corps who had been invited along with journalists, artists, young Japanese army officers and a sprinkling of Japanese businessmen. When the less intimate of the guests left about ten o'clock, a number of geisha girls were summoned to the house and for the next few hours the noises emanating from the rickety structure testified to the orgy going on within. The neighborhood listened unhappily until the early hours, when the girls left accompanied by the majority of the remaining guests, all, that is, except Voukelitch, Ozaki, Klausen and Miyagi, whom Sorge pressed to finish the last bottle with him. In the comparative quiet that followed, and before the four guests eventually left with the first light, Sorge had given his spies their first briefing.

Sorge's parties soon became the talk of Tokyo, and if watching *Kempei tai* agents noticed that his four best friends always stayed after the other guests had left, they saw nothing suspicious in that.

A spy normally draws the least possible attention to himself. Sorge worked from the other extreme. Not only were his wild parties the talk of Tokyo, but his relationships with women became notorious. He was a very highly sexed individual, and his attitude toward the unfortunate women who fell under the spell of his great charm and consummate wooing was fundamentally one of contempt. He soon grew bored with his victims, and within a few weeks of the opening of an affair he cast them off and looked around for new excitement. This reputation also served him as "cover." Any man who attracted so much attention to himself could not be a spy, seems to have been the argument.

With his ring well established Sorge went to work, and it was not long before he was justifying the confidence which his Moscow masters had placed in him by a series of brilliant espionage coups.

The first of these coups was achieved by the agency of Ozaki, whose family background and his work as a political correspondent for Japan's most influential newspaper gave him the entrée to high political circles. His political acumen and his tremendous knowledge of Chinese affairs were such that when, toward the end of 1935, the foreign minister prepared a report for the cabinet on Japan's economic and political aims for 1936, Prince Konoye, the prime minister, readily agreed to a proposal that he should be allowed to see a draft copy and to give his independent views of those sections referring to China.

Ozaki was permitted to study the document for the greater part of a day in a private room at the Foreign Office. Completely undisturbed, he photographed it page by page. The report made it quite clear that Japan had no intention of attacking Russia in the near future and that the invasion of south China would depend on the development of heavy industries in Manchuria.

In search for confirmatory evidence, Sorge obtained private interview with the German ambassador, Dr. Herbert von Dirksen, on the excuse of writing a report for his newspapers. By clever questioning he learned that the

Japanese high command had hinted to the German military attaché that the withdrawal of German officers instructing the Chinese armies would be taken as a sign of friendship.

At the same time Miyagi discovered from a Japanese staff colonel, whose portrait he was painting, that large-scale models of certain parts of south China were being constructed for practice purposes.

All this information taken in conjunction satisfied Moscow that their spy had supplied them with material of truly vital importance; and if before they had acknowledged him as a master, they were now prepared to promote him to miracle worker.

Such a coup so early in his career might have influenced another spy to rest upon his laurels. For Sorge it merely set the standard for his future activities.

Realizing the importance of Ozaki's contacts in high political circles—he presently became the private and confidential adviser of the prime minister himself—he set about acquiring similar contacts himself at the German Embassy. There he soon became the confidant of the military attaché, Colonel Eugene Ott, who was later to become much more valuable when he replaced von Dirksen as ambassador.

Voukelitch also consolidated his own position at the French Embassy while Miyagi extended his friendships with the younger military clique, with whom his work was popular.

Sorge's path was not always smooth. His involvement with women at times threatened his security. Klausen, though a first-rate radio operator, was not good agent material, and on more than one occasion narrowly escaped arrest.

But in some strange way the *Kempei tai* remained deceived. For seven years Sorge and his ring operated, pulling off coup after coup, each more brilliant than the last. He warned Russia of the impending German attack on the U.S.S.R. and, as we have seen, brought his career to a climax by obtaining the approximate date for the attack on Pearl Harbor.

He had been in prison awaiting trial less than seven weeks when his cell door opened one morning and the guard brought in his breakfast. As the man set down the bowl he said: "This morning our air force destroyed the American fleet in Pearl Harbor."

The prisoner looked at the homemade calendar he had scratched on the wall. It was December 8th. He had told Moscow it would be December 6th. But he was only one day out, for in Honolulu, because of the International Date Line, today would be December 7th!

CHAPTER 21

The Smoke and Noise of Climax

Normally the aircraft warning station at Pearl Harbor closed down at 7 A.M. On December 7th, 1941, however, two private soldiers under training who were operating a set on the north shoulder of Oahu decided they would carry on until their relief arrived.

At two minutes past seven they picked up on their instrument indications that a large formation of aircraft was flying on a bearing almost due north of them at a distance of roughly 130 miles, but rapidly approaching. Their first reaction was that something was wrong with their apparatus. But when they checked all was in order.

They telephoned the central station. It had shut down dead at its customary time and they could get no reply. Eventually they did manage to contact the air lieutenant in command, who told them to forget about it; it might be merely some aircraft coming in from the mainland.

The soldiers plotted the aircraft until they were so close that the echoes from the sea and the surrounding hills blotted out the echoes of the engines. Then they, too, closed down.

Thirty-two minutes before the soldiers had picked up the flight of aircraft the U.S.S. *Ward* had sighted a small submarine in the prohibited area outside Pearl Harbor. For fifteen minutes she stalked her prey and at 6:45 A.M. attacked with her four-inch guns and depth charges. The incident was noted in the destroyer's log, timed 6:53 A.M., and a warning was sent to shore.

No action was taken, no alert sounded and not even the antitorpedo net protecting the harbor was closed, with the result that at least two Japanese submarines got right inside the harbor net defenses without being seen.

The fact was that a lack of cooperation between the military and naval commanders at Hawaii had led to a complete disregard for the defense of Pearl Harbor. On this Sunday morning in December 1941 the army's aircraft warning system was not operating; no regular reconnaissance or inshore patrols were maintained either by the army or the navy; the antiaircraft and coastal batteries were unmanned, and if they had been manned they would have been absolutely ineffective because not one of them was supplied with ammunition.

True, the likelihood of an attack by Japanese submarines and possible sabotage had crossed the minds of Admiral Kimmel and Lieutenant General Short; but it would seem that they were not impressed by the risk and had promulgated the taking of only a few minor precautions. Warnings had been issued from Washington, where negotiations between Japanese representatives and the secretary of state had been dragging out for weeks but, for some reason or other, these, too, were ineffective.

Fifty-three minutes after the soldiers had picked up the approaching aircraft they arrived over Pearl Harbor, where no less than seven of the eight battleships of the United States Pacific Fleet were moored along the shore of Ford Island and over eighty other warships—cruisers, destroyers, minelayers, minesweepers and auxiliaries—were at anchor. The formation consisted of forty torpedo bombers, fifty-one dive bombers, forty-eight horizontal bombers and forty-three fighters. Their first objective was to put out of action the fighter aircraft packed tightly at the moorings in Kaneohe Bay and on Wheeler and Hickham airfields. Their second objective was the ships in Pearl Harbor.

These objectives they reached and those attacking the

aircraft obtained success beyond their own expectations. The survivors of the Americans were for the most part rendered ineffectual by the cratering of the runways, which prevented their taking off, but a few planes were able to take off and joined forces with seven patrol aircraft which were in the air when the engagement began.

By a fortunate coincidence Admiral Halsey, in the aircraft-carrier *Enterprise,* was returning from an exercise and immediately put his planes in the air. Four of these were shot down and one was so badly damaged that it had to withdraw.

In the attack on the ships in the harbor the Japanese made eight runs. In the first, one of the battleships opened up immediately with machine-gun fire and accounted for two of the torpedo planes. Within ten minutes of the opening of the attack, all ship-borne antiaircraft batteries had come into action.

The Japanese pressed their attack until 8:25. Then they drew off and there was a lull until 8:40. Dive bombing and precision bombing attacks were then made on the port and airfield installations and completely destroyed them. For another hour and five minutes the battle raged until, at 9:45, the Japanese finally broke off.

When they had gone, the American Pacific Fleet had had all its battleships knocked out, and a large proportion of its other forces. Almost 2,500 men had lost their lives, nearly a thousand were missing, and more than 1,200 were wounded. American sea strength in the Pacific was for the time being but a tiny fraction of the power it had been one hour and three-quarters before.

For the greater part of this time, up in her attic Ruth Kühn was watching the results of the attack through her binoculars, and her father, at her side, was flashing with his signal lamp the information she gave him.

Pearl Harbor was to be the climax of Japanese espionage against America. It has been suggested that the reason why Japan did not take immediate advantage of the great success she achieved that day was that the magnitude of it took her by surprise. Whatever may be the reason, all the work of her spies in the United States and in Central America was to be of no avail. There was to be no base in

Mexico, no seizure of the Panama Canal, no landing on the California coast. All the work of years, the efforts of the language students, the brothel keepers, the dentists, the barbers, the soda water bottlers, the coolies, the farmers, the doctors and fishermen was to be put to no account.

To call Pearl Harbor the climax of Japanese espionage is not to impute too great importance to the work of their intelligence. It was undoubtedly a coincidence that so great a proportion of the Pacific Fleet should be in Pearl Harbor on December 7th, 1941, but the Kühns had been plotting the movements and locations of all the units of the fleet for weeks, and at the moment of attack the Japanese knew exactly what their target was, though it was then too late to make preparations to follow their attack up as logic demanded. It was the climax of the Kühns's spying, too. Even had they escaped, nothing in the future could have been quite so successful.

Fate seems to have a penchant for tying up loose ends. With the part played by the Kühns at Pearl Harbor, the greatest achievement of Japanese espionage, the denouement was neater than any man-devised denoument could ever have been, for at the most crucial time and in the most crucial spot it was countrymen of Wilhelm Stieber's who made the victory possible, just as it had been Stieber's precepts and tuition which had been the basis for all Japan's spying.

With the American Pacific Fleet powerless the Dutch East Indies were easy prey, defeated by espionage before the Japanese invasion though they were in any case. The Pacific islands were equally at Japan's mercy. So were Singapore, Malaya and Burma.

As the armies of the divine emperor spread over a quarter of the globe and took possession of the lands they had formerly secretly invaded, the role of espionage lost in importance and gradually its great force was retracted. Then as the tide turned and Japan began to fight for her life, it was no longer a case of preparation for attack; and retreat needs no preparation by espionage.

So, brilliant as her first fifty years of espionage had been, Japan was to see herself destroyed before the second fifty years were completed; and in that destruction espionage had played a major if indirect role. For had she not used espionage to prepare for her attack, and if she had not attacked, she would not herself have felt the blast of atom bombs on Nagasaki and Hiroshima.

Post-Mortem

It is not usually difficult to be wise after the event; and post-mortems cannot change the result of the game. But standing back from events in time places us in a position from which we can see what was happening, events, trends, failures and successes unable to be seen at once by those involved because of their very nearness to them, or if seen, not in the right perspective because, again, too close proximity throws them out of focus.

Whatever happened in the past, whatever may happen in the future, the meteoric development of Japanese espionage will always remain a phenomenon not only in the records of espionage but in the wider field of history.

Had the perpetrators of State Shintoism been asked and had been prepared to give an honest answer, they would have explained that the third tenet—"to bring the whole world under one roof"—was originally designed not as a basis for expansionist policy but as an instrument for stirring the pride of the individual Japanese and diverting it into a channel where it might operate for the good of the country. A people used to discipline, as the Japanese had been under their feudal structure, is lost if that discipline is relaxed, and rapidly degenerates into a goal-less people without ambition or direction. Such a development in Japan would have automatically removed every possibility of the nation's benefiting from its new contact with Western civilization.

The industrial and economic, political and military growth of Japan presents a phenomenon of no less proportions than her espionage. In it is revealed a flair for organization and imitation unsurpassed so far by any other nation in the world. Though it is easy to sneer at the imitation, it is nevertheless a fact that this imitation was responsible for converting Japan into a great power in the space of a generation and a half.

It was this conversion to power, rather than the third tenet of State Shintoism, which made it absolutely essential for Japan to secure her position in Eastern Asia, and it was this necessity which gave rise to the need for espionage. Only later, when the rulers were imbued with fascist arrogance, was the third tenet of Shintoism taken as the basis for policy. The doctrine of the Master Race, the need for *lebensraum* and the creation of slave nations were as much part and parcel of the credo of the Japanese leaders of the thirties as they were of the contemporary leaders of the Third Reich. But whether the necessity to secure her position or the third tenet of State Shintoism was the motive or excuse, Japan's resulting actions were the same.

In seeking to establish her position in Asia securely, Japan saw herself faced with the need for controlling immense physical areas. Siberia, Eastern and Central Asia cover a vast proportion of the earth's surface. Accepting the theory of espionage preparation being essential for success in war, it appeared to Japanese leaders that large numbers of spies were required to cover the area of operations.

It was, perhaps, fortuitous that the most up-to-date system of espionage at that time should also be based on the use of vast numbers of agents. This point certainly gave the Stieber system an added appeal in the eyes of the Japanese. Indeed, it is doubtful whether any other system would have suited their purpose.

So enthusiastically did they take to espionage, and so greatly were they encouraged by the ease with which their spies operated on account of the lack of opposition everywhere, that they let themselves be run away with by the idea of numbers. The defeat of Russia and the conquest of Manchuria were first-rank espionage successes, but there is no doubt that they could have been no less brilliant had one-third of the agents been used.

The Japanese became obsessed by espionage, and if

total war was an invention of their National Socialist German friends, the original concept of *total espionage* must certainly be conceded to the leaders of Japan. In essence, their theories were right. The infiltration of the Moslem Russian minorities of Central and Western Asia by agents who fomented a state of constant unrest which made the minorities a sword point constantly tickling the ribs of Russia had everything to commend it in theory. The Nazis were not too proud to copy and use the method with great effect in Danzig, with the Sudeten Germans in Czechoslovakia and, after the Second World War began, the Croats in Yugoslavia. But exactly how much good accrued to Japan from these efforts is not easy to define. Had she occupied Central and Western Asiatic Russia, then her activities there would have been fully justified. As it was, she seemed to have involved large numbers of men and spent many millions of dollars in these distant areas merely to keep Russia preoccupied. She could have achieved the same result with fewer men, and at far less expense, in Siberia itself.

So it was in every field in which she was involved, particularly in China, where the chaotic state of the government and of the economy produced already a mature condition for the imposition of foreign control. With a hundred or two agents, instead of the thousands actually employed there, carefully and cunningly placed, she could have kept the China caldron on the boil.

Nevertheless, it would be wrong to denigrate the brilliance of Japan's espionage achievement, when reckoned in terms of the implementation of national policies, during the first fifty years of spying. It is the next fifty years which surprise, almost bewilder, certainly mystify.

When Japan turned her attention to the American continent, she turned on it the same weight of espionage which has already been described. Granted that preparing Mexico as a base might require the efforts of many men, as the years passed it must have become only too obvious that the achievement there was falling far below expectations.

There was, however, a very different set of conditions facing the Japanese in America from those which aided her in Asia, the Dutch East Indies and elsewhere. Here the economic structure was sound and there was no national unrest. This called for different tactics, and the only tactics which she could devise—and which American military activity, or the lack of it, allowed—were the tactics of ordinary, straightforward espionage. She did not understand, however, that this type of spying is impeded rather than helped by large numbers.

In California and the Panama Canal Zone she was working very closely to Stieber's methods when he was preparing France for the Prussian invasion of 1870. Her spies were instructed to discover and report every small detail, not only in connection of the armed forces, but concerning the economic and structural potential of the destined area of invasion. But in doing this she outdid Stieber in the number of spies she employed, with the effect that three-quarters of the information she received when it was not misinformation was unimportant, and far better results would have been achieved with a few highly trained, highly organized, strategically placed cells.

Nothing points the ineffectiveness of the vast armies of Japan's secret servants with greater emphasis than the successes, against the vast organization of the *Kempei tai* in Japan, of Richard Sorge and his four companions; and even more so, the achievement on their behalf of the trio of Kühns in Honolulu. Had they worked on similar principles of operation elsewhere they would surely have gained more for less effort and expense.

The more one considers it the more is one impelled to the conclusion that Rudolf Hess was right when he suggested that spying is ingrained in the whole Japanese nation. This being so, even without Stieber's model the Japanese leaders would probably have organized their espionage on a grand scale, since they would know that every subject of the emperor was prepared to be his divine and imperial majesty's secret servant. In such circumstances, the temptation might have been too great to resist.

But if Hess was right, are there in the suggestion any implications for the future?

Under the instrument of capitulation the Japanese were

forbidden to operate a secret service. But the questions nag for an answer: can a people in whom the principles of espionage are so deeply ingrained ever be compelled to refrain from spying by an injunction placed upon them?

Bibliography

The following are original documents from the Japanese Foreign Office archives which have been consulted:

1. Investigation of the military preparedness of Honolulu, Sections 1 to 4, March 1907 to December 1926.
2. Intelligence from the Japanese Naval General Staff, November 1922.
3. Weekly reports from the Army Intelligence Bureau at Hawaii.
4. Miscellaneous documents relating to proposals by foreigners concerning the sale of documents containing military secrets, September 1908 to September 1922.
5. Miscellaneous documents relating to the movement of Russian forces, June 1897 to April 1903.
6. Documents relating to the despatch of Tsuruok Nagataro, Yamane Takusaburo and Ioya Toyoto of the Japanese Legation in China to investigate the movements of the Russian Army in the hinterland of Manchuria, April 1903 to February 1904.
7. Diary of Lieutenant Colonel Morita's travels in Inner Mongolia, March 1908.
8. Reports from intelligence agents in connection with the Russo-Japanese War, October 1897 to April 1906.
9. Documents relating to the investigations of intelligence offices in various foreign countries, June 1936 to March 1938.
10. Documents relating to appointments of Japanese army officers for intelligence work in the U.S.S.R.
11. Documents relating to the eastward journey of the Russian Baltic Fleet at the time of the Russo-Japanese War, June to November 1904.
12. Documents relating to secret information, August 1930 to September 1931.

Other documents consulted are:

1. Records of the patriotic societies.
2. Documents relating to Japanese espionage in the Dutch East Indies.
3. The report on Japanese espionage compiled by Rudolf Hess.
4. The papers of the trial of the Kühn family in Honolulu, 1942.
5. The files of various American national newspapers for the trials of Thompson and Farnsworth.

The following is a list of printed works consulted, to which the author acknowledges his indebtedness.

1. *Honorable Spy* by J. L. Spivak (1939)
2. *Secret Service in America* by H. O. Yardley (1940)
3. *Total Espionage* by Curt Reiss (1941)
4. *Betrayal from the East* by Alan Hynd (1943)
5. *Passport to Treason* by Alan Hynd (1943)
6. *Japan's Secret Service in the Hawaiian Islands* by K. D. Singer (1944)
7. *Japanese Attempts at Infiltration among the Muslims in Russia* (U.S. Office of Strategic Services, 1944)
8. *Japanese Infiltration among the Muslims in China* (U.S. Office of Strategic Services, 1944)
9. *Hearings on American Aspects of the Richard Sorge Case* (U.S. Congressional Committee on Un-American Activities, 1951)
10. *History and Mission of the Counter Intelligence Corps in World War II.* (U.S. Counter Intelligence Corps School, 1951)

HER
MOTHER'S
GRAVE

HER
MOTHER'S
GRAVE

LISA REGAN

GRAND CENTRAL
PUBLISHING

NEW YORK   BOSTON

Copyright © 2018 by Lisa Regan

Cover design by GhostUK.
Cover images by Shutterstock.
Cover copyright © 2020 by Hachette Book Group, Inc.

Grand Central Publishing
Hachette Book Group
1290 Avenue of the Americas, New York, NY 10104
grandcentralpublishing.com
twitter.com/grandcentralpub

Originally published by Bookouture in 2018.
Bookouture, an imprint of StoryFire Ltd., Carmelite House, 50 Victoria Embankment, London EC4Y 0DZ

First Grand Central Publishing Edition: November 2020

Grand Central Publishing is a division of Hachette Book Group, Inc. The Grand Central Publishing name and logo is a trademark of Hachette Book Group, Inc.

The publisher is not responsible for websites (or their content) that are not owned by the publisher.

The Hachette Speakers Bureau provides a wide range of authors for speaking events. To find out more, go to www.hachettespeakersbureau.com or call (866) 376-6591.

Library of Congress Control Number: 2020935809

ISBN: 978-1-5387-0124-9 (trade paperback), 978-1-5387-0125-6 (mass market)

Printed in the United States of America

CW

10 9 8 7 6 5 4 3 2 1

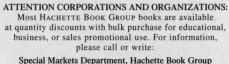

ATTENTION CORPORATIONS AND ORGANIZATIONS:
MOST HACHETTE BOOK GROUP books are available at quantity discounts with bulk purchase for educational, business, or sales promotional use. For information, please call or write:

Special Markets Department, Hachette Book Group
1290 Avenue of the Americas, New York, NY 10104
Telephone: 1-800-222-6747 Fax: 1-800-477-5925

For my brother, Andrew Brock,
for showing me you can always rewrite your own story!

PROLOGUE

She started the fire in the nursery. Her lips curved into a smile as amber flames licked the walls and spread throughout the room, consuming the perfectly matching furniture and the carpet from which she'd spent so many hours scrubbing invisible marks. The gossamer crib canopy she painstakingly arranged every day went up in a satisfying whoosh. *Don't wake the babies. Don't go in there till the children are up. Don't, don't, don't.* This'll teach her.

As the air thickened and began burning her nose and throat, she backed out of the room. Tendrils of thick, black smoke slipped around the edges of the door, coating the ceiling and chasing her out into the hallway. She used her forearm to cover her mouth as she ran. Soon the flames would rage through the house, burning up every fancy thing that spiteful, snobby bitch owned. It was going to be wonderful.

She fled downstairs, stopping to hold a match to the heavy drapes and valances that adorned each window in the living and dining rooms until the taste of fire in her throat became unbearable. She made her way to the kitchen, intending to leave through the back door before she was caught. She was never supposed to set foot in the house again after they'd accused her of stealing.

She was halfway there when a glimpse of something in the family room stopped her dead in her tracks. A frisson of excitement spiraled inside her. Here was something even more destructive than fire, a way to bring down that bitch for good. The grin spread further across her face as she darted into the room, hands outstretched.

CHAPTER 1

Six-month-old Harris Quinn giggled from his high chair as the small plastic pot of pureed baby peas hit the kitchen floor with a splat, covering Josie's sneakers with drab green mush. Startled, Josie took one look at his little food-covered face and laughed too; it was impossible to get mad at him. Plucking a paper towel from above the sink, she bent to clean the mess from the floor, muttering "Rookie mistake" to Harris, who banged his palms against the tray in delight. Throwing things on the floor and watching Josie pick them up was his new favorite game.

Dumping the clump of paper towels into the garbage can, she turned back to see Harris's pea-covered little fists pressed into his eyes for just a moment. Josie looked at the clock on Misty's microwave. "Time for a nap, little man," she told him.

She looked around her for any further traces of food on the floor or walls of Misty Derossi's immaculate home. It wasn't often that she asked Josie to look after her son, but every once in a while, if Harris's grandmother wasn't available, she would get the call. Josie looked forward to these rare visits and didn't want to jeopardize her status as one of Harris's trusted babysitters by leaving a mess for his mother.

Grabbing a cloth from the sink, she cleaned Harris's face and hands as he squirmed and wailed in protest. "All done," she announced as she unfastened the straps of the high chair and lifted him out of it, marveling at how big he had grown in such a short amount of time. She could still remember the first time she had held him, pinned against her chest after rescuing him from the deathly cold currents of the Susquehanna River. He had only been a few days old then, tiny, frail, and lucky to be alive. Now he was chunky and solid, his blond locks growing thicker each day, with a real personality beginning to emerge.

Now that Harris was older, Josie enjoyed making him giggle, watching him spread his meals across his rosy cheeks, cleaning him up and then falling asleep together in the rocking chair that Josie had bought for Misty. It was one of only a handful of modern pieces of furniture in the house, and completely out of place in the sitting room, which looked as though it had been torn from the pages of *Victorian Homes* magazine.

Harris rested his head on Josie's shoulder as she settled there now, using her feet to gently rock the chair back and forth. From the cloth pocket beside her, Josie pulled out one of Harris's pacifiers, which he reached for greedily. Shifting him a little lower so that his cheek rested on her chest, Josie stroked his hair until he slipped into a deep sleep. There was nothing quite like this feeling, she thought as she began to doze off herself.

The digitized beat of her cell phone broke into the silence, and Josie's eyes snapped open, alert and searching. The sound was muffled and coming from the other side of the room, where her jacket was slung over the back of the couch. If it was important, whoever it was would call back. Looking down at Harris, she was relieved to find him undisturbed, his pacifier teetering just on the edge of his bottom lip, about to fall. A pool of dribble fanned across her T-shirt below his head. Josie smiled, running her hand up and down his back and nudging the chair into a gentle rocking motion. The phone stopped ringing, and she closed her eyes again. If it was a true emergency, Lieutenant Noah Fraley and Detective Gretchen Palmer knew where to find her.

She had just drifted back into a warm drowsiness when her phone rang again. This time, Harris stirred. Josie tucked the pacifier back into his mouth as quickly as she could, and he sucked loudly for a moment before crinkling his brow in preparation for what she suspected would be an unhappy howl. She held her breath in anticipation, but his features smoothed and he let out a little sigh instead. Silently, Josie cursed her phone, knowing there was no way to get them both across the room to her jacket without waking him. Not that it mattered—a moment later she heard the front door open and close, and Misty's voice called out, "I'm home!"

Harris stirred again, eyes scrunching, pressing his face into Josie's chest as Misty's voice drifted in from the hallway. "Josie? You in the living room?"

Harris lifted his head, his blue eyes bleary with sleep as he searched the room for his mother. She appeared in the doorway, a huge smile lighting her face at the sight of him. One side of her mouth still drooped, like an invisible finger was drawing it downward, but she had regained a lot more function since the assault she'd survived the day Harris was born. Clapping her hands together, Misty crossed the room and scooped him off Josie's body, cooing and smoothing his wayward locks down. "Hi, baby," she murmured to him. "Did you have a good nap?"

Josie stretched and adjusted her T-shirt. She looked up at Misty. "How did it go?"

Grinning, Misty pointed to her top front teeth. "Got my permanent implant. Feels great. I'm so glad to be done with it."

When she'd had one of her top front teeth knocked out during the attack, she'd been given a temporary crown in the hospital, but it had taken a few months for her to save up the money to have it permanently repaired. Josie had been helping her when she could, but Misty used all the funds Josie gave her for Harris's needs first. Before Harris came along, Misty made a lucrative living dancing at the local strip club, which had enabled her to purchase and furnish her lavish home. She had used her savings for an in vitro procedure to get pregnant with Harris and decided not to return to stripping once she gave birth—even if she wanted to, the injuries she'd sustained placed dancing again firmly outside the realm of possibility.

Josie stood and moved over to the couch, riffling through her pockets to find her cell phone. "Looks good," she told Misty.

Misty shifted Harris from one hip to the other. He rested his head on Misty's shoulder, the pacifier bobbing in his mouth. "Did he eat?"

"Some fruit puffs and a bit of mashed peas. He was more interested in seeing how it looked on the floor."

Misty laughed. "Oh yeah, that's his new thing. No worries. I'll see if he'll take a bottle."

Josie pulled up her missed calls. Both from the same number. Not one she recognized.

"Thank you again," Misty said, although she had thanked Josie about a dozen times before she left for the dentist. "If Mrs. Quinn wasn't so sick, she would have watched him. Some kind of stomach bug."

Josie pulled on her jacket and walked over, patting Harris's back. "No problem. We don't want him catching whatever's going around. You can call me. We're finally finishing up all the paperwork for the district attorney on our last big case, so things are slow."

"That drug dealer, right? Lloyd Todd?"

"More like a kingpin," Josie said.

"Hard to believe he had such a big operation," Misty remarked.

Lloyd Todd had been considered a pillar of the community in the small city of Denton. His general contracting company was one of the busiest and most well-known, but as Josie and her team had found out in the last two months, it had been mostly a front for a large drug-dealing operation. Todd had had nearly two dozen young men and a couple of young women working for him as mules and low-level dealers. He'd been supplying about eighty percent of the city's illegal drugs to needy customers. It was no surprise to Josie that the number of overdoses had gone down sharply after his arrest. Of course, they'd go back up once Todd's customers found their fixes elsewhere.

"It was a shocker," Josie agreed.

Misty followed her through the labyrinth of lavish rooms until they reached the front door. Once on the front porch, Misty said, "Want to stay for lunch?"

It wasn't the first time she had asked Josie to stay a little longer, but while Josie would love to spend more time with the baby, she wasn't sure her relationship with Misty was quite ready for a girls' lunch. It had taken them a long time to reach the civil place they found themselves in now. Several years earlier, when Josie's marriage to her late husband, Ray Quinn, fell apart, he had started an affair with Misty. Ray had cared deeply about Misty, and his dying wish had been for Josie to respect his choice. It was a difficult task, even on her best day. It had taken the assault on Misty and the birth of Ray's son to finally bring the two women together. Still, Josie knew she could be abrasive, even when she tried not to be, and she was afraid the fragile relationship she had developed with Misty would be ruined if they spent more time together. "I have to work," she lied.

Misty's mouth sagged with disappointment, the partial paralysis of her face making the expression even more acute.

Josie felt a prickle of guilt. "Maybe next time."

Misty's gaze dropped to the wooden floorboards. "You always say that. Listen, I know we haven't always gotten along, but I want you to know that I—"

The ring of Josie's cell phone interrupted Misty's speech before it had started. Both women stared down at Josie's jacket pocket. Fishing the phone out, Josie gave Misty a sheepish smile and glanced at the screen. It was the same number as earlier. Desperate to avoid the topic of their reconciliation, Josie quickly swiped answer and pressed the phone to her ear.

"Quinn," she said.

A man's voice answered. "Josie Quinn?"

"Yes. Who is this?"

"I—I—you can call me Roger."

"I can 'call you' Roger? Who is this?"

Hesitation. Then, "I'm calling about your ad. You know, on craigslist?"

A sinking sensation swept through Josie's stomach. She glanced up at Misty, who was looking at her with puzzled concern. Josie stepped off the porch, using her free hand to mimic bringing a phone receiver to her ear and mouthed, "Call if you need anything."

She turned away from Misty and strode to her car, turning her attention back to Roger. "My craigslist ad? Which one was that?"

"Which one?" Roger asked, and again Josie heard more hesitation in his voice. "You don't—do I have the right number?"

"You called me, Roger."

More dead air. Then Roger said, "You don't sound like you're looking for fun."

"Being pranked through craigslist isn't my idea of a good time, Roger."

But Roger had hung up. Josie glanced back toward Misty's house, but she'd gone inside with the baby. With a sigh, Josie got into her Ford Escape and started the engine. She used the internet app on her phone to pull up Denton's craigslist site. It took a couple of minutes of browsing to find the ad. This time it was under Casual Encounters. It had been posted three hours earlier. *Kinky girl seeks playmate—Woman seeking man.*

Dread froze her finger over the screen. She didn't want to read it, didn't want to know what it said, but she had to look. Better to do it now, in the privacy of her vehicle, than to do it at the police station with her lieutenant and detective reading over her shoulder. The first time it happened, her face had taken fifteen minutes to recover from the flush that had reddened her cheeks. She took a deep breath, held it, and pressed the link to the ad.

Looking for some kinky fun. Hot girl early thirties seeking afternoon delight. A tongue so skilled I will never leave you unsatisfied. Always clean, always discreet. Call to hook up.

Below that was Josie's name and cell phone number.

She let out the breath she'd been holding and tossed the phone onto the passenger seat as though it had burned her hand. A movement in one of the windows of Misty's house caught her attention. It was likely Misty peeking from behind the curtain, wondering why Josie was still sitting curbside. Josie pulled away and headed to the police station. It was her day off, but this couldn't wait.

CHAPTER 2

The calls had started just after Lloyd Todd's arrest a month earlier. They were always the result of a craigslist ad that gave her name and cell phone number, some so disgusting and graphic she could barely get through reading them. She'd changed her number three times already. Whoever was writing the ads managed to get hold of her new number each time. She'd tried to figure out how—in fact her entire staff had come under suspicion—but she still couldn't track it. She'd gone to the cell phone store, even gone so far as to bring in the store associates for interrogation, but that lead had fallen flat pretty quickly. Even if someone at the cell phone store was giving out her new number each time she changed it, she had no way of proving it. She'd switched cell carriers after the last ad, but it was now obvious that hadn't worked.

Josie wove through the streets of downtown Denton. Her city was roughly twenty-five square miles, many of those miles spanning the untamed mountains of central Pennsylvania, with their one-lane winding roads, dense woods, and rural residences spread out far and wide. The population was edging over thirty thousand, and it increased when the college was in session, providing plenty of conflict and crime to keep Josie's team of fifty-five pretty busy. She arrived at the police station in only ten minutes, parked in the chief's spot in the municipal parking lot, and went in the front door. Her desk sergeant nodded to her. "Is Lieutenant Fraley here?" she asked him.

He pointed to the ceiling. "Upstairs finishing the paperwork on the Todd case."

"Great," Josie said.

She took the steps two at a time and found Noah at his desk, staring at his computer screen, a gnawed pen hanging from his mouth and his thick brown hair in disarray. Without moving his head, his eyes tracked her. "I hate paperwork," he mumbled, pulling the pen from his mouth. "Did I mention that?"

Josie perched on the edge of his desk. "You might have," she said.

He tossed the pen onto his desk, used his mouse to close out the programs on his computer, and turned his attention to her. Brow furrowed, he said, "What's going on?"

She held up her cell phone. "I got another one."

He glanced at the phone, then stood up, nodding toward her office where they could speak in private. Noah closed the door behind him and already had his notepad out by the time Josie rounded her desk. She plopped into her chair, pulled up the ad on her phone, and read it aloud to him as his pen flew across the page and his face grew increasingly stern. She told him about the call from Roger and rattled off the phone number.

"I'll flag this as prohibited and fax another warrant over to the craigslist offices," Noah said.

Josie sighed. "And that will get us nowhere, just like the last three times."

"But we need to build a case. When we find out who's doing this, we need to have everything in order to be able to put them away."

"We know who's doing it. Lloyd Todd and his legion of assholes."

"Fine, then we need to be prepared to put those assholes away."

"Like we did when they slashed the tires of all the cars in the police lot? Or when they egged the downstairs windows? They're angry because we arrested their boss and took away their drugs, and now they're all unemployed and in withdrawal. They're blowing off steam."

"Directed specifically at you," Noah pointed out.

"Because I'm the one who gets the job of going on TV every time something big or bad happens in this town."

"Yeah," Noah said, smiling. "I know that's your favorite."

She glared at him.

"You should hire a press liaison," he suggested.

Josie rolled her eyes. "We can't afford a press liaison. Just get today's ad taken down, would you?"

"Fine, but I'm faxing over a warrant as well."

"So you can get dummy email addresses and IP addresses that don't help us find the person who's doing this? Knowing the person posted the ads from an IP address somewhere in the city of Denton doesn't exactly narrow it down. Who knew these idiots were so tech-savvy?"

"Last time we narrowed it down to the Starbucks near the college," Noah pointed out.

"Yes," Josie said. "Someone piggybacking on their wifi. We have no idea if that person was even in the store, or if they were in a car or across the street. There was no way to tell from the video footage inside the cafe whether it was one of the patrons. Everyone in that place is on a damn computer or a phone."

"It's still worth looking into," Noah said. "We might catch a break. This is getting serious. I think these craigslist ads rise to a higher level than pranks, Boss."

"Noah."

He stared at her, and she knew what was coming. "Don't even say it," she said.

"Boss, let me put a detail on you. Just until we catch these punks."

"I don't need a detail," Josie said. "Not for this. This is dumb high school shit."

"You've got men calling you for sex."

"Men who think I'm someone I'm not. Believe me, I'm not worried about the Rogers of the world. That guy couldn't even handle a phone call with me. I doubt he's going to try to track me down."

"I'm not worried about Roger," Noah said. His eyes bored into her. "I'm worried about the jerk placing the ads. Are you certain this is coming from Lloyd Todd's camp?"

"Well, I've put a lot of people away as Chief of Police. It could be anyone, but it started after we arrested Todd, after I'd given at least three press conferences. If his lackeys are looking for someone to direct their rage toward, I would be that person. But listen, this is just a nuisance. It hasn't risen to the level of putting a detail on me."

He opened his mouth to speak again, but Josie stopped him with a raised palm. "I'm not ruling out the possibility of a detail—although I can certainly take care of myself—but not now, okay? Right now, I have to go back to the phone store and get my number changed. Again."

He knew her well enough by now not to push her. "Fine," he said. "I'll get to work on this. Text me with your new number."

CHAPTER 3

The Spur Mobile store was completely empty, for which Josie sent up a prayer of thanks. Even more annoying than calls from unwitting men looking for sexual encounters was waiting in line to have her number changed. The disinterested kid behind the counter pulled a pair of headphones from his ears as she approached the counter. He didn't ask many questions, even when he pulled up her account and saw how many times she'd changed numbers in the past month. A half hour later she was all set. Outside in her vehicle, she texted her most important contacts with the new number. Putting a call through to her grandmother, Lisette, she breathed a sigh of relief when it went straight to voicemail; she didn't feel like explaining the craigslist situation, especially not to her grandmother.

Her phone buzzed in her hand just as she was putting it back in her pocket—a return message from Trinity Payne. *A new number again already? WTH is going on?*

Trinity was the only reporter that Josie would consider a friend, and even that was a stretch. Trinity had shot to stardom in the national news market straight out of college, only to fall from grace after a source fed her a bad story. She had been doing penance reporting for her hometown television station two years ago when Josie cracked a big missing girls case that had made them both famous. Trinity had been an indispensable ally during the fallout from that case, and since then, an excellent source of information on just about everything under the sun. Josie kept in contact with her for that very reason.

None of your business, Josie texted back.

Did you think about what I said? My producers would love it if I did a story on you. Small-city chief cracks big cases. It would go national.

Trinity had been after a profile of Josie ever since she solved a string of murders that ran the length of the East Coast. *No way,* Josie texted back.

It only took a moment for Trinity to answer. *Some other time, then. I'll be in town in a couple of weeks for a retrospective piece on the missing girls case. We'll do lunch. What about the Lloyd Todd arrest? That would make a great story for a national news magazine. How about an exclusive?*

Josie shook her head, chuckling. Trinity was nothing if not persistent. Josie didn't bother to respond. She was sure that Trinity would get what she wanted eventually. She decided to wait it out until she needed a favor from her, and then she'd use the Lloyd Todd story as leverage.

A loud growl emanated from Josie's stomach as she got back into her car. She should have taken Misty up on her offer of lunch—so much for a relaxing day off! In her mind, she catalogued what waited in her fridge at home, and headed off in the direction of the nearest drive-thru.

She had just polished off a burger when her phone rang. A glance at the screen showed it was Noah calling. Pulling over, she abandoned the bag of fries on the passenger seat and swiped a greasy finger over the answer icon. "What've you got?" she said.

"It's not about the ads—or Todd's crew."

She could tell by the slight strain in his voice that whatever he was calling about was serious. "What is it?"

"Some kids found human remains behind the Moss Gardens Trailer Park. You know it?"

She knew it all right. "Yes," she said, surprised by the steadiness of her voice. A stillness overtook her. Movement felt impossible. "What kind of human remains?"

"Skeletal. Old. Gretchen's over there now. Dr. Feist is on her way."

"I'll meet you there," Josie said. Forcing her limbs out of their momentary paralysis, she put her vehicle in drive, the smell of the French fries suddenly nauseating. Pulling back into traffic, Josie headed toward the trailer park she hadn't visited since she was fourteen years old, the trailer park she used to call home.

CHAPTER 4

"Hey, JoJo, want to play a game?"

Josie heard her mother's words drifting down the dark hallway of the trailer, slithering under the door to her bedroom. The red crayon she clutched in her right hand froze, hovering over the coloring book her mother had given her earlier that day. She hardly ever gave Josie presents, so Josie had taken it and run off to her bedroom, closing the door and spreading out on the floor with all of her crayons before her mother could think about taking it back. She had already colored four full pages.

"JoJo," came the voice again. "Mommy wants to play a game."

Josie stared at the half-colored flower beneath her hand. Her mother rarely wanted to play games. "Coming," she called back.

She stuffed her crayons back into their box, closed her coloring book, and snatched up her small stuffed dog, Wolfie. Racing into the living room, she found her mother sprawled across the lumpy brown couch. Across from her, the television played a newscast on mute. Dust motes floated in the late-afternoon sun that streamed through the windows. "JoJo," her mother said in a sing-song voice. "Come closer."

Josie took a step forward. "What kind of game are we going to play, Mommy?"

Soft laughter carried through the air. "The kind where we see how fast you can get me a beer from the fridge."

"Oh." Josie knew from experience it was only seven steps from where she stood to the fridge. Her mother always put her beer cans on the bottom shelf so Josie could reach them easily. Sometimes her mother counted off the seconds as Josie raced back and forth to the fridge, but not today. As she handed her mother a beer, she saw the belt loose around her upper arm, and on the couch beside her, a blackened spoon, a lighter, and a needle. Josie never asked what these things were for, but they made her feel funny inside. She was staring at the small dark scab in the crook of her mother's elbow when the trailer door burst open behind her.

Wolfie fell from her grasp as she turned to see a man standing in the doorway.

CHAPTER 5

Moss Gardens sat on top of a hill behind the city park, a collection of about two dozen trailer homes spread far enough apart that if you screamed, your neighbors might not hear you. Josie knew this to be true.

When she had lived there, the entrance was marked by a large boulder by the side of the road with the words MOSS GARDENS emblazoned on it in black calligraphy. Today, the boulder was overshadowed by a wrought-iron archway that announced the name of the park in large, ornate letters. Beyond it, Josie saw that the drab brown trailers of her youth had all either been replaced or refurbished. The park held none of the dreariness she remembered. Almost all the trailers were brightly painted and well kept; some even had potted plants outside. She knew it was meant to feel welcoming, but knowing what she did about the place made the vibrant colors and homey touches seem garish and unnerving.

She passed the lot where her childhood home had once been. The trailer she'd lived in with her parents had long since been removed—or torn down—and now the nearest resident was using the space for extra parking. A few pipes that poked from the yellowed grass were the only sign that anyone had once resided there.

Toward the back of the park was a wooded valley that lay between the trailer park and one of Denton's working-class neighborhoods. There was no marked path, but Josie remembered a shoulder-width break in the brush where the local kids trampled the tall weeds to cut through. At the very back of the park, beyond the last row of trailers, was a paved one-lane road that ran alongside the edge of the woodland. Josie spotted Noah's department-issue SUV parked in one of the driveways. Two patrol cars sat in the middle of the road, their front ends facing the old path like arrows. As she pulled past, Josie saw the metal gate with a No Entry sign across the opening. She remembered the day the gate and sign were installed. It was shortly after her father had walked down that very path and put a bullet in his head.

Unfortunately for the landowner, a No Entry sign in Denton was generally considered to be an invitation to explore, and Josie and her late husband, Ray, had spent the majority of their childhood in those very woods. They should have felt afraid in the dark, dangerous woodland, but compared to their respective homes, the forest had offered a sacred and much needed respite. It wasn't cold, but Josie felt a chill envelop her as she parked behind the medical examiner's small white pickup truck and got out of her vehicle.

Josie was relieved to see that news of the discovery hadn't spread, and no nosy neighbors lolled about the perimeter of the scene, craning their necks for something to gossip about. Only Noah and some of Josie's other officers stood along the road—Hiller next to his patrol car, Wright guarding the gate. They nodded to her as she approached Noah, who leaned up against the other patrol car, his notepad and pen in hand.

"What've you got?" Josie asked.

Noah pointed to the backseat of the cruiser. "Couple of kids playing in the woods found some bones."

Josie peered through the window into the backseat of the cruiser, where the faces of two young boys stared back at her. They couldn't be older than ten or eleven, twelve at the most. They both had dark eyes and brown hair—one short and spiked, the other nearly covering his eyes. Both were covered in mud.

"Gretchen went to get their mom," Noah said. "Apparently their dad is no longer in the picture."

"They're brothers?"

Noah nodded.

"Who called it in?"

"One of the neighbors. Barbara Rhodes. She watches the boys while their mom works at the Denton Diner. She let them play in the woods. When she called them in for dinner, one of them was carrying what we think is a jawbone. She called 911."

Josie looked back at the boys. The long-haired boy stared back at her, chin jutted forward in defiance. His eyes, wide with fear, told another story. Beside him, his brother chewed on his fingernails. "Where's the jawbone now?" she asked.

"Gretchen took it into evidence," he replied. "The evidence response team is down there now with Dr. Feist processing the scene."

"The neighbor?"

He gestured toward the last row of trailers. "Third one from the left, number twenty-seven. The white one. I took her statement and sent her back home. The fewer people out here, the better."

Josie nodded, glad they didn't have to contend with a crowd of onlookers—at least not yet. The sound of a car drew their attention. Gretchen's Chevy Cruze turned a corner and pulled up behind Josie's vehicle. Before the car even came to a stop, a woman dressed in black jeans and a polo shirt with a matching black apron leapt out of the passenger's side and ran toward Josie and Noah. The long-haired boy pressed a hand against the window of the cruiser, and Josie reached back and opened the door. The boys tumbled out in a pile of gangly limbs and raced toward their mother. She swept them up in a tight hug, kissing both their heads and then studying their faces one by one. The younger, short-haired boy looked relieved. His brother did not. Josie, Noah, and Gretchen met the three of them in the middle of the road.

Gretchen introduced the woman. "This is Maureen Price, the boys' mother. I explained to her that we can't talk to her boys without her permission."

Maureen squeezed the long-haired boy's shoulder. "This is Kyle, my oldest. He's twelve, and this is Troy. He's eleven." She smiled tightly. "Irish twins," she explained.

Up close, Josie could see Maureen was quite young, probably not even thirty-five. There was something familiar about her round face and clear blue eyes. Her chestnut-colored hair was pulled back into a tight bun. Josie wondered if she'd gone to Denton East High School. She would have been a few years ahead of Josie and Ray.

"Chief Quinn," Josie said, extending a hand. "This is Lieutenant Fraley. Why don't you boys tell us what happened?"

Maureen looked down at their two heads, their thin bodies wedged against hers. "I thought I told you two to stay out of those woods."

"Aww, Mom," Troy said. "It's boring at Mrs. Rhodes's house."

"What were you guys doing in there?" Noah asked.

"Playing," Kyle answered. His eyes were still wide and wary.

Troy jumped away from his mom and mimicked holding a rifle, spinning around and squinting one eye as though he were looking through the sights. "We were playing war!"

"War?" Gretchen asked.

Maureen rolled her eyes and tried to gather Troy back to her side. "They've been watching the military channel. They're obsessed."

Noah raised a brow. "The military channel?"

Troy said, "We wanted to make foxholes. Like in the World Wars."

Josie glanced at his older brother, but he said nothing. "Where did you get the shovels?" she asked.

"Mrs. Rhodes," Troy said.

Finally, Kyle spoke. "We borrowed her gardening shovels. She said it was okay."

Maureen chewed her bottom lip. "Boys, really. You shouldn't

be bothering Mrs. Rhodes with stuff like that. Why can't you just play video games till I get home?"

Josie said, "How many foxholes did you dig?"

"Three," answered Troy. "We stopped when we found the, you know, bones."

"How far down?" Josie asked, looking directly at Kyle.

The older boy shrugged. "When we stand in them, they come up to about here." He pointed to his solar plexus. So, a few feet down.

"Which one of you decided to bring one of the bones home?" Noah asked.

From the flush of young Troy's face, Josie knew it had been him. Neither boy answered. Maureen gave them each a stern look. "Boys, you answer the policeman."

"You're not in any trouble," Gretchen told them. "We're just trying to put together exactly what happened."

Troy looked to his brother, but Kyle's gaze had dropped to the asphalt. With a sigh, he said, "It was my idea. I didn't think Mrs. Rhodes would believe us. But as soon as I showed her, she called 911 and told us to stay away from the woods."

"Did one of you show Detective Palmer where the body was when she got here?" Josie asked.

Both boys nodded, and haltingly, Kyle raised a hand.

"Lieutenant Fraley tells me the piece of the skeleton you brought back was a jaw bone," Josie said. "Tell me, was it loose already? Separated from the skull? Or did you break it off?"

The two boys looked at one another. The older brother chewed on the nail of one of his index fingers.

"It's okay either way," Josie told them. "Even if you broke it off, you won't be in trouble. We just need to know so that we can tell what happened to these bones before, and after, you uncovered them. You understand?"

Young Troy nodded. "You want to make sure the killer didn't do it!" he exclaimed.

His mother swatted his shoulder. "Troy!"

"It's okay," Josie said. "We don't actually know what happened, but it helps us to figure it out if we know all the details."

"We snapped it off," Kyle said, his tone flat. He looked at his feet. "Sorry."

Gretchen smiled at them. "It's fine," she assured them. "Thank you for telling the truth."

She pulled a business card out and gave it to Maureen. Addressing the boys, she said, "If you think of anything else that might be important, you can give me a call. You will have to stay out of those woods though, at least until we're finished gathering evidence, okay?"

"That means no more foxholes," Maureen told her children pointedly. She grabbed Troy by his collar and pushed him along, toward their trailer. Josie guessed it was the one next to Mrs. Rhodes's trailer with two bicycles propped against its side.

Once the three of them were inside the trailer, Gretchen clapped her hands together and looked at Noah and Josie. "Let's go see what Dr. Feist has unearthed."

CHAPTER 6

Josie hoisted herself over the gate and walked into the woods. Behind her, Gretchen and Noah followed, twigs snapping beneath their feet. The path was exactly as Josie remembered it, leading them deep into the trees before disappearing where the forest grew too dense. Josie stopped and turned back to Gretchen. "Which way?"

Gretchen pointed to the left and Josie felt goosebumps erupt all over her body; the woods were nearly three miles long and yet she knew, almost instinctively, that they were heading toward the one section she dreaded revisiting the most. Wordlessly, Josie gestured for Gretchen to take the lead, and Noah fell in behind her. They picked their way through brush, weaving through the thick trunks of red maples and northern oaks to a giant Norway maple tree encircled with a strip of yellow crime-scene tape.

Josie felt her stomach sink as she stopped abruptly, and Noah's chest bumped into her back. "Boss?" he said.

It was hard to say how she knew, how her body remembered, but it did. She had only been six when her father had shot himself beneath this tree. She wouldn't have known which tree it was had her mother not insisted on marching her through the woods to look at it whenever she was feeling particularly cruel.

Josie heard her mother's voice like a whisper soughing through the leaves over her head. "This is where your precious daddy came to die."

Noah's hand slid under Josie's elbow, a gentle nudge. His

voice was softer this time, meant only for her to hear. "Boss, you okay?"

Josie gave her head a shake. "Fine," she mumbled.

Tearing her eyes from the tree, she counted up the three foxholes the Price boys had dug in a half circle around the base of the tree. The evidence response team moved around in white Tyvek suits with clipboards, cameras, and evidence flags, documenting everything.

"Those don't look like foxholes," Josie said.

"They were dug by kids, Boss," Gretchen pointed out.

The holes were sloppily dug, and the larger of the three, more of a rectangular shape, had been cordoned off with string and evidence flags. The voice of the county medical examiner, Dr. Anya Feist, floated out from inside the hole. "Chief? That you?"

"I'm here," Josie called. "What've you got down there?"

Dr. Feist's head shot up, a white evidence cap holding her silver-gold hair away from her face. A camera hung round her neck. "I'll let you know. You just stay over there. I don't need any more people traipsing around this hole. With all the rain we've had, the soil is pretty soft as is. I've just got to excavate without this damn thing collapsing on me." She held up her gloved hands—in one was what looked like a paint brush, and in the other was a small trowel. "My assistant is on his way. He's done this kind of work before. He'll help. What I need you folks to do is keep everyone away from here. And to answer your question, Chief, there's not much I can tell you until I get these bones back to the lab."

"You won't even hazard a guess as to how long the body has been there?" Josie asked.

Dr. Feist rolled her eyes but said, "Nothing but bones, a body buried this deep, unembalmed? My best guess is it's been here at least eight years, probably longer. Could even be thirty or forty years. All I can tell you is the skull has a hell of a fracture."

Josie felt Noah's eyes on her. She could practically hear his thoughts. Two years ago, Denton's famous missing girls case had unearthed dozens of remains buried in a wooded area on a mountaintop and led to the discovery of two serial killers who had been operating in the area for decades. This scene felt like déjà vu. "It's not related to the missing girls case," she said. "We don't even know it's a woman."

He gave her a weak half-smile. "You can read my mind now?"

Josie managed her own wan smile. "I'm getting better at it." She motioned around them. "We're at least fifteen miles away from the mountain where those girls' bodies were found. This is something else."

Noah frowned. "We have no matching open missing persons files, Boss. None that would be old enough to be this decomposed."

"I know that," Josie said. She knew exactly how many missing persons cases there were in her city at that exact moment—and in the county. She even knew their names. Noah was right. The oldest open missing persons case they had was from three years ago, and that young man was a habitual drug user and had been deemed a runaway. She took a careful step forward, her shirt brushing the crime-scene tape, and peered over the edge of the hole where Dr. Feist was painstakingly carving dirt away from a skull. "Then it's someone who hasn't been reported missing. One way or another, we'll find out."

CHAPTER 7

Josie's heart skipped several beats until she realized it was just her daddy standing in the doorway. She ran to him, but he didn't scoop her up and spin her around like he normally did. Instead, he placed a hand on top of her head and stared past her toward where her mother lay on the sofa. Josie turned to see a smile curve across her mother's lips as her eyes fluttered open and closed. "Shit," her mother said. "I thought you had to work."

"I do," he said. "But I wanted to see—" he broke off. His hand moved to Josie's shoulder, and he pushed her back toward the hallway, his eyes never leaving the sofa. Josie watched her parents stare at one another for a tense moment, and a strange shaky feeling started in her legs. The room felt full of something—something bad, but Josie didn't know what.

"Go to your room, JoJo," her daddy said. "Now."

CHAPTER 8

The next morning, Josie, Noah, and Gretchen stood around a sheet-covered metal examination table in the Denton City Morgue. The drab, windowless room was situated in the basement of Denton Memorial Hospital, an ancient brick building on top of a hill that overlooked most of the city. Josie could never get used to the smell—a putrid combination of chemicals and decay. Beside her, Noah looked pale, almost green, while Gretchen, completely unaffected, looked almost bored. Josie remembered that Gretchen had seen a lifetime of autopsies during her tenure as a homicide detective with the Philadelphia Police Department before coming to Denton.

Josie elbowed Noah lightly.

"I'm fine," he mumbled from the side of his mouth.

Dr. Feist breezed in from the small office she shared with her assistant just off the main autopsy room. Her hair was tied back in a loose ponytail, and she now wore dark-blue scrubs. "I've already recorded my initial findings," she told them with a smile. "So, I'll allow questions."

Carefully, she removed the sheet. The bones seemed small and insubstantial lined up in a perfect body shape across the examination table. The dirt had all been brushed away from the bones, which now looked off-white. The four of them stood around the table sharing a moment of silence for the stranger who had been murdered and forgotten for so long that only the thin, yellowing framework remained.

Josie knew before Dr. Feist even spoke that they were

looking at the remains of a young woman; she had seen more than her share of female skeletons while concluding the case that had made her chief.

"I believe we are looking at female remains," Dr. Feist announced. "I'd estimate the height to be about five foot two, five foot three." She pointed to the mandible, which had been separated from the skull. "The chin is rounded, where men tend to have more squared-off chins." She pointed to the forehead. "The frontal bone is smooth and vertical. The mastoid process"—Dr. Feist's finger moved to a small, conical bone behind the jaw, where the girl's ear would have been—"which is this bone here that kind of protrudes where certain neck muscles attach to it. As you can see, it's small. In men, it is very pronounced."

Gretchen scribbled on her notepad. Josie stepped forward and pointed to the pelvic bone. "The pelvis gives it away."

Dr. Feist smiled, her eyes alight, looking at Josie as though she were a prized pupil. "Yes, it does. Why is that, Chief?"

Josie pointed to the pelvic girdle. "This opening here is broader and rounder—so women can give birth. Also, here, this angle—" she pointed to the bottom center of the pelvic bone.

"The pubic arch," Dr. Feist put in.

"Right. This angle where the two sides meet is more obtuse in females. Greater than ninety degrees."

Noah said, "For childbirth as well?"

Both Josie and the doctor nodded.

"How old was she?" Gretchen asked, pen poised over her notepad.

"Between sixteen and nineteen years old," Dr. Feist replied.

"That's quite specific," Noah remarked.

"Well, the growth plates—or lack thereof—make it pretty easy to determine," Dr. Feist said. "The long bones in the body have three parts: the diaphysis—that's the shaft—the metaphysis, which is the part where it widens and flares at the end, and then the epiphysis, which is basically the end cap of the bone or the growth plate. In children, there is a gap between the epiphysis and the metaphysis."

Gretchen, busy sketching on her notepad, said, "You mean there's a space between the growth plate and the knobby end of the bone."

Dr. Feist's head bobbed from side to side. "Basically, yeah. As you get older, your growth plates and the 'knobby end,' as you call it, fuse together. The growth plates fuse at pretty predictable ages. For example, the epiphysis of the femur at the proximal end—that's where the femur goes into the hip socket—fuses between ages fifteen and nineteen, give or take six months on each end."

One of her gloved fingers ran up the length of the girl's right femur, stopping at the hip socket and pointing to the very top where the bone inserted into the pelvis. "It's fused, which means she could have been as young as fifteen, fifteen and a half, and as old as nineteen or nineteen and a half."

"But you said sixteen," Josie pointed out.

"I'm estimating, of course," Dr. Feist responded. "But the distal radius fuses at around sixteen, and hers are fused." Her gloved finger found the long bone of the arm on the thumb side of the girl's right hand. Touching the flared part where the radius met the intricate bones of the hand, Dr. Feist said, "No space. The epiphysis has fused to the metaphysis."

"When does the last growth plate fuse?" Gretchen asked.

"The medial aspect of the clavicle fuses by age thirty at the latest," Dr. Feist answered. "However, we don't see epiphyseal fusion of either the medial or lateral aspect of the clavicle until age nineteen, and this young lady doesn't have it."

Josie leaned in and peered at the girl's collarbones.

Noah ran a hand through his thick brown hair. "I'm trying to remember my college anatomy class."

"The lateral is the part that goes into the shoulder," Gretchen said. "The medial attaches to the sternum."

"Show-off," Noah muttered.

Gretchen kept her head down, her pen sketching the skeleton at a furious pace.

"That's correct," Dr. Feist said. "More or less." She pointed to the gap between the epiphysis and the metaphysis on each end of the collarbones. "If she were nineteen or older, these growth plates would be fused."

"So, this is a teenage girl," Josie said, acid in her stomach fizzing.

"Yes," Dr. Feist agreed. "It's possible to estimate a year on either side of the range—perhaps fifteen to twenty—but I believe you're looking at a sixteen- to nineteen-year-old female. Oh, and this teenage girl gave birth at least once."

Josie could see by Dr. Feist's raised brow and amused smile that she enjoyed tossing out that little surprise. Hands on her hips, Josie matched the doctor's expression and said, "Just how can you tell that this girl gave birth?"

Dr. Feist beckoned them all closer to the table. They gathered round, and she pointed to one of the flat planes of pelvic bone, where Josie could make out a smattering of small holes roughly the size of shotgun pellets. "It's called parturition scarring, or pitting," Dr. Feist said.

"Par-nutrition?" Noah said.

"Parturition," Dr. Feist corrected slowly. "Childbirth. When a woman gives birth, her pubic bones separate to allow the baby to fit through, and sometimes the ligaments attached to the bones tear and leave these small scars. It's not always one hundred percent accurate, but in a girl this young, I'd say these are from her having given birth."

Josie frowned. "No way to tell how old she was when she had her baby—or anything about the baby?"

"I'm sorry, Chief, but no. All I can tell you is that she had a baby before she died."

"Maybe someone killed her and took her baby," Gretchen suggested.

Dr. Feist shrugged. "I can't speculate on why she was

murdered or what happened to her child—but she was definitely murdered. You can see the fracture better now that she's
cleaned up."

She moved around to the head of the table and reached up,
adjusting the large, circular lamp that hung from the ceiling so
that its beams shone directly onto the girl's skull. Josie shuffled
closer to Dr. Feist, and Noah and Gretchen followed, craning
their necks to see the top of the skull. "See these," Dr. Feist
said, pointing to faint squiggly lines running down the center
of the skull from front to back and then across the front from
temple to temple. "These are called sutures. They're openings
where the skull plates fit together. These are normal, and you
can see they're still partially open, which is also normal for a
teenager. Most of the skull's sutures close well into adulthood."
She pointed out other sutures in the back of the skull and above
where the ears would be. Then she pointed to a large depression
on the top of the skull, on what would have been the girl's left
side, about midway from the front of her head to the back. Jagged cracks extended from where the bone had caved slightly.
"This is not normal," Dr. Feist said.

Noah gave a low whistle. "What could have caused that?"
he asked.

Dr. Feist shrugged. She used her thumb and index finger to
frame the size of the fracture. "A hammer maybe? The blunt
side, not the sharp edge. It's big enough that whatever she was
hit with would have been blunt, but we're still talking about
something relatively small."

"A baseball bat?" Gretchen asked.

Dr. Feist frowned. "Maybe, but it's more likely something
smaller and heavier."

"Tire iron?" Josie offered.

The doctor nodded. "That's more likely. Whoever hit her
used a great deal of force. It's hard to say from just bones,
but I'm not sure the struggle—if there was one—lasted long.
She doesn't have any other fractures. Of course, she may have

sustained bruising or lacerations, but we'll never know that now."

"How about the angle?" Josie asked. "What would you say? Someone taller than her? Shorter? Same height?"

Dr. Feist held up a finger. "I estimate her to be about five foot three. I would say she was killed by someone about the same height, but using an overhead strike." She motioned to Gretchen, who was about her height. Gretchen moved closer, and Dr. Feist approached her from the side, slightly to her rear, both arms raised high over her head as though she was clutching something in them. She brought her invisible weapon down on Gretchen's head, stopping before she made contact. "If it was someone taller than her, or if she had been kneeling, I would expect the fracture to be more depressed, because there would be more follow-through with the strike."

"All right," Gretchen said. "So we suspect she was struck over the head by someone close to her own height, and then she was buried in the woods."

"And we suspect whoever killed her was a woman," Josie said.

"How do you figure that?" asked Noah.

Josie said, "How many men do you know who are five foot three?"

"Not many, but they exist," Noah countered.

"I'm aware," Josie answered. "But if I had to make an educated guess in this instance, I would say we are more likely looking for a female assailant." Josie turned back to the doctor. "No way to tell if she was killed there in the woods, or if she was killed elsewhere and then moved to the grave?"

"I'm afraid not."

Noah turned his gaze to Dr. Feist. "No way to tell if she was sexually assaulted?"

Dr. Feist gave him a tight smile. "There's no way to tell a lot of things. This poor girl has been buried for a long time."

She walked over to a table along the wall and picked up a

brown bag, which she emptied out onto the exam table near the skeleton's feet. Dirty scraps of fabric came first, and then a larger garment. It was dirt-covered and faded, and some of it had disintegrated, but Josie could see that it was a windbreaker—dark blue with squares of what used to be bright yellow, teal, and pink on the shoulders and where the pockets were. There was only one sleeve left, and as Dr. Feist held the garment up, Josie could see several swaths of fabric missing from the back, the collar, and the waist—worn away by time and the earth's erosion.

"This is what's left of her clothing," the doctor said.

Gretchen raised a brow. "No chance there are any identifying items in her jacket pockets?"

Dr. Feist laughed and placed the jacket carefully onto the countertop. "The insides of the pockets are gone. Decomposed. The rest," she waved at the scrap pile, "is just buttons, a shoe sole, and what are probably scraps of leather."

Josie stepped forward and looked down at the sad collection of items: a rusted zipper, a couple of blackened grommets from shoes requiring laces, a few small scraps of leather, the tiny folded nickel clasps of a bra, and a grimy rubber shoe sole deteriorating around the edges. Josie looked from the pile to the jacket and then pointed to the jacket. "What material is that made from?"

"My guess is nylon."

"Looks like something from the 1980s," Gretchen said. "Windbreakers were all the rage back then, especially the style with the blocks of bright colors."

Josie nodded. "How long does nylon take to decompose in the ground?"

Noah pulled out his phone, his fingers working fast over the screen. A moment later, he said, "Thirty to forty years."

"Seems about right," Dr. Feist said. "The challenge in a case like this is figuring out how long the body has been in the ground. Usually the items we find along with the bones—if any—are the most helpful in trying to pin down a time frame. I was going to have a friend of mine from the college's Archeology Department consult, but thirty to forty years would be a place to start."

"That's all fine and good," Josie said. "But you know as well as I do that we don't have any missing teenage girls in the entire county going back that far."

Dr. Feist grinned and raised a finger in the air. "Oh, I may be able to narrow it down for you."

Josie, Noah, and Gretchen stared at her. Gretchen's busy pen finally stilled in anticipation.

"Wait till you see this," Dr. Feist said as she returned to the head of the table and grasped the sides of the skull with both hands. She lifted it away from the lower jaw bone and held it under the overhead light so they could see inside what would have been the roof of the girl's mouth. All three police officers leaned in.

"Holy shit," Noah said. "Are those fangs?"

Behind the two front teeth were two additional, conical teeth that came to points.

"Supernumerary teeth," Dr. Feist explained.

"Extra teeth?" Josie asked.

"Yeah, pretty much. The condition is called hyperdontia. It's an inherited defect. Extremely rare. Something a dentist in a city this small would remember, especially given the fact that her supernumerary teeth actually looked like fangs. I did a little research. Supernumerary teeth can appear anywhere in the dental arch. Not all patients present with extra teeth that look so fanglike. Trust me, this girl would have been memorable to look at."

Josie met Noah's eyes, and then Gretchen's. "Well," she said. "Start tracking down dentists who were practicing in the city thirty to forty years ago."

CHAPTER 9

A week passed, and every night Josie dreamed of the tall maple tree in the woods behind the trailer that was her childhood home. Sometimes her father was there, a hole in the top of his head, a macabre smile on his face. He beckoned her. "Come," he said. "I have to show you something." Each time, Josie was too afraid to get close to him. Sometimes Ray, her ex-husband, was there—only it was Ray at nine years old, crashing through the woods behind her, telling her not to get any closer. She woke sweaty and thrashing in her king-sized bed, her limbs twisted in the sheets.

Today was no different. Her eyes snapped open, her heaving chest and gasping breaths slowing gradually in the warmth of the sunlight streaming through her bedroom windows. She sat up, pulling her sweat-soaked T-shirt away from her skin, and looked around the room, taking in the high ceilings, the large windows, and the walls painted a soothing cream color. It was her favorite room in the house, open and airy in a way she usually found comforting, but still she shivered as the sweat on her body dried, leaving her clammy. She would have just enough time to shower and stop for coffee before reporting to work.

Twenty minutes later she was locking her front door, her mind on the performance evaluations and equipment requisitions waiting on her desk at the station, when her cell phone rang. It was Noah.

"What've you got?" Josie answered.

Noah's laughter filtered through the phone line. "You're getting better at the small talk, Boss. I'm fine, thank you."

Josie smiled as she made her way from her stoop to where her Escape waited in the driveway. "I'm glad to hear that, Fraley," she said. "I'd really love a latte from Komorrah's Koffee. Maybe you could make your way over there before I get to the station. How's that for small talk?"

"The latte is already on your desk," he responded, making Josie smile.

"You may need a raise," she joked. "Now, what've you got?"

"I've got a preliminary ID on our mystery girl. We didn't get any hits in Denton, so Gretchen expanded the search area. We tracked down a dentist in Bellewood who inherited his father's practice about ten years back. His dad practiced for decades before he retired. Apparently, his dad repeatedly mentioned the patient with hyperdontia he treated in the late '70s, early '80s, because the condition was so rare. Gretchen is over there now getting the chart so Dr. Feist can see if they're a match."

Josie stood beside her Escape, feeling a tingle of excitement. An ID in a week. It was a good start. "That's great," she said, fishing her key fob out of her jacket pocket.

"Yeah, we lucked out with her having those fangs."

"Extra teeth," Josie corrected. Ever since she'd seen them, she couldn't help but wonder what the poor girl had been through because of them; kids could be exceptionally cruel.

"Sorry," Noah said. "Supernumerary teeth. Anyway, we might have never tracked down her identity if it weren't for them."

Josie lifted her shoulder and used it to keep the phone pressed against her ear as she reached for the handle of her Escape. On the underside of the door handle, her fingers sank into something cold and mushy. "What's her name?" she asked.

The smell reached her nose the moment she took her hand away from the door handle—foul and stomach-clenching. She held her fingers up in front of her face, the brown color confirming her guess. "Shit," she muttered.

"What's that?"

"Nothing. Her name?"

"Belinda Rose. Date of birth October 15, 1966."

Josie felt the color drain from her face, the clamminess of the early morning returning and coating her skin like a greasy film. In that moment, she wasn't sure what made her feel queasier—the excrement covering her fingers or hearing the name from Noah's lips.

She held her hand away from herself, looking around, realizing she'd have to go back inside to clean up. But her legs felt heavy and stuck in place, and her lungs were filled with lead.

"Boss?"

"That's not possible," Josie croaked.

"What's not possible?"

"Belinda Rose can't be dead—she can't have been dead for over thirty years."

"Oh yeah? Why is that?"

"Because Belinda Rose is my mother's name, and as far as I know, she's still alive."

CHAPTER 10

The trailer only seemed too small when her mother was angry. When she got really worked up, her fury filled the whole place like thick clouds of steam from a hot shower. Her rages were inescapable, even when Josie hid beneath the kitchen table and watched her feet stalk back and forth, back and forth. It was never good when she started pacing.

"I don't know who he thinks he is," her mother growled, spittle flying from her mouth. The refrigerator door opened and slammed closed, and Josie heard the snap of a beer can opening. She clutched her threadbare Wolfie to her chest, shrinking back as far as she could, out of reach from her mother's hands, which she knew would thrust under the table and drag her out eventually.

But they didn't come. Josie's eyelids grew so heavy she could barely keep them open. She stifled a yawn and tried to ignore the cold that seeped from the tiles into her nightgown. It was late. She knew because it was dark outside.

"That bastard," she heard her mother mutter, her feet suddenly moving again across the kitchen.

Josie tried to tune out the sound, listening hard for the sound of her daddy's truck outside. She wished he would come home. Next, she heard the sound of kitchen drawers being torn from their homes and silverware clattering to the floor. Then her mother's voice again, thick and slurred this time, talking though no one else was there. "You're not going to get away with this. Goddamn you. I'll destroy everything you love. Everything."

Then suddenly—terrifyingly—her mother's face appeared in the tiny space beneath the table. She smiled at Josie, and Josie got that sick feeling in her stomach she always got when her mother did bad things. She reached out a hand to Josie.

"You come here now, girl."

CHAPTER 11

Josie went inside and got cleaned up without making a mess anywhere. But even after she had scrubbed her hand several times and assured herself the excrement hadn't gotten on any of her clothes, the smell still lingered deep in her nostrils. She'd ended the call with Noah abruptly, but he was on his way to her house, and that knowledge settled her agitation a little. She went into one of her spare bedrooms, where she kept her laptop on a small desk in the corner of the room. She pulled out the chair, sat, and booted it up.

She'd had a security camera installed in her driveway a month earlier, after she'd found all four of her tires slashed—just a week after all the department vehicles at the station house had suffered the same fate. Replacement tires for her Escape had cost her a small fortune, and she wouldn't let the vandal get away with it a second time.

She queued up the footage from the moment she'd pulled in the night before, and then fast-forwarded until she saw a figure slink into the driveway. Josie looked at the time stamp: 3:12 in the morning, when she had been fast asleep. The person wore baggy pants and a hoodie pulled down low over their face. She couldn't tell if it was a man or woman, but based on the height—she guessed about six feet—Josie thought it was probably a man.

She watched the hooded figure reach into a paper bag, come out with a handful of dark matter, and push it up under the door handles of Josie's car. So she would have to clean all four handles.

"Great," she muttered to herself.

When the figure was done, Josie could see him peeling off latex gloves, shoving them into the paper bag, and then jogging off down the street, bag in hand. Resetting the footage to when the figure first appeared, Josie leaned back in her chair and sighed. At three in the morning, none of her neighbors would have been up. Even if they were and had seen the guy, it was unlikely they'd seen anything more than what Josie had caught on camera.

Noah arrived ten minutes later. She let him in, and they reviewed the footage together. Josie saved it to a flash drive and handed it to him. "I want a report filed. By you. No one else."

Noah sighed. "You're documenting this, but you're not letting me do anything about it."

Josie gave him a dismissive look as she stood. "There's nothing to be done. These are little teenage pricks doing pranks. I don't need a detail."

He knew better than to start that argument with her again. Instead, he took the flash drive from her and dropped it into his pocket. "The craigslist ad is a dead end. You were right. All we can get from the IP address is that it was somewhere here in Denton—this time near the mall. Probably someone piggybacking off the free wifi of one of the stores, or something like that."

"Figures," Josie said.

Noah didn't move from the doorway. His gaze made her face feel hot. She put her hands on her hips. "What?" she said.

"We need to talk about Belinda Rose—and your mother."

CHAPTER 12

The hospital was big and bright, with endless tiled hallways and ugly blue curtains for walls. Behind every curtain Josie could hear hushed voices and sometimes cries of pain. Nurses dressed in periwinkle scrubs rushed up and down the halls and in and out of the curtains. After a long, agonizing wait while her whole head throbbed, one of them stopped by her cubicle, snapped on a pair of latex gloves, and prepared a smelly, folded piece of gauze to clean the wound on the side of Josie's face.

"This is gonna sting, hon," the nurse told Josie. She beckoned for another nurse to hold Josie to the bed before pressing the wet pad against her jawline.

It felt like her skin was ripping open and they were setting it on fire. The more she squirmed against their big hands, the harder they pressed her against the plastic mattress. The nurse holding her head loosened her grip for a moment to check the wound, and Josie looked down at her blood-soaked nightgown. Her heart did cartwheels in her chest. Had she died?

No, she thought. She hadn't died.

She hadn't died because Needle had shown up just at the moment her mother's knife had sliced down the side of her face. Needle wasn't his real name. Josie didn't know what he was really called, only that he came to the trailer when her daddy was at work, and he always brought sharp, dangerous needles. He wasn't a nice man, but when he'd walked in that night, he had looked scared, and that terrified Josie more than her mother's white fury, and more than any blade.

It was Needle who'd pried the knife away from Josie's mother. It was Needle who'd insisted that Josie needed to go to the hospital, scooping her off the floor and carrying her to the car. Josie couldn't remember if he had come with them, but she definitely hadn't seen him at the hospital. Needle was gone.

She couldn't be dead if Needle had made her mother stop. But the blood. There was so much blood. She struggled against the nurses, fighting for her life.

"Josie, honey, you have to hold still." Her mother's voice came from somewhere beside her.

"I'm sorry, hon. I know it hurts. We're almost done," said one of the nurses.

She wanted her daddy.

Finally, they stopped. Her breath came in heavy gasps. Gently, one of the nurses turned her onto her back. "I'm real sorry, hon," the nurse said, a pained smile directed down at Josie. The big light behind the nurse's head burned Josie's eyes.

The other nurse turned to her mother. "She's gonna need stitches. You wanna tell us what happened?"

CHAPTER 13

Josie watched Noah circle her Ford Escape, leaning over to get a good look at the shit caked under her door handles. He wrinkled his nose, snapped some photos with his phone, and turned to her. "Want to send a sample to the lab? See if it's human?"

Her stomach turned. "No," she answered. "I'm not spending department money on a bad joke."

"How long is the backlash to Lloyd Todd's arrest going to last?" Noah asked.

"Hard to say. Hopefully not much longer. We'll take your car. I want to get back to the station before my latte gets cold."

Noah smiled. "And leave this crap caked under the handles all day? I don't think so. I'll clean this up for you while you tell me about your mom."

Josie stood in her driveway, arms crossed over her chest, while Noah moved in and out of her house gathering latex gloves, paper towels, surface cleaner, and a plastic bag. He went to work on the driver's door first, talking as he cleaned. "So your mom's name was Belinda Rose."

Josie didn't answer.

Once he got all the sludge out from under the handle using paper towels, he sprayed it with disinfectant and used more paper towels to wipe away the remnants, depositing all the dirty towels into the plastic bag. The smell wafted over to where Josie stood. Her nose wrinkled, but Noah seemed unaffected.

"Used to dealing with crap, are you?" she asked.

He smiled. "Don't change the subject."

"It's just that the smell at the morgue turns you green in seconds, but you're practically face-deep over there, and it's not bothering you at all."

"There could be more than one Belinda Rose," he pointed out, moving to the next handle.

"With the same birthday?"

"I thought your maiden name was Matson, not Rose," Noah said.

"It was. Matson was my dad's last name. My parents never got married."

"Where's your mother now?"

Josie's chin dropped to her chest. She didn't like talking about her mother; she'd been actively trying not to think about the woman for the past sixteen years. Her mother had taken enough from her. She didn't deserve any more of Josie's time or mental energy. "I don't know," she said. "I haven't seen her since I was fourteen. She left."

Noah turned and looked at her, one brow raised. "You never tried to find her?"

Josie's hands found the lapels of her jacket and tugged them closer together. Her eyes drifted away from Noah. "She's not the kind of person you go looking for."

"How tall is she?" he asked, and Josie knew he was thinking of their post-autopsy meeting with Dr. Feist.

She sighed. "Tall enough to have hit this girl over the head with a hammer or tire iron. Probably about five four."

"Do you have a picture of her? We could work from that."

"No, I don't."

"That bad, huh?"

You have no idea, Josie said silently. Out loud, she told him, "She destroyed every picture there was of her in the house before she left."

At the time, Josie had thought it was exactly in keeping with the kind of spiteful, vengeful monster her mother had always been—mostly because the only photos Josie had of her mother also had her father in them. Josie remembered coming home to find the whole trailer smelling of smoke, and finding the last slivers of photographs in a pile of ashes in the stainless-steel kitchen sink. Belinda hadn't left Josie a single photo of her father. Back then, Josie figured her mother was just trying to hurt her, like she always did, but now she wondered if there was a more sinister reason for destroying the photos. It sure didn't make Josie's job of tracking her down any easier.

"What about your dad?" Noah asked. "Would he have any?"

"He passed away when I was six."

She waited for more questions, and her body went loose with relief when they didn't come. Instead, moving to the other side of the car and starting on the handles there, Noah said, "I'm sorry to hear that. Well, look, we can talk more about your mom later if it turns out we need to find her. Right now, I think the first order of business is to confirm the dental records. We'll have a look at the chart Gretchen's pulling and go from there."

CHAPTER 14

Josie's mother paced the cramped curtained area. One hand pressed against her heart while the other clutched a tissue, dabbing at the tears that fell freely from worried eyes. Josie stared at her, shocked and confused to see her mother cry for the very first time.

"I was sleeping," she explained. "I woke up to go to the bathroom and went in to check on JoJo. She wasn't in her bed, so I searched the trailer. Didn't find her. The back door was unlocked, so I got a flashlight and went looking for her. I found her lying on the ground in the woods, covered in blood." A wail tore from her throat. "My baby. My little baby. She was just co-co-covered in it."

Josie glanced at the two nurses watching her mother cry, their faces unreadable.

"She must have fallen," Josie's mother went on. "I mean, it was dark and those woods are filled with trash and glass, all kinds of things children can hurt themselves on."

"Did you ask her what happened?" one of the nurses asked in the same kind of voice Josie's kindergarten teacher used when the students didn't put all their stuff into their cubbyholes.

"Of-of course I did," Josie's mother said. "She told me she fell. That's how I know she fell."

The two nurses exchanged a skeptical look. Then one of them said, "The doctor will be in soon."

They left, one of them tossing a concerned look over her shoulder at Josie before disappearing through the curtain.

Seconds later, Josie's chin was gripped tightly in her mother's hand, fingers squeezing against the bone and pulling at the skin around her wound. Her eyes watered with the pain. "Mo-mommy," she gasped.

Her mother's blue eyes were almost black with fury. When she spoke in an angry whisper, spittle sprayed across Josie's nose. "You don't say one fucking word, you got that?"

"You told lies." Josie squeaked through the part of her mouth that was still mobile.

Her mother's fingers tightened, making Josie feel like her face would tear apart.

"I told you to shut up. Not one word. What I say is what happened, you got that? If you tell one person—just one person— what happened, you're going into the closet. Forever. And Daddy and Gram won't be able to save you. You understand that?"

Fear set her entire body into a quiver, and she felt a hot wetness spread down her legs and through her nightdress. She whispered, "I promise." At last, her mother let go, moving to the other side of the room to peek through the curtain. Hugging herself, Josie wished she had thought to bring Wolfie. Then she remembered—the last time she saw him he had been lying just out of reach in a puddle of her blood on the kitchen floor.

CHAPTER 15

Noah had done a good job cleaning up Josie's door handles, but she was still convinced that the smell clung to her. Standing beside him in the morgue, she sniffed the air but could only smell the chemical odor of death that saturated Dr. Feist's small basement empire. They had stopped for coffee on the way, but now Josie held her full paper cup in one hand, feeling too queasy to drink it.

Dr. Feist breezed into the room with Gretchen in tow and headed over to the ancient x-ray viewer that hung on the wall. Dr. Feist snapped it on, and the fluorescent lights inside flickered to life. She took two films from Gretchen and hung them side by side. It didn't take an expert to see that the dental x-rays Dr. Feist had taken during Belinda Rose's autopsy were a perfect match to the ones that Gretchen had retrieved from the dentist. Josie's heart skipped painfully in her chest; if Belinda Rose had been buried in the woods for over thirty years, who the hell was the woman who called herself Josie's mother?

"Well," Dr. Feist said, turning back to the officers. "Now you've got your victim's identity. Guess you just have to find her killer."

"How old was she when those x-rays were taken?" Josie asked Gretchen.

Gretchen put her reading glasses on and riffled through the thin file she had brought with her. "Looks like the last exam was done when she was fourteen years old."

"What else is in that file?" Josie asked.

Gretchen shuffled more pages around, frowning.

"What is it?" Noah asked.

"Looks like she was a ward of the state," Gretchen said. "There's a notation here. She lived in a group foster home in Bellewood."

Bellewood, the county seat, was forty miles away from Denton. Josie crossed the room and peered over Gretchen's shoulder, studying the address. "That place was torn down when I was in high school. There's a strip mall there now. Is there a contact listed? Someone had to bring her to her dental appointments, sign off on treatment and stuff."

Gretchen turned a page. "Maggie Smith."

"Let's find her. If she's still alive. We'll write up some warrants and see if we can get this girl's file from Child Services," Josie instructed.

Noah stepped forward. "I'll run Belinda's name through the databases." He glanced at Josie. "We think someone might have been using her identity after she was killed."

CHAPTER 16

It seemed like an eternity before the doctor came. He was young—he looked young like her daddy—and he asked a lot of questions. Her mother answered them all with the same sad, tear-stained face she used when she talked to the nurses.

"What about Josie's father?" he asked. "Where was he when all this happened?"

"He works overnight at the gas station out by the interstate."

"Have you called him?"

Josie's mother gave a wavering smile. "For a little cut? No, I didn't want to bother him."

The doctor raised an eyebrow and walked to the bed where Josie lay. Gently, he lifted Josie's hair and leaned in, studying the side of her face. He frowned at Josie's mother. "This is not a little cut, Ms. Rose. I'm afraid your daughter is going to require several stitches."

Josie's heart did a somersault. Tears threatened, and she concentrated as hard as she could on holding them back. The doctor's palm was warm on her shoulder. When she looked up at him, he smiled. "I'm going to give you some medicine so they won't hurt, okay, sweetie?"

She nodded, not sure whether to believe him or not.

The doctor looked at Josie's mother again. "I think Josie's father should be here. Why don't you go call him?"

Alone with Josie, the doctor called in another nurse, and they asked her a lot of questions: Did her mommy hurt her?

How did she get the cut? What was she doing in the woods, and was there another person there who hurt her? And last of all, was she scared of her mommy? Josie knew better than to tell the truth. She kept mumbling, "I fell," again and again like a broken toy. At first the lie was hard, but the more she said it, the easier it became, until it was as normal as breathing and her body didn't know she was lying anymore.

The doctors and nurses insisted on checking her limbs and torso for injuries as well, and they asked more questions until Josie could barely keep her eyes open. By the time the doctor started the stitches, Josie didn't even care what they were or whether they would hurt. She just wanted to go to sleep. She didn't have to be held down. No one had to tell her to hold still. She just turned on her side and closed her eyes. The doctor was right. She felt the needle he gave her to make her face numb, but that was it. She didn't feel a thing.

Her daddy came while the doctor was hard at work on her cheek. She knew he was there because she could hear him fighting with her mother outside the curtain. She only heard some of the words he said. "You ... your fault ... sick ... leaving ... never see ... police ... abuse ... custody ... hate you."

CHAPTER 17

Josie sat behind her desk at the station house, laptop open before her. Gretchen was off writing warrants to get the Department of Human Services foster care file on Belinda Rose. Noah was getting more coffee. Josie opened up the first of several databases to enter in Belinda Rose's information, but her hands froze over the keyboard. Her scalp prickled. Once she started down this road, there would be no turning back. She had hoped to leave her mother firmly in her past, but that was impossible now. The Denton Police Department had a murder to solve. They needed to know who the girl buried in the woods had been. Since Josie's mother had clearly stolen the girl's identity sometime after her death, there was little choice but to track her down, or at least find a connection between the two women.

The door to her office swung open, and Noah stepped through, a steaming mug of coffee in one hand. She nearly lunged for it. He laughed. "Whoa! Feeling a little tired, are you?"

Curling both palms around the mug, she sat back down in her chair and sipped it. "Looking for a distraction," she said. "Close the door."

The sounds of her officers moving about in the bullpen outside receded as Noah clicked the door shut. He sat in the chair across from her and raised a brow. "What's going on, Boss?"

"I'm trying to figure out a way to solve this murder without actually having to get back in contact with my mother."

"Not sure that's possible," Noah said. "You know we have

to follow all the leads, and if your mother was using this girl's identity—not that long after the murder—that makes her a significant person of interest. I mean, Belinda Rose doesn't show up on any of our missing persons lists, so how would your mother have known so soon after her death that she could use her identity?"

Josie put her mug down on the desk and traced the rim of it with her index finger, keeping her eyes on the steam rising from inside the mug instead of on Noah. "I understand what you're saying."

He waited a beat. Then he asked, "You have no interest in finding out who your mom really was?"

Josie met his eyes. Her fingers reached up and pulled her black hair down over the long scar on the right side of her face. She swallowed once to quell the dryness in her throat. "Oh, I know who she really was."

But I don't know if I want the rest of the world to know, she added silently.

"Boss," Noah said.

"Yeah."

"You know who you are too. Don't forget that."

It was exactly what she needed to hear, delivered perfectly.

"Thank you," she said.

Noah leaned forward, pulled a rolled-up bunch of papers out of his back pocket, smoothed it out, and pushed it across her desk. "I already did a search using the name Belinda Rose with the October 15, 1966 birthdate to look for a last known address."

Josie snapped her laptop closed and looked at the report. As her eyes roved over the addresses associated with Belinda Rose, Noah stood and moved around the desk next to her. He pointed to the first address, which Josie recognized immediately. "This was the foster home run by Maggie Smith," he said. "We're still trying to track her down. I've got Lamay running some searches. He'll have something for us soon—as long as she's still alive."

Noah's fingers continued moving down the list. "The next address was an apartment in Fairfield. The real Belinda Rose would have been eighteen when she lived there."

"That's almost an hour away from Bellewood, in Lenore County," Josie said. "I wonder if she actually lived there, or if she was already dead by then. It might have been my mother living in that apartment under her name."

"I'm sure we'll be able to make a better guess as to when she died once we have the DHS file and once we talk with Smith," Noah said.

"Look at this," Josie said. She pointed below the Fairfield address. "She had a bunch of apartments throughout Alcott and Lenore Counties before she came to the trailer park—all of them at least forty miles away from Bellewood, if not more. Well before my mother came to the trailer park. I don't think this is the real Belinda Rose." Josie remembered vividly how often and how abruptly her mother came and went, abandoning her for months at a time and then returning when she least expected it like a tornado tearing through her life, destroying everything.

"Okay, so we know it was your mom who lived in the trailer park," Noah said. "And you think these half-dozen apartments before that were probably her too. Should I have someone go out to these buildings and talk to landlords?"

Josie leaned back in her chair and took another swig of coffee. "I'm not sure it's worth it," she said. "That was over thirty years ago. Some of these places might not even be standing anymore."

"Nosy neighbors?" Noah suggested.

"Make some inquiries," Josie instructed. "You never know."

"Is there anyone still living in the trailer park who would remember her?"

"I doubt it," Josie said. "But you can send someone over to ask around."

There is someone, she thought to herself, *though he isn't at the trailer park anymore.* Josie didn't even know if he was still alive; she hadn't thought about Dexter McMann in sixteen years, had put that entire episode out of her mind, just as she tried to do with everything else connected to her mother. She doubted he would know more than she did anyway. She didn't want to turn that slippery stone over unless she absolutely had to.

"I think we really need to look at where she went after the trailer park, and there's only one address listed for Belinda Rose after that," Josie said.

According to the report, the year that Josie turned fifteen, her mother had lived in an apartment in Philadelphia, two hours away from Denton. "After that, there's nothing," Josie added. "She used this identity until 2002, and then stopped."

"Maybe she died," Noah said.

"I wouldn't be that lucky," Josie mumbled.

"What's that?"

"Nothing, nothing. She must have found another identity to assume. Or went back to her real identity—whatever that is."

"Did she have any family?" Noah asked.

Josie shook her head. "No. I mean, if she did, she never told me about them. I was a kid. I never asked her." *I tried not to talk to her at all.*

"I'll send someone to all the places on this list, see if we can come up with anything," Noah said. "Even if we don't find anything that way, we'll dig into the real Belinda Rose's life. Maybe they knew one another."

CHAPTER 18

Fingers trailed over Josie's scalp, stroking her hair gently. Nestled in her bed, her small hands clutched the fuzzy pink blanket her gram had given her for Christmas. It was her favorite thing in the world after Wolfie. Poor Wolfie, she hadn't seen him since the night at the hospital.

"JoJo," her daddy whispered.

Her eyes snapped open and she smiled, a hot spike of pain shooting from her ear all the way down to her chin, making her wince. She'd nearly forgotten. Her daddy's face floated above her bed, half-smiling, half-worried. She knew his worried look. One of his eyebrows always went up like a fuzzy caterpillar bending in the middle. Reaching up, she traced a finger over it, trying to smooth it down.

"Daddy," she said. "Is it wake-up time?"

Again, he brushed her hair away from her face, careful to avoid the dressing. "No, honey, it's still nighttime."

"Don't you have to go to work?" Josie asked.

He smiled, and his worried caterpillar brow arched more. "Not tonight, sweetie. I need to talk to you. We're going to go to Gram's, okay?"

"Will Mommy come?" she asked.

Her daddy looked away from her, at the closed door, and then back. "No. Mommy's staying here."

Josie tried to hide how happy this made her.

"JoJo," her daddy said, shifting on the edge of her bed. "I

need you to be very quiet, okay? At least until we get out to my truck. Can you do that for me?"

Wide-eyed, Josie nodded.

He got up and walked over to a small duffel bag near the door, shoving things into it—her clothes and toys. She was just about to ask how long they were going to be at Gram's house, when there was a thump against her bedroom door. Both of them jumped. Her daddy turned just as another loud blow shook the door. Then her mother's voice shouted, "Goddamnit, Eli, what are you doing in there?"

Her daddy didn't answer. He just stood there in the middle of Josie's room, duffel bag in one hand.

"Unlock this door, Eli. Right now," she snarled.

"Daddy," Josie whispered. "I'm scared."

CHAPTER 19

One week later, Josie found Gretchen and Noah standing awkwardly in front of her desk. "What do you mean we have a
problem?" she asked.

Noah sat in the guest chair while Gretchen began pacing,
her notepad in hand. She took out a pair of reading glasses and
perched them on the bridge of her nose before flipping a few
pages. She read off the names of every person she had talked
to at the Department of Human Services. None of them meant
anything to Josie.

"Stop," Josie said. "You're telling me you talked to all of
those people, and they *all* told you the same thing?"

Gretchen looked up at her. "Yes. The Belinda Rose file is not
there. The Department of Human Services does not have it."

"Not there?" Noah asked. "Meaning it could be somewhere
else? Do they have off-site storage?"

"No, they don't. All the county records are stored in one
place—at the main office in Bellewood—and Belinda Rose's
file is not among them," Gretchen said.

"So, they lost it," Josie said.

"They wouldn't go that far," Gretchen replied.

Noah laughed. "Which means they lost it. Or it was
destroyed somehow, and they don't want to take the heat."

Josie ran a hand through her hair. "Okay, well, surely they
had some kind of file for Maggie Smith. She ran the home
Belinda lived in."

Gretchen waved her pen in the air. "Yes. That's the only

lead we've got at this point. Turns out Maggie Smith got married in the late '90s, moved on from the foster home program, and became Maggie Lane. She and her husband traveled the country in an RV until he died of a heart attack."

"That was in her personnel file?" Noah asked, perplexed.

Gretchen smiled. "No, I got that from one of the DHS workers. Office gossip. She was new to the office when Maggie left to get married. Maggie had been running the group home for almost thirty years, so it was quite the hot topic of conversation at the time."

Josie asked, "How old was Maggie when she got married?"

"In her sixties. That was the other reason for all the gossip. She waited her whole life to get married, and then her husband was dead within ten years. It's terrible."

"She gave up her position at the group home in the late '90s," Josie remarked. "That was twenty years ago. Which means she would be in her mid-eighties. Is she—is she still alive?"

"Yes," Gretchen said. "She is currently a resident at Rockview Ridge, right here in Denton."

CHAPTER 20

Josie pulled the covers over her head, curling into the tightest ball she could manage. Smaller, she needed to be smaller. The shouts from just outside her door punched through the air, penetrating the flimsy wood and slapping against her small bed. Again, Josie wished she had Wolfie.

"She is my daughter too, Belinda," her daddy said.

"So what? You're just going to take her and leave me? Leave me here alone?"

"I told you last week this wasn't working."

Her mother's voice became a screech. "Go then. Leave!"

Something thudded against Josie's door. She squeezed her body tighter, pressing her forehead to her knees.

"I'm taking my daughter," her daddy said.

"She's not yours! She's mine!"

"The hell she is."

There was a series of thuds and then a crash, and Josie heard what sounded like glass breaking. Then her mother's voice, mean this time, like the way it sounded in the hospital when she grabbed Josie's face. "I told you, you're not taking her. She stays here with me."

"You forfeited your right to be her parent when you put a blade against her face. You think I don't know you did that? Twenty-seven stitches, you sadistic bitch."

"You can't prove a goddamn thing. Now get out. You're not taking her."

"Get out of my way, Belinda."

"You think you can take the only thing I have and leave?"

"That's what I'm doing, isn't it? You've got some real serious problems, Belinda. Josie's not safe here. I'm taking her to my mother's."

"Oh sure, run to your mommy."

Josie heard a rustling, then a thump. Then her daddy said, "I don't want to hurt you, Belinda, but I will if it means protecting Josie. I'm taking her. Now get out of my way."

Her mother laughed, and Josie's body stiffened. Her heart felt like it was taking too long between beats.

More crashing. Then her daddy's voice came again, and this time he sounded different. "Belinda," he said. "Where did you get that?"

"You're not taking her, Eli."

"Let's talk about this."

More of her mother's laughter. Josie felt a strange feeling like she might pee herself. She tried to hold it in. Her mother would be *really* mad if she wet the bed.

"Oh, sure, now you want to talk," came her mother's voice from the other side of the door.

"But not here," her daddy said. "Let's take a walk, okay? Get some fresh air? We can talk this through."

"We can talk all you want, Eli, but you're not taking her."

CHAPTER 21

Sitting high on a rock-strewn hill at the edge of town, Rockview Ridge was Denton's one and only skilled nursing facility. Josie's grandmother, Lisette Matson, had been a resident there for several years now. Lisette was Josie's last living relative—besides Josie's mother—and her best friend. Josie visited her regularly and knew exactly where to find her at this time of day. She spotted Lisette's silver curls the moment she walked into Rockview's cafeteria; lunch was over, but several residents lingered, reading magazines, watching the communal television and, like Lisette, playing cards. She looked up and smiled, waving Josie over.

"You're never here this early in the day," she said as Josie leaned in for a kiss.

"I know. Work stuff." Josie took a seat across from her grandmother.

A game of solitaire was spread out before Lisette. She snapped a card down onto one of the piles and said, "I guess you don't have time to play."

"Sorry, Gram. Listen, I need to ask you some questions."

Lisette frowned. "Is everything okay? What's going on?"

Josie reached across the table and patted Lisette's hand. "Don't worry. No one is missing, or shot, or dead. Okay, well, that's not entirely true."

She told Lisette about the discovery of the real Belinda Rose's remains behind the trailer park. "We believe that my mother stole this girl's identity. I need you to tell me everything you remember about her."

Lisette's gaze slipped to the table. Slowly, she gathered her cards and began shuffling them. "Josie," she said, and her tone filled Josie with dread. It was the tone she had used when she caught Josie drinking at age sixteen, the tone she had used when she found out that Josie and Ray were having sex; it was her warning tone, the tone that said, "I can't stop you from traveling the path you're on, but I'm telling you to be careful."

Josie's heart did a quick double tap. "Gram," she said softly. "If my mother did something to this girl, I have to know."

Lisette still didn't look at her. "That woman is best left in your past, Josie. Have you forgotten how hard it was to get her out of our lives?"

"Of course I haven't. Believe me, if I had a choice, I would run screaming in the other direction. I don't even care that she's not who she said she was—but I have a murder to solve, and she has a connection to the victim."

Lisette stopped shuffling and placed her deck on the table, tapping the sides one by one until the cards were in perfect order. Josie thought she saw her eyes glisten over.

"Gram, please."

Suddenly her grandmother's fingers were digging into Josie's forearm with a strength and fierceness that belied her eighty-five years. Eyes wide, voice low, Lisette leaned in and said, "You think I don't know the things she did to you, Josie?"

Josie resisted the urge to pull away, even as pain spiked through her arm. "Don't," she choked out.

"I know, Josie. I know about what she did."

"Please, Gram. Don't."

"That's why I fought so hard for you. That's why I did the things I did. You remember that."

Josie couldn't catch her breath. Lisette's fingers dug in deeper, and Josie swore she felt her skin bruising.

"I should have killed her when I had the chance," Lisette added.

"Gram!"

Josie looked around, but none of the residents in the room were paying attention, and Gretchen, who had accompanied her to the home, was still at the front desk making inquiries about Maggie Lane.

"I would have," Lisette went on. "I wanted to, believe me. It would have been the best thing for all of us, but I was afraid I'd get caught and then you'd have no one."

Josie peeled her grandmother's fingers from her arm one by one and placed Lisette's hand on the table. "Gram, please. That's in the past. Just like you said. I'm not trying to resurrect all of that, but this case has to be solved."

"You can't be the one, Josie. You have to stay away from her. You've got officers beneath you. Let them do this."

Josie covered Lisette's hand with her own. "And they'll come in here and ask you the same questions I'm about to ask. I'm the chief of police, Gram. No, I don't have to lead the investigation, but I do have to oversee it. Just tell me what you can remember."

"You promise to stay away from her?" Lisette said.

"As much as I can," Josie answered.

Lisette pulled her hand away and stared down at her lap. "I don't know much more than you do, I'm afraid. Your father brought her over a few times in the beginning, introduced her as Belinda Rose. We had no reason to disbelieve her."

"What about her past?" Josie asked. "Did she ever talk about family or where she was from?"

Lisette was silent for a moment, and Josie could tell by the way her gaze drifted upward to the ceiling that she was searching her memory for any scraps that remained from before Josie's birth. "She didn't have any family," Lisette said. "That's what she said. Grew up in foster care. I remember that because I felt sorry for her. She was quite beautiful, your mother. When I met her, she was young, and I remember wondering why wouldn't any family adopt such a sweet, pretty girl?" She humphed. "Well, now we both know why. Unfortunately."

"I thought I heard her tell people her family was dead," Josie said.

Lisette shrugged. "She told a lot of different stories. She told your father and me that she had grown up in foster care. But after she left, I talked with the attorney who represented her in all the custody disputes. He said he didn't even know where to begin looking for her because she'd told him that her entire family perished in a house fire."

"Did she ever say where she was from?"

"Bellewood. Said she grew up around there, but that she had been moved from home to home all over the state."

"Did she have friends? A job?"

"No friends that I ever met. She used to clean houses though, I remember that."

"For a company or on her own?"

"Oh, I don't remember. I didn't ask. She stopped working after you were born anyway."

"Where did she and my father meet?"

Lisette gave a wan smile. "Where else? A bar. There used to be one down the way from the trailer park, but it was torn down ages ago."

"The trailer we lived in—whose was it?"

"Your father's. Well, he rented it from the park owner. When he died, she just kept making the payments. The owner tried to charge me for the damage to the place when she left since it was still in Eli's name."

"Do you know if she lived in the trailer park also? Before she met Dad?"

"I really don't know, love," Lisette answered. "I don't think she did. Your father said there were a lot of drugs in the park back then. He always worried about that with you. I wanted him to move back in with me after you were born, but he said your mother wouldn't allow it. Anyway, I think maybe she knew people from the bar who lived in the trailer park or went there to get high."

Josie sighed. The bar her grandmother referred to was long gone, and the drug activity that had plagued the trailer park had been eradicated during Chief Harris's tenure. Josie could have someone canvass the park, but she doubted anyone would have useful information sixteen years after the fact. Besides, by the time Josie's mother met her father, she had already been using the Belinda Rose identity for over a year, at least.

"Gram, do you have any photos of her?"

Lisette's mouth formed a straight line. A moment later, she said, "I don't think so. Your mother didn't like having her photo taken, and back then we didn't have phones with cameras, so we didn't take pictures every single day of our lives. We had actual cameras with rolls of film that had to be developed, and that cost money—"

"Gram," Josie said, trying to keep Lisette on track.

Lisette smiled. "I'll give you my photo albums before you leave, and you can go through them."

Gretchen appeared in the doorway of the cafeteria. She nodded at Lisette, and Lisette waved back at her. "You're not just here to talk to me, are you?" Lisette asked Josie.

"I'm afraid not, Gram. Do you know Maggie Lane?"

"I know who she is—she doesn't come out of her room much. Had a stroke a couple of years ago and hasn't felt like socializing since. Therapy brought her brain and her speech back, but she doesn't get around very well now. Only ever talked about her husband, and he's been gone a few years now. Don't worry, she's still lucid, but I think she's just one of those who's waiting to die. I can take you to her room if you like?"

CHAPTER 22

Her mother shook her from sleep, pinching Josie's shoulder so hard that pain shot all the way down her arm. Josie opened her bleary eyes to see her mother's face floating above her in the lamplight. "JoJo," she whispered. "Wake up."

Josie felt her body stiffen. Slowly she sat up in the bed and looked at her mother. Strands of her mother's black hair floated around her head. Frizzies, her mother called them. They only appeared when it rained. Wet black streaks ran down each of her cheeks. She was crying.

Something was wrong. Very wrong.

"Mommy?" Josie said.

Her mother's soft, sympathetic smile punched fear into Josie's heart faster than if she'd held the shiny knife to Josie's face again. "Wh-where's Daddy?" Josie asked.

Her mother shifted on the bed and took Josie's hand. "Baby, I'm so sorry... your daddy did something very bad tonight."

Josie stared at her, confused. "What happened?"

Her hand gently stroked Josie's forearm, causing the hairs to stand to attention. Josie suddenly wished her mother wouldn't answer; each word of her reply was like a barb in Josie's skin.

"Your daddy left us tonight, JoJo. He's gone forever and ever. Do you know what it means when someone dies?"

Josie didn't answer, but she sort of knew. She knew that when people died they went to a place called heaven. That's what her daddy and her gram said. Heaven was really, really good, except that you didn't get to see your family anymore.

CHAPTER 23

Frail and thin, Maggie Lane sat hunched in a wheelchair, her long gray hair tied back in a ponytail. Although Josie knew Maggie was about the same age as her grandmother, time had been far less kind to her. Maggie's face seemed to have twice as many wrinkles as Lisette's, and her hands curled in her lap, fingers knobby and bent permanently inward toward her palms. Contractures, Josie knew they were called—when the joints or muscles shortened from lack of movement, causing permanent deformities. Josie glanced at Maggie's feet, turned inward toward one another in a pair of plain white sneakers, and suspected she probably had them in her feet as well.

Maggie raised her head up as Josie and Gretchen entered the room, and Lisette shuffled off back to the cafeteria with her walker. "Mrs. Lane," Gretchen said.

Maggie stared at them, her rheumy eyes flitting back and forth between the two unexpected visitors. Her wheelchair was sandwiched between her bed and a small dresser. Beside the dresser was a recliner, which Gretchen sat in while Josie remained standing. They introduced themselves, and Gretchen explained that they were there to talk to her about a girl who used to be in her care.

"In my care?" she said in a voice that sounded scratchy, perhaps from years of smoking cigarettes.

"A girl who lived with you in the group home on Powell Street in Bellewood," Gretchen said. "This would have been the late '70s, early '80s. Her name was Belinda Rose." Gretchen pulled out her trusty notepad and flipped through a few pages. "Birthday, October 15th."

Maggie lifted a gnarled hand and waved it. "I remember Belli. That's what I called her. Sweet thing. Till she got to be a teenager. Then she was hell on wheels."

Gretchen and Josie exchanged a look. Josie said, "How long did she live with you?"

A series of coughs erupted from her lungs, causing her whole body to shudder. Just as Josie was wondering if she should fetch one of the nurses, Maggie settled. "When I got Belli, she was about five. She was in a couple of foster homes before that, with families looking to adopt her, but it never worked out. One of them foster dads had different ideas about raising a girl, if you know what I mean."

Josie's stomach turned.

"So, you got her at five," Gretchen said. "Did they tell you anything about her real parents? Why she was in foster care to begin with?"

"Well, they don't tell you much, but if I'm remembering correctly, she was one of the girls that came from a couple of teenagers fooling around who weren't ready to be parents. Back then, having kids when you was a kid was . . . what do they say? Frowned upon. So we got quite a few kids come to us from teenage parents."

"What was she like?" Josie asked.

Maggie smiled, and her top dentures slipped a bit. She clamped her mouth shut, sucking them back into place. Then she said, "Sweet. She was a sweet one. Liked to help me around the home. Liked to do things for the other girls. Could always count on her for chores and such. She was affectionate too. A lot of those girls didn't have no affection growing up, and so they didn't want none or give it out. Some of them been hurt real bad—only knew a 'bad touch,' if you know what I'm sayin'."

"You said Belinda was a sweet girl until she became a teenager," Gretchen said. "What happened then?"

Maggie shrugged. Her shoulder blades rose as if she were going to have another coughing fit, but when she exhaled, all that came out was a long wheeze. She replied, "Don't know, really. Sometimes girls just go bad once they get a certain age. She started failing in school, staying out past curfew, smoking and drinking. Police caught her out in the woods drinking with some other kids a bunch of times."

In that part of Pennsylvania, it seemed every high school had an area out in the woods where teens congregated to get drunk or high, smoke cigarettes, or simply cut school. When Josie was in high school, they all went to a place known as The Stacks, a spot where multiple slabs of rock had fallen from the side of a mountain in stacks. "So, she went to school in Belle-wood?" Josie asked.

"All my girls did," Maggie answered.

"Do you remember any of the kids she hung around with?" Gretchen asked.

"Had plenty of girls of my own to keep track of," Maggie said. "I couldn't be doing with their friends."

Josie said, "What about the girls in your care? Was she close to any of them?"

Maggie's lungs whistled again. She held up a hand, and they waited several seconds for her to catch her breath and speak again. "Not really. She kept to herself. She shared a room with Angie...oh dear, I don't remember her last name, although she went and got married after college, moved out by Philadelphia. Belli was closer to Angie than any of them."

If Angie had gone to college, gotten married, and moved to Philadelphia, then she wasn't Josie's mother. Still, they'd find her and see what she knew about Belinda and the people she associated with. "I'm sure we can track Angie down through the old files," Josie said. "That's very helpful."

Gretchen asked, "What did Belinda look like?"

"My Belli was short and chunky, with the curliest blond hair you ever saw. A nuisance it was."

"How long was she in your care?" Gretchen asked.

"Well, she was supposed to be with me till she was eighteen, but she ran away a couple of times."

Again, Josie's and Gretchen's eyes met. "When was that?" Josie asked Maggie.

Maggie leaned her head back and gave a tired sigh. Her face was ashen. The interview was taking a lot out of her. "Well, once for a few months when she was about fifteen or sixteen. Can't remember exactly. I was so mad at her. Someone at the high school had got her this job at the courthouse doing filing and answering phones a few hours a week. She did so well at first and was bringing in her own money. She stopped cutting school, stayed out of trouble, mostly. But she started fighting with my other girls a lot."

"About what?" Gretchen asked.

Another shrug. "Who knows? What do teenage girls fight about? There were always squabbles about their things—this one used the other one's hairbrush, that one took the other one's sweater. Then the other girls said she thought she was better than them 'cause she had a fancy job. Silly kid stuff. Then they teased her 'cause she put on some weight after she started working. She started eating everything in sight; I couldn't keep up. I never got paid that much for any of my girls. I had to stretch what little the state gave me to feed all of them. Anyway, we had a fight 'cause I said she was eating me out of house and home, and she started crying and ran off. Came back a few months later."

"Was she still overweight when she returned?" Josie asked.

"A little. But she'd calmed down a bit."

Gretchen wrote something down in her notebook, and Josie knew she was marking the timeline. Belinda Rose had suddenly gained weight and started overeating after working at the courthouse for a while. She'd left and come back thinner and with less of an appetite. Perhaps it hadn't been obvious to Maggie, but Josie knew exactly what had happened. "Mrs. Lane, did Belinda ever have any . . . health issues?"

Maggie turned her head in Josie's direction. "What do you mean, health problems?"

Josie shrugged. "I don't know. Anything."

Gretchen saw where Josie was trying to go and reached forward, placing a palm on Maggie's thin forearm. "Mrs. Lane, we have reason to believe that Belinda may have given birth at some point."

Maggie stared at her, uncomprehending. Then she laughed, her thin shoulders bouncing. "You're mistaken," she told Gretchen. "Belli never had no baby."

Gretchen looked to Josie, and Josie gave a swift shake of her head. Clearly, Maggie hadn't known about the pregnancy, so there was no point in pursuing that line of questioning with her. Gretchen asked, "Did you report her missing?"

"Course I did," Maggie said. "I had to. Police never found her. One day she just came back."

"Did she talk about where she had been?" Gretchen asked.

"No, and I didn't have time to pry it out of her. I had a lot of girls, and if you don't know, teenage girls aren't exactly easy."

"Mrs. Lane, can you try to remember exactly when that was? Was Belinda fifteen or sixteen?" Josie asked.

Maggie sucked on her upper dentures again. "Sixteen. She just turned sixteen."

"So, it was the fall?" Gretchen prodded.

She took a moment, then said, "It must have been. It was real cold. I remember 'cause we had all these extra heaters in the house, and I was afraid one of my girls was gonna start a fire with 'em. It was right before Christmas too. They were all just waitin' for that Christmas break to come, but holidays were hard 'cause they were all foster kids. A lot of 'em got depressed around the holidays—led to a lot more fights. I hate to say it, but when Belli ran off that first time, it was sort of a relief."

So Belinda Rose had been fairly late in her pregnancy in the fall of 1982, just after she turned sixteen, and had gone off to give birth and returned with no one the wiser.

"Can you tell me," Gretchen asked, "did she have a boyfriend? Any lads she hung around with regularly or was interested in?"

"There was one she went to high school with. Oh, what was his name? Lonnie or Lyle or something. He had two first names."

Josie suppressed a groan. "Lloyd Todd?"

Maggie raised an arthritic finger in the air. "Yes, that's it! They were together almost a year."

Josie knew that Lloyd Todd had grown up in Bellewood. He had moved to Denton when he started his business, because Denton was significantly larger than Bellewood and offered many more clients for both his contracting business and his drug venture.

Gretchen made another notation. "You said the first time— when did she go missing the second time?"

"Couple years later. She was seventeen; had about six months to go till she was eighteen. I remember 'cause we were trying hard to figure out what she was gonna do after she aged out. She wanted to stay with me, but I told her she couldn't. It was around Easter, I remember that. She went to work at the courthouse after school like she always did. She was supposed to be home around seven, but she never came back. I called the police again, made a report."

"We've checked records for the entire county," Josie said. "She's not listed as a missing person."

"Oh, 'cause she's not, dear. I got a postcard from her a few months after she left. It was after her eighteenth birthday, so she was free to do what she wanted. Never gave an address and never came to pick up any of her stuff though."

Josie felt a tingle race up her spine. "Where was the postcard from?"

"Philadelphia. Said she was sorry she left suddenly, but she met a man there and they were getting married. Thanked me for everything."

Gretchen said, "You don't still have that postcard by any chance, do you?"

Maggie laughed. "Oh honey, I didn't keep anything from my care home days once I married my husband. We took the RV on the road. Wasn't a lot of room for nostalgia. But I did give it to the police so they could mark their case closed."

CHAPTER 24

JOSIE – SEVEN YEARS OLD

Josie woke, thrashing and sweat-covered from a nightmare. Her eyes snapped open, and she had a moment of terror at the unfamiliar surroundings before the fog of sleep receded and she remembered where she was—at Gram's house, in Gram's bed. Ever since her daddy died, she had been staying here. She had her own room, but she usually preferred to curl up beside Gram. Josie sat up and blinked, her hands searching the bed covers for her grandmother's warmth, but it wasn't there.

"Gram?" she called.

There was no answer. Fear wrapped its calloused fingers around her heart, squeezing hard. She climbed down from the bed and tiptoed along the hallway toward the sliver of light coming from beneath the bathroom door. As she got closer, she heard her grandmother wailing, a high-pitched keening sound that made goosebumps break out all over her skin. She stood frozen in the hall, wondering if she should knock or call out to her. The pressure in her chest got tighter, and she ran back to Gram's bed and pulled the covers all the way over her head. She wished more than anything that her daddy would come back from heaven, but deep down she knew she would never see him again.

She was just wondering if Wolfie was in heaven with him when she heard her gram's footsteps in the hall. Josie shut her eyes and pretended to be asleep when Gram returned, not moving an inch when she climbed back into bed and wrapped her arms tightly around her.

When she woke, Gram was gone again, and sunlight streamed through the windows of the bedroom. Hearing voices downstairs, Josie hopped out of bed and went to the top of the steps to listen.

The sound of her mother's voice made Josie's whole body go cold. "She's mine. You'll never get her, Lisette."

"Please, Belinda," answered her gram. "She's happy here. I'll take care of her."

"Over my dead body," Josie's mother said. Then she shouted, "JoJo! Come down here."

Slowly, like her limbs were moving through mud, Josie made her way down the stairs. Her mother smiled at her. Not in the scary way she sometimes did just before she did something mean, but in the way she did on the rare occasion that she was nice to Josie—like when she gave her the coloring book. She knelt so that she was face to face with Josie and gently smoothed Josie's hair out of her eyes. "JoJo, you want to come home with Mommy, right?"

Josie didn't know what to say. She didn't want to leave Gram, but she liked it when her mother was nice to her. When she didn't answer, her mother said, "I've missed you, JoJo. Don't you want to come home with me? We'll color and play games and do girl stuff together; what do you say?"

Josie looked at Gram, whose face had gone all stiff.

"JoJo?" her mother said.

She wanted to do all those things with her mother. They could play hide and seek and tag, and maybe they could paint their nails together. One of Josie's friends from school had spa days with her mother where they played with makeup and did each other's hair. Josie wanted that more than anything.

Josie nodded, and before she knew it, her mother was stuffing her into the passenger's seat of her blue Chevette and slamming the door. Josie looked up to where Gram stood on the porch, tears glittering in her eyes, waving slowly. Josie's mother got into the driver's side and started the engine.

"Mommy," Josie said. "I forgot my clothes and my blanket."

"Shut up, JoJo."

CHAPTER 25

It took nearly four hours to get their hands on the Belinda Rose file. Josie considered it a miracle that the tiny Bellewood Police Department still had it. Their chief was gracious enough to let Josie, Noah, and Gretchen search their dusty back room filled with old, closed files. It didn't appear that they had ever thrown anything away.

"Gotta love small-town departments," Noah remarked as he pulled box after box off the storage shelves for Josie and Gretchen to look through.

Josie was just beginning to lose hope of ever finding it when she finally put her fingers on it. The ink on the yellowed file tab was so faded that Josie could barely make it out, but there it was: Belinda Rose.

After signing the requisite forms, the three of them left with the file in hand and headed back to their own station house, Gretchen sneezing the entire time from the hours spent kicking up dust. Josie's eyes burned like hell. They rode most of the way back to Denton with the windows of Josie's Escape all the way down, letting the cool March air blow away the past for a little while.

Once in Josie's office, they spread the contents of the file across her desk. It was thin, and the reports were faded and typewritten with an old-fashioned typewriter. There wasn't much more than what Maggie Lane had told them. Josie noted the names of the officers who had taken the two missing persons reports. A quick call to Bellewood PD revealed that both had retired long ago.

"Here," Noah said, plucking an old color photograph from the pile of pages. It was slightly bigger than an index card and showed a heavyset teenage girl standing in the small garden outside the care home. Sunlight streamed down on her, the light bouncing off her tight blond curls, and she squinted against it, smiling. A shapeless floral-print dress draped over her large middle, stopping midway down two pale, thick thighs. Josie saw the strap of a backpack on one shoulder, and in one of her hands she held a brown paper bag.

"First day of school," Gretchen said.

Josie took the photo from Noah's hand and turned it over. Someone had written *September 1982.*

"She was pregnant in this photo," Josie said. "If we've got our timeline correct."

"Is there another photo?" Gretchen asked, her fingers shuffling the contents of the file once more. "From before the second time she ran away?"

Josie found it paper-clipped to a second set of reports that had been prepared over a year after the first set. In the photo, Belinda was descending a flight of stairs in what Josie guessed was the foster home—the background was all dark wood paneling and ratty gray carpet. The photo didn't look posed for as the last one had—more like someone had caught her coming down the steps and snapped the photo. Belinda was considerably smaller and thinner than in the first photo they had found—she looked half the size she had been in September of 1982. Her hair hadn't changed; tight blond ringlets hung to her shoulders, offering a splash of life to the otherwise drab background. Without the sunlight in her face, her blue eyes shone wide and clear over a thin smile. This time she wore a tight pair of jeans and the same nylon windbreaker that Dr. Feist had unearthed along with her body. Peeking out from the collar of the jacket was a small gold locket in the shape of a heart.

"Look at that," Josie said, pointing to it. "That wasn't found in the grave."

"Maybe she wasn't wearing it when she died," Gretchen offered.

"She was a foster kid. It's quite a nice locket," Josie pointed out.

"Could be costume jewelry, Boss," Noah pointed out.

"It could also be important," Josie insisted.

She herself hadn't grown up in foster care, but her situation hadn't been much better; not until after her mother left. Josie hadn't owned jewelry even remotely as nice as that locket until she'd turned eighteen, when Ray had given her a diamond pendant he'd saved up for months to buy. She'd worn it nonstop through most of college. She still had it.

"Gretchen," Josie said, "when we're done here, take a picture of this photo with your phone and go back to Rockview and talk to Maggie Lane. She said that Belinda left her things the second time she disappeared. Ask her if this locket was among them, would you?"

"Sure thing, Boss," Gretchen said, snapping a picture of the photo with her cell phone.

"When was that picture taken?" Noah asked.

Josie took the photo back from Gretchen, turned it over, and read off the month and year. "March 1984."

"Maggie said she went missing around Easter in 1984," Gretchen said, bringing up the internet browser on her phone. Josie watched over her shoulder as she punched in her query. "Easter was April 22nd of that year," Gretchen added.

Josie picked up the report that Maggie had made. "This is dated the 26th," she said.

"So we can estimate the date of the murder then," Noah said. "Sometime on or after April 26, 1984."

"Yeah, but that doesn't tell us anything about who did it," Josie answered. "But there are names here of people who were interviewed back then. Here—" she snatched up another piece of paper. "They interviewed Lloyd Todd and his brother, Damon." She skimmed the faded typewritten words. "Lloyd said they'd been dating on and off since early 1983, broke things off around Christmas of 1983. He saw her at school that day and she seemed fine. He was at track and field practice that evening. His brother and father confirmed this as they were both at the athletic field that night too."

"It's going to be impossible to talk to Lloyd Todd," Gretchen noted. "I mean, he's in county jail right now awaiting trial. No way is he going to talk to any cops about anything without his lawyer."

Josie nodded. "He might not even agree to speak with us. Track down the brother then. If the Bellewood PD thought he was worth interviewing back then, maybe he can help us now."

Gretchen marked down the brother's name on her notepad. Then she said, "There are some names of people she worked with at the courthouse here too."

"Track them down as well," Josie said. "Someone might know who she used to hang around with. Also, see if the DHS has a list of all the girls under Maggie Lane's care for the time period that Belinda was there. I want names and photos if you can get them. Track as many of them down as you can. I want the most complete picture we can get of this girl's life in the months before she was killed."

Noah searched through the rest of the file as Josie spoke. Finally, he came up with a postcard. The Liberty Bell took up one side, the words *Greetings from Philadelphia* in red letters above it. He handed it to Josie, and she turned it over, staring at the writing on the back of it while her blood turned to ice in her veins.

Maggie: I'm sorry I left without telling you. I met the most wonderful man. We're in love! He's whisked me away to Philadelphia and we're getting married! Please don't worry about me. Thank you for everything! Belinda

It was dated the day after Belinda Rose's eighteenth birthday, postmarked out of Philadelphia, and written in Josie's mother's handwriting.

CHAPTER 26

Josie's stomach clenched and burned. She didn't remember ever being so hungry. Her mother hadn't come out of her room in days. Inside the fort of sheets she had made in her bedroom, her belly groaned and felt like it was trying to fold in on itself. She squeezed her eyes shut and pressed her hands together, whispering, "Dear God in heaven, please bring my daddy back, and Wolfie too, and let me see Gram again, and also please bring more food for me and my mommy."

As she said the words, she heard voices outside her door. Her mother and a man; it must be Needle. She couldn't hear what they were saying, but she heard them walk past her door, and then heard her mother's bedroom door close.

Then she smelled it. Pizza. It was unmistakable, and her favorite. The smell of it filled her mouth with saliva. As quietly as she could, she opened her door and snuck into the hallway. Her feet were light and soundless on the worn carpet that led from the hall into the living room, ending at the kitchen tile.

The big white box sat on the kitchen table, smells of deliciousness seeping from its creases. Josie's stomach made a noise so loud, she was sure her mother and Needle heard it. But no sound came from the back of the trailer. She climbed onto a kitchen chair and opened the box. Glancing back to make sure they were still in the bedroom, she picked up a slice that seemed bigger than her head and started eating. She ate until she felt sick and woozy but fuller than she had felt in weeks.

She was on her third slice when a hand came down hard on the back of her head, knocking her from the chair she squatted on.

"Jesus, Belinda," Needle said as her mother grabbed her by the arm and dragged her out of the kitchen.

"Did I say you could eat that pizza?"

Josie said nothing. Her throat felt like it was full of concrete. Tears stung the backs of her eyes, and she concentrated as hard as she could on not letting them fall.

"Belinda," Needle said. "Come on."

"You shut up," she told him.

The closet door opened in front of Josie, coats hanging from a bar above a dusty, brown bit of carpet. It smelled like cigarette smoke and stale air. Josie screamed, "No! Mommy, no!"

Josie's mother pushed her inside. "Shut up."

The carpet was scratchy against Josie's cheek. "Mommy, you said," Josie choked out, unable to stop the tears now, "you said if I didn't tell, I wouldn't have to go in the closet. Mommy!"

Needle said, "Jesus, Belinda. She's a kid."

Her mother pointed a finger at Needle. "You stay out of it."

"Mommy, please!" Josie cried.

Then the door slammed shut, and the darkness closed in all around her.

CHAPTER 27

"Are you sure this is your mother's handwriting?" Noah asked.

Josie plopped into her chair, the first painful throbs of a headache starting behind her eyes. When Josie didn't answer him, he said, "Do you have a sample? Something that has her handwriting on it so we could compare?"

"I don't need a sample," Josie said.

From the guest chair in front of Josie's desk, Gretchen said, "Lieutenant Fraley, did you learn to forge your parents' signatures when you were a teenager?"

He looked at her. "What? No. Why would I need to forge their signatures?"

Gretchen shook her head, a look of mock sadness turning the corners of her mouth downward. "Well," she said gravely, "you must come from a long line of goody-goodies."

In spite of herself, Josie laughed long and loud, grateful to Gretchen for easing the tension in the room. Josie felt the tight muscles in her shoulder blades loosen a fraction as she laughed.

Noah raised a brow. "What?"

Josie said, "You're kidding, right? You can't forge *either* one of your parents' signatures?"

His gaze snapped from Gretchen to Josie. "No. What are you—"

Gretchen cut him off by standing and flipping her open notebook to face him. Josie stood so she could see the page too. On it, in two radically different types of handwriting, Gretchen had written: *Agnes Palmer* and *Fred Palmer*. "My grandparents' signatures," she offered. "I lived with them during high school. How do you think I successfully cut school seventeen days of my senior year?"

Noah shook his head, but a small smile played on his lips. "So you were an overachiever then, were you?"

Gretchen slapped his shoulder with her notebook but laughed just the same.

Josie took a piece of paper out of the printer on the corner of her desk and signed her mother's name as she had known it: *Belinda Rose*.

Both Gretchen and Noah stared at it, wide-eyed. It was a near-perfect match to the handwriting on the postcard. "I started cutting school when I was twelve," Josie explained. "Also, my mom wasn't around much, and she didn't care about school or doctor's appointments or much else when it came to me, so learning to forge her signature came in pretty handy until she left. Then when I moved in with my grandmother, she caught me trying to learn her handwriting and grounded me for a week."

The levity in the room leached away as Josie placed her forged signature next to the postcard. She didn't look at her officers. The throbbing behind her eyes had become a full-on pounding, like a heartbeat. She choked out the words, "Looks like my mother just graduated from person of interest to prime suspect."

CHAPTER 28

Josie pounded her fists against the closet door. "Mommy, please!" she cried. "I have to finish my homework."

There was the sound of something sliding across the living room carpet, then a bang against the closet door. Josie jumped back. The shard of light at the bottom of the door disappeared. Her breath froze in her lungs. The last few times she'd locked Josie in the closet, her mother had pushed one of the living room chairs up against the door so Josie couldn't get out.

Josie put her hand in front of her face, but she couldn't see it. Her heart pounded so hard, the sound seemed to fill up the tiny dark space. She sank to the floor, curling into a ball and trying desperately to think of things that made her feel happy, like visiting Gram and going to school. The thought of school made tears sting her eyes; her teacher was going to be disappointed in her when her homework wasn't finished. It was so unfair. She hadn't even done anything wrong. She'd come home from school and started her homework, then her mother had stormed in like a tornado, tossing Josie into the closet like an old coat.

When Josie heard the muffled voice of a man, she suddenly understood why. One of her mother's special friends was there. Josie always had to go into the closet when they came. Sweet-smelling smoke wafted under the door and made her dizzy. The man's voice was loud and angry. "I told you to have my fucking money, Belinda," he said. "Where's my money?"

It wasn't Needle. Josie had heard this man's voice before, but she had never seen his face.

Her mother said, "Relax. I told you, I'm good for it."

"No, you're not. If you were good for it, you would have it and I wouldn't have to wait. What do you think this is? I don't give shit away for free. What do you have? What can you give me right now?"

There was the sound of rustling, drawers being pulled out, things being knocked over. Then her mother said, "All I got is seven dollars."

A louder sound came; a heavy crash. Josie heard her mother cry out. When she next spoke, her voice sounded all squeezed and strange. "Come...on...let go...we'll work something out, I promise."

"Oh yeah? Like what? I want payment now, and I'm going to get it one way or another."

"You know what—I don't have money, but there are other things I can do to pay you back."

"Yeah? Like what?"

"I have a girl. You can take her in the back. Do whatever you want."

"What do you mean, a girl?"

"What do you think I mean? A kid. You can have her. I'll talk to her. She'll do whatever you want."

"How old?"

Her mother didn't answer.

"Wait a minute," the man said. "You mean that little kid? The one with dark hair just like you?"

"I only got one kid," said her mother.

There was a long, silent moment. Josie knew they were talking about her, but she didn't understand what they were saying.

When the man spoke next, his voice was filled with disgust. For a moment, he reminded Josie of the way her daddy talked to her mother near the end, before he went away to heaven. "Are you kidding me? You're kidding, right? You think I'm some kind of pervert?"

"No, no. I didn't say that."

"I don't mess with little kids. That's disgusting. You're fucked up, you know that? Give me my shit back."

Josie heard crashing sounds, grunts, gasps, and then her mother, breathless, begging, "No, please. I can pay you. Just wait." There was more rustling, the sound of a zipper being pulled down, and then the man took in a sharp breath. Josie's mother said, "I can take care of the payment myself."

CHAPTER 29

"You didn't find any pictures of your mother in your grand-mother's photo albums?" Gretchen asked.

Josie stared straight ahead from her place in the passenger's seat of Gretchen's department-issue Cruze. "I found two photos of her in profile—she was with my dad—but that was it. In both, her face was turned too far away from the camera for them to be of any use to us. My grandmother never liked her and never got along with her, so I'm not surprised she didn't take that many photos of her."

"Sounds like a lot of people didn't get along with her," Gretchen noted.

Josie turned her gaze toward the window, watching the working-class neighborhoods of Denton give way to the more affluent areas. They were entering the mayor's neighborhood, where the houses stood tall and regal on acres of meticulously kept land. Apparently, Damon Todd had also moved from Bellewood to Denton after high school, and had done quite well for himself. It had only taken Gretchen a day to locate him, and when she called him, he had agreed to speak to them with the understanding that it had nothing to do with the charges pending against his brother.

When Josie didn't speak, Gretchen said, "Boss, I know you don't want to talk about her, and I don't need to know...the things she did, but I am one of the lead investigators on this case. It would help if I had a better idea of what she was like."

Josie knew Gretchen was right. In any investigation Josie

ran herself, she would ask family members the same questions. You had to know who you were dealing with—what you were walking into when the day came to confront the person you were hunting.

Gretchen pulled over in front of a large white-and-brick colonial with pillars holding up a portico, bougainvillea lining the front of it. She turned the car off and shifted in her seat, pulling her polo shirt from where it was tucked into her khaki pants and lifting it up, revealing pale flesh beneath.

"What are you doing?" Josie asked.

Gretchen was in her forties and carried some excess weight around her middle. Rolls of doughy skin jostled as she lifted her shirt up to just beneath her breasts.

"Gretchen," Josie said, slightly alarmed. "I don't think—"

She stopped speaking when she saw the scars. They crisscrossed Gretchen's upper abdomen, some of them silver and thin and others purple-pink and thick like cords of rope. "Exploratory abdominal surgery," Gretchen explained. "Do you know what Munchausen by proxy is?"

Josie swallowed. "That's that syndrome where parents make their children sick for attention?"

Gretchen smiled and lowered her shirt, tucking it back into her waistband. "Yes, exactly."

"Your—your mother did that to you?" Josie asked.

Gretchen shook her head. "No, various doctors did it over many years. My mother made them think I needed it."

"I'm so sorry," Josie said, feeling stunned, as though Gretchen had just punched her. Gretchen was notoriously private. She had been with them almost a year, and no one knew anything about her. Most of the time she wore a beat-up leather jacket that, combined with her short, spiked hair, gave her the look of a biker, but as far as Josie knew, she didn't own a motorcycle. The jacket clearly had a story behind it, but no one on the police force had had the nerve to ask about it. Josie understood this need for privacy; she was the same way. Gretchen had always done her job well, and neither Josie nor anyone else on the team had felt the need to pry.

"Look," Gretchen said, "I know this stuff isn't easy to talk about. It's not easy to bare your scars, yeah?"

Josie swallowed and gave a stiff nod.

"Even when those scars are here." Gretchen tapped an index finger to her temple. "Or here," she added, tapping the same finger against her heart. "But I know a thing or two about toxic mothers."

"How did—when did your mother stop?" Josie asked.

"When she killed my sister," Gretchen said. "She's been in prison ever since. Muncy. Inmate number OY8977."

Josie said nothing.

The front door of the colonial opened, and a tall man in his late forties with wavy salt-and-pepper hair walked toward the car.

"Well," Josie said as she opened her door, "maybe my mother will join her."

Gretchen smiled as she opened her own door. They met Damon Todd halfway up his driveway and made introductions. Up close, Josie could see that he was good-looking for his age—tan and fit with an easy smile. The polar opposite of his burly, gristle-faced brother. He wore a blue polo shirt and khaki pants, as if he were about to head out golfing. He invited them inside, walking them through a large, high-ceilinged foyer with bags of sports equipment pushed up against one wall.

Damon smiled sheepishly as he motioned to it. "Sorry. I've got three teenage boys and they all play sports—and now I've got Lloyd's boys as well. The foyer is kind of the dumping ground when they come in."

To the left of the foyer was the living room. The hardwood floors were dominated by a gray microfiber U-shaped sectional that faced a large television. Josie counted three different video game systems on the entertainment center beneath the television. The sleek, dark coffee table with matching pedestal tables on either side of the room boasted faux floral arrangements. Between those and the heavy, gray, pleated drapes, it was obvious that the messy, sports-loving Todd men still had a woman in their lives. Josie knew from the research that Gretchen had done that Damon was now a physical therapist who worked closely with the student athletes on Denton University's campus.

"So," Damon said, taking a seat on one side of the sectional. "You're here to talk about Belinda Rose. I always wondered what happened to her."

"I'm sorry to tell you that she was murdered," Gretchen said, taking a seat across from him. Josie remained standing.

Beneath the tan, Damon's skin paled. "What? When...How?"

"We believe she was killed sometime on or after the night she disappeared," Josie cut in. "April 26, 1984."

His brow furrowed. "Disappeared? Word at school was she met someone, and they ran off to Philadelphia together. How do you know she was murdered?"

"We recently found her remains in the woods out behind the trailer park," Josie answered.

He hung his head. "My God. I don't know what to say." They gave him a moment. He took in a few breaths, and when he looked back up at them, he said, "What does this have to do with me?"

Gretchen said, "We're trying to get a picture of Belinda's life before she died—who she hung around with, what she was like, places she went, that sort of thing."

"Oh, well, we didn't know each other that well."

"Her foster mother said she dated your brother, Lloyd," Josie said. "Your brother gave a statement to a police officer after she disappeared stating he was her boyfriend, and you confirmed it."

"I wouldn't have said that, and neither would Lloyd. Maybe that's what the police inferred. That's what everyone inferred. I mean, people just assumed that."

Gretchen asked, "Why would people assume that Belinda and Lloyd were dating?"

"And why would Lloyd let them?" Josie added.

He clasped his large hands together and pressed them between his knees. "Well, she spent a lot of time at our house junior year."

"But she and Lloyd weren't an item?" Gretchen said.

"No, not the two of them."

"Then who? You and Belinda?"

His mouth twisted. "I guess it doesn't matter now," he mumbled, almost to himself.

"What doesn't matter, Mr. Todd?" Josie asked.

"Belinda was seeing our dad," he blurted. The effort of pushing the words out seemed to make him short of breath.

Josie and Gretchen looked at one another. Then Josie said, "Your dad?"

"He's dead now," Damon said. "Died a few years back of pancreatic cancer. He was an algebra teacher at the high school. Back then, my mom had left us right before my freshman year, so it was just the three of us—me, Lloyd, and Dad. He was tutoring Belinda after school, and things...progressed."

"That's one way of putting it," Gretchen said. Her notebook was out, and she began frantically making notes. "When did the affair start?"

"Right before the summer after sophomore year."

"1983?" Gretchen asked.

"Yeah. That's right. It was the summer before she disappeared."

"Did you or Lloyd ever talk to her or your dad about what was going on?" Josie asked.

"We tried. We were both pretty disgusted with him. I mean, we weren't ready for him to date at all, let alone carry on an affair with someone we went to school with. Lloyd was furious. I thought him and my dad were going to come to blows over it, but my dad made it clear he wasn't going to stop seeing her, and finally Lloyd just gave up. They didn't speak for a long while. I tried reasoning with Dad, but he said it was something I couldn't understand until I was older. He said we could be mad at him all we wanted, but he only asked that we not tell anyone, because it would ruin his career and he could go to jail."

Josie and Gretchen stared at him.

He spread his hands in a plaintive gesture. "Look, I know it sounds terrible. Looking back, I realize how bad it was, but Lloyd and I were kids. All we had was my dad. If he went to prison, we'd be on our own. I think that's why Lloyd stopped fighting with him over it. He kept saying it would fizzle out eventually and that as upsetting as it was, it wasn't worth our dad going to jail, so I just kind of...fell in line."

"What about Belinda?" Gretchen asked. "Did you ever talk to her about their relationship?"

"Yeah, a couple times. She said she wouldn't stop seeing my dad and asked me not to tell anyone. She said Lloyd had already agreed to do the same. Like I said, ultimately, Lloyd didn't want our dad to go to jail. He was in the same year as Belinda, so when people assumed that she was coming over here to see him all the time, we let them think that. She told people at school she and Lloyd were a thing, and he didn't deny it. She followed him around, and even though he barely gave her the time of day, people saw them together and just assumed they were an item. You know, she had...this is going to sound strange, but she had fangs. Only on the top. They weren't even really noticeable, but by high school, almost everyone knew she had them."

"It was noted in the autopsy," Josie said. "Supernumerary teeth."

"Is that what they're called? Sorry. No disrespect intended. I only bring it up because she got made fun of a lot in school for them. She didn't have a lot of friends—none, really—and when Lloyd didn't deny that they were together and let her follow him around, all of the teasing stopped. I think sometimes she didn't want to bother with guys her own age because all they ever did was pick on her. She never said that. That's just my take on it. I mean, I told her she should be dating someone her own age, but she said—" He broke off and looked away from them.

"She said what?" Josie prompted.

"She said she liked older men—that they were nicer to her and more sophisticated and treated her better. She made it sound like she'd been with older men before."

Gretchen's pen hovered over her notepad. "Did she name anyone?"

Damon shook his head. "No. I thought she was making it up, trying to make herself seem more mature."

"Did your father ever give Belinda any gifts? Jewelry or anything like that?" Josie asked.

"No. He wouldn't have. He was pretty paranoid about being caught. People knew he was single, so if he bought jewelry, the town would have been talking. She always wore this locket 'round her neck, but it wasn't from him."

Josie narrowed her eyes. "Really? Did she ever say who gave it to her?"

"I never asked her, and she never talked about it. Lloyd didn't care enough about her to ask her. The other girls at school would bring it up sometimes, but she just said it was from someone special, and that's all she would say. I used to think maybe she bought it herself. Belinda was a nice person, but she liked attention, and the more mystery she could surround herself with, the more attention she drew."

"Mr. Todd," Josie said. "Did Belinda ever mention being pregnant or having had a baby?"

His eyes widened. "What? No. Never."

Josie knew that Belinda's affair with Damon Todd's father would have started four or five months after she'd given birth, but it was worth a try to see if perhaps she had mentioned it to Damon. Josie wondered if Belinda had hidden the pregnancy from everyone. Had she had even one friend to confide in? Would anyone out there know what had happened to the baby?

"So, what happened between Belinda and your father?" Gretchen asked, picking up the line of questioning once more.

"Oh, it didn't last. By the time the new year came around, they were finished."

"Who broke it off?" Gretchen asked.

"She did. My dad was crushed. I think he really liked her. She would have been eighteen that fall. They could have been together for real—at least that's what my dad kept saying. Took him months to stop talking about her. Then that fall there were rumors around town that she had met some guy in Philadelphia and was getting married. I never saw my dad so depressed— well, except for when my mom left."

"Where did these rumors come from?" Josie asked.

"One of the girls who'd lived at the care home with her was in her senior year, and after their foster mom got a postcard from Belinda, it was all the girls at the home could talk about. Word spread from there. Eventually my dad overheard some of the kids talking about it in class."

"Do you remember any of the names of the girls she lived with at the care home?" Josie asked.

He rattled off a few of them, mostly first names that were so common they'd be impossible to track down with any accuracy. But within a few days, they'd have the list of former care home girls from the Department of Human Services, and they'd be able to match those names with the names Damon remembered.

"I know you said she didn't have many friends, but do you remember if she had any close friends that she hung around with? Most teenage girls have at least one."

"I'm sorry, but no, I can't think of anyone. She wasn't popular, and she didn't really have friends at school—other than the girls who lived at the care home. I mean, if she had friends outside of school, I don't know. She had a job at the courthouse—she might have made friends there that I didn't know about. Like I said, she was seeing my dad. It was weird. We covered for them, but it wasn't like her and I were friends, you know? You could always check the yearbooks. All the girls from the foster home went to Bellewood High."

Josie wanted to kick herself for not thinking of it. "The yearbooks," she said. "Does the school keep copies that far back?"

"I don't know, but if you want, you can have my dad's. He kept one for every year he taught. They're in the garage with a bunch of his other stuff. I didn't know what to do with them. Seemed wrong to throw them away."

Gretchen stood up. "That would be great, Mr. Todd. We would certainly appreciate it."

"Sure. My wife will be happy to be rid of them."

CHAPTER 30

Josie dragged a piece of blue chalk across the sidewalk outside of her grandmother's home. A series of squares stretched from one end of the pavement to the other in a pattern: two squares, then one, then two, then one, and so on. They played hopscotch at school all the time, but Josie had never drawn the boxes before. She'd squealed with delight when her grandmother presented her with a pack of colored sidewalk chalk. There were four colors: blue, pink, yellow, and green. Josie liked blue best of all, so that's what she started with. Once the boxes were all complete, she went to one end and started jumping. One foot, two feet, one foot, two feet—all the way to the end.

"Josie," her grandmother called from the front door. "Time to get ready."

Carefully, she put her chalk back inside its cardboard box and skipped up the front walk and inside.

"Wash your hands," Lisette told her.

Josie ran to the kitchen and did as she was told. "Do you think I'll fall, Gram?" she asked.

Lisette smiled as she pulled their jackets from the closet in the front hallway. "Probably. Everyone falls their first time roller skating. It's unavoidable."

Josie dried her hands on the dish towel and ran to Lisette so she could slide her jacket on. "How long does it take to get to the skating rink?"

"Oh, not long," Lisette told her, picking up her purse and keys. "Maybe ten minutes."

"Did you remember the present?" Josie asked.

Lisette picked up a brightly wrapped birthday present from the foyer table. "Of course, dear."

"I can't wait!" Josie exclaimed. "I never got invited to anyone's birthday before. Especially not at a skating rink!"

A bright smile stretched across Lisette's face. She knew Josie had been looking forward to this for two whole weeks. It was all they talked about. Lisette had even said that she might put skates on.

Her smile died the moment she opened the front door. Josie's mother stood on the stoop in a pair of torn jeans and a dirty blue T-shirt that hung off one shoulder. A cigarette smoldered in one hand. Her cheeks were sunken, and her long, black hair looked dull. She smiled a mirthless smile that sent a chill all the way down Josie's spine.

CHAPTER 31

Josie and Gretchen lugged several boxes of Bellewood High School yearbooks back to Josie's office at the station house. While Gretchen went to check on the warrants, Josie pored over the yearbooks from 1981 through 1985, looking for her mother's face among the hundreds of photos.

"There's nothing here," she said when Noah appeared.

He sat across from her. "So, she didn't go to school with Belinda Rose. We still have the care home girls, and I set up an interview tomorrow with a lady from the courthouse who worked there at the same time as Belinda."

With a sigh, Josie pushed the last yearbook away and spun her chair to look out the window behind her desk. Night had fallen, which meant it was time for her to go home, alone, to her empty house, a bottle of Wild Turkey, and the now stirred-up memories of a mother whose greatest kindness to her had been to leave.

"You okay, Boss?"

She spun back around and offered him a wan smile. "Fine," she lied. "What's up?"

"Maggie Lane says that Belinda's locket was not among the personal effects left behind at the care home. She says she doesn't know who gave it to her, but Belinda started wearing it around Christmas after the first time she ran off. I already had someone go back to the crime scene and take another look. Nothing turned up."

"Interesting," Josie said. "Maybe we'll find out more when we track down some of the girls who grew up with her."

"Hopefully." He motioned toward the dark window behind her. "It's pretty late, Boss."

"I know."

Noah was always looking out for her. She thought about asking him to go for a drink, but decided against it. Two years ago, she'd had an easy answer to this cloying sense of dread and anxiety: sex. Two years ago, she'd been in a committed relationship where sex with her fiancé was readily available, uncomplicated, and—above all—numbing. Her body yearned for the kind of physical sensation that would blot out the blackness creeping into her head. She knew Noah wouldn't say no, the same way she knew it was a bad idea. She pushed the thought away; she didn't need to make her life any more complicated. She stood and fished under the piles of yearbooks for her car keys.

"I'm going home," she said. "I'll see you tomorrow? I'd like to be there for the courthouse interview."

"You got it."

Josie left the station behind, wending her way through Denton's quiet streets, her mind on the bottle of Wild Turkey waiting on top of her fridge—the next best thing to sex—but she knew something was wrong as soon as she pulled into her driveway. The lights in her bedroom windows glowed bright and gold in the darkness.

Someone was in her house.

CHAPTER 32

"Belinda," Lisette said, her voice sounding odd and stilted. "What are you doing here?"

"What do you think I'm doing here, Lisette? I came to get my kid."

Lisette glanced at Josie, and Josie took a step behind her grandmother. "Just like that? You left her here, Belinda, without a word. It's been months. Almost the entire school year!"

Her mother rolled her eyes. "So what? She's my kid." She extended a hand toward Josie. "Let's go, JoJo."

"Belinda, this coming and going, it's not good for Josie. She needs stability."

"Just shut up, Lisette, would you? No one asked you what you think."

Lisette's voice shook with anger. "You don't need to ask me what I think. You leave this child on my doorstep whenever you get tired of raising her. That means I'm involved. I'm her grandmother. I love her. I want her here."

"And I'm her mother. And I'll do whatever the hell I want. Now come on, JoJo. I said let's go."

Lisette didn't move. Her body blocked Josie from stepping toward her mother. "She's doing well here, Belinda. Her grades are up, she's happy. She's made friends at school. Just let her stay."

"Goddamnit, Lisette. Give me my kid."

"Just listen. Just let her finish the school year here with me."

Josie's mother put a hand on her thin hip and narrowed her eyes at Lisette. "I said no. Now I'm taking my daughter and we're going home."

"Belinda, please."

"Don't push me, bitch. I can make sure you never see her again."

It was then that Josie realized she wouldn't get to go to the skating party after all. She had been making calculations in her head as the two women went back and forth. There had been times that her mother agreed to do what her Gram asked, but those times were few and far between. Josie knew that this time, her mother would win. She could tell by the smoldering look in her dark blue eyes and the way she held her whole body stiff like a sharp edge. Josie was headed back to the old, smelly trailer and the dark, lonely closet. To hunger and the sounds of her mother's special friends moving in and out of the trailer at all hours. She had been silly to think she could do what other kids did. Silly to think she could have real friends. Now everyone in her class would be talking about the skating party but her. Well, her and that boy Ray who was always nice to her. She would be left out again, and she wouldn't even have her Gram to console her. Tears welled up in her eyes, but she held them back. Lisette put a hand on Josie's arm, but Josie knew it didn't matter.

"Okay," Lisette said. "Fine. Take her, but at least let her go to her friend's birthday party. We were on our way there now." Lisette held up the gift. "I even bought a present. It will only be a few hours. I'll take her and then drop her off to you afterward."

Her mother pushed Lisette aside and clamped a hand down on Josie's bicep, yanking her across the threshold. "I don't give a damn about some stupid kid's birthday party. Let's go, JoJo. And you, Lisette, I don't know who you think you are, trying to make decisions about my daughter's life. You'll never get her. I'll never let you have her. You just remember that."

CHAPTER 33

After calling in a robbery in progress, Josie parked across the street under a neighbor's large oak tree. She got her bulletproof vest out of the back of her Escape, strapping it on before checking her Glock. After that, she circled the house twice, her steps silent, her movements covered by darkness. She knew where her own motion sensor lights were and carefully avoided them. It only took one lap to figure out that whoever was in her house had broken in through one of her kitchen windows.

Anger boiled inside her, warring with the anxiety that raged beside it. Who was in her house? What were they doing in there? Just the thought of strangers in her private space, touching her things, felt like a violation. She had bought the house with her own money after she'd left Ray. It was huge and airy, with plenty of windows to let in the sunshine—the exact opposite of the coffinlike trailer she had grown up in. This home held only good memories for her. It was her safe place in a world that never ceased to horrify her—her sanctuary. Or it used to be, until tonight.

She was pulled from her thoughts by the arrival of two marked units, followed closely by Noah in his own vehicle. Vest already on, Noah jogged over to her, checked his weapon, and signaled for the uniformed officers to join them. They formed a small knot behind her Escape, heads bent together as Josie gave instructions. "There are two points of entry—front and back. The screen door out back is locked from the inside, so there's no getting in there from the outside—at least not quietly.

They broke in through a kitchen window out back. I have no idea how many are in there, or if they're armed. I couldn't hear anything. Please exercise extreme caution." She held out a set of keys, which Noah took from her. "We'll go in the front using these. Lieutenant Fraley and me on one team, and two of you on another. You two stay out here and keep eyes on the house. Lieutenant, you have a notebook?"

Noah pulled a folded notepad from his back pocket. One of the other officers handed her a pen. She quickly scratched out a diagram of the layout of her house. "Lights are on here," she said, pointing to the square representing her bedroom. "Fraley and I go this way, you two go that way; we clear the first floor and then go to the second and proceed down this hall."

Nods all around.

Adrenaline shot through Josie's bloodstream as she and Noah crept up to the front door, followed by two of her uniforms. She'd done this dozens of times before, but never in her own home. Again, fear pushed itself to the front of her mind.

"Boss." Noah's whisper interrupted her thoughts.

She had to keep focus. This was just a regular house with potential burglars inside it. That was how she had to think of it. She clamped a hand onto Noah's shoulder, and he slid a key into her front door. The door swung open without a sound, and they padded over the threshold in a column, two teams splitting off, moving soundlessly until they met back up at the steps, giving all-clear signals. No one was on the first floor.

As they ascended the stairs, Josie heard the sound of voices—two, from what she could gather. Noah must have thought the same, lifting his hand to signal with his index and middle fingers—two perpetrators—then he pointed down the hall toward the last door, Josie's bedroom, where a sliver of light outlined the doorframe.

The voices coming from within were male. "Yo, is he coming back or what?"

"Nah, he said he got what he needed. We'll just mess this

shit up real good and get going. He said this bitch ain't ever home anyway."

There were three empty rooms between them and the master bedroom—the bathroom, the guest bedroom, and a room full of surveillance equipment Josie used as a home office. Stealthily they checked each of the rooms with flashlights, but each one was dark and empty. Finally Noah stopped outside of Josie's bedroom, and the rest of them stilled behind him. Inside her chest, Josie's heart took two extra beats. Josie gave the hand signal for go, and then they were through the door with a bang, weapons panning the room, voices hollering, "Freeze! Police! Hands up! Get down on the ground!"

Two teenage boys in sweatpants and hoodies froze, dumbstruck. One of them stood on top of her bed, a can of red spray paint in one hand. On the wall above her headboard he had sprayed the letters S, L, and U. Josie guessed the last letter was probably a T. Across from him, the other boy had been yanking drawers out of her dresser and dumping the contents all over the floor. He immediately threw his hands up. The other boy dropped the can in his hand and made to jump down from the bed, only to fall face-first onto the carpet. Within seconds, the uniformed officers had both of them cuffed and ready to be transported to the station. Both teens were read their rights, then patted down, but they had none of Josie's personal property on them.

"Yo, dude," Spray Paint said as the officer pushed him into the hallway. "I hit my head. Hey, be careful all right?"

Her officer said nothing, and the sound of the other boy telling his friend to shut the hell up faded as they were both led out of the house. Josie stood, gun at her side, eyes roving every inch of the room. The word WHORE had been spray-painted on one of the other walls. Most of her pillows had been slashed open, their stuffing pulled out and tossed all over the room. Clothes had been pulled from her closet and strewn everywhere. Muddy boot prints punctuated her clean carpet and her bedspread. The mirror over her dresser was shattered. Her nightstands were overturned, the lamps broken but still lit, casting strange shadows across the destruction. Her jewelry box lay in pieces on the dresser-top.

She strode over and sifted through the remains. "Oh God," she whispered.

Noah put a hand on her shoulder. "Boss," he said, "I think we should have the evidence response team come through. You heard what I heard in the hall, right? There was someone else working with them. You can come through after and figure out if anything is missing."

"My jewelry," she said. She didn't have much, but she had amassed a small collection of earrings, necklaces, and bracelets over the years. Gifts from her grandmother, Ray, and her fiancé Luke when they'd been together. Pieces she'd bought for herself for different events. Most of it she could live without, but there were three pieces of jewelry she owned that she really cared about.

"My wedding ring," she croaked. "My engagement ring from Luke and the diamond pendant Ray gave me when we graduated from high school. They're gone."

She couldn't stop staring at the dark wooden shards spread across her dresser. The jewelry box hadn't even had a lock on it. There was no need to break it, but they had anyway. Why? Why so much destruction? The rest of the house was untouched. Why had they destroyed the room in her home that she loved most? What had they done with her jewelry?

"Those little bastards," Josie blurted. Finally, she looked at Noah.

His face wore an uncomfortable expression. He wanted to comfort her, she realized, but he had a job to do, and he knew she would want him to do his job first. She holstered her weapon but remained in place, staring at Noah, focusing on his face instead of the detritus around her. Gently, he took hold of her elbow and guided her out of the room.

"We'll get to the bottom of this, Boss," he said as they moved down the stairs, his mouth so close to her ear she could feel his breath tickling her hair. "I promise."

CHAPTER 34

Their steps echoed loudly in the halls of the county courthouse. Josie walked behind her mother, cold air flying up the stiff brown skirt her mother had made her wear. She stopped at a water fountain and gulped greedily before her mother could slap her and hiss at her to hurry up. But it didn't come. They were in public, in the courthouse where things were formal and official, and everything was cold and grown-ups stared at you like you were a bug.

"JoJo," her mother said sweetly, smiling. "Let's go, hon."

Josie knew she was the only person who could hear the edge beneath her mother's words. Hanging her head, she followed her mother to a set of large, wooden doors that opened into a huge, shelf-lined room filled with more books than Josie had ever seen. A massive desk sat in the middle of it. In front of the desk, several chairs were lined up. They were divided into sides, and Josie's gram sat in one of them, a man Josie didn't recognize beside her.

Josie followed her mother deeper into the room. Her gram reached over and squeezed Josie in a hug while Josie's mother glared. "Remember what I said," Lisette whispered into her ear before releasing her.

A tiny pinprick of fear spiked Josie's chest. How could she forget?

Her grandmother had decided months ago—after missing the skating party—that she would simply sue Josie's mother for custody. There had been endless meetings and appointments and lots of stuffy grown-ups asking Josie all kinds of questions she knew she couldn't answer honestly. She'd even had to meet with a psychologist. Of course, what none of them understood was that every time Josie was forced to talk to them, it made her mother more enraged and crueler than usual behind closed doors. She was careful not to leave any marks on Josie's body, but she didn't have to—she knew how much the closet terrified her daughter. The only reason Josie had coped with the increasingly long periods of time in the dark cell was the backpack Ray had given her to hide inside the closet. It contained a flashlight, extra batteries, a dog-eared copy of the first *Harry Potter* book, a Stretch Armstrong doll, and a couple of granola bars. As she waited out the endless nights, shivering in her nightdress from fear and cold, Josie liked to imagine that Ray was there with her.

The only good thing to come out of the custody battle was that Josie's mother was forced to let her spend short periods of time with Lisette. It was purely strategic on her mother's part. Josie had overheard her mother's lawyer say that in her petition to the court, Lisette had painted her mother as unreasonable, mean-spirited, and spiteful. He said that allowing Josie to spend time with her grandmother would go a long way toward debunking Lisette's claims. But Josie's time with Lisette was mostly spent being grilled over what her mother did to her. When Lisette realized that Josie would never confess the things that her mother did, she spent the rest of their time together trying to convince Josie that if she told the truth, she would get to live with Lisette forever.

"Josie, this is very important," she had said. "You have to tell the judge what your mother does to you. If you are very brave and tell the truth, your whole life will change. I know you're scared of her, but I'm telling you that you don't need to be. I can help you. I can protect you, but I can only do that if you tell the truth."

But Josie knew that no one could help her. Not her father from heaven, not her grandmother, not the teachers at school or the psychologist she had seen, and certainly not the judge who swept into the room and started shaking everyone's hands.

Josie sat beside her mother, her legs swinging nervously. She reached into the pocket of the cardigan she wore and felt for the Disney figurine Ray had given her. He had pressed the miniature fairy godmother from *Sleeping Beauty* into her hand the day before when they met in the woods between their houses. "Keep it," he told her. "Maybe a real fairy godmother will come and save you."

Now her fist closed around it, and she concentrated hard on the pain in her palm instead of the grown-ups all around her, talking in serious voices about her as though she wasn't there. Nobody had any power over her mother. She may only be ten, but Josie wasn't stupid.

"Miss Matson," the judge said. "Josie Matson."

Her mother leaned in and lightly touched Josie's arm, her hissed threat ringing in Josie's ears: "You be a good girl now, JoJo. Go on."

CHAPTER 35

Josie sat in the viewing room at the station house, staring at a large, closed-circuit television that showed one of the teenage boys they had arrested at her house. A mug of coffee sat untouched on the table beside her. She felt numb and exhausted. Her mind kept returning to the havoc they had wreaked on her bedroom, the window they had broken, the thought that strangers had been inside her home and violated her sanctuary. The door creaked open, and Gretchen stepped through it with a newly minted manila file in her hands.

"This one is Austin Jacks. Nineteen. Graduated from Denton East last year, hasn't been doing a hell of a lot since then. Works part-time at a fast-food place. Got picked up for possession of drug paraphernalia last year, but the charges didn't stick."

"No connection to Lloyd Todd?"

"Not that we can find."

"What about the other one?" Josie asked.

"Ian Colton. He's a minor. Sixteen. He's in holding till his parents get here. He's a junior at Denton East. No record. No arrests. He works with Jacks. That's how they know one another."

Josie doubted that they'd be able to get to Ian Colton. The moment his parents showed up, they'd likely demand a lawyer, who would agree to let Josie's team question the boy but then instruct him not to answer any questions. She saw it all the time.

"Our best bet to find out who else was involved is this kid,"

Josie told Gretchen, motioning to the screen. On it, Austin Jacks fidgeted in his seat. His heels bobbed up and down, drumming an uneasy beat on the floor. His teeth tugged at a hangnail on his thumb while his other hand rubbed the top of his head, brushing back and forth over blond hair that was short like peach fuzz.

"Noah's going in," Gretchen responded, pulling out a chair and sitting down beside Josie.

They watched the boy squirm, his movements growing more frenetic by the second until Noah sauntered in fifteen minutes later. He slid a crushed pack of cigarettes across the table, and Austin snatched them up. A lighter appeared in Noah's hand, and he gave the boy a light before pocketing it and leaning against the wall. Austin sucked in several hungry lung-fuls of smoke, closing his eyes briefly to enjoy it. The fevered movements slowed a little, but not much.

Noah read him his rights again, and Austin acknowledged that he understood them. He didn't ask for a lawyer, so Noah plunged right in. "Do you know whose house you were arrested in earlier tonight?"

The boy shrugged. "Don't know. Some police lady. Don't care."

"Why were you there?"

He blew smoke in Noah's direction. "Why do you think? It don't take a rocket scientist to figure that out."

"You and Ian were there to rob this police lady, and yet nei-ther one of you had any of her personal property on you when we arrested you. How do you explain that?"

His gaze flicked around the room, looking anywhere but at Noah. "You caught us before we could take anything, man."

Noah stepped toward the table. "Her jewelry is missing."

Austin's knees bounced beneath the table. "I don't know what to tell you."

"Who else was there with you?"

Another shrug. "You know who was there—you got him too."

Noah placed both palms on the table and leaned in toward the kid. "We know there was a third guy, Austin. He came and took the jewelry and left you and Ian behind to wreck the place. Who is he?"

A tenuous smile flitted across Austin's face and disappeared. He put out his cigarette in the ashtray Noah had provided and balled his hands up in his lap. "I don't know what you're talking about."

Noah sighed. "Fine. We'll get prints from the kitchen window. It won't take long to run them. Unless Ian tells us first and saves us the time. That kid is scared shitless. I'm sure him and his parents will be interested in the reduced charges the DA is offering for information on the third perp—and for throwing your sorry ass under the bus."

Without hesitation, Noah turned and left the room, leaving Austin's mouth hanging open, his skin paling beneath his acne.

Ten minutes later he stood beneath the eye of the camera, waving both arms. "Hey man, come back," he called. "I got something to say."

CHAPTER 36

JOSIE – TEN YEARS OLD

Josie stood frozen in place until finally a hand pushed her closer to the judge's desk, and her feet shuffled forward until she was nearly touching its edge.

"Young lady," he said, "I'm going to ask you some questions now, and I want you to answer them as truthfully as possible, do you understand?"

Josie nodded. She felt her mother's eyes on her like a white-hot laser beam. Her mother had been smiling for the benefit of the other grown-ups, but Josie had seen the glint in her eye; they both knew that no matter what she told the judge, Josie was going home with her mother. Josie also knew that what she said right now could either make things better for herself, or much worse.

So, she lied.

With each lie that poured from her lips, Lisette's frame crumpled a little bit more beside her. Guilt was a sour taste in the back of Josie's throat, so she looked away from her gram, instead focusing on her mother's face, which shone brighter with satisfaction with each one of Josie's denials.

As expected, the judge said Josie was to return home with her mother, but that Lisette should have visitation rights. Before they left the judge's chambers, Lisette grabbed Josie up in a bear hug, and Josie felt her gram's lips against her ear once more. "I'm not done, Josie. I'll get you away from her. I promise."

When Lisette let go, Josie smiled bravely at her, holding back the tears and digging the point of the plastic fairy godmother's hat deep into her palm. "It's okay, Gram," she told Lisette. "I'll be fine."

Another lie.

CHAPTER 37

Noah made Austin Jacks wait it out, let him sweat. Just when Josie expected him to start climbing the walls like some kind of jumping spider, the door to the room opened and Noah poked his head in. "Was that you hollering?" he asked.

Austin stood beneath the camera and pointed to it. "Yeah, it was me. You don't have someone watching me right now?"

"We're pretty busy right now, Mr. Jacks. I've got to use my people on witnesses who have something to say, like your buddy Ian. What do you need? Bathroom break?"

"You talked to Ian?"

"We're in with him now, yeah," Noah said, already retreating out of the room.

"He told you about the guy under the bridge?" Austin said.

Noah didn't miss a beat. "Yeah, but he said he didn't know the guy's name."

"'Cause we never knew his name," Austin replied. "He's just, like, the guy under the bridge."

Josie knew there were only two bridges in Denton that crossed the Susquehanna River, and only one of them offered enough space and privacy for homeless squatters and drug transactions. Noah knew this as well.

"Austin," Noah said patiently, "there's more than one guy under that bridge. You think we don't run busts down there once a week?"

The kid rubbed his scalp with both hands. "I can tell you what he looks like. You could get, like, an artist or whatever to come in, and I can tell him how to draw the guy. You know, like on TV."

Beside Josie, Gretchen laughed. Everyone thought real-life police work was like what they saw on television, but things like sketch artists cost money. A lot of money. The kind of money no police department would spend on a simple burglary—even for its chief of police.

Noah stepped inside the room, pulling the door closed behind him and motioning for Austin to sit again. This time, the whole chair rattled with his agitation. Noah said, "How about you just tell me what you know about the guy and we'll go from there."

Austin's teeth gnashed on his dirty fingernails. "You gonna help me out, or what? Like with the DA?"

"I can see about some reduced charges, sure."

Annoyance flashed in Austin's eyes. "Reduced charges? Come on, man. You could get me out of here. I didn't even do anything. I mean it wasn't even my idea."

Noah leaned back in his chair, relaxed. "Reduced charges is the best I can do, Austin. I don't make these decisions. You should know, the police lady whose house you broke into was Josie Quinn."

Austin's mouth dropped open. "The chief of police? The hot one who's always on the news?"

"Uh, yeah. We only have one chief of police."

"Shit."

"You see my dilemma? I want to help you out here, but my hands are tied. Unless of course you have some information about Lloyd Todd or any of his associates."

Austin's brow furrowed momentarily. "Who?"

"Lloyd Todd," Noah repeated slowly.

The creases in Austin's forehead deepened. "You mean that big drug dealer you guys busted last month? Todd's Home Construction?"

Noah nodded.

"I don't mess with Lloyd Todd," he said. "Never did."

Noah tapped his fingers on the table as though bored. "How about someone in Todd's crew? They've been pretty pissed since we put him away. Did someone in his organization ask you to do this job?"

Austin shook his head. "Nah, dude. I told you, I never messed with Lloyd Todd. I'm not trying to get involved in all that. I mean, like, one day I want to go to college and shit. Those guys get in deep with him. He like, controls them."

"Yeah, we know. How about your guy under the bridge? He work for Todd?"

"I don't think so. I never saw him talking to any of Todd's guys. He's on his own down there, I'm pretty sure about that."

"What else can you tell me about him?"

Austin rubbed at his cheeks until the skin pinkened. Finally, he said, "Reduced charges, right? What do you want to know?"

"Reduced charges," Noah repeated. "Tell me whatever you know about him."

"He's old, dude. Like, way old."

"Can you estimate his age?"

"I don't know, like fifties or sixties."

Next to Josie, Gretchen let out a lengthy sigh. "Nice to know that fifty is 'like, way old.'"

Josie laughed at her impression of the kid.

"He's really skinny," Austin continued. "I mean, dude's whacked out most of the time. You know Lloyd Todd don't take no whackos. You have to be on point to work for him. Anyway, I think this guy lives under the bridge, like, all the time. He's always got the same old green jacket on, even in the summer."

Noah narrowed his eyes. "I thought you didn't know much about him. Sounds like you see him a lot."

Austin slumped in his chair. "Come on, man. You trying to bust me for something else? So me and Ian go down to the river a lot, okay?"

"To buy drugs," Noah filled in.

"I'm not saying that. You asked me about the guy, I'm telling you about him."

"Okay, he's in his fifties or sixties, skinny, green jacket..."

"Stringy-ass gray hair, wears this old pair of work boots that look about twenty years old."

"You don't know his name?"

Austin shook his head. "The people you see down there—you don't ask for names, you get me?"

"Fair enough. How'd he get involved in your robbery?"

Austin put a hand to his chest, fingers splayed. "My robbery? Dude, that wasn't my robbery. I'm not trying to rob the chief of police and shit. It was his idea."

"Who?"

"The guy under the bridge. We get stuff from him sometimes, you know?"

"What kind of stuff?" Noah asked.

"Like stuff, you know? You really want to know? 'Cause if I tell you, you can't, like, bust me, right?"

Noah sighed. "I'm only interested in what you know about the robbery. I don't care what 'stuff' you were getting from this guy, okay?"

"Okay, okay. We were getting some weed and pills and shit from him—me and Ian—and we were a little behind in payment, so this guy said we could get caught up and get some more stuff if we did a job for him."

"He approached you with it?"

"Yeah, I guess. He said it would be easy. He'd go with us to the house, get us inside, and then we were supposed to take some shit and mess the place up. But there was nothing in there, you know? Nothing this guy wanted. He didn't want electronics or anything. He said to look in the bedroom for jewelry and cash, so we did."

"Who brought the spray paint?"

"He gave it to us. Said we should write something real nasty on the walls."

"So 'slut' and 'whore' were your idea?"

Austin's face flushed. "No, man, not ours. We didn't even know this bitch—I mean the chief. I said to him, 'What do you mean by nasty?' and he said to write 'slut' or 'whore' or something. He said, 'Bitches don't like to be called slut or whore.'"

Noah let out a heavy sigh. "Women don't like to be called bitches either."

Austin's head bobbed. "Hey, man, I know that."

Next to Josie, Gretchen hung her head. "Progressive," she muttered.

"Did this man tell you why he wanted you and Ian to do these things?" Noah asked the kid.

"No. We just figured he had a beef with the lady. I mean, he said it was a police lady and she lived alone, 'cause we were like, we don't want to go into no house if there's people there or a big dog and shit. He said she was always working. Anyway, he was there, and once we found the jewelry, he left. Said he'd meet up with us later when we were done. Ian said he should stay, 'cause what if we got caught, then we'd take the fall for all of it, so he said he might come back, but I knew he wouldn't."

Noah folded his arms across his chest. "Where were you supposed to meet up later?"

"Under the bridge, where else?"

Josie shook her head. "God, this kid is stupid."

"That's why the guy used him," Gretchen agreed.

"You think he's lying?" Josie asked. "About this man under the bridge?"

"Well, we know from what you heard in the house there's someone else involved. Hard to say if it's someone they're protecting, or if he's telling the truth about this drug-dealer guy. But there's one way to find out."

"He's not going to be under the bridge," Josie said.

"Probably not," Gretchen agreed. "But it's a good place to start. I'll head over there with a couple of marked units. Let you know what we find."

CHAPTER 38

Her mother's small blue Chevette sat outside the trailer looking like a discarded toy, slumped to one side, its front passenger-side tire flat. Red paint streaked the bumper where her mother had hit a shiny red Mustang when they left the liquor store. It had been two days, but Josie's neck still hurt.

Her homework was spread out on the kitchen table. Fractions. Josie hated fractions. They had started them in the fourth grade, and she still hadn't mastered them. Her mother paced from the kitchen through the living room and back, stopping at the front door on each pass to stare at the broken-down car and curse under her breath.

Josie heard the sound of a car jolting over the large pot-hole two trailers down before the same red Mustang pulled up beside the Chevette. From the kitchen window, Josie could see that it was waxed to perfection, except for the long thick streak where the paint had been gouged from the front of the driver's side to the back. Josie watched a man climb out of the Mustang, flicking a cigarette into the grass as he walked toward the front door of their trailer. He was tall and thin, older, but not as old as Josie's gram. Dull brown hair peeked from the back of a worn blue ball cap. The sleeves of his white T-shirt had been torn away, revealing wiry arms with faded black tattoos that Josie couldn't make out. Beneath a long, bulbous nose, a wide moustache stretched across his upper lip. Old stains dotted his faded blue jeans, and the toe of one of his boots had a hole in it.

When he banged on the door, the sound reverberated through the whole trailer. Her mother stood frozen between the kitchen and living room. She brought an index finger to her lips, signaling for Josie to be quiet. They waited without moving as the man kept knocking, harder and harder. The minutes ticked by. Then he began shouting, "I know you're in there, dammit. Just answer the door. You're not getting away with this. You hit my car and then drove off."

More knocking. More shouting. "I know who you are, Belinda Rose. The lady at the liquor store knows you. Told me all about you. Now come on out here or I'll call the police."

At this, her mother took a few tentative steps toward the door. "Shit," she muttered.

"I'm giving you ten seconds," the man hollered. "You don't come out in ten seconds, I'm leaving, and I'll be back with the police."

Josie's mother pulled the door open. "Okay, okay," she said. "Here I am."

"You gonna make me stand out here, or you gonna invite me in? Least you can do is offer me a drink after you wrecked my car."

Her mother rolled her eyes and stepped aside, letting the man inside. "I hardly wrecked your car," she remarked.

The man stood in the middle of the living room, eyes panning the trailer until they landed on Josie. He offered her a toothy smile. "Hey, sweetheart."

Josie lifted a hand in a half-hearted wave. Her mother went to the drainboard and snatched up a glass, filling the bottom of it with the vodka she'd bought at the store. She handed it to the man, and he knocked it back in one gulp, handing her the glass back. She put one hand on her hip and stared at him. "What do you want?"

Again, he smiled. "What do you think? I need a paint job and you're gonna pay for it."

"Oh yeah? How's that? I don't got no insurance."

He laughed, his eyes drifting to Josie and then back to Josie's mother. "Of course you don't."

"How much is a paint job?" her mother asked.

He looked out the front door at the Mustang. "For a beauty like that? At least five hundred."

"Five hundred dollars?" her mother exclaimed. "Are you shitting me? For some paint?"

"Honey, that's a 1965 Mustang GT. A classic car. Took me years to restore it."

Josie's mother sighed and threw her hands in the air. "I don't have no five hundred dollars. You come back in a week and maybe I'll have something for you."

The man walked over to the couch and sat down. "I don't do payment plans, and if I leave, I told you, I'm coming back with the cops."

Her mother followed him, standing between his legs, staring down at him. "Cops don't solve nothing," she told him. "Stop bringing them into this. This is between you and me."

He stretched his arms out across the back of the sofa and smiled at her like they were old friends. "Is that right?"

CHAPTER 39

As Josie predicted, the man Austin Jacks described was not under the bridge. Gretchen unearthed a handful of people who knew him, but only as Zeke. It wasn't a lot to go on. Josie didn't know anyone named Zeke, and she had no idea what the drug dealer would want with her—particularly if he wasn't associated with Lloyd Todd, as Austin had said. She left Noah at the station house to book the teenagers while she returned home to assess the damage and start cleaning up. She went in through her front door and moved through the first floor slowly, flipping on light switches as she went. The downstairs hadn't been disturbed at all. Everything was exactly as she had left it—it was impossible to tell that anyone had been there. But Josie knew. The house felt different to her now—emptier and colder somehow, like it was missing something. Something she didn't know if she could get back.

She hesitated before turning on the kitchen light, knowing the sight of the broken kitchen window was going to stir up all the feelings of unease and rage she'd been tamping down since the teenage boys had been taken out of her bedroom in cuffs. The entire ride home she'd been worrying about that point of entry—the glass broken now, her home open and vulnerable. Now anyone could slip inside unheard until she had it fixed. Then there was the cost of the window.

The kitchen lights flickered on, and Josie's breath caught in her throat. In the window, a large, thick board had been fitted into the window frame, sealing it off. It wasn't the responsibility of Denton PD to clean up crime scenes, and certainly not to board up windows, but her team had done it for her. She walked over and tested if it was secure. Tears of gratitude burned her tired eyes as she pressed against it and it didn't budge. She rushed upstairs, taking the steps two at a time. Her bedroom had been straightened, the night stands had been placed upright once more, her lamps reassembled as best as they could be. The stuffing torn from her pillows had been removed, and the torn pillowcases were neatly folded and placed at the foot of her bed. Someone had stripped the muddied sheets and folded them as well. Even the broken pieces of her jewelry box had been neatly arranged on the top of her dresser. She walked over to the dresser, where all the drawers had been put back in their places, clothes folded and placed inside each one. She studied the carpet and saw that someone had vacuumed. Many items would need to be replaced, but everything in the room was clean and orderly. Only the nasty red words shouted from the walls, marring the tidy room.

She sank onto the bed and squeezed her eyes closed against the sting of tears. In her jacket pocket, her cell phone made a pinging sound. A text message from Noah. *I'm outside*, it read. *Can I come in?*

He waited on her doorstep, a brown bag in hand that smelled deliciously like meatball subs. "You didn't eat," he said as he stepped past her. He gestured toward the bag as he made his way to the kitchen. "All I could get were sandwiches from that minimarket over near the college. We'll probably pay for this later."

Josie glanced at her microwave clock and saw it was almost three a.m. "Noah," she said softly. "You don't have to—"

"I think you should come stay with me for a day or two. Just until you get everything back in order here." He didn't look at her as he spread the contents of the bag across her kitchen table. Her stomach clenched as the smell grew stronger. He was right. She hadn't eaten. She was starving.

"That's not necessary," she told him.

Together they sat down and dug in. Under normal circumstances, Josie knew she probably wouldn't enjoy a minimarket sandwich, but in that moment, the cheese- and sauce-covered meatballs were the best thing she'd ever tasted. Noah waited until her stomach was full before trying again.

"You can take my bed; I'll sleep on the couch."

"I'm fine," Josie insisted.

He raised a brow. "So, you're saying you'll be able to sleep here tonight?"

He had a point.

"I wanted to go with you guys tomorrow for the courthouse interview on the Belinda Rose case," she said.

"Then you should definitely get some sleep. Stay at my place—at least for tonight."

CHAPTER 40

Josie watched as her mother's body language changed. Her posture was looser, and she had that fake smile she often used on her special friends when she didn't have enough money for needles or pills. She moved closer to the man, her legs touching the inside of his. "Between you and me, I think we could work something out, don't you?"

"What do you mean?" he asked. "Like a trade?"

Josie's mother reached down and ran a hand up his thigh to his belt. "Something like that. I do something for you, and we forget all about the paint job. Call it even."

He chuckled. "Even, huh?"

She straddled him. His hands reached for her hips, but his eyes traveled over her shoulder to where Josie remained paralyzed at the kitchen table. Her mother followed his gaze, glancing at Josie. Then she turned back to him, using an index finger to bring his attention back to her. "We'll go in the back," she said.

His hands snaked down and around her mother's back, cupping her rear. He leaned into her and whispered something in her ear. At first she laughed, but then he whispered something else. There was a lengthy discussion that Josie couldn't make out. Then she heaved off his lap. She went back to the sink and rinsed a glass out, filling it with vodka. Josie waited for them to disappear into her mother's bedroom so she could concentrate on her fractions, but instead, the glass of vodka appeared in front of her. Her mother pushed it across the table until it was under Josie's nose. From the couch, the man smiled widely.

"JoJo," her mother said, "you drink this."

Josie stared at her mother. "Mom, I can't drink alcohol. I'm not supposed to."

Her mother tapped an index finger against the rim of the glass. Josie could feel the man's eyes on her. She looked at him again, but this time his smile looked different—hungry and a little bit greedy. Josie's heart skipped several beats and then raced ahead. The room seemed to close in on her.

Her mother said, "I'm your mother and what I say goes. Now you're gonna drink this down, and then you're gonna go into the back with this nice man."

"In-into the back?" Josie said, her voice cracking.

Her mother rolled her eyes. "Yes, the back. You can use my bedroom."

"Use it?"

She pushed the glass closer, and the liquid sloshed over the rim, spilling across Josie's math homework. She lowered her voice. "Don't ask questions, JoJo. You go into the back room with this gentleman and just do whatever he tells you to do, you got it?"

The vodka stung so badly, Josie gagged on it. "Jesus, JoJo," her mother complained. She went to the fridge and searched through it until she found a carton of orange juice. She poured some into the cup, diluting the vodka. Even with the juice, it smarted all the way down, burning Josie's mouth and throat and leaving a funny numb feeling on her tongue.

Josie's mother made her drink another glass after she finished the first. When she grabbed Josie's arm and pulled her up out of her seat, the room spun. Josie's feet wouldn't work. She couldn't tell if it was from the vodka or from the way the man was looking at her. Her mother's bedroom door was at once a million miles away and too close for comfort.

She didn't want to do whatever the man told her to do.

She had a panicky feeling inside that he would want to do the disgusting things her mother did with men. Josie had seen them many times. Sometimes her mother was too drunk or high to remember to put Josie into the closet or to go to her own bedroom with her special friends. There had been several times that Josie was at the kitchen table when they started taking their clothes off. No one noticed her, and she was too afraid to try to run past them to her room and draw attention to herself. The things the men did to her mother looked painful and scary.

"Mommy, I don't want to," Josie choked out.

"Shut up, JoJo." Her mother pushed her down the hallway and she stumbled, reaching for the dark paneled walls to steady herself. The man followed.

Josie felt his hand in her hair, and she jumped. His laughter was hot on the back of her neck. "Relax, sweetheart. I'm going to make you feel good."

Nausea roiled in her stomach. The vodka and orange juice threatened to come back up. He was so close. Too close. The heat of his body closed in on her. Tears stung her eyes. His hand slid down from her neck, tracing her spine, moving down until one of his fingers hooked inside the waistband of her cotton shorts.

She stumbled again, and her shorts, caught on his finger, pulled down a little, exposing her. The man gave a low whistle. "This is gonna be fun," he said, making Josie's heart thud so hard in her chest, it hurt. She shut her eyes as she closed her hand around the handle of the bedroom door, and turned . . .

Suddenly, the trailer's front door banged open behind her and the man jumped back, snapping his hand away from her body. She turned, looking past him, to where Needle now stood just inside the trailer. Without moving, he looked from her mother to where Josie and the man were frozen in place. His dark beady eyes narrowed at the man in the hallway. "What the hell's going on here?" he asked.

All eyes turned to Josie's mother. For a fraction of a second,

Josie thought she saw fear in her mother's eyes. It was quickly replaced with a flash of anger. She stepped toward Needle. "Nothing that concerns you," she told him.

But Needle remained rooted to the spot. He gestured toward the man. "Who the hell's that?"

Her mother rolled her eyes. "None of your goddamn business. Did you bring anything?"

Needle ignored her. "JoJo," he called.

Josie said nothing. Her fear, mixed with the effects of the vodka, robbed her of speech. Her eyes pleaded with him.

"Hey," her mother said irritably. "I told you to stay—"

"Shut up," Needle said. He held out a hand in Josie's direction. "JoJo, come on now. Come over here."

Somehow, Josie's feet scuttled toward him. His hand touched the top of her head, and he nodded toward the front door. "Go on outside and play now."

"You son of a bitch," her mother growled, but Needle ignored her, pushing Josie toward the door.

She didn't have to be told twice. She practically tumbled out into the cool air, running into the woods as quickly as her feet would carry her.

CHAPTER 41

Josie surfaced from a deep sleep, her bleary eyes taking in unfamiliar surroundings. Light-blue walls, a four-drawer dresser scuffed from top to bottom, masculine items scattered across its surface—an electric razor, cologne, a black wallet. Then there was the smell. Not unpleasant. Just different. It was Noah's smell, she realized. As the fog of sleep cleared, she sat up in his bed, listening. She thought she heard noises from downstairs. She had slept peacefully, considering she was in a strange bed and was still reeling from the intrusion of her home. She looked around the room once more, noting how little light it got compared to her own bedroom. The furnishings were utilitarian, although in the six months since she had last been to his house, Noah had outfitted the downstairs with new, modern furniture and appliances. It still had the half-finished look of a bachelor pad, but it was far more welcoming and comfortable.

A knock sounded on the door. Before Josie could answer, Noah walked in, a steaming mug of coffee in his hands. He froze when he saw her. "Oh, I'm sorry. I guess I should have waited for you to say 'Come in.'"

"It's okay," Josie said.

"You might have been changing," he pointed out. "I—uh—I'm really sorry."

He started to retreat, but Josie stood and reached for the coffee. "It's fine," she said. "Really. Thank you."

She sipped the coffee standing there, suddenly aware of how she must look wearing Ray's faded old Denton PD T-shirt and a pair of threadbare sweatpants. She put the mug on his nightstand and patted her hair down. Beneath her fingers, she felt a thick lump of knotted hair in the back of her head.

"Guess I should, uh, use your bathroom," Josie said.

She went to move past him as he tried to get out of the doorway, but they both moved in the same direction. The awkward dance continued as they tried to get out of each other's way, only succeeding in bumping chests. The heady scent of Noah's aftershave invaded her nostrils. She wished she'd had time to brush her teeth before their first conversation of the day.

"I'm sorry," Noah said, finally backing out of the room. He pointed to his left. "Bathroom's that way."

Josie smiled tightly. "Got it. Thanks."

She showered, brushed her teeth, and dressed quickly. In the kitchen, Noah whipped up a breakfast of bacon and eggs, which they ate in silence. Only once they left to meet Gretchen for the interview of the former courthouse employee did the awkwardness between them dissipate. As they drove to the Bellewood home of Alona Ortiz, the retired district court clerk who had once worked with Belinda Rose, Josie tried hard not to dwell on what had happened in her home the night before.

Ortiz lived in a two-story brick home near the courthouse in the center of Bellewood. Her front porch was cluttered with potted plants and children's toys. When Ortiz emerged, a knit shawl wrapped around her hunched shoulders, she smiled and waved at the mess. "Grandkids," she explained. "They're like little tornadoes. Come in, come in. Sit."

Her living room was equally full of plants and toddler toys— brightly colored blocks, worn stuffed animals, a plastic tool set, and a dress-up trunk filled with glittery pink and purple dresses and several sparkly tiaras. Gretchen made small talk with her while Josie and Noah found their places on her threadbare burgundy sofa. Ortiz sat in a recliner across from them, tucking strands of her shoulder-length silver hair behind her ears. Josie knew she was in her sixties, but she had a youthful look about her, her olive skin still relatively smooth except for the deep laugh lines bracketing her mouth.

"Three of you," she observed. "This must be important. What did young Belinda get up to? Is she in trouble?"

Gretchen perched on the arm of the sofa. "I'm sorry to tell you, Mrs. Ortiz, but we believe Belinda was killed in 1984, possibly the same day she went missing. We found her remains in Denton last week."

Mrs. Ortiz's mouth turned downward. Her brown eyes found the floor. "I'm sorry to hear that," she said gravely.

"We were wondering what you could tell us about Belinda and her job at the courthouse," Josie said.

Mrs. Ortiz leaned back in her chair and folded her hands over her stomach. "That was some time ago, but I wouldn't have told you to come over if I didn't remember her. Hard to forget those blond curls, but mostly I remember her because she was quite a flirt. Caused a little bit of conflict around the office while she was there."

"What did she do at the courthouse?" Noah asked.

"Oh, you know, mostly filing, getting the mail ready, making sure the coffee pot was full. It was a part-time job. Myself and one other woman worked there as clerks. We had gone to the high school to see if we could get one or two students to come in and help out. There were a handful of candidates, but Belinda got the job. She was very sunny. Never had any problems with her work. I mean, she was a bit unreliable. I didn't think we should let her come back after the few months she missed, but we needed help and she did her job well. Like I said, I never had a problem with her work."

Josie leaned forward, her elbows on her knees. "But you had other problems with her?"

Mrs. Ortiz gave a tight smile. "Well, not just me. We had several judges, some assistant district attorneys, and some public defenders who worked out of the courthouse. They had their own staff who didn't appreciate the way Belinda flirted with their bosses."

Noah asked, "Was the staff primarily female?"

Mrs. Ortiz smiled at him knowingly. "We're talking the early eighties, son. The judges and lawyers were male, and the staff was female. So yes, all female. I think many of them were just jealous. She was a very vivacious young woman, and she did turn the heads of a lot of men."

Josie said, "Did Belinda have relationships with any of the men?"

Mrs. Ortiz frowned. "She was a teenager," she said, as if that precluded the possibility of an affair.

"Well, was there anyone she flirted with more than the others?" Gretchen asked.

"I suppose she had quite an interest in Judge Bowen."

The name was vaguely familiar to Josie, but she couldn't place it.

Gretchen scribbled something on her notepad. "How did Judge Bowen react to her interest?"

Mrs. Ortiz waved her hand. "Oh, he loved it. Of course, he had to be careful because he had a young wife, and she worked there too, as a secretary. The flirting caused some arguments between them at first, but then Mrs. Bowen became friendly with Belinda. They were close in age."

"How close?" Josie asked.

"Oh, well, Mrs. Bowen was only twenty. It was quite the scandal when she and the judge got married because he was fifteen years older than her, but she was of age and they seemed in love."

"How old was Mrs. Bowen when they got married?" Noah asked.

"Eighteen," Mrs. Ortiz answered.

Noah looked at Josie with a raised brow. She knew what he was thinking. If the girl was eighteen when the judge married her, they had likely been seeing one another before she became of age. Which meant he may have had a predilection for young girls. Belinda had gotten pregnant shortly after starting her job at the courthouse. It was too big a coincidence to ignore.

"What was Mrs. Bowen's first name?" Gretchen asked.

"Sophia."

"Did the Bowens stay married?" Noah asked.

Mrs. Ortiz nodded. "Oh yes. They were married right up until Judge Bowen passed. Cancer. That was about ten years ago. Their children were already grown, thank goodness. They had two boys."

"Do you remember Belinda being pregnant?" Gretchen asked, steering the conversation back to their reason for being there.

Three horizontal lines appeared on Mrs. Ortiz's forehead. "Pregnant? Belinda was never pregnant. She was just a child."

Josie wondered if Belinda had really been that skilled at hiding the pregnancy, or if all the adults in her life had simply been that oblivious. Mrs. Ortiz seemed a bit naïve in Josie's estimation, although what Josie saw in her job day in and day out had made her jaded. Josie said, "You said that Belinda was friends with Sophia Bowen. Was there anyone else she was close to? Someone she may have confided in?"

Two of Mrs. Ortiz's fingers tapped her chin as she thought about it. "There was that one young lady from the cleaning service. Oh, what was her name?" She pursed her lips. Several seconds slipped past. She sighed. "I can't remember her name. She worked for the housekeeping company that came in in the afternoons and evenings to clean. Actually, the three of them were thick as thieves now that I think about it. I used to catch them out back smoking cigarettes and giggling about this or that. No one would have noticed if it was just Belinda and the cleaning girl, but Sophia—well, people expected a judge's wife to act a certain way. I talked with her a few times about not acting like a teenager cutting school."

"Do you remember the name of the cleaning service?" Josie asked.

"No, no I don't."

"What about the girl from the service that Belinda and

Sophia used to hang out with?" Noah asked. "What did she look like?"

"Oh, she was very pretty," said Mrs. Ortiz. "She had long, black hair. Almost down to her rear end. Blue eyes. She was very thin—not like Belinda or Sophia. No, the cleaning girl was thin as a rail."

"How old was she?"

"I'm not sure, dear, but she was young. Maybe in her twenties."

Josie felt Noah's eyes on her but didn't look at him. Her mother had to have been young enough to pass for eighteen when she stole Belinda's identity. She had blue eyes and had always worn her black hair down to her backside. By fourteen, Josie had outweighed her mother. It was the drugs, Josie knew now. Her mother had survived almost entirely on drugs, and not much else. Food had never been a priority in their trailer. Josie shot Noah a quick glance, communicating with her eyes. It could be her. He nodded almost imperceptibly.

"Do you remember who owned the cleaning service?" Noah asked. "Or the names of anyone else who worked there?"

Mrs. Ortiz shook her head. "I'm sorry, I don't. They went out of business decades ago. Maybe someone on your staff would remember? They had municipal contracts with all the police departments in the county as well. They had different cleaning crews that went to different buildings, but if you're just looking for the name of the company, any one of the police departments would have had a contract with them in the early '80s."

CHAPTER 42

Sergeant Dan Lamay ran a hand over his thinning gray hair and shook his head slowly. "A cleaning service?" he said. "In the '80s?" He took another moment to think about it while Josie, Gretchen, and Noah stared at him. Lamay was the oldest officer on the force, and the only one who had been around in the 1980s. His career had survived the ushering in and out of four different chiefs of police, as well as one mighty scandal. He was nearing retirement age, with a bad knee and a paunch that stretched his uniform shirt more each day. But Josie knew that with his wife battling cancer, and a daughter in college, he needed both his income and health benefits, so she kept him on and assigned him to the lobby desk.

"Anything you can remember would be helpful," Josie prodded.

He scratched over his left ear. "I'm sorry, Boss," he said. "I don't remember. I don't even remember there being a cleaning service back then. I was on patrol, you know? Brand new from the academy. Didn't spend much time in the station house."

Josie sighed and waved toward her office door. "Thanks anyway, Sergeant."

Lamay lumbered toward the door but stopped before crossing the threshold. "Boss," he said, "I bet there are records of it upstairs. I had to go up there last year to get an old case file. There were records going back to the '70s—not just closed cases, but receipts and stuff too."

Excitement propelled Josie out of her chair. "Let's take a look," she said.

*

They hardly ever used the third floor of the Denton Police Department. The old, historic building didn't have elevators, and no one particularly wanted to climb another set of steps, so it was used primarily for storage. Josie had only been up there a few times, mostly to help the women from the historical society lug holiday decorations back and forth from one of the storage closets. She had never noticed all the document boxes stacked in the hallways—or rather, she had never noticed just how many of them spilled out of the various rooms and into the hallway.

She, Noah, and Gretchen stood at the mouth of one of the hallways, staring at the stacks of boxes. Beside her, Gretchen said, "This is worse than the Bellewood PD storage room."

Noah said, "This looks like a fire hazard."

"Do we really have that many closed files and old records?" Josie asked.

They moved down the hallway, and Josie swung the door to the first room open. Inside were shelves along each wall, all of them packed with more boxes covered in dust nearly a quarter-inch thick.

Noah said, "Chief Harris kept everything."

"So did everyone who came before him, by the looks of it," Josie said.

Gretchen sneezed.

"I think none of them had the time to organize any of it and shred the old stuff," Noah explained.

Josie sighed. "Well, I'm not authorizing overtime to clean up this mess, that's for sure, but have a couple of people start doing it bit by bit on the slow days, would you?"

"Sure thing," Noah said.

"All right, let's see what we can find."

They split up, each one taking a different room, quickly searching the boxes for old receipts and contracts from the mid '80s. An hour later, Josie's back ached from leaning over the boxes and riffling through their contents, when she heard Gretchen call from the hallway, "I got it!"

Josie and Noah met her in the hallway, where she dragged an old white document box along the floor. "Here," Gretchen said, wiping sweat from her forehead with the back of one hand. "Handy Helpers Cleaning Service. They had contracts to clean the building after hours in 1981, 1982, and looks like 1983. No personnel records, only the contract between the service and the police department. I don't see anything after 1983. It must be in a different box."

Josie said, "That's okay. Pull what you've got. What we really need is the name of the owner. I doubt they'd keep personnel records over thirty years old, but the owner might remember my mother, or know someone who would."

CHAPTER 43

"You've got to be kidding me," Josie said, looking from Gretchen to Noah, who stood in front of her desk like a couple of school children being reprimanded by the principal.

Noah shook his head, a mournful look in his eye. "I'm sorry, Boss. Handy Helpers Cleaning Service went out of business in 1984, when the owner died. Car accident. Not long after Belinda disappeared."

"I talked to a couple of his relatives—a niece and nephew. No one kept any of the records from the business," Gretchen said.

"So there wouldn't be any personnel records," Josie said.

"Sorry, Boss," Noah offered.

Gretchen said, "There is still Sophia Bowen, the judge's wife. If she used to hang around with Belinda and the girl from the cleaning service, maybe she can offer us a lead. She said she can meet with us later today, and she lives in Denton now."

Josie considered this. Interviewing Sophia Bowen had been a priority to begin with, but she had really hoped that the cleaning service personnel records would give them something more solid than someone's memories. A first and last name. A date of birth. A social security number. Anything that might tell them the identity of Josie's mother before she stole Belinda Rose's life.

"I'll go with you," Josie said. "Where are you with the list of girls who lived in Maggie Lane's care home during the time Belinda was there?"

"Well, that's the good news," Gretchen said, pulling a sheaf of papers from her back pocket and handing them to Josie. "I have a complete list, and Angie is on her way to the station to talk to us."

The disappointment Josie felt just moments earlier gave way to hope. "That's great."

Gretchen helped Josie spread the pages across her desk. "There are fourteen girls in all who lived at Maggie Lane's care home while Belinda was there. Two of them we can eliminate because they were adopted out before Belinda turned ten. Three of them are dead. One is in prison. Two were moved to different foster homes before Belinda reached high-school age. That leaves six of them, including Angie Dobson—that's her married name—who is on her way here."

Gretchen pointed to a photo of a woman in her early fifties with long brown hair just starting to show strands of gray. The photo looked as though it had been pulled from a social media account. In it, Dobson stood on a beach at sunset, smiling with sunburned cheeks, a Hawaiian-print sleeveless sundress wrapped around her thick frame. The straps of her bathing suit peeked from beneath the dress, cutting into her tan shoulders. "She lives outside of Philadelphia, but her daughter goes to college here, and she's in town to visit. She graduated the same year that Belinda would have graduated."

"What about the others?" Josie asked, studying each of the photos, most of which had been pulled from social media. There was one mug shot and the photos of the three women who had already passed on, accompanied their obituaries. All looked to be in their forties or fifties. None resembled Josie's mother.

"I've spoken to them all," Gretchen said. "They didn't have much to offer. Belinda did her own thing. Most of them didn't like her because Mrs. Lane seemed to favor her. Then she got the job at the courthouse and was hardly ever home. They confirmed her gaining weight shortly after she started at the courthouse, running away for three months, and then when she came back, always being over at Lloyd Todd's place. A couple of them said they suspected that she was pregnant, but they couldn't say for sure. None of them recall her talking about where she went when she ran away. Two of them said they thought she had a few friends at the courthouse, but they don't remember any names. None of them remembered the names of any of her friends other than Lloyd and Damon Todd."

"So, this Angie is our last hope as far as the care home girls go," Josie said.

Gretchen nodded. "Yeah, hopefully she knows something the others didn't."

"Well if Belinda didn't confide in anyone at the care home," Noah piped up, "there's still Judge Bowen's wife."

CHAPTER 44

Angela Dobson made herself comfortable at the head of the conference room table while Gretchen flipped to a new page in her trusty notebook and Noah got them all coffee. Her shoulder-length hair showed even more gray than in the Facebook photo that Gretchen had found. When she smiled, clusters of crow's feet appeared at the corners of her brown eyes. A variety of colorful butterflies dotted the sweater she wore over a pair of pressed jeans. "I always wondered what happened to Belinda," she told Josie and Gretchen. Her hair swished as she shook her head. "So sad. I didn't believe she had met prince charming and gotten married, but I never thought she was dead. Murdered too. How sad. How did it...how did it happen?"

Gretchen and Josie exchanged a look. Josie said, "I'm sorry, Mrs. Dobson, we're not at liberty to divulge those details yet."

Angie nodded sagely. "I understand. I guess it will all come out eventually anyway."

Noah appeared with three coffee-filled paper cups squished together between his palms. He doled them out and then produced packets of sugar, creamers, and plastic stirrers from his pockets. Angie smiled at him. "My kind of guy," she remarked.

Leaving her coffee untouched, Gretchen began, "How well did you know Belinda?"

Angie dumped three sugars into her coffee and stirred. "Pretty well, I guess. We were the same age, you know. Our birthdays were only a month apart. I came to the care home two years after Belli though. That's what Maggie called her. Did she tell you that?"

"Yes, she did," Josie answered.

Angie rolled her eyes. "None of the rest of us had nicknames, but Belinda did. Maggie would never say it, but we all thought Belinda was her favorite. She was a nice lady, Maggie was, but she didn't hide her preference for her precious Belli."

"Maggie said that Belli became quite the troublemaker in her teens, though," Noah remarked.

Angie waved a dismissive hand. "Oh sure, we all were. Belinda just got caught more often."

"Did you and Belinda spend a lot of time together?" Gretchen asked.

"At Maggie's we did, but that was about it. Especially once she got the job at the courthouse. She was never home."

Josie said, "Did Belinda ever talk to you about her pregnancy?"

She expected shock and surprise, but Angie simply laughed and said, "She didn't talk to anyone about that pregnancy."

"You knew about the pregnancy?" Noah asked.

"Well, I suspected. She never came out and admitted it, but she didn't deny it either. One time I caught her raiding the fridge in the middle of the night, and she asked me not to tell Maggie. I said, 'I won't tell her you were sneaking food, but that's the least of your worries 'cause she is gonna flip when she finds out you're pregnant,' and she didn't say anything. Didn't even blink. She just waddled off to bed. That's when I knew I was right."

"Did you ever ask her about who the father was or what she intended to do about the baby?" Gretchen asked.

Angie shook her head. "No, not like that, anyway. I got her in private a few times and told her if she wanted to talk about it, she could tell me anything and I wouldn't tell Maggie, but she always walked away from me."

"You noticed she was pregnant," Josie said. "How come no one else did?"

Angie shrugged and sipped her coffee. "Belinda was one of

those girls who gained weight all over when she was pregnant. She didn't really have a belly, she just got wider everywhere, so it looked like she was just putting on weight. I only knew because we shared a room, and she was always throwing up in our trash can. Plus, the foster mother I was with before Maggie got pregnant right before I was transferred, so I knew what to look for. Actually, that's why I ended up at the care home, because once she had her own baby, she was finished with us foster kids. I guess I just knew the signs—the morning sickness, the big appetite, the weight gain—and like I said, if we didn't share a bedroom, I might not have even known. We hardly saw her at the care home. She worked all the time back then. She'd leave for school with the rest of us in the morning and not come home till half the girls were already in bed. Maggie was so overwhelmed, she didn't have time for noticing things."

This last statement was without malice. Even when Angie complained of Maggie playing favorites, her tone betrayed quite an affection for the foster mom.

"Did you say anything to anyone when she ran away in the winter of 1982?" Gretchen asked.

"No," Angie said. "It wasn't my place."

"You were a couple of fifteen-year-olds," Noah said. "Your foster sister was hiding a pregnancy. You didn't mention it to Maggie when Belinda disappeared? Weren't you worried about her?"

"Look," Angie replied, "Belinda was pretty independent, you know? Yeah, she hid the pregnancy, but she didn't seem like she was in trouble. She wasn't the kind of girl you worried about. She always got by. Sure, Maggie was worried about her, but Maggie also had the rest of us to care for, and before Belinda left, the fights those two used to have were off the charts. I hate to say this, but it was kind of a relief when Belinda took off. I knew she was getting close to delivering, and I figured she had made arrangements. Plus, it wasn't my secret to tell, you know? Then she was back a few months later like nothing ever happened."

"Did you ask her what happened to her baby?" Josie asked.

"Of course I did. She would only say that everything worked out. She was really cryptic about the whole thing."

"She didn't tell you what she did with the baby?" Gretchen asked.

"No, not a word."

"She never gave you any indication as to where she was during those three months?" Josie asked.

"None. She just said that she was fine and that everything had worked out."

"Assuming she carried to term and the baby was born healthy, she couldn't have gone through any official channels," Noah remarked. "No way she gave birth at a hospital. If a minor showed up at a hospital—particularly one who's already in the foster-care system—to give birth, there's no way that would have gone unnoticed or unreported. And an adoption—the courts would have had to be involved."

Angie finished off her coffee and set her cup on the table. "That is true."

"What do you think happened to the baby?" Gretchen asked.

Angie thought for a moment. "I honestly don't know. But someone must have helped her. I mean, she had to stay somewhere those last few months, right? Maybe someone took the baby from her. Did you know that if you have a home birth, you can fill out the birth certificate whenever and mail it in to the state?"

Josie frowned. "Don't you need a midwife to file that paperwork?"

"No, you can have an unassisted birth in Pennsylvania. I had my first daughter at home in the bathtub. Same thing. I mean, I went to a real doctor throughout my pregnancy, but my husband helped me deliver. We were lucky there were no complications. But all I had to do was fill out the paperwork to file for a birth certificate. I don't know what the laws are now, but back then, you just needed two witnesses to sign a form saying you were pregnant. Not impossible to come up with."

"You think that's what happened to Belinda's baby?" Noah asked. "That she found someone to take it?"

Angie stared at the table, her face looking drawn. "It's better than the alternative, isn't it?"

"Which is what?" Noah asked.

Josie knew what Angie was going to say before she said it. "That the baby died, and Belinda buried it somewhere."

"Do you think she was capable of dealing with something like that?" Josie asked.

Angie held her gaze, dark eyes penetrating, sending a chill from Josie's scalp to her toes. "When you're a fifteen-year-old foster kid with no resources and no good choices, you're capable of dealing with just about anything."

"Did she ever talk about who the father was?" Gretchen asked.

"No. She wouldn't talk about him."

"Was she seeing anyone before she got pregnant?"

Again, Angie shook her head. "No, not that I know of. Maggie would have killed her anyway. We weren't allowed to date until we were seventeen. Most of us did anyway, starting at thirteen or fourteen, but we kept it a secret. Obviously, Belinda was seeing someone, or she couldn't have gotten pregnant, but I don't know who it could have been."

Gretchen said, "Or she could have been sexually assaulted."

Angie considered this. "I guess that's true, but I think she was seeing someone. I mean, she wasn't torn up or anything. Although by that age, most of us had been assaulted or molested at one point or another."

Angie said this in such a matter-of-fact way, Josie didn't know whether to be saddened or in awe of her strength and candor. "Come to think of it," Angie went on, "she did come home after the pregnancy with this pretty little locket. She never took it off and would never tell anyone who gave it to her. So, wherever she was and whoever helped her—I don't think it was against her will."

Josie said, "What about friends? Do you remember who she hung out with?"

Angie's lips twisted as she thought for a long minute. Then she said, "No one at school, that's for sure. People teased her mercilessly, especially about her teeth. You know about those, right?"

"We're aware," Noah said.

"In her junior year she started seeing that Todd kid—I think he's the same one who just got arrested. That's something isn't it?"

Steering her back to the topic of Belinda, Gretchen said, "How about people she worked with?"

"Oh yeah, there were a couple of girls she was friendly with at the courthouse. One was a judge's wife, if I'm not mistaken. The other one worked there too."

"Do you remember their names?" Josie asked.

"I'm sorry, I don't."

"We have the name of the judge's wife," Gretchen told her. "Sophia Bowen. We don't know the name of the other woman she hung out with."

Angie said, "I know it began with an L, but that's all. Linda? Lilly? Laura? Something like that. She was a few years older than Belinda. I remember that because Belinda kept talking about how cool she was that she had her own apartment."

"Did she say where that apartment was?" Josie asked.

"No. I just assumed it was in Bellewood."

Gretchen made a note on her pad. "Do you remember anything else that Belinda said about her?"

"I'm really sorry, but I don't."

CHAPTER 45

Noah drove them to Sophia Bowen's home, recapping what they knew as they moved through the streets of Denton. "Belinda starts working part-time after school at the courthouse sometime in early 1982. By the fall, she is pregnant, but the only person who notices is her roommate. She disappears for three months and returns no longer pregnant, but with a nice locket for her trouble. We have no idea where she went, who she stayed with, or what happened to her baby. As far as we know from the people we've talked to, she never told anyone what happened. She came home and resumed her normal life. A few months after that, she starts having an affair with a teacher, whose sons help to cover it up. Eventually she dumps the teacher, and three or four months after that, someone smashes her head in with a tire iron, or something similar, and buries her in the woods. Six months later, the boss's mother starts using her identity here in Denton."

"Belinda kept a lot of secrets," Gretchen said. "Any one of them could have gotten her killed."

"Or none of them," Josie muttered.

She felt Noah's eyes on her. "What do you mean?"

"I mean my mother could be impulsive, crazy even. It's possible that none of the things we've learned about the real Belinda Rose did anything to set her off. Maybe she just looked at my mother the wrong way that particular day, and she decided to smash her head in."

As the campus of Denton University passed by outside her window, Josie became aware of the heavy, awkward silence in the car. She turned to see Noah glancing at her out of the corner of his eye and then craned her neck toward the backseat where Gretchen was studying her. With a sigh, she said, "You guys said you needed to know more about her."

"According to Angie and Mrs. Ortiz, they were friends," Noah said.

Josie laughed drily. "My mother didn't have friends. She was only interested in what people could do for her."

"Well, obviously she had a relationship with Belinda long before she stole her identity," Gretchen said. "So, what would Belinda have been able to do for her?"

Josie didn't have time to answer as Noah pulled up in front of a large gable-style house with a faux-stone patterned exterior, complete with curved windows bracketed by board and batten shutters and hemmed in by wrought-iron window boxes. They were empty, but Josie could imagine them filled with colorful flowers come springtime. The front door opened before they were even out of their car, and a woman stepped out onto the stone steps. She was short and rotund, dressed tastefully in a long red skirt and white blouse with a red scarf draped around her neck. Thin blond hair swept away from her face, pinned in a bun at the back of her head.

"Mrs. Bowen?" Noah said, extending a hand for her to shake as they climbed the steps.

Introductions were made, and Mrs. Bowen ushered them inside her home. It was large and tastefully decorated in muted pastel colors. Potted plants dominated the foyer and the large sitting room, which was bright and airy. Two light-gray, button-tufted Chesterfield sofas sandwiched a circular, glass-topped coffee table with a large vase at its center, fresh flowers reaching out from it.

The three officers sat on one sofa, and Mrs. Bowen sat across from them, perched on the edge of the opposite sofa, her ankles crossed primly, hands clasped in her lap. "Can I offer you some coffee or tea?" she asked.

"Thank you, but we're fine," Gretchen said, notebook and pen ready in her hands.

Sophia's gaze dropped to her lap momentarily. "I'm so sorry to hear what happened to Belinda. I would never have suspected. Everyone thought she ran off with a man."

"Where did you hear that from?" Josie asked.

Sophia shrugged. "Oh, I'm not sure now. I think Mrs. Lane came around and told someone at the courthouse. We were all concerned. She stopped coming to work. Malcolm and I had brought home our first son by then, so I had stopped working, but I heard all the office news when Malcolm came home each night. So, what can I help you with all these years later?"

Gretchen said, "We're just trying to get a sense of what Belinda's life was like in the weeks leading up to her death. The people she spent the most time with, that sort of thing. Alona Ortiz mentioned that you and Belinda were good friends."

"Oh yes. We were quite close. We used to take smoking breaks together and talk about what had happened on *Dynasty*."

"Mrs. Ortiz mentioned that Belinda was very flirtatious with your husband," Noah said. "Was that a problem between you two?"

Sophia laughed, the sound like wind chimes tinkling, and waved a hand in the air. "Oh that. Yes, well, Belinda flirted with everyone. That's just how she was. She liked attention, just like all of us young girls did. It is true that at first, I was concerned with how much attention Malcolm paid to her. I was a young bride and quite insecure. What I didn't understand at the time was how difficult things were for girls like Belinda."

"Girls like Belinda?" Josie echoed.

Sophia smiled. "Foster children. No family or support system. She had a foster mother of course, but no father figure in her life at all. My Malcolm was just trying to provide guidance to her, give a strong male figure to look up to. He used to say it was the Christian thing to do."

Josie wondered what else Malcolm had tried to provide

for Belinda Rose, but she kept silent. Gretchen said, "So you became friends with Belinda."

Sophia nodded.

"Did she confide in you?" Gretchen continued.

"Well, sure."

Josie asked, "Did she talk to you about her baby?"

Sophia's measured smile froze on her face. "Her what?"

"Her baby," Noah said.

Sophia's eyelids fluttered as she struggled to keep a polite smile on her face. "Belinda didn't have a baby."

Josie said, "Her autopsy showed she gave birth before she died."

"No," Sophia said. "That can't be. Belinda was never pregnant."

"It would have been in 1982," Josie told her. "She would have given birth sometime in late 1982."

Sophia placed a manicured hand on her chest. "My God. I didn't know. I knew she went missing that winter. She had been fighting a lot with her foster mom, I remember that much. But I certainly don't remember her being pregnant."

"She came back to work at the courthouse afterward. Did you ever ask her where she had been?"

"Yes, of course I did. We all did. She didn't want to talk about it. I didn't push. You know, she probably just stayed with a friend, but Belinda loved to generate drama."

"Yes," Josie said. "We've heard that."

"Speaking of friends," Gretchen said. "Who else did Belinda hang around with?"

"Oh, I don't know who her friends were; well, besides the girl she roomed with at the care home. I'm sure she had friends at school, but I only ever saw her at the courthouse, so I really couldn't say."

Josie said, "We understand she hung around with one of the girls from the cleaning service, as did you."

Sophia did her wind-chime laugh again. "Oh, Handsy's helpers?"

Noah said, "You mean Handy Helpers."

"No, we called them Handsy's helpers because the owner was a little...um...handsy, if you know what I mean."

"You mean he sexually harassed his workers?" Gretchen asked pointedly.

Her smile still in place, Sophia humphed. "I suppose that's what it would be called today. He had a lot of young girls working for him, and word was that he couldn't keep his hands to himself. That's why the turnover was so big. For such little pay, who would want to deal with their boss groping them all the time?"

Josie swallowed the biting replies that came to mind, as well as the lecture about why your pay shouldn't matter—a woman should never be groped or harassed, in her workplace or anywhere else. It seemed completely lost on Sophia that she had been a teenage secretary to the judge before they were married. Instead of pointing this out, Josie asked, "Were you friendly with any of the young women from the cleaning service?"

"Oh, well, not really. Like I said, there was a big turnover so none of them were around for very long. Plus they really only came right toward the end of the day when the rest of us were getting ready to leave."

"Mrs. Ortiz said you and Belinda were quite close with one of the young ladies," Noah said. "Thin, with long, dark hair and blue eyes. Does that ring a bell?"

Josie added, "Her name perhaps began with an L? Linda, Lilly? Something like that? Laura, perhaps?"

Sophia's brow furrowed. Her gaze flitted up to the ceiling. "Hmmm," she said. "That does sound familiar. I mean, I wouldn't say I was 'quite close' with any of them, but there were probably one or two who were there longer than the rest that I talked with. I'm ashamed to say that I used to smoke, and those cleaning girls would sometimes join Belinda and me outside for a cigarette."

Gretchen asked, "Do you remember a specific woman whose name began with an L?"

"I don't doubt that there was a young woman, a Linda or a Lilly—that sounds a bit familiar—but I don't specifically remember one. I'm so sorry."

Another dead end. How was it possible that Josie's mother had been so forgettable to so many people that none of them even remembered her name? Had it been by design? Or was someone lying? Were multiple people lying? If so, why? Josie couldn't see any reason for Mrs. Ortiz to lie. Damon Todd also had no reason to lie, especially after divulging his father's scandalous secret. He, his brother, and their father all had alibis for the night that Belinda disappeared. Angie Dobson had been more forthcoming than anyone they'd talked with. She had given them their first real clue as to Josie's mother's real identity—or at least the identity she'd been using before she stole Belinda's. Josie couldn't think of any reason for Sophia Bowen to lie, but she was certain she wasn't being entirely truthful.

"When did you stop working at the courthouse?" Josie asked her.

"Oh, it would have been the summer of 1983 when we brought our eldest son home. Then a couple of years later, our other son was born, and I never looked back. They're grown now, of course. Andrew is a lawyer, you know, right here in Denton."

It was then that Josie realized why the name Bowen was so familiar to her. Andrew Bowen had been to the police station many times to defend his clients. Josie had never spoken directly with him, but she had passed by him many times over the years. "Does your son practice criminal law?" Josie asked.

Sophia's smile widened. "Yes, that's right. He does a little family law and other civil matters, but his primary area of practice is criminal defense. My other son is a doctor. He lives in San Francisco."

There were a few more minutes of conversation between Sophia and Gretchen that Josie didn't bother to pay attention to. She was on her feet, wandering around the room, aware that Sophia's eyes kept darting toward her, although she couldn't imagine why she was making Sophia nervous. They thanked her for her time, asked her to call them if she remembered anything else, and started toward the front door.

It was then that Josie noticed the framed photographs hanging on the wall toward the back of the foyer. There were several of two handsome young men, probably only a few years older than Josie, one brown-haired and the other blond—high school graduations, college graduations, candid shots of them playing various sports, and even a photo of one of them on top of a mountain peak. Josie recognized Andrew Bowen. It was an impressive display of the accomplishments of Sophia Bowen's seemingly perfect offspring, but that wasn't what made Josie's throat seize up. Her finger pointed to the large portrait that presided over all the other photos—Sophia Bowen as a much younger woman seated in a rigid pose next to her husband, Judge Malcolm Bowen.

Noah stepped up beside her. "What is it, Boss?"

Josie's mouth opened, but no words would come.

"Boss?" Noah repeated.

She squeezed out, "Him."

Sophia walked over to them. "That was my Malcolm," she said lovingly. "Of course, that was taken ages ago."

Gretchen sidled up to Josie on her other side, looking from Josie to the portrait and back. "You knew Judge Bowen?" she asked.

"What's that?" Sophia asked, an edge of uncertainty creeping into her tone.

Finally, Josie's voice came to her. "I didn't know him, but he knew my mother."

"Oh, did he? Who was your mother?" Sophia asked.

"Boss," Noah said, a note of concern in his voice.

Josie ignored Sophia and turned to Noah. "There was a custody hearing. No, not a hearing, a private mediation. Just me, my mother, my grandmother, their attorneys, and Judge

Bowen. I was nine or ten. My grandmother wanted custody. She lost. Mostly because I lied about all the things my mother did to me. I was too afraid to tell the truth."

Now Josie wondered if telling the truth would have made a difference. Her grandmother had sued her mother under the name Belinda Rose, and Judge Bowen had known the real Belinda Rose who had worked at the courthouse in 1982. Josie was now willing to bet that he was the father of Belinda's baby. He would have known in 1997 when Josie's mother appeared before him that she wasn't Belinda Rose. He might have even remembered her from her days on the Handy Helpers' staff. Or had he simply believed there was more than one woman by that name in the county?

Josie tried hard to think back to that day, examining her memories for any small clue that the judge and her mother had been in league together. If Josie was right, and it was Judge Bowen who had impregnated Belinda Rose, it was possible that her mother had known about the affair and used it to blackmail the judge. There were a number of judges in the county. Why had her case fallen on his docket, and for a private mediation rather than a hearing?

Again Sophia asked, "Who was your mother?"

But now the judge was dead. His records and the docket would only reflect that a woman named Belinda Rose was awarded custody of her own daughter. Josie wondered if he had been the judge to sign off on the custody order when her mother finally left once and for all. The only person who knew that her mother wasn't who she said she was had passed away, leaving Josie with nothing but a ghost and more questions than answers.

"I don't know," Josie answered. "I have no idea who she was."

CHAPTER 46

"She's lying," Josie said.

Back at the station house, she, Noah, and Gretchen had gotten takeout and planted themselves in the conference room, their notes and materials from the Belinda Rose case spread out over the table.

"Boss," Noah said, "she stopped working at the courthouse long before your grandmother tried to get custody of you. I doubt she even knew about any of it."

"Unless Malcolm came home and told her," Gretchen said. "It seems like he liked to come home and share the office gossip with her. You don't think it would have occurred to him to come home and say, 'Hey, remember that girl who used to work at the courthouse who disappeared? Well, she showed up today at the courthouse only she wasn't the same girl.'"

"Or," Noah said, "there's more than one Belinda Rose in the state. We don't even know that Malcolm Bowen knew Josie's mother from when she worked for the cleaning service. Do men like that really notice the help?"

"He noticed Belinda Rose," Josie pointed out. "My money's on him as the baby's father."

Gretchen nodded her agreement. "I was thinking that too."

Noah made a noise of frustration. "That still doesn't mean he knew your mother in the early 1980s, or remembered her."

"My mother had something on him," Josie said with certainty. "I know she did. How ballsy was it to go to the courthouse you used to clean using the identity of a girl you used to work with there?"

"We're talking fifteen years later, Boss," Noah said.

Josie was going to argue her point, but her cell phone vibrated, dancing noisily across the glass-topped table. Seeing Misty's name flash across the screen, Josie snatched it up and answered, listened for a moment, then said, "I'll do it. Give me a half hour, okay?"

She hung up and, as she stood, she noticed Noah and Gretchen staring at her. "Misty needs me," she explained. "Both her and the baby are sick. Mrs. Quinn took them to the doctor, but she has to work. Misty needs me to pick up a prescription for the baby."

They continued to stare, and Josie realized that it was out of character for her to walk away from work in the middle of an active case, even though as chief, she didn't need to be there. She was supposed to be getting better at delegating. "I'll be back in an hour," she said. "In the meantime, draw up some warrants. I want a search for any female foster children in the care of the state between 1962 and 1982 whose first name is Linda, Lilly, or Laura."

Noah groaned. "Boss, with all due respect, that's like looking for a needle in a haystack."

Gretchen was already taking notes. Josie raised a brow at Noah. "Do you have any better ideas?"

"Is there anyone else your mother knew who might be able to shed some light on who she was or what happened to her?" Noah asked.

"No," Josie said. "Everyone who knew her would have known her as Belinda Rose. That doesn't help me. Most of the people she knew were heavily involved in drugs in one way or another. I don't know their names. I only know them by the nicknames I gave them when I was a child. Most of them are probably dead now."

Gretchen asked, "Did she have any boyfriends? After your father passed?"

Again, Dexter McMann rose up in her mind. "There was

a man," she admitted. "A boyfriend. But I don't think he will give us much to work with. He would only have known her as Belinda Rose, same as me. I don't know what happened to him."

"Do you have his name?" Gretchen asked.

"I don't—I don't remember," Josie lied.

Gretchen gave her a penetrating look. Then she said, "Try to remember. People you date usually keep photos. Could be worth paying him a visit. In the meantime, we'll get to work tracking down the Lindas, Lillys, and Lauras of the foster care system."

CHAPTER 47

There was a man in her mother's bed. This wasn't at all unusual, except that it was the same man who had been in her mother's bed every morning for the last two weeks. The noise of their vigorous nighttime activities was hard to sleep through in the tiny trailer, but she made sure to be up, showered, dressed, and out the door every morning before either of them got up, taking the shortcut through the woods to wait for Ray on his back porch. Josie's mother and the new guy weren't around in the afternoons, usually returning to the trailer after dinner, by which time Josie was firmly barricaded in her room. Josie didn't like it when men stayed over, but she loved it when her mother had a reason to ignore her.

When she finally met him, it was by accident. A stomach virus had kept her up most of the night, and as she was stumbling from the bathroom to the kitchen to get a glass of water, she stumbled smack into his bare chest. The impact sent Josie flying backward, her ass hitting hard against the kitchen tiles. The lights switched on, and Josie threw up a forearm to avoid the sudden glare. Standing over her, looking impossibly tall, was a guy who had to be closer to Josie's age than her mother's. Shaggy brown hair fell across his face. He wore only boxer shorts, and the muscles of his long torso rippled when he reached down to help her up.

"Hey," he said. "You okay?"

She nodded, suddenly very aware that she must smell like vomit.

"You don't look so good," he told her. "I'm Dex, by the way. Your mom said she'd introduce me, but you're never here."

Oh, I'm here, Josie thought. All her mother had to do was knock on her bedroom door, but now Josie saw why her mother wouldn't want them to meet. She couldn't take her eyes off his flat stomach and the trail of hair that dipped into the front of his boxers. She'd seen Ray shirtless a dozen times, but Ray didn't look like this. "How—how old are you?" Josie asked.

Dex laughed. "I'm twenty. I know, I know, there's a bit of an age difference, but your mom, you know, she's really cool."

Josie didn't bother responding to that. Dex didn't seem like he was there as the result of a drug-and-alcohol-fueled bender like most of them. He actually wanted to be there, which made him either really stupid or every bit as cold-hearted as Josie's mother. Josie's money was on stupid; she'd seen her mother manipulate men before. She pushed past him and got a glass from the overhead cabinet, filling it with water and gulping it down. Immediately she regretted it as nausea roiled in her stomach.

"You sick?" Dex asked.

Yeah, he definitely wasn't the brightest.

Ignoring him, Josie tried to push past him, but before she could get through the living room, the nausea overcame her and vomit exploded across the carpet in front of her. Holding her stomach, she swayed on her feet. It was only the water she'd just had, but the smell was rank. Her mother was really going to make her pay for this.

Then Dex was at her feet, blotting the carpet with paper towels. He left and came back with cleaner he'd found under the kitchen sink. "You should go lie down," he said. "I got this."

Josie knew she should thank him, but she was afraid if she didn't get into her bed that instant, she might not make it. She ran to her room and clambered into her bed, pulling the covers up to her neck, letting the illness pull her under its choppy waves.

She didn't even remember falling asleep, but when she woke up, on her nightstand were four cans of ginger ale and two sleeves of saltine crackers. She sat up, confused and sure she must be dreaming. Reaching over to examine one of the cans, her feet bumped into something hard and plastic beside her bed. A bucket. For her to throw up in. For a moment, Josie wondered if her grandmother had been there in the night, but she knew better. Her mother never allowed Lisette inside the trailer. There was no chance it was her mother, so it had to be…Dex?

It was two weeks before their paths crossed again, and when they did, she only managed a mumbled "Thanks." It made her nervous when men were nice to her. It always came at such a heavy price—her mother's rage, a bargaining chip, or something worse. Occasionally Dex would invite her to join him and her mother while they ate or watched television, but she always declined. He invited her to go to the movies with them or out to eat, but again she refused. He always looked a little disappointed, but he had no idea of the way things worked in her mother's world.

Then he started approaching her when her mother wasn't home. He had practically moved in by this point, and while her mother was off doing whatever she did to earn money to keep the trailer roof over their heads, Dex tried to draw Josie out, offering her rides to and from school, wanting to take her for ice cream, asking if she needed help with her homework, trying to get her to watch TV with him. One day he brought home a dozen donuts and offered her some, pointing out that he had gotten six of her favorite kind: French crullers. How he even knew that was beyond her. Had she told him?

As if sensing her question, he said, "The last two times your mom got donuts, the French crullers mysteriously disappeared. I took a wild guess."

Josie stood in the middle of the tiny trailer kitchen, her stomach growling at the sight of the donuts, and put a hand on her hip. "Look," she told him, "I've already got a boyfriend, I don't need anyone's help, and I sure as hell don't need another one of my mom's pervy boyfriends trying to be 'nice' to me. I wouldn't touch you for a million donuts, so just cut it out. Okay?"

For a moment, he stared at her wide-eyed, shock slackening his jaw. Then, slowly, a smile spread across his face and he began to laugh. He bent at the waist, holding his belly, just laughing his ass off. Josie shot him the dirtiest look she could muster.

Finally, he said, "You're pretty sassy, you know that? How many 'pervy boyfriends' did your mom have before I moved in?"

Josie walked away from him, taking up position on the living-room couch where her homework was spread out. "Enough," she said.

"I'm not being nice to you because I want something from you, and I'm certainly not a pervert."

"That's what they all say," she muttered as she picked up her pencil and tried to focus on her homework.

A French cruller on a folded paper towel appeared next to the worksheet in front of her. "We're living together," he said. "I'm dating your mom. I don't want anything from you. I'm just trying to talk to you, to maybe make you look less miserable once in a while."

"Well, don't try being my dad either," Josie snapped.

"I'm not trying to be anyone's dad," Dex replied. "Your mom and I, we're just having fun."

"I know," Josie said. "I hear you every night."

Again, he laughed. "You're a whip," he said. "Anyway, have some donuts, don't have some donuts. I'm going out. If you want a ride to school tomorrow, I can take you."

He flashed a smile at her, his green eyes vibrant beneath a shock of dark hair, and left the trailer. Josie listened to the sound of his car pulling away and wondered how long he would be in their lives.

CHAPTER 48

Josie emerged from the pharmacy with Harris's antibiotics in one hand and her cell phone in the other. Misty rattled on while Harris screamed in the background, the sound making Josie want to race to him and scoop him into her arms. But when he was sick, she knew all he wanted was his mother. Fetching the medication was the best way she could help. "I got some more infant Tylenol too," Josie said. "I'm only a few minutes away."

"Oh great," Misty said. "You're a lifesaver."

A man stood leaning against the driver's-side door of Josie's Escape as she found her vehicle in the parking lot. She hung up with Misty and stopped dead in front of him. It was dark, and the parking lot was deserted except for them and a couple of other vehicles, but Josie could see dark eyes glinting from beneath his baseball cap. He wore faded blue jeans and a blue down vest over a flannel shirt. She estimated him to be in his forties. His hands were hooked in the belt loops of his jeans, one of his feet flat against the door of her car. A smile snaked across his face as she looked him up and down.

"Can I help you?" Josie asked.

He kept smiling at her in a way that made the hairs on the back of her neck stand up. One of her hands slipped inside her jacket and rested on the handle of her service weapon.

"Now that's not very nice, is it, Chief?" he said.

"Do I know you?" Josie asked.

"No," he said, "but you want to."

"Yeah, I don't think so," Josie said. "Out of my way. There's someplace I need to be."

He stepped aside slightly and put a hand on the door handle, as if to open it, but Josie hadn't disengaged the locks yet. She didn't want to get any closer to him, much less cross his path to get into her vehicle. "Allow me," he said with fake politeness.

"I can take it from here," Josie told him.

The hand on her gun was reassuring, but she knew she had to be careful—the mayor would have her ass if the chief of police was caught pulling a gun on a guy who was simply trying to open her door for her.

The man didn't move, so Josie said, "What do you want?"

"Just trying to have a conversation with you, sweet thing."

Josie kept her voice clear and firm. "My name's not sweet thing, and I really don't have time for this. I told you, there's somewhere I need to go. Someone is waiting for me."

"You know, you could be nicer to a gentleman just trying to be polite," he told her, his sickening smile holding firm.

She'd had enough already. "Get out of my way," Josie told him.

The punch came fast and hard, whizzing past the left side of her head as she ducked under it just in time, barreling into him with the full weight of her body and slamming him against her Escape. Josie heard him gasp the word, "Bitch." Then everything else happened at once—she took a step back, her hand emerging from her jacket with the Glock, but before she could take a shooter's stance, his fist swung out wildly, catching her on the side of her face. She felt the skin of her cheek swell. Stumbling to the side, she tried to keep her balance, lifting the Glock toward him once more. Lightning-fast, his other arm lashed out at her wrist. The Glock clattered to the ground and the man's hands closed around Josie's throat. He swung her around, and her body crashed into the side of the vehicle. Pain shot across the back of her skull.

The man held her there, squeezing her throat until her vision started to gray as she clawed at his fingers. "You said you wanted it," he breathed into her face. "I'm gonna give it to you, Chief."

Josie's heart froze in her chest and then kicked into overdrive, jackhammering against her sternum. One of his hands left her throat and reached between her legs, tearing at her jeans, pulling them downward. It was all the opening Josie needed. She brought one elbow up and sliced downward onto the man's forearm, breaking his hold. Her other elbow came up fast, smashing into his nose. He staggered backward, muttering the word "bitch" once more and holding his hands to his face. They came away bloody. He stared at them and then looked back at her. "Oh, so you really want this to be real, then. Well, now I'm taking what I came for."

He lunged toward her, and she stepped out of the way, snagging one of his wrists and twisting his arm high behind his back. She kicked between his feet, spreading his legs and putting him off balance. Her forearm knocked his face into the window of the Escape once, and then again for good measure. Josie didn't have cuffs, but she took his other wrist and twisted that behind his back as well. "Get on your knees," she commanded.

She felt him struggle against her hold, and she twisted his wrists until he cried out in pain and his knees buckled. Pushing him onto the ground, she readjusted her grip on his wrists, both now bent at unnatural angles. Josie knew the pain was the only thing keeping him from coming after her again. Once his face was against the asphalt, she put one knee on his back and one on his neck. "You're under arrest," she said, and read him his rights.

"What the fuck is this?" he cried.

Josie took one hand away long enough to fish her phone out of her pocket and dial 911, dropping the phone onto the pavement so she could keep him pinned as she shouted into it. She rattled off the address. "Officer needs immediate assistance. Send nearest units. Contact Lieutenant Fraley."

The man squirmed beneath her. "Are you fucking kidding me?" he spat. "This was not what we agreed on. This wasn't part of the deal."

Josie leaned closer to his face. "What?"

"You promised not to arrest me," he cried.

"Promised not to arrest you? I don't even know you."

"It's me," he said. "Keith. I answered your ad."

Josie felt her stomach sink. "My ad? What ad?"

He continued to struggle, bucking against her, grunting. "Your ad on craigslist, you crazy bitch."

CHAPTER 49

Noah arrived just behind two marked units, jumping out of his car and racing toward her before the patrol officers were even out of their seatbelts. Blue and red lights pulsed in the darkness. Dropping to his knees, Noah grabbed the man's wrists, securing them with two plastic zip ties he pulled from his pocket.

"I've already read him his rights," Josie told Noah as they lifted Keith from the ground and handed him over to the patrol officers to put in the back of a cruiser. Josie stalked around the perimeter of the Escape, locating her gun and holstering it before going in search of the pharmacy bag she'd discarded during the attack. Luckily it hadn't been crushed. She held it up as Noah approached. "I need to get this to Misty," she said.

Noah studied her, and she saw the change in his face—the hardened professionalism giving way to shock. Even under the whirring red and blue lights, she could see his pallor. Looking down, she saw that the zipper on her jeans was torn open to reveal the waistband of her black panties beneath.

"Josie," Noah said.

She held out her free hand. "Give me your jacket, Fraley."

Slowly he took it off and handed it to her. Trading him the pharmacy bag for his jacket, she tied the jacket around her waist, knotting the sleeves at the small of her back. "Misty needs that, do you understand?"

He stepped closer to her. The patrol officers waited several feet away, standing by their cruiser. "I don't care about Misty right now," Noah said.

Josie looked away from him. "Well, you should. If you want to help me right now, you can get that to her and meet me at the station." She signaled for one of the officers, and he jogged over. "The store probably has footage of what just happened. Go in and see if they've got cameras out here in the parking lot. I want whatever they have."

"You got it, Boss," he said, and headed off to the store.

Noah's face was set with frustration. Josie raised a brow at him. "Do we have a problem, Fraley?"

He shook his head, but a muscle ticked in his jaw.

"Good," Josie said. She panned the ground again. "I need you to get to work. That guy was answering an ad, and I'm pretty sure this time it was for much more than 'kinky fun.'"

Noah swallowed. "What are you saying?"

"I think the ad that was posted was for a rape fantasy."

CHAPTER 50

"His name is Keith Gibbs," Noah said. "He's forty-four, a resident of Denton. Single, no kids. Works at the potato-chip factory. He says he found your ad a few days ago, that the two of you exchanged emails and set up the scenario. That was all I could get out of him before he asked for an attorney."

Josie followed Noah into the closed-circuit viewing room, smoothing down the T-shirt and jeans she had changed into in her office. Unfortunately, these extra clothes had been stuffed inside one of her desk drawers for so long, they were plagued with wrinkles. But they would have to do. "Did you get the emails?" Josie asked.

"He sent them to Gretchen from his phone. She's printing them now."

They watched the large television screen that provided them with a view into their interrogation room, where Keith Gibbs paced.

"Did you find the ad?" Josie asked.

She glanced at him just long enough to notice the flush creeping from his throat to the roots of his hair. He handed her a sheet of paper. On it, the subject line of the ad read: *Fulfill My Fantasy...Looking for a Forced Connection*. Beneath that, the text went on, *Thirty-something hot female cop looking for a big, strong stud to fulfill rape fantasy. Don't reply unless you're willing to come at me hard and you like a good fight. If you want something fun and taboo, hit me up.*

Nausea stirred the dinner Josie had eaten an hour earlier in the conference room. "My God," she said.

Noah took the page from her hand and placed it facedown on the table. "I read the emails. There are only four of them. Basically, whoever is posing as you gives your name and address, says you're the chief of police. Lays out this scenario where he follows you for a day or two and approaches you in a public place and rapes you. You will fight back, but he is not to stop, and you promise not to arrest him."

"The email address?" Josie asked.

"It's a free email address anyone can open with a dummy name. It's registered in your name, obviously. I drew up a warrant—for the email provider and craigslist—but I doubt we'll turn up much. Whoever is doing this is tech-savvy enough to remain anonymous. I mean, maybe if we were a bigger department or the FBI, but we don't have a lot of resources for this kind of thing. I can pass this along to the state police or ask someone at the college to consult, if you want."

Josie shook her head. She had someone else in mind. "I'll handle it. Just get me what you can, okay?"

"You know someone?"

"I know someone who knows people," she answered. She took out her phone and fired off a text to Trinity Payne. *Hey, are you still coming to town? Still interested in that Lloyd Todd story? I'll give you an exclusive, but I need your help with something. ASAP.*

To Noah, she said, "I want to talk to Lloyd Todd."

"Boss."

"I don't care what you have to do, get me a meeting with him. I'll drive over to the county jail and talk to him. He can have seven lawyers if he wants. This ends now."

Her cell phone rang. It was Trinity. "I'm coming into town this evening," she said when Josie answered. "I'll be staying at the Eudora, and yes, I'm still interested in the Lloyd Todd story. I'm more interested in doing a story on you."

"Don't hold your breath," Josie said.

Trinity laughed. "Never say never, my dear. I know you well

enough by now to know that you don't call me unless you need something. What am I trading for the Todd story?"

"I need your help with some...computer crimes. You have connections, right?"

"Oh, honey, I know some of the best hackers you'll never meet. But I'm not sure the Todd story is big enough to warrant me calling in those favors."

Josie groaned. "You can't be serious."

"You've been involved in some of the most intriguing cases in the entire country just in the last two years. The network thinks a story on you would bring in huge ratings."

"I really don't have time for this, Trinity. Not to mention that I have absolutely zero interest in having my face splashed all over the national news again."

"I knew you would say that. Just hear me out. We'll talk about it in person. Alone. No producers, no cameramen. Just me. Just come over tomorrow, okay? I'll help you with your computer crimes case."

Josie felt Noah's eyes on her. She really didn't have the time or inclination to hear Trinity out about this particular matter. She hated doing press, and the last thing she needed was to be under a microscope on national television. But she knew that Trinity's contacts would locate whoever was placing the craigslist ads in a matter of hours, where it could take weeks through official channels. After the last few days, she was desperate for this assault on her life to stop, even if that meant humoring Trinity's pitch for a few hours.

With a heavy sigh, Josie said, "Fine. Text me your room number when you get here."

The squeal of delight Trinity gave could be heard all the way across the room where Noah stood. It startled him.

She knew it was futile, but Josie pushed the phone closer to her mouth to remind Trinity, "I didn't say I'd do it. I only said I would hear you out." But Josie could picture Trinity's predatory grin. She always got what she wanted.

"Whatever," she told Josie, hanging up just as Gretchen came in with a sheaf of papers in her hand. Josie took the pages from her but didn't read them.

Gretchen said, "Your would-be rapist, Keith Gibbs, has no known association with Lloyd Todd. He was just a twisted guy answering an ad."

"I figured that," Josie said. "We'll find out who's behind the ads and go after them."

Gretchen looked at the CCTV screen, where Gibbs had finally taken a seat, then back to Josie. "Boss," she said, "we can't hold him."

Josie stepped toward Gretchen. "What?"

"You know this," Noah said. "He thought he was answering an ad for a consensual sexual encounter. Technically, he did nothing wrong. At least, that's what his attorney will argue."

"I don't give a shit about his attorney," Josie snapped. "He assaulted me. He stuck his grimy hands on me. He did not take no for an answer."

"Because he thought that was the arrangement," Gretchen said. "Look, I agree, the guy's a shithead, and he assaulted you, yes, but he thought this was an arrangement the two of you had agreed on. He had no reason to believe that you were not the person behind the ad or emails. He's got no priors. Not even traffic tickets. Clean as a whistle."

"I want to press charges," Josie said.

"The DA will toss them out," Noah told her. "I know you know this, Boss."

Anger flared in Josie's chest, burning up her skin. "I don't give a shit. I'll talk to the DA myself if I have to. He is not leaving here tonight. Charge him."

Gretchen and Noah looked at one another and seemed to come to some kind of agreement. "Okay," Gretchen said. "I'll do the paperwork."

CHAPTER 51

The glowing numbers on Noah's cable box showed it was nearly one a.m. Curled beneath a blanket on his couch, Josie shook herself awake long enough to register the old 1990s sitcom playing on the television. She tried to focus on it, but every cell in her body felt heavy with longing to go back to sleep. Her ears tuned to the sounds coming from the kitchen—dishes clinking, the microwave whirring, and another sound that Josie couldn't identify. A warm sense of calm pulled her back toward sleep again. She was safe here. She could relax—just for a little while. She picked up the remote and turned the volume up a little, filling the room with canned laughter and letting her eyelids flutter closed once more. She was almost there, almost all the way under, when she felt Keith Gibbs's hands press down on her, smelled his moist breath. Her insides curdled, and she thrashed against him.

"Boss!" Noah's voice startled her awake. He stood over her looking worried, two large coffee mugs in his hands.

Josie shifted to sit up and wiped sweat from her brow. "Sorry," she said. "I-I, uh, fell asleep."

"You were dreaming," Noah said.

Not dreaming, she thought. *Remembering.* Her mind was trying to process those terrifying, chaotic moments now that it wasn't focused on work.

"You okay, Boss?" Noah asked.

Ignoring his question, she said, "You know, you can call me Josie—I mean, at least when we're here together."

She patted the space next to her, and Noah sat down, handing her a cup. White foam with what looked like ground cinnamon steamed from inside. It smelled sweet and spicy, with a faint scent of whiskey. "What is this?"

Noah smiled and lifted his cup. "A dirty chai latte—coffee, spices, and single malt. I thought you might like it. I can make you something to eat too, if you want."

Josie smiled and sipped the drink, slowly savoring it. "Not necessary," she said. "This is perfect, thank you."

They drank in silence, lost in the images playing on television for several moments. Then Noah said, "Are we going to talk about tonight?"

"No," Josie replied.

"Bos—Josie, you know you can talk to me."

"And you know that I'm not a talker."

He laughed. "True. All right, how about that detail we talked about? One unit on you all the time until we get this sorted out?"

She was grateful to him for not pushing. The only way she had survived what she had was by blocking out the terrible things that had happened and all the dark feelings that went with them. The only option she had ever had was to keep moving forward. She knew this wasn't healthy—a therapist she'd been forced to see in college had told her that one day it would all catch up with her, but so far she had been able to stay just ahead of her demons. She planned on keeping it that way.

The latte made her feel warm and drowsy. She put her coffee mug onto the table and stood, offering him a small smile. "Can we not talk about that right now? I think the best thing for me right now is just to go to bed."

Looking surprised, Noah set his own cup on the table. "Oh, sure, okay. I mean, unless you want to hang out. We don't have to talk about work."

"Thank you, but I really just need some sleep."

She felt his eyes on her back as she left the room. Upstairs, she collapsed into his bed and straight into a deep, dreamless sleep.

*

A few hours later, she woke; her back and neck felt stiff from the assault, but the memory of Keith Gibbs attacking her was a little duller in her mind than it was before. Soon the memory would be small enough to lock away in her mental vault with all the other horrors she'd endured.

Heading downstairs, Josie tiptoed past Noah, who lay sprawled on the couch snoring, and found her phone charging in the kitchen. It was almost the time she would normally get ready for work. There was a text message from Gretchen from twenty minutes earlier.

Todd has agreed to meet with you. Ten a.m. county prison.

There was also a text from Trinity. *Room 227. I'll see you later today, right?* Josie didn't answer it.

She went back into the living room and gently shook Noah awake. "Fraley," she said. "Wake up. You're my detail today."

CHAPTER 52

The Alcott County Jail was located in Bellewood and managed by the sheriff's office. The jail acted as a hub for all the police departments in the county, processing their prisoners and holding them over for trial. Although Denton police had a holding area in their station house, it was mostly for drunk college students and other people guilty of minor offenses. Once it came time for someone to be arraigned and booked, the sheriff transported them from Denton and processed them through the county facility.

Because Lloyd Todd's lawyer insisted on being present for their meeting, the deputies had placed them in a private meeting room. Lloyd sat hunched over the table, his hands cuffed and threaded through an iron loop fixed to the tabletop. The orange jumpsuit he wore stretched tight across his broad shoulders. Dark eyes glared from beneath a pair of bushy eyebrows, and gray shot through his short, spiked brown hair and the patchy beard that stubbled his cheeks. He looked much older than his brother, although Josie knew they were only two years apart. Noah waited outside.

"This is highly irregular," Lloyd's attorney said from where he stood behind his client, looking sharp and imposing with his slicked-back black hair and a charcoal suit that probably cost more than Josie's car.

"Your client agreed to it," she said.

The attorney bristled. "I advised him against it."

No one was more surprised than Josie that Lloyd had agreed to meet with her, but as Trinity Payne often said: *People always want something, you just have to figure out what it is.* It wasn't normally Josie's style to bargain with people, but she had two major issues she needed to address with Todd, and whenever possible, she preferred to go directly to the source.

Lloyd, however, gave nothing away.

Josie started close to home. "I met with your brother the other day."

Nothing.

"Your boys are doing well there."

A flicker in his eyes, barely perceptible. He folded his hands together, chains clinking. Josie forged ahead. "I was there to talk to him about Belinda Rose. Do you remember her?"

"We went to high school together," Lloyd said.

"That's right," Josie said. She recapped everything Damon had told them, and Lloyd agreed that all of it was accurate.

"You wouldn't be coming around asking about her unless something bad happened to her," Lloyd said.

"She's dead," Josie told him. "Someone caved her head in thirty-three years ago and buried her in the woods in Denton."

Lloyd's expression didn't change, but he offered, "Sorry to hear that."

"Mr. Todd," Josie said, "do you remember anyone that Belinda hung out with? Any of her friends? Perhaps from the courthouse?"

"Why are you asking me?"

"Damon said you and Belinda spent a lot of time together," Josie said.

"Damon also told you she was seeing our father, so you know that me spending time with her—it was all fake."

Josie raised a brow. "But you did spend time with her. Surely the two of you talked now and then."

Lloyd chuckled. "Belinda talked a lot, Chief. I don't remember everything she said."

"I'm not asking you to remember everything she said," Josie told him. "I'm asking one question. Surely you remember Belinda talking about her friends."

Lloyd sighed. "She was friends with a chick named Angie from the foster home," he said.

"Anyone else?" Josie prodded.

"That's more than one question."

"It's the same question. I want to know who Belinda's friends were."

"There were a couple of girls from the courthouse."

"Names?" Josie asked.

"Come on, Chief—" he began.

"You remembered the name of her friend from the care home; what were the names of her friends from the courthouse?"

He sighed, shaking his head as though what she was asking was ridiculous, but seemed to give it some thought. Lines creased his forehead until, finally, he said, "Sophia. Sophia and Lila. That was the other one, Lila."

Josie hoped her excitement didn't show on her face. Her spine straightened, and she leaned forward slightly. She hadn't expected him to remember. Not Linda or Lilly or Laura.

Lila.

It was like unlocking a secret code. She felt slightly breathless. "Do you remember Lila's last name?"

He shook his head. "Nah, sorry. I never met her or the other one. Just heard Belinda talk about them all the time. She talked a lot, and like Damon told you, I let her follow me around at school sometimes so no one would get the wrong idea about her and my dad."

Josie was sure that Noah was already on his phone, asking Gretchen to get into the county foster-care records, but she glanced meaningfully at the camera over the door anyway. "There's one more thing," she told him.

"I think that's quite enough," the attorney interjected. "My client has been more than helpful on this matter. He didn't have to meet with you today."

Lloyd glanced over his shoulder and silenced the man with a look. He turned back to Josie and opened his palms, inviting her to go on.

"I want you to get word to your people to stop harassing me. You crossed a line last night."

"Chief Quinn," the attorney said, approaching the table.

Once again, Lloyd silenced him. "I'm afraid I don't know what you're talking about," he said.

"Okay, fair enough," Josie said. "Maybe your minions don't keep you abreast of all their activities in here, but since your arrest, the department's vehicles have been vandalized, the station house has been egged, someone put shit under the handles of my car doors, robbed my house and destroyed my personal property, and worst of all, someone placed sick personal ads on craigslist under my name. Last night, a man tried to assault me in the parking lot of a pharmacy because he was responding to an ad someone placed in my name for a rape fantasy."

The attorney said, "These are very serious allegations."

Josie kept her eyes fixed on Lloyd, whose expression had not changed. "I'm not accusing him of anything," she said. "I'm accusing people he associates with. I believe if he had a conversation with these people and encouraged them to stop these behaviors, it would greatly help his situation."

The attorney opened his mouth to speak, but Lloyd said, "My situation?"

Josie leaned forward again, both elbows on the table. "I'm not stupid, Mr. Todd. I know you didn't have to meet with me. You didn't have to talk to me about Belinda Rose. You did something for me. Now, what can I do for you? What can I do for you that might make you more amenable to talking to these associates?"

"I don't have associates," he responded. "But if I did, they wouldn't be doing shit like robbing your house or putting ads online."

"What are you saying?"

"I'm saying, anyone I associated with might pull off some harmless pranks."

"Slashed tires and shattered windshields of the department's entire fleet is hardly minor," Josie pointed out.

Lloyd shrugged. "I told you, I don't have associates. I'm speaking hypothetically."

Josie resisted the urge to roll her eyes. "Okay, hypothetically, what are you telling me?"

"That the other stuff you're talking about—robbery and personal ads—my hypothetical associates had nothing to do with that."

"The man who robbed my house is in his fifties or sixties, thin, with gray hair, always wears a green jacket, can be found under the bridge, and goes by Zeke. Hypothetically, he wouldn't be someone you associate with?"

Lloyd laughed, his shoulders shaking. "You're talking about Larry Ezekiel Fox. He's an old burnout. No one associates with him. He's a pirate with absolutely no loyalty. He's been using since you and I were in diapers. Used to go by Larry. Started using his middle name a few years back. Now everyone calls him Zeke."

"So, hypothetically, he wouldn't have robbed my house in retribution for my department arresting you?"

The attorney's face flamed red. "Really, Chief, this is highly irregular. I must—"

This time Josie put a hand up to silence him.

Lloyd answered, "Hypothetically, no. If Zeke wanted to rob your house, he had his own reasons."

"Where can I find him?" Josie asked.

"Can't help you there."

"But you can help me with my hypothetical problem with the vandalism and 'minor' property damage?"

A smile slid across his face. "If you can help me with my son. My oldest. You see, he got caught up in this mess—me being falsely accused and all that. He's been charged with some things he didn't do."

"I'm sure he has a good lawyer," Josie said pointedly.

"Oh, he does. But it never hurts to have the chief of police have a conversation with the district attorney."

Normally, Josie would have taken great pleasure in telling a man like Lloyd Todd to go fuck himself. Somehow she doubted his oldest son was as innocent as Todd portrayed him, but she understood a parent's need to protect his child. She also knew that Todd wouldn't offer everything he knew and then ask for a favor after the fact. He was holding on to something, and the only way to get it was to make a show of good faith.

"Let me make some phone calls," she said.

*

Two hours later, she was back in the conference room across from Lloyd, handing his attorney the paperwork concerning Lloyd Todd Jr. "I couldn't get the charges dropped," she told him. "But I did get them reduced. Plus, he can enter an accelerated rehabilitation program. He goes to therapy, drug and alcohol counseling, job training. He does community service and pays some fines, and if he completes all the requirements, his record is expunged of these charges. That's the best I can do. He'll still get a clean slate. This time."

Lloyd bristled at the barb, but looked over the paperwork his attorney pushed in front of him, nodding as Josie spoke. He didn't hurry. After a solid five minutes, he looked up at her and said, "There's a strip mall on Sixth Street. That laundromat that's been there for decades."

"I know the one," Josie said.

"Zeke hangs out there when he's not under the bridge. So I've heard. Hypothetically."

Josie stood. She couldn't believe the words were coming out of her mouth, but they did: "Thank you, Mr. Todd."

Her hand was on the doorknob when Lloyd called out to her one last time. "Bowen and Jensen," he said.

Josie turned her head. "What?"

"Belinda's friends. Their last names. Bowen and Jensen. I remember because together they made the initials B.J. You know, like blow job?"

CHAPTER 53

"Lila Jensen."

Noah drove as Josie sat in the passenger seat, staring straight ahead but seeing nothing. She kept saying the name. Trying it out. It wasn't what she'd expected. Then again, Josie wasn't sure what she had expected. Lila Jensen sounded so normal, pretty even. Not at all like the devil she knew her mother to be.

"Lila Jensen," she said again.

"Gretchen's already on the phone with DHS trying to expedite a search of their records. She's also checking the databases to see how many Lila Jensens there are, or were, in the state, looking for any born between 1958 and 1964—assuming she was between eighteen and twenty-four when Belinda first met her at the courthouse. We know she was older than Belinda, but not by much."

Josie blinked, the flashing mountain scenery coming back into focus. "That won't help you find her."

"What?"

"So we know who she was before she stole Belinda's identity. She shed her own identity for a reason. She wouldn't go back to it. She doesn't want to be found."

The strange exhilaration of discovering one of her mother's secrets was now replaced with a sense of disappointment. Maybe they would find out some things about Josie's mother before she had become Josie's mother, but she knew in her gut it would not lead them to her. They still had no way to track her. No photos, even.

"Dex," she whispered.

Noah looked over at her for a second. "What's that?"

Josie cleared her throat and spoke more loudly. "Dexter McMann. The boyfriend I mentioned to you. I remembered his name. I need you to find a current address for him. He would be thirty-seven now."

"You think he would have photos?"

"I doubt it," Josie said. "It's probably a dead end, but Gretchen is right, I have to at least try talking to him. But first, I want to find Larry Ezekiel Fox and have a little chat with him."

CHAPTER 54

Her biggest mistake was letting herself enjoy life with Dex around. He'd been living with them for almost a year, and he was right: he wasn't a pervert, and he didn't want to be her father. They'd developed a strange kind of friendship restricted to the hours that Josie's mother was out of the trailer. She watched *ER* with him, and he watched *Ally McBeal* with her. Lisette would have said Josie was too young to watch television shows with such adult themes, but Dex didn't seem to think it was an issue. He drove her to school each day, picking up Ray along the way, and sometimes even picking them up at the end of the day as well. He took her for ice cream sundaes, swimming in the river during the summer, and sledding in the winter. Once during a snowstorm he'd driven into an empty parking lot and done donuts in the icy slush, provoking screams and giggles from Josie and somehow not crashing the car into any of the light poles.

If her mother noticed their rapport, she didn't comment on it. As usual, Josie stayed out of her way, and Dex focused all of his attention on her when she was there. For a time, Josie thought they could go on forever that way. But it couldn't last forever. That was the silly dream of a naïve fourteen-year-old.

The first signal came the day Josie sliced her hand open working on a science project. She had chosen to take and compare fingerprints and, after taking her own and Dex's prints, had broken a glass while reaching for some paper towels.

A wedge of glass protruded from the meat of her palm.

There was a lot of blood, but she didn't even feel the pain until she heard Dex say, "Holy shit!" He sprang into action, wrapping her hand up in a dish towel and rushing her to the hospital. At the ER, they removed the glass, stitched her up, and sent her home, where her mother was waiting for them.

Josie could smell the booze on her before they were even through the door. She stood next to the bloody glass debris they had abandoned in the kitchen, hands on her hips, glaring at the two of them. Josie knew from the way her eyes narrowed that she was in deep shit now. But when her mother spoke, she was looking at Dex. "Just what the hell do you think you're doing?"

From the corner of her eye, Josie glanced at him, seeing the confusion on his face. He smiled as though he wasn't sure if this was some kind of joke. "I'm sorry," he said. "What did you say?"

"Where were you?"

"I took JoJo to the hospital. She cut her hand pretty bad. She had to get stitches. I—"

"Did I give you permission to take my fourteen-year-old daughter to the hospital?" Her mother's voice was hard and cold, sending a shudder up Josie's spine.

Dex looked mystified. "Didn't you hear what I said? She needed stitches. She was bleeding all over the place."

"I didn't hire you to be a babysitter, Dex," her mother said. "You're mine."

He placed a hand on his chest. "I'm sorry, what?"

"JoJo takes care of herself. She doesn't need your help with anything. You're here for me."

"She's a kid," Dex argued.

"Yes, she's my kid. Not yours. You stay away from her and stay out of our business, you got that? I don't care if her goddamn hand is hanging off. And what the hell is all this?" she waved toward the makeshift fingerprint kit that Josie had left on the coffee table.

"I was helping her with a science project," Dex said. "But let me guess, you don't want me doing that either?"

A smile curved her mother's lips. "Now you're catching on."

Dex took a step toward her. "Let me ask you, Belinda, when's the last time you helped your kid with her science project? Or helped her with her homework, or—"

"Dex," Josie said, "don't."

The smile dropped from her mother's face, replaced by a look of pure rage. She looked from Josie to Dex and back again. Then, in a mocking tone, she mimicked Josie: "Dex, don't."

"Belinda," Dex said.

"I see what's going on here. You thought that JoJo was part of the deal. And you"—she turned her wrath toward Josie— "you're just a little whore after all, aren't you?"

"Hey!" Dex shouted. He moved in front of Josie and pointed a finger at her mother's chest. "Watch it."

Her mother looked him up and down as though he was beneath her. "Oh? What if I don't?"

He sniffed the air, moving his face closer to hers. "You're drunk," he said.

"So? That doesn't make what you're doing right."

"I'm not doing anything, and neither is JoJo. She's a kid, Belinda."

"And so are you. Get the *hell* out of my house."

With that, she sauntered off to her bedroom at the back of the trailer. Josie let out the breath she'd been holding. The center of her palm was on fire. Dex stared at her for a long moment. "You okay?" he asked.

Josie nodded.

She assumed he would leave. They always did. But she was wrong. Instead, he followed her mother down the hallway, kicking open her door with a loud bang and slamming it closed behind him. Josie stood rooted to the spot, listening as the shouting turned to gasping, and the familiar sound of her mother's bed springs creaking filled the small trailer—faster, louder, and longer than Josie had ever heard before. She fled to Ray's house, staying until well after midnight, but when she came home, she could still hear them.

CHAPTER 55

As much as Josie wanted to arrest Zeke herself, if she intended to press charges against him for the robbery of her house, she knew it would make things much easier on the district attorney if she had one of her patrol officers pick him up. Just as Lloyd Todd had promised, they found Zeke sleeping across two plastic chairs in the back corner of the laundromat.

Once he was brought in, Noah had him put into the interrogation room. He didn't ask for an attorney. As his teenage accomplice had told them, he wore a drab green jacket, frayed at the edges and missing all of its buttons. His face was creased with lines from age and hard living, and his long gray beard was yellow at the end. Across his forehead he wore a bandana that had lost all of its color and was now a dingy gray with a faded pattern on it, scraggly white hair snaking out from beneath it. Josie watched him on the closed-circuit television as he chain-smoked the cigarettes Noah had left with him, lighting one from the end of the last.

"A thousand cigarettes will not cover up his stink," Noah remarked as he walked in, handing her a file. "This guy needed a bath ten years ago. Homeless most of the last decade. Did a handful of stints for drug possession, manufacture, intent to sell—that sort of thing. No known associations with Lloyd Todd, just like Todd said."

Josie flipped through the pages of the file, which contained arrest reports, docket entries from his various convictions, and a few old mugshots. There was one photo from seven years earlier that caught Josie's eye, and something niggled at the back of her mind. She riffled through more pages until she found another one from thirteen years ago. With fewer lines on his face, his features were a little clearer. They were familiar, she realized. But why?

"Do you think Todd was telling the truth about the robbery and the ads?" Noah asked.

Josie didn't take her eyes off the file in her hands as she looked for more photos. "You know I don't make a habit of trusting lowlifes like Todd, but I don't see why he would give me so much information but lie about something like that. He hypothetically admitted to the most costly of the incidents. Why hold out on the other stuff? There's no benefit."

"I guess. But that begs the question: Who is behind the robbery and the craigslist ads?"

Josie motioned to the television. "Maybe Zeke can tell us."

She suddenly found what she was looking for: a third mug shot, this one taken twenty years earlier when Josie was ten. A gasp escaped her throat as the rest of the contents of the file fluttered to the floor.

"Boss?" Noah said. "What is it?"

Josie could hardly get the word out: "Needle."

"What's that?"

She looked up at the television screen. "I have to talk to him."

Noah was hot on her heels as she dashed out of the viewing room and down the hall to the interrogation room. "Boss," he called out, but he wasn't fast enough.

The door banged open and Needle stared up at her. She walked slowly to the table as Noah slipped in behind her and closed the door. She could sense that he wanted to say something, to stop her, but he kept silent. Josie placed a palm flat on the table and leaned toward him, the smell of smoke and stale body odor nearly overpowering her. "Do you remember me?"

He stared at her, a toothless smile splitting his face.

"Do you?" Josie demanded.

"Little JoJo."

Behind her, Josie sensed Noah startle. No one ever called her anything but Josie or Boss. Only Ray had had the privilege of shortening her name to Jo. Hearing her childhood nickname after so many years gave her a jolt as well, but she did her best to hide it.

"You knew my mother," Josie said. "What was her name?"

Needle laughed. "You know your mother's name."

"I want to hear it from you."

"Belinda," he said easily. "Belinda Rose."

"Her real name," Josie demanded.

A look of genuine confusion crossed his face. "Be-linda Rose," he repeated.

So her mother hadn't confided in this man. Josie changed tactics. "Why did you rob my house?"

"I didn't rob no one's house."

Josie rolled her eyes. She slapped her palm against the surface of the table to keep his attention focused on her. "Cut the shit, Zeke," she said. "I have two witnesses who not only put you there, but will testify that you put them up to it. Why? Why me? Why now?"

His fingers fumbled to get a cigarette out of the crushed pack in front of him and light it off his last. "You were a cute kid, you know that, JoJo?"

Josie said nothing.

"Made your mom a little crazy, I think. Having such a pretty thing around. Everyone always paying so much attention to you. Your dad—he didn't care a lick for your mom once you came along. That never sat well with her, you know."

Without conscious thought, Josie's hand reached up and traced the scar that went down her jawline. Needle motioned to her face. "That was the worst I ever seen her," he said. "Well, up until that night."

"You stopped her," Josie said.

He nodded. "She scared me that night. I seen her do a lot of things, but that was something different."

"Did you take me to the hospital?"

"Yes."

Josie's throat felt like it was in danger of closing up altogether. When she asked her next question, it came out nearly a whisper. "Why didn't you go inside and tell them what she did?"

He shrugged. "Wasn't my place. Besides, you don't cross a woman like that." He took a long drag from his cigarette, the ash glowing bright orange. "You oughta know that better than most."

She said nothing. Smoke hung in the air, unmoving. Quietly, Noah took a step closer to the table, watching the two of them. Finally, he shifted his gaze to Needle and said, "Zeke, we've got you on the robbery. Just tell us what you did with the jewelry. Did you sell it?"

Needle shook his head.

Noah said, "You didn't sell it?"

"I don't know what happened to it."

"It just disappeared from your hands, did it?" Noah asked.

"Did you know it was my house?" Josie interjected.

Needle met her eyes, and she was taken back to her childhood, hiding behind the couch or under the kitchen table, Needle catching her eyes, smiling at her, offering her a piece of his sandwich or a sip of his soda. She was always hungry. Then there was the day he had walked in on her mother trying to sell her for a paint job and told her to go outside and play. Josie never knew what had transpired after she ran off, but when she'd returned home, the man was gone. The paint job was never spoken of again. Needle had been in the right place at the right time. He had been kind to her. As kind as someone like him could be.

He smiled a sad smile. "I'm sorry, little JoJo."

"Why were you nice to me when I was a kid?" she asked.

He shrugged. "No reason not to be. Seemed like you were in a pretty bad situation there, especially after your dad passed."

Again, she was struck by the fact that his kindness and sympathy had only gone so far. Yes, he had been nice to her, had recognized what could only be called abuse, but he hadn't gone so far as to help her out of the situation. The world was full of people like Needle. People who noticed when others were in trouble, but whose sense of self-preservation ultimately outweighed their sense of justice.

"Why?" Josie tried again. "Why did you rob my house?"

Needle shook the pack of cigarettes, but there were no more left. He stubbed out the last butt in the ashtray Noah had provided and let out a lengthy sigh. "You're smart, JoJo. You can't figure it out? You haven't figured it out yet?"

Josie felt the cold fingers of fear scuttle up her spine. "Figured what out?"

Needle leaned back in his chair and folded his nicotine-stained hands over his stomach. "I'm about done here. If you're gonna charge me, charge me, and I'll take that lawyer you said would be appointed for me if I can't afford one. I got nothing else to say."

Noah and Josie stared at him for a long moment, waiting to see if he would change his mind or ask for something, but he was relaxed in his seat, whistling an unrecognizable tune to himself. Finally, Noah walked to the door and Josie followed. He held the door open for her, and she was about to step through it when Needle spoke again.

"Don't know what you ever did to her, little JoJo."

Her heart seized in her chest. She turned back to him. "What did you say?"

"She said you'd find me. I said no you wouldn't, you'd never know I was involved. But she was right. You got me. You even recognized me."

"Who said I'd find you?" Josie asked, frozen in the doorway. "What are you talking about?"

He met her eyes. "She wanted me to give you a message. She said she'll destroy everything you love."

CHAPTER 56

"Boss," Noah said as she fled past him down the hallway. The distance from the interrogation room to her office seemed endless, like she was in one of those nightmares where no matter how fast you ran, you never moved, and the end was always just out of reach. Breath came in short gasps, her palm clammy as it closed around the door handle at last.

Noah was only a few feet behind; she heard the sound of his feet slowing on the tiles behind her. "Boss," he called again. "What the hell was that about?"

She slammed the door in his face, locked it, slumped against it, and slid down to the floor. Her heartbeat thundered in her chest. Too fast—it was going too fast. Dizziness assailed her. Noah called to her from the other side of the door, but she couldn't answer. She looked around her office, but all she saw were flashes from her childhood—her mother stalking the darkness of the trailer, waiting for Josie's dad to return, muttering words Josie would never forget:

I'll destroy everything you love.

It was her all along. How long had she been back? What had brought her back after all these years? Where was she? The memories of the things Belinda—no, Lila—had done to her awoke and screamed into Josie's mind, black and cloying. She squeezed her eyes shut, but that only made it worse. Clambering to her feet, she moved behind her desk, hands searching for the framed photo of her and Ray as nine-year-olds. She focused on his face, remembering all the ways he had helped her face the monsters in her head. She was suddenly glad Ray was dead—it meant her mother couldn't hurt him.

She looked up to the corkboard above her desk where she had pinned several photos—Josie and her predecessor, Chief Harris, at one of her promotion ceremonies years earlier. Photos of people she'd never met—victims whose grateful families had written her letters after she'd solved their cases. A photo of Josie and Lisette from Lisette's last birthday. The most recent photo was a candid shot of little Harris Quinn, giggling with smashed baby peas all over his face.

"Oh Jesus," Josie mumbled to herself.

She sprang up and opened the door to her office to find Noah still there, his arms folded across his chest, his eyes piercing.

"I need a detail on Misty Derossi and my grandmother," she said.

"What was that guy talking about, Boss?" Noah asked.

"He's talking about my mother. She's back. She's here, or somewhere nearby. She's behind all of this—the ads, the robbery. She's coming after me and the people I love; no one is safe. You need to get someone over to Rockview. I'd bring Gram home with me, but it's not safe. And Misty and Harris—she'll find out about them. I can't let anything happen to them. Not because of me."

Noah's arms dropped to his sides as she spoke. "Let me go at this guy. He must know where she is. We'll get to her first."

"No," Josie said. "He doesn't know where she is. Not that he would tell you anyway. She's smarter than that. She would have come to him. If she knew that I was going to find him, she wouldn't make it that easy."

Behind Noah, Gretchen approached, a piece of paper in her hand. She reached past Noah and handed it to Josie. "Found that boyfriend. Fraley told me his name. Dexter McMann lives in Fairfield now."

It was a little over an hour away. Josie could get there in half that time.

"There's a phone number there," Gretchen said.

"I don't need it," Josie told her. She went to her desk and found her car keys. "I'll be back in a few hours."

"I'm going with you," Noah said.

"No, you're not. I need you to stay here, make sure Zeke gets properly booked, get someone out to Misty's place and Rockview."

Her phone buzzed in her pocket. She pulled it out and saw another text from Trinity reminding her she had agreed to meet that day. *Something came up at work,* Josie shot back. *I'll try to stop by tonight, but it will probably have to wait till tomorrow.* In reply, Trinity sent her a pouty-face emoji. Josie rolled her eyes, pocketed her phone, and left the building.

CHAPTER 57

There were other instances that caused cracks in the tenuous peace inside the trailer since Dex had moved in. One evening her mother had come home early from work and found them sitting side by side on the couch, laughing at a movie on television. She had flown at Josie, raining down open-hand slaps onto her head until Dex pulled her away. Josie had fled to her room and stayed there until the arguing died down. That night Dex did leave, and he didn't come back for a week.

There was the time it was raining—pouring in sheets—and Dex left her mother at the trailer to pick Josie up from school so she wouldn't have to walk home through it. At first, her mother hadn't made much of it, but when Dex was asleep she had burst into Josie's bedroom, pouring a bucket of cold water over her as she slept. Startled awake, Josie found herself on the wrong end of an expletive-laced tirade. If Dex had noticed how tired Josie was the next few days while her mattress dried out and she slept on the floor, he didn't comment.

The forensic science books that Dex had found at a thrift shop for Josie were burned in the metal barrel outside of the trailer while he was at work. When he asked if she was enjoying them, she didn't have the heart to tell him what her mother had done. Maybe she should have. Maybe he would have left. Or maybe he would have simply followed her mother into her room and banged her some more. Josie never understood their strange relationship. She never understood anyone's relationship with her mother. Except Lisette's—her gram hated her mother fiercely.

The death knell of that mostly bright year was all Josie's fault. Perhaps having someone there to talk to her, to care about her, to show interest in her, had made her bolder. Or perhaps it had simply made her just as stupid as Dex. There was a freshman dance coming up—a formal dance—and Ray had asked her to go with him. His father had been gone for a year, and he was finally feeling his freedom—he wanted them to be normal and go to a dance like boyfriend and girlfriend. Josie figured she could do her own hair and makeup, like she'd seen a few of the other girls at school doing theirs in the bathroom. But she knew she needed a dress, and she didn't have much money.

She had asked Dex if he would drive her to the thrift store and then, later that evening, drive her and Ray to the dance. But Dex, being Dex, had gone above and beyond, dropping her outside a dress shop and telling her there was a deposit behind the counter for whatever dress she wanted. Her heart sang as she chose a slinky but fairly modest blue dress that the saleswoman said brought out her eyes. Dex also had a cousin who owned a salon, and he'd arranged an appointment for her there once she was done.

Josie barely recognized herself in the mirror as Dex picked her up to take her back home so she could change before the dance. "Ray won't know what hit him," he told her, smiling.

Josie couldn't wait to see Ray's face when they picked him up. In her bedroom, she put on her dress and twirled in front of her mirror, feeling pretty for the first time in her life. Her bedside clock showed that she only had a few minutes before Dex would take her to get Ray. Her mother would be at work all night, and Josie hoped she would never find out about the dance, or the dress, or the makeup, or the way Ray had made her feel when he asked her to be his date.

Dex's eyes lit up when he saw her. "Wow," he said. "You look amazing."

"Thanks," Josie replied.

They were standing by the front door, ready to leave, when Dex stopped her. "Wait," he said. He took her shoulders and peered into her face. For a moment, a bolt of fear shot through her, and she flinched as he lifted a hand, licked the pad of his thumb, and rubbed at a spot just below her left eye. "Mascara," he said.

Josie laughed nervously. The palm that remained on her one shoulder was warm. She hadn't ever been this close to Dex. The proximity—mixed with her anticipation of going to the dance—was dizzying. He grinned at her. "JoJo," he said softly. "You make sure you have a good time tonight, okay?"

She nodded.

"Ray's a lucky guy, kiddo."

A sudden impulse made Josie rock up onto her toes and plant a kiss on Dex's cheek. Surprise lit his face, and they stood frozen in time for a moment—Josie's lipstick on his cheek, his hand on her shoulder—smiling stupidly at one another. And that's when the door opened; her mother stood there, a six-pack of beer in her arms. She stared at them for a long time, taking everything in: Josie's dress, makeup, and hair, the way they stood close to one another, Dex's car keys now dangling from his free hand.

Josie's heart stopped, and she counted two long seconds before it thundered back to life like an angry beast trying to claw its way out of her chest. She waited for her mother's fury, for her to throw the beer cans at Josie's head, or to fly at her, tearing at her dress and hair until Josie was too unkempt to be seen in public.

But her mother did nothing. She simply stood there. Then she asked, "What's going on here?"

Dex said, "JoJo has a school dance. She's going with Ray. I told them I'd drop them off."

Her mother turned her gaze to Josie. "Your grandmother sneak you that stuff? That interfering bitch."

Josie would have let it go. That would have been best. But Dex jumped in before she had a chance to formulate her response. "No, I did, and I didn't sneak it. JoJo needed a dress for the dance, and my cousin does hair and makeup, so I asked her to help out."

Her mother narrowed her eyes at him. "*You* did this?"

"Come on, Belinda. You never went to a school dance? Give the kid a break. You won't let her see her grandmother. Her dad's dead. The only person she ever sees is that scrawny little Ray. So she wants to go to a dance; let her have some fun."

Josie braced herself for the attack she knew was inevitable. She closed her eyes and took a deep breath, waiting for the blows, the tearing of her beautiful dress, the bruises on her face that would render her makeup useless.

But it didn't come. She felt something brush by her, and when she opened her eyes, her mother was seated on the couch, popping a can of beer. Both Josie and Dex stared at her in shock, but she simply sipped her beer, picked up the remote control, and turned on the television. When she realized they were both still looking at her, she said, "Well, you better get going then."

They walked outside, letting the trailer door flap closed behind them, a fizz in the air like they had narrowly escaped something huge. They didn't speak or look at one another the entire route to Ray's house.

Ray seemed oblivious, possibly mistaking her nervous energy for jitters about the dance. She tried to have a good time, to focus on Ray and the way he kept looking at her like buried treasure, but her mind kept returning to the terrifying calm of her mother, sitting placidly on the sofa, drinking beer.

When Dex brought Josie home from the dance later that night, her mother looked as though she hadn't moved an inch, except for the bottle of vodka in front of her. Dex said, "I'm going to bed. You coming?"

"No," she said. "I think I'll stay up awhile. Might sleep out here by the TV."

CHAPTER 58

Anxiety gnawed at Josie's insides as she drove alone to the address Gretchen had given her for Dexter McMann. Before she had made it to her car, Noah had redoubled his efforts to come along, but ultimately he did as he was told, staying behind and sending patrol cars to monitor Rockview Ridge and Misty Derossi's house. From the car, Josie called Misty and awkwardly explained that some people had been harassing her lately because of her job, and that she wanted to make sure that harassment didn't extend to those around her. Luckily for Josie, Misty was too ill and too exhausted from dealing with a sick baby to ask many questions. Josie had a similar conversation with the administrator of Rockview, who promised to tighten up their security measures. Gretchen was busy finishing up the paperwork on Needle's arrest. They would have their hands full until Josie returned.

Fairfield was a tiny town in Lenore County, which was south of Alcott County. Most of Lenore County was made up of farms and state gameland. The Escape hugged the curves of the winding mountain roads until they gave way to rolling one-lane roads snaking across miles of farmland. If the thought of seeing Dex again wasn't making her sick to her stomach, Josie would have enjoyed the idyllic scenery.

The address Gretchen gave her brought her to a one-story house with dingy white siding and several poorly constructed additions built onto the side. It sat two acres back from the road at the end of a gravel driveway. An old red pickup truck sat outside the front porch. Josie saw several cut tree trunks standing like sentries in the grass in front of the house. As she got closer, she saw that several of them had been carved into the shapes of animals—a bear, an eagle, and a large owl. One trunk had a man's face carved into it, with a long flowing beard that reached the ground. They were stunning. She parked her Escape and walked over to where they stood. There were several smaller ones in the long grass at her feet—a duck and a sleeping coyote.

A man's voice called out, "They start at three hundred. The eagle is already sold, I'm afraid. I've got more in the back. Just finished my first mermaid."

She heard his steps moving toward her. She didn't want to turn, to face him, but she was here, and there was no running away.

"I, uh, also have a couple of dragons if you're into that sort of thing. Lots of people looking for those these days. There's a big demand for mythical creatures all of a sudden. I was thinking I might try a unicorn, but I don't—" His words died on his lips as Josie turned to look at him.

Frozen in place, he stared at her. He'd always been tall, and in the years since she'd last seen him, he'd put on some weight. He looked sturdier now, strong and burly in a pair of stained, torn jeans and a black T-shirt that clung to his chest. He had always been handsome. Until the fire.

She had hoped that maybe the scars would get better over time, or that he'd find a plastic surgeon who could restore what had been lost, but looking at him now, his face still bore the heavy, indelible marks of her mother's wrath.

"Haven't seen you in almost twenty years, JoJo," he said, his voice husky.

"Josie," she said. "My name is Josie."

He smiled, and the side of his face that hadn't melted lifted. "I know," he said. "Josie Quinn. Married Ray after all. I was sorry to hear about his death. You were two peas in a pod."

"We turned out to be very different people," Josie said.

He nodded. "Yeah, well, I guess that's true, isn't it? I see you on the news all the time since you solved that case of all those missing girls and became chief. You've done well for yourself."

Josie took a step closer to him. She ran a finger along the side of the enormous bear sculpture. "Looks like you have too."

He shrugged. "I do okay. Beats going to a job every day and dealing with the public." He motioned to the side of his head. The burns had taken a portion of his hair behind his left temple. "It gets old answering the questions, you know?"

She didn't know, but she nodded anyway. "They gave you a glass eye," she said. "It looks good."

His fingers touched just beneath his left eye socket. "Yeah, makes me look more human, I think."

An awkward silence unfurled between them. Josie turned and looked back at the sculptures. "These are amazing, Dex. I had no idea you knew how to do this."

"What are you doing here, JoJ—Josie?"

Josie pointed to his front porch. There were no chairs, but there were a couple of steps they could perch on. "Can we sit?"

He ushered her over, and they sat side by side on the stoop. For a couple of minutes, they stared at his open front yard, watching the breeze ruffle the tops of the trees lining the road. Then Dex said, "I never told you this—never had the chance to—but it wasn't your fault."

Josie swallowed over the instant lump in her throat. "Bullshit. It was entirely my fault. I'm so, so sorry, Dex."

He knocked his thigh against hers. "Stop. We don't even know that she did it. It was just odd timing."

"Someone sets fire to your hair while you're sleeping? On a night when she just happened to fall asleep on the couch, out of harm's way? You know as well as I do that she did this to you. And she did it because of me."

"You were a kid. Belinda was crazy."

"Lila," Josie said. "Her real name was Lila Jensen."

"What? What do you mean by that?"

She told him everything, and he didn't speak for a long time after she had finished. Then he said, "Makes you wonder what else she's gotten away with, doesn't it?"

Josie nodded.

"What do you need from me?"

"A photograph," Josie answered. "If you had any—or kept any. I know it's a long shot. I probably wouldn't have kept a picture of the woman who disfigured me."

He stared out at the road. "I didn't."

Disappointment sat heavy on Josie's shoulders. Before it could settle into full-blown despair, Dex said, "But I kept a picture of you. And your mother happens to be in it as well. All this time, I thought that was unfortunate."

CHAPTER 59

Josie woke to the sound of Dex screaming like a wild animal caught in a trap—a sound that would haunt her dreams for years to come. She sprang out of bed and ran into the hallway to find smoke billowing from her mother's room. Inside, Dex's head was a ball of flame, and he was running around throwing himself against the walls like he was stuck in a pinball machine. On the bed, one of the pillows was alight, and fire was spreading quickly across the bedspread. A gust of air from the open window billowed the curtain into the flames and set them alight too. Dex slapped his hands furiously against his skull, but the flames were taking over faster than he could snuff them.

Josie ran back to her room and snatched her comforter from her bed. Back in the main bedroom, she screamed Dex's name to get his attention, but he seemed not to hear her. Finally, she climbed onto the bed, trying to stay on the side that wasn't burning, and as he passed by her, she threw the comforter over him. Her hands found the round hardness of his skull, and she pounded it with both palms. He kept screaming. She had to get him out of the room. Jumping down off the bed, she guided him toward the door. He stumbled and fell into the hallway. Josie pulled the door closed behind her, trying to contain the fire, and tried to find his arms beneath the comforter. Her hand closed around one of his. "Dex," she said. "Come on. We have to go."

He teetered but came to his feet. The comforter was still

over his head, tendrils of smoke floating from beneath it. The smell of burnt flesh singed Josie's nostrils as she guided him out into the living room, toward the front door. Her mother watched them from the couch, unmoving, a glass of vodka in one hand and a satisfied smile on her lips.

CHAPTER 60

Josie paused before getting in the car to snap a picture of Lila's face with her phone. She sent it to Noah and Gretchen so they could get it out to the news outlets as quickly as possible. As she drove, the photo sat on the passenger's seat of her Escape, drawing her gaze toward it again and again. Her mother standing outside of their trailer, slender but shapely in a pair of jeans and a lavender V-neck T-shirt. Long, shiny black hair cascaded down over her shoulders. Her thin face, high cheekbones, square chin, and blue eyes set on the slightest angle gave her a slightly exotic look. Josie remembered well the steady flow of male attention that Lila Jensen attracted—when she wanted to.

Josie's thirteen-year-old self stood beside her mother in a sleeveless sundress that was two sizes too large for her, her blue eyes vacant. I'm here but I'm not really here, said the look on her face and her stiff posture, her body leaning away from her mother even though they stood shoulder to shoulder.

Josie didn't remember the photo being taken. Few people they knew had cameras, and Lila hadn't generally allowed them when they did—now Josie understood why. Josie was grateful that Dex had kept this one photo. It was the most tangible lead yet.

Back at the station house, Gretchen reported that there were four Lila Jensens in Pennsylvania, and only one of them was within the age range that Josie's mother would be—and she'd had one apartment in Bellewood in 1983 before disappearing off the grid forever. It was a dead end. All they knew for sure was her true birth date. Not in October, but July. Josie faced a mound of paperwork on her desk from administrative duties she'd been putting off all week. Jitters ran through her body, making her fingers tap her pen in a drumbeat on her desk as she sat in her chair, trying to focus. She called and checked on Misty and Harris. Then she called Rockview again. No reports of anything out of the ordinary.

Gretchen had tracked down Lila Jensen in the foster-care system, but in a county many hours away whose DHS office was having difficulty locating such an old file. Josie had a sinking feeling that the Lila Jensen file had gone wherever the Belinda Rose file had gone. She wondered if Judge Malcolm Bowen had had anything to do with it before he died. He was the only person who would have had enough influence to make two foster care files disappear. Again, the thought that Sophia Bowen hadn't been truthful when they interviewed her niggled at Josie's mind. Now that they had a photo, perhaps they could bring her in, question her formally, and see if they could get something more from her. She called Bowen's home but got the voicemail. She left a message asking if Sophia could come to the station for formal questioning and gave her office and cell phone number. It was Sophia's move.

Giving up on the idea of getting any paperwork done, Josie decided to drive over to the Eudora and face Trinity. But there was no answer when Josie knocked on the door to her room. She waited in the hall for fifteen minutes, texting Trinity that she was there, but got no response.

Night fell around her as she drove away from the hotel and aimlessly around the city until fatigue burned her eyes. She wanted to keep moving, keep doing anything that would keep the memories at bay. But the clock on her dashboard said midnight, and Noah had texted her twice already to remind her that she needed rest; he suggested she stay with him again for her own safety.

Noah.

smile. He cupped both her cheeks. "No," he said with abso-
conviction. "You're not damaged. You're extraordinary."

It was like their bodies had caught fire as her mouth crashed
own onto his, and then both of them were reaching, pulling at
ne another's clothes. With Noah's frenzied hands and mouth
n her body, the trauma of the last several days fell away. There
as only him and the sensations he provoked in her body. It
as like trying to stop a forest fire with a watering can, but
omewhere deep inside, the more reasoned part of her made
er pull back. She didn't want to be this person anymore—a
woman who used the heat and ecstasy of sex to hold back her
demons whenever she thought they might overwhelm her.

"Stop," Josie said. "We have to stop."

Her last two relationships had been colossal failures. Maybe
not entirely because of the sex and whiskey she used to escape
her feelings, but they'd failed nonetheless.

Noah's mouth was hot against her throat. She pushed him
away gently, disentangling herself and standing up. She needed
some distance between them, even as every cell in her body
yearned to be close to him again.

His chest heaved. "What is it?" he gasped, staring up at her.
She'd managed to get his shirt off. The scar near his right shoulder from where she'd shot him during the missing girls case
drew her gaze. He had forgiven her easily, but her guilt lived on.

"You deserve better than this," she said.

A crease appeared over the bridge of his nose. "What?"

"I'm not—I'm not good enough for you."

He jumped up. He was down to his boxer shorts, and she
uld see that he was ready for her. "I think that's a judgment I
ed to make, not you," he said.

She was suddenly aware of the air on her skin. She looked
und but didn't see her T-shirt anywhere. She folded her arms
r her bra and met his eyes. Emotions of every kind roiled
hin her. She tried to find some kind of focus. "Noah," she
, "this just isn't a good idea."

The lights of his little house glowed brightly as she pulled
up in front of it. Wordlessly, he let her inside. His thick brown
hair was still wet from a shower, and he wore shorts and a
Denton PD T-shirt.

Josie went upstairs and changed into a pair of sweatpants
and a T-shirt. She took up position on Noah's couch again, staring at her reflection in the blackness of the television screen:
drawn face, haunted eyes.

Noah joined her on the couch. There were no dirty chai
lattes. No meatball subs. He didn't even ask if she had eaten.
She knew he was truly angry with her this time; she hadn't been
forthcoming with him about Needle, and then she had run off to
talk to Dex alone. "I'm sorry," she said.

"I'll respect your boundaries," Noah said. "You don't need
to shut me out."

"I'm not—I didn't, I—"

He waved a hand. "It's okay. Just let us protect you. You've
got a whole department at your disposal. If anyone on your staff
had been robbed and attacked in the same week, you'd want
someone on them—you know you would."

This was true. It was also true that she didn't like admitting
weakness or vulnerability, and she certainly didn't want her
staff to view her that way. "I'll try," she said.

"Lila Jensen's photo ran on the eleven o'clock news," Noah
said. "It's already up online on all the local news sites. You'll be
notified immediately if any good tips come in."

"Thank you," Josie said.

"Gretchen tried to get something out of Zeke, but he
wouldn't talk."

Josie kept her eyes on her reflection in the television. "I
told you he wouldn't. He's got nothing to lose. He meant what
he said—he wouldn't cross my mother even if he knew where
she was."

"Josie, do you really think she's that dangerous? That she
would go after your grandmother or Misty and the baby?"

She shook her head. "Maybe not directly. You've seen—she had someone else rob my house. I doubt she is very computer-savvy. She probably had someone else place the craigslist ads. One of those teenage idiots working at the Spur Mobile store has probably been giving her my number—hell, that same teenager is probably the one placing the ads. She uses people; there were always people willing to do things for her for drugs or favors or because she had something on them. She's been working at this for over a month now. She won't stop until everything I love is gone."

Noah let a moment pass. She sensed him trying to figure out a tactful way to ask the question. "Why...why does she—"

Josie met his eyes. "Why does she hate me so much?"

He looked away.

"It's okay. Look." She pulled her hair away from her face, turning so that he could see the long, silvered scar running down the side of her face. "She did this to me when I was six. The man you brought in tonight? Zeke? He stopped her. I used to call him Needle because I didn't know his name, and that's what he always brought with him."

"I'm sorry," Noah said.

"That was probably the least horrible thing she did to me. The man I visited today was her boyfriend. She was angry with him because of something I did, so she set fire to his hair when he was sleeping. Or at least, I suspect she did. There was never any proof. They both smoked, and it was assumed he must have fallen asleep with a lit cigarette in his mouth. But I just know she did it."

"Jesus."

"In my sophomore year of college, I had some...struggles. I was depressed. Drank too much. I had to see a therapist. I didn't go for long, but what I got out of that experience was the realization that my mother hates everyone—not just me." She laughed, a mirthless sound. "In other words, it's nothing personal. She only cares about herself, which means she cares

about other people only if they have somethin needs. Once they've served their purpose, she in making them suffer. She is spiteful, jealous, and most of all, she's unpredictable. And very, ver

"I had no idea," Noah said.

"Of course you didn't. No one knows. It's not talk about. Ever. Only Ray knew what she was rea even he didn't know everything. For a long time, I thing keeping my dad around. Once he was gone, s from my grandmother just to be cruel. So, the answ question—she hates me because that's just who she don't know is why she's come back. Why now?"

A feeling of bone-deep fatigue spread through h spoke. She closed her eyes, and a moment later she fe hand slide into hers, squeezing gently. There was n could have said to comfort her, and she appreciated t silence he let her have. She squeezed back.

When she opened her eyes again, she caught hi at her intently. As tired as she was, the electricity their clasped hands gave her a jolt. With his other ha reached over and pressed a palm to her cheek. It was v Josie let her head sink into it. Tears sprang to her eye blinked them back. She wasn't sure if she could take of tenderness. He searched her face and leaned in s lips inches from hers, testing the air between them her lips to his, and he kissed her, long and slow an her legs felt weak and her whole body tingled. Kiss strange and nothing like she had expected; it wa anything she'd ever expected, and that terrified h

He broke the kiss but held onto her, pressing hers, the two of them breathing into one another

"Noah," she said. "You don't—you shouldn'

"What?"

"You don't want me. You're so good and I'm

He moved his head back just enough so

He lifted a hand to touch her, but she moved back, out of his reach. The edge of the coffee table cut into the backs of her calves. The confusion in Noah's eyes was replaced with hurt. The sight felt like a knife in her chest.

"I'm sorry," she managed. "I just don't think we should—"

The sound of their cell phones ringing simultaneously cut her off.

Noah tore his eyes from her, looking around blindly for his phone.

"On the table," Josie said as she looked around for her own. She found it between the cushions of the couch. It had stopped ringing, but the missed call was from the police station. Noah was already talking to someone. "Yeah, I got it," he said. "I'm on my way."

"What is it?" Josie asked.

He sighed and pushed a hand through his hair. He wouldn't look at her. "Big college party at one of the off-campus houses. You know those big ones up on Turner Hill?"

"The ones with the big drop-off behind them?"

"Yeah, the creek runs behind them. One of the neighbors called police because of the noise. Patrol showed up, a bunch of kids ran out the back, and one of them fell from the drop-off trying to get away. He's alive but had to be life-flighted to Geisinger."

"My God."

Noah found his T-shirt on the floor next to the couch and pulled it on. "They've got a bunch of underage drinking arrests. I'm going to head over and help out."

He disappeared up the steps. Overhead, Josie could hear him opening and closing drawers in his bedroom. When he came back down, he was wearing jeans and his shoulder holster.

Arms still folded over her semi-naked torso, Josie stepped toward him. "I'll go with you."

He shook his head, snatching his keys from the coffee table. "I can handle a college party. Go upstairs. Go to sleep."

Josie watched his back as he walked away from her toward the foyer, and felt a panic start deep in her chest. "You have to be careful," she blurted, running after him. "My mother—she'll try coming after you too. She'll know—"

Noah's hand was on the doorknob, but he still wouldn't look at her. "Know what?"

She reached for his back, her fingers brushing his shirt. A hot flush crept up her cheeks. "That I..." She broke off. Beneath his shirt, she saw the muscles of his shoulders tense. She tried again. "That I care about you."

He pulled the door open. Over his shoulder he said, "Somehow, I don't think that's true." Then he was gone.

CHAPTER 61

The glowing green numbers of Noah's digital clock announced that it was after ten a.m. Josie sat up with a start, throwing the covers off her. Sunlight peeked around the edges of his bedroom shades. Why the hell hadn't he woken her up? Was he really that angry with her? Had he come home at all? Snatching her cell phone off the nightstand, she saw she had no messages. Something wasn't right. She threw on some clothes and went downstairs. Everything was exactly as she had left it when she'd trudged up to Noah's bedroom the night before. The coffee pot was empty, a sure sign he hadn't come home.

A small kernel of unease settled in the pit of her stomach. Since she had been chief, there hadn't been a single day that she hadn't gotten at least three phone calls before ten a.m. Even on her days off. She raced upstairs to grab her things before dashing to her car. Hopping into it, her right foot searched for the gas pedal but didn't find it. It was then that she noticed how far back her seat was from the steering wheel.

"What the hell?"

A slow panic tingled through her. She slid her seat back up and broke three traffic laws getting to the station house. Sergeant Lamay sat at the lobby desk. Josie could tell by his wide eyes that something wasn't right. She passed through the door that separated the public from the rest of the building and advanced on Lamay. "What the hell is going on?"

Lamay spoke in a whisper. "There's been an incident. Well, a murder. Bad one. Boss...I know it wasn't you. We all do. But the fire marshal called the mayor 'cause he didn't trust Fraley or Palmer to handle it. Least, that's what he said when he showed up here with her a few hours ago."

Josie's heart began to race, the tingle in her body now a hard vibration. "A few hours ago?" she hissed.

Lamay looked behind her to make sure they were still alone. "They were going to pick you up."

"Pick me up? You mean arrest me?"

Lamay nodded. He leaned toward her, and the chair creaked beneath his rotund frame. "You can still go, Boss," he told her. "I'll take care of the cameras."

Josie put a hand on his shoulder. "Thank you, but that's not necessary."

"Boss, it's bad."

"I'm not going anywhere. I am the chief of police in this town, and this is my department, my station house. Where are they?"

Lamay's shoulders rounded. He fidgeted with one of the buttons on his uniform shirt. "Conference room."

Josie turned to go but stopped before she reached the hall that would lead her deeper into the building and closer to her doom. She thought of her grandmother, then Misty and baby Harris. A sick feeling invaded her stomach. "Lamay," she said. "The victim. Was it a woman? Or a child?"

"No," he said. "It was the owner of that body shop over on Sixth and Seller. Not too far from where Zeke was picked up the other night."

The color drained from her face.

"You okay, Boss?" Lamay asked.

No. She was not okay. Words failed her. She steadied herself with a hand against the wall.

"Did you know him?" Lamay inquired.

Bile rose in the back of her throat. "Sort of."

CHAPTER 62

Mayor Tara Charleston presided over the conference room table with a cold stare that made Josie's skin crawl. The two had never gotten along, and Josie knew that Mayor Charleston was just waiting for any opportunity to remove her from her post as chief. Or "interim chief" as Tara liked to call her. Josie didn't know what the hell was going on, but whatever it was, there was a good chance it could end her career.

"Chief Quinn," she said when Josie walked through the door. "We were going to send someone to find you."

"I bet you were," Josie said.

Gretchen and Noah sat next to one another on one side of the table. Both looked haggard and distressed. Dark stubble covered Noah's face. When he met Josie's eyes, the look of pain and confusion was like a physical slap. She wished things hadn't ended so awkwardly between them the night before. Gone was Gretchen's easy smile. Every line etched into her face by her forty-four years was evident. Both of them looked as though they were being held against their will. Perhaps they were; she couldn't imagine either one of them not trying to warn her. Unless Noah was really that hurt. Then she saw their phones sitting side by side near Tara's right hand.

"What's going on?" Josie asked, pulling herself up straight and tall.

"Boss," Gretchen said.

"Detective," Tara cautioned.

Naked anger flared on Gretchen's face as she looked at

Tara. Noah nudged her with an elbow, a silent request for her to keep her cool. She kept quiet but shook her head, a vein in her forehead throbbing. Josie couldn't remember ever seeing her so angry.

"Sit," Tara said.

Josie folded her arms across her chest. "I think I'll stand."

"Suit yourself." Tara swiveled slightly in her chair and punched a button on a department laptop, bringing the screen to life. "During the night last night, at approximately three a.m., you, or a woman looking remarkably like you, drove your Escape—or a vehicle identical to yours with your same license plate number—to Ted's Auto Body, where the owner, Ted Heinrich, was tied to a chair, beaten, and set on fire. He did not survive."

Josie swallowed but said nothing.

Tara turned the laptop toward Josie so that she could see the screen. She pressed another button and a video began to play. At the top left-hand side of the media software, Josie could make out the words ROWLAND INDUSTRIES. Ted Heinrich had obviously sprung for some high-definition video surveillance equipment. Top of the line. Her gaze returned to the bird's-eye view of the front of his body shop. A concrete driveway with a giant grease stain led to two large garage doors, their windows painted white. To the right of the garage doors was a regular door with a sign above it: OFFICE. Creeping into the corner of the frame, Josie could see part of Heinrich's red 1965 GTO Mustang. The sight of it made her feel sick.

A few seconds later, an Escape pulled up and covered the grease stain completely. When Josie saw her own license plate staring back at her, she wished she had agreed to sit down. The brake lights died, and the driver's-side door opened.

And then, Josie stepped out of the car wearing a yellow T-shirt, jeans, and a pair of white sneakers. They looked new. Josie felt three pairs of eyes drilling into her, but she maintained composure while her brain worked at warp speed to make sense of what she was seeing. For a split second, she actually questioned herself. Had she been drugged? Sleepwalking? Had she driven to Ted Heinrich's business during the night and killed him? She'd certainly fantasized about it over the years. But no, she realized, remembering that her driver's seat had been out of position when she got into her car that morning. This was something else.

On screen, the woman closed her door, took two steps away from the Escape, and looked around. Her eyes searched upward, panning until she found the camera. She looked into it, and Josie's own face stared back at her. In the conference room, Josie counted off the seconds. One, two, three, four. Then the woman reached up and gathered her long, black hair into both hands as if she were pulling it into a ponytail, dragging it to the side so that all her hair rested over her left collarbone. Her head tilted to the left a bit, almost as if she were listening to something. But she wasn't listening to anything. She was exposing her profile. The right side of her face was soft, smooth, and unblemished in the moonlight.

"Trinity," Josie murmured.

Trinity went into the office door, and Tara reached over and fast-forwarded the video, stopping it when Trinity came back out, her clothes mussed and covered in something dark—oil or blood, or both, Josie guessed. This time, in her rush to get to the Escape, she didn't bother looking at the camera. Within seconds, both Trinity and the Escape were gone. Tara closed the laptop.

Gretchen said, "The mayor ordered patrols to go to your house and collect you and your vehicle—for evidence processing—but you weren't there."

Noah had known where she was, but he hadn't told. Because he was protecting her or because he knew that if the mayor found out she'd been sleeping at his house, he'd be in the hot seat as well?

"Chief Quinn," Tara said, "the only reason you are not

being booked into county jail right now is because Lieutenant Fraley tells us that that cannot possibly be you in that video. Primarily because, unlike the woman in this footage, you have a scar running down the right side of your face."

Josie lifted her hair and turned her face so that Tara could get a good look at the mark her mother had left on her at the tender age of six.

"Well," Tara said. "It seems you have a doppelganger."

"There's more," Gretchen said. "Tell her."

Tara looked reluctant but added, "We found what we believe is your old wedding ring at the scene, but Detective Palmer tells me that all of your jewelry was stolen from your home only a few days ago, so there is no way you could have left it at the scene."

"This is obviously a setup," Gretchen said.

Josie said, "You should talk to Trinity Payne, the reporter. She's staying at the Eudora Hotel. Room 227."

"Why would Trinity Payne kill a man and try to frame you for it?" Tara asked.

Why would Trinity kill a man at all? Josie wondered. What nagged at Josie even more was why Heinrich, and why now? What connection did Trinity have to the man?

The story.

Josie almost blurted the words out loud, stopping herself at the last minute. Trinity would do anything for a story, and she had wanted to do a story on Josie. But then Josie had blown her off repeatedly. Had she gone off on her own and started digging into Josie's past? Even if she had, how had she turned up the connection to Heinrich? No one knew about him. Not even Ray had known. There were only four people who knew what nearly happened between him and Josie all those years ago—Heinrich, Josie, Needle, and Lila.

Fucking Lila.

"Trinity had to be under duress," Gretchen said. "Whatever happened inside that body shop—Trinity's hand was forced.

She's the face of a national network. Why would she do something like this if she wasn't under duress?"

"She didn't appear to be under duress," Tara pointed out. "And she was alone. She drove up, went inside, spent almost an hour there, and came back out alone. How could she be under duress when she went there willingly?"

Trinity would have gone willingly if it meant getting a story. Lila must have fed her something. But how? Had Trinity somehow tracked down Lila? No, the entire Denton PD hadn't been able to track the woman down. Trinity had some of the best resources for finding both people and information, but surely she hadn't been able to find Josie's mother when the rest of them had been smacking into wall after wall.

Which meant that Lila had somehow contacted Trinity. Trinity would have agreed to meet Lila. She would have been interested in Lila's take on Josie's childhood. All the juicy secrets—the juiciest of all being what Heinrich had almost done to Josie at eleven years old. Lila would lie and spin it, of course. When she told Trinity the story, she would fail to mention that she had sold Josie for a paint job. No, she would make Josie out to be some tween seductress, and she would leave out the part where Needle showed up and stopped the whole thing. But if Trinity had gone to Heinrich's for a story, why go in the middle of the night, and what had happened to result in his murder?

"Someone threatened her," Gretchen said.

"So, you're saying someone made her steal the chief's car and drive to Heinrich's to murder him. Then why would she make a point to show the camera that she doesn't have the chief's scar?" Tara argued.

"Because she knew the police would pull the video, and she wants us to know she's being coerced," Gretchen shot back.

Josie's thoughts spun on. It was one thing for Lila to lure Trinity to Heinrich's shop with the promise of a big story, but quite another for Trinity to kill him. Had she actually murdered the man? Josie tried to imagine Trinity killing him. It wasn't hard. Josie had imagined killing the man for decades. She had also seen how ruthless Trinity could be, but did that cutthroat behavior in her work necessarily translate into being able to murder someone? Was Trinity capable of beating a man and setting him on fire while he was tied to a chair? Josie thought she knew the answer, but maybe she was wrong.

Tara shook her head. "We don't even know for sure that's Trinity. Makeup can cover up a scar."

"It's her," Gretchen insisted.

"Maybe it is," Tara said. "Or maybe it's not. Chief Quinn, do you have an alibi for last night?"

"Of course I—" Josie broke off. She didn't have an alibi. She had been at Noah's alone, and he had been here at the station house. Even if he wanted to, he couldn't lie for her, not that she would ever expect him to do that.

Tara smiled coldly. "Well, the DNA will tell. Given the unique circumstances, I've spoken with one of my high-level contacts at the state police, and he has agreed to expedite testing. We should have it back within forty-eight hours. In the meantime, I've instructed your staff to carry on with their day-to-day operations. Lieutenant Fraley and Detective Palmer will spearhead the investigation. They'll speak with Ms. Payne so that she can shed some light on this unfortunate situation."

"You've instructed my staff?" Josie said.

"In light of the fact that you are now a suspect—"

"Person of interest," Gretchen interjected, drawing a nasty glare from Tara, which she shot right back.

"Person of interest," Tara echoed. "I don't think it's appropriate for you to continue on as chief. I'm therefore suspending you pending the outcome of this investigation. You are not to leave this town, do you understand?"

Josie heard her mother's words once more. *I'll destroy everything you love.*

She had underestimated her mother, read the situation all

wrong. Josie loved nothing in the entire world more than her job. It had been quite a challenge when she took over as Chief, and she often found it stressful, but if she was forced to choose between being chief and no longer being a police officer, she would choose chief every time. Lila Jensen had truly gutted her—worse than the knife slice, worse even than being sold.

Josie had sacrificed everything to become a police officer, rising through the ranks of the Denton Police Department rapidly, becoming the first female lieutenant, then the first female detective, and finally the first female chief of police in Denton history. She had fought and forfeited to bring justice, peace, and protection to the citizens she served. This was her life's work, and while she'd slept, her mother—using Trinity Payne—had taken it away from her.

"I'll need your credentials and your gun," Tara said. "And we'll need you to turn over your car so that it can be processed for evidence."

God only knew what Lila had told Trinity, but Josie was sure that Trinity would never throw away her own career to kill a pedophile. Exposing her unblemished face to the camera was a clear message to Josie. The question was: What message was Trinity trying to send?

"And you're not to set foot in this building again until I authorize it," Tara went on.

In the last two years, Trinity had tried many times to get Josie to confess the origin of her scar. She had never remarked on the resemblance between them, but if Josie noticed it every time they were together, she was certain Trinity had as well. Trinity knew that she would be mistaken for Josie. Was Trinity in league with Lila, or was she Lila's unwilling pawn? Did Lila have something on her? Was Trinity just twisting the knife in Josie's back, or was she trying to tell Josie that she hadn't gone there willingly?

"Ms. Quinn, do you understand me?"

Tara's words seemed to come from far away, and the room

had gone out of focus. Josie blinked, and Tara's piercing, gleeful stare sharpened again. Josie took her badge and police ID from her pocket and tossed it onto the table. The Glock slid out of her holster. She ejected the magazine and handed it to Gretchen together with the pistol. Then she took her car key from her keychain and handed that over as well.

"I'll get this back to you," Gretchen said, ignoring the scathing look Tara sent her way.

Josie nodded. She looked at Noah, but he wouldn't meet her eyes. That hurt almost as much as giving up her gun and badge. There was nothing left for her to do but leave, so she thrust her chin forward and gave Tara one last challenging look before turning and walking out of the room, and her station house.

CHAPTER 63

With no car and no job, Josie sat on a bench across the street from the station house, staring at what just hours ago had been her domain. Her mind raced as her body went numb. Heinrich was dead. Her childhood bogeyman was gone. Finally. How many times had she wished for him to be punished for what he'd intended to do to her? Even though Needle had saved her from going into that bedroom, she still had nightmares about what might have been. She had to admit to feeling a small sense of peace now that this monster had been vanquished. But mostly she felt empty. Heinrich's death changed nothing. Her soul remained scarred. He wasn't, after all, the one who had made the deal. Lila had.

She tried to shift her focus away from the conflicting feelings raging inside. Lila was still out there, working to destroy Josie's life; and then there was Trinity. There were at least a half-dozen things she needed to do immediately, but she had no transportation. It would take a couple of days for her vehicle to be returned to her, and she had a feeling that Tara would do all she could to stretch that timeframe even longer. She didn't even have a way to get home, or to Noah's to pick up the things she had left there. Her texts to Trinity went unanswered, and when she called Trinity's cell phone, it went straight to voicemail. Josie didn't leave a message.

"Boss?"

She looked up to see Sergeant Lamay standing beside the bench. She hadn't even noticed him leaving the station house or crossing the street.

"I'm not your boss anymore, Lamay," she said.

"Would you say we're friends then?"

"Well, I wouldn't go—" She stopped, blinking to bring him into focus, concentrating on his eyes, which glinted with mischief. "I mean, of course we're friends, Dan."

He held out a set of keys to her. "Then the mayor wouldn't have an issue with me lending my friend my car. Right, Josie?"

Josie couldn't help the grin that spread across her face. As her hands closed around the keys, tears of gratitude stung the backs of her eyes. Her arm froze in midair, keys jangling. "Wait," she said. "I can't borrow your car. You need it. Your wife has chemo—"

"My daughter is away at college," Lamay interrupted. "She left her car at our house. We'll just use that until you get yours back. My wife and I pay the insurance on it anyway."

Before she could think about it, she leapt to her feet and squeezed Lamay in a quick hug. "Thank you, Dan," she said. "I won't forget this."

She drove to the Eudora, sneaking past a long line of people waiting to check in at the front desk, and made her way up to Room 227. She banged on the door several times, but there was no answer, and Josie could hear no movement behind the door. Back in the lobby, Josie waited behind the last guest in line. Once the concierge had checked the man in, Josie stepped up. The young blond man with the permanent toothy smile recognized her at once, the genial look in his eyes instantly replaced with contempt. She had stood in this very spot six months ago while working a case involving a casino mogul who had rented out the hotel's penthouse.

"Chief Quinn," the man sneered, his painted-on customer service smile still in place. "Is there something I can help you with?"

Her suspension hadn't been made public, and the concierge hadn't asked for her credentials. "I'm here for a welfare check on one of your guests—Trinity Payne in Room 227. I tried knocking on her door. There's no answer. No one has heard from her in twenty-four hours, and we have reason to believe she might be in trouble."

He eyed her skeptically. "Well, if you've knocked on her door, and she didn't answer, there's not much more I can do to help you, I'm afraid."

"You can have someone on your staff check the room," Josie said.

"We don't like to violate the privacy of our guests."

"I'm not asking you to violate the privacy of one of your guests, I'm asking you to check and make sure she's not dead or injured inside that room. What is hotel policy, by the way, if you believe one of your guests may be in imminent danger? How many hours are you required to wait before you check inside the room?"

His fake smile never faltered and yet, somehow, he managed to glare at her. "Is it the Denton Police Department policy to send the chief of police to do welfare checks?" he asked.

Josie leaned her elbows onto the counter, moving closer to him. "Trinity Payne is a close personal friend of mine. She's also a bit of a celebrity, as I'm sure you know. If she is, in fact, injured or dead inside her room, do you really want to bear the scrutiny of nationwide press because you refused to allow the police to do a proper welfare check when they made it clear to you that Ms. Payne may be in danger?" Josie read off an invisible headline above his head. "Concierge refuses welfare check. National news reporter, Trinity Payne, dies. I can see that going viral."

With a sigh, he tapped the keyboard of the computer. Then a keycard appeared in his hand. "Let me have my associate take you to her room." He made a phone call, and five minutes later a different man led Josie back to room 227.

Wordlessly, he let her into the room and stood by the door with his hands clasped at his waist while he watched Josie nose around. The bathroom and closet were clear. Trinity wasn't there. Josie felt both reassured and anxious. She hadn't really expected to find Trinity's dead body in the hotel room, but she was relieved all the same. But if Trinity wasn't in her hotel room, then where the hell was she? Where had she gone after killing Heinrich?

"Are you finished?" the man asked.

"Just a second," Josie said. Trinity's open suitcase lay across the bed. On the small circular table in the corner of the room was a closed laptop, a Gucci purse, a set of car keys, and Trinity's phone. The sight of her phone sent a prickle up Josie's spine. Trinity never went anywhere without her phone. Josie pulled a pair of latex gloves from her jacket pocket—even as chief, the habit had never died—snapped them on, and picked up Trinity's phone, pressing its power button to bring up the lock screen. It asked for a password.

Josie had no idea what Trinity might use as her password, and she couldn't spend much time trying to think of it. Tara was clearly focused on Josie for Heinrich's murder, but Josie knew that once she let Gretchen and Noah out of her sight, their first line of inquiry would be Trinity Payne. They'd be on her heels any moment. Gretchen would know how to get the phone unlocked, Josie was certain.

Josie turned to the man. "I'm going to need to see your CCTV of this hallway, the entrance, and possibly the parking lot."

The man looked bored. "Let's go back to the lobby," he told her. "I'll call the manager."

The manager, a balding blond man in his forties, was both more personable and more helpful than both the concierge and the man who had let Josie into Trinity's room. He didn't ask for her credentials either, and within moments of meeting him, Josie understood why. "I saw you on TV after the Lloyd Todd arrest," he said. "You're much more attractive in person—and I don't mean that in an inappropriate way."

Josie smiled uncomfortably as they stood behind one of his

staff members in the CCTV room behind the lobby, waiting for the young woman to pull up any footage of Trinity she could find. The manager prattled on, "Anyway, I just wanted to personally thank you. My son has been hooked on drugs for years now. We haven't been able to help him. Turns out his dealer was one of Todd's guys. Soon as those guys were arrested, my son went into rehab."

"I'm glad to hear that," Josie said.

"Who knows if he'll stick with it, but we're very hopeful. You know, since the day he was born, he was always giving us trouble."

Before the manager could launch into the story, the employee seated in front of the screens said, "Here you go—she left her room yesterday afternoon around two p.m."

On screen, they watched Trinity emerge from her hotel room wearing the same clothes she had on in the Heinrich surveillance. She held nothing in her hands as she rushed down the hallway. At the elevators, she pressed the down button frantically and was through the doors before they were even fully open.

"Here she is in the lobby," the woman said, pointing to a different screen. Both Josie and the hotel manager watched as Trinity exited the elevator in the lobby. She made a beeline for the door, walking so fast she was nearly jogging.

"And here she is in the parking lot," the employee added. She indicated three of the other screens, and they watched Trinity make her way through the parking lot to the outermost edge of the camera's view, where she walked rapidly off-screen. "I'm afraid that's it," the woman said. "That's as far as these cameras go."

Where had Trinity been rushing off to without her phone or car keys or even a purse?

"What about the rest of the day and night? Can you see if she ever came back to her room?" Josie asked.

The employee turned her attention to the screen showing the

hallway outside of Trinity's room, fast-forwarding the footage until it caught up to present time. Trinity never returned.

Josie turned to the hotel manager. "Thank you for your help," she said. "My colleagues will be back to collect some evidence. If you hear from Ms. Payne, please call the police department immediately."

"Of course," he said.

As Josie drove out of the parking lot in Sergeant Lamay's ten-year-old Camry, she passed Gretchen with a patrol car trailing behind her. Neither Gretchen nor the patrol officer even glanced her way.

CHAPTER 64

From the Eudora, Josie drove to Heinrich's auto body shop, but the entire building was cordoned off with police caution tape, and a patrol car sat outside. Of course. Tara knew Josie's first instinct would be to go to the scene herself and investigate. She pulled away and drove through town, pushing back the strange mixture of relief and emptiness that had come over her since she'd heard about Heinrich's death. She tried to figure out her next move. She kept coming back to Trinity. The reporter had left her hotel room willingly. There was no one with her, no gun to her head. She must have gone to meet with Lila, and from there, stolen Josie's car, driven to Heinrich's, murdered him, and then left—alone—to return Josie's Escape to the street outside Noah's house.

But if Trinity had driven the Escape back to Noah's house, why was the seat pushed all the way back? Trinity was the same size as Josie. She would have no reason to adjust the seat. Which meant that somewhere between the body shop and Noah's house, Trinity had met up with someone and turned Josie's car over to them. Someone taller than both Trinity and Lila. Lila was even shorter than Josie, so she wouldn't have pushed the seat back.

So, who had been in her car?

Josie pulled over and took her phone out. She started to text Gretchen about the car but then realized that her Evidence Response Team would print the car anyway. If the person who had driven it had left prints, they would be found. Josie put her phone away and pulled back into traffic, the need to keep moving consuming her.

Where was Trinity now? she wondered. Was she hiding because she had killed a man, or was Lila holding her somewhere? Josie had no doubt that Lila was behind Heinrich's murder somehow, and that Trinity had gone to meet Lila because Lila had promised her a story. But what would make Trinity kill a man so willingly? Josie thought about what it would take for her to throw away her life and career and commit a murder. What would make her desperate enough to do that? Not a threat against her own life. She'd rather die than go down and lose everything. But would she trade her career and her morality to save someone she loved? It was then that Josie realized she didn't know Trinity at all. She knew nothing personal about the reporter, her life, her family, her loved ones.

Josie turned the vehicle around and headed back to her home. She hadn't been inside for days, and the rooms had an empty, sterile feeling to them—as if they weren't really hers anymore. She hoped that one day it would feel like a safe place again. But until then, she would startle at every little noise, like she did when she was in the spare room booting up her laptop and her neighbor's garage door screeched open. Bringing her laptop down to the kitchen, she made herself a pot of coffee, still unable to shake the feeling that she was in someone else's space now.

As the coffee brewed, Josie pulled up her internet browser and typed in Trinity Payne's name. The search returned more results than Josie could possibly sift through in a few hours, or even a week, so she typed in *Trinity Payne biography*, and that narrowed it down somewhat. She clicked through several sites, turning up the same information again and again. She had gone to NYU, where she'd graduated summa cum laude with a degree in journalism. She started out as a roving reporter for WYEP in the Denton area, then she moved quickly to the network's morning magazine show in New York City, working as a national correspondent until a source gave her a bad story. Her fall from grace had landed her back at WYEP, until she had helped Josie crack the missing girls case two years earlier, and the network wanted her back on the national stage.

Josie knew all this. She clicked through the sites faster, skimming over repeat information, looking for something more. Finally, on an NYU alumni website, she found a more detailed article about Trinity, written three months earlier—*NYU Journalism Alum Rises from Tragedy to Network Royalty.*

The first paragraph read: *Network darling Trinity Payne is no stranger to controversy. Her travails with bad sources as well as her recent rise to fame helping to crack some of the biggest criminal cases in the history of her home state are well documented. What most people don't know about Payne is that her life was inexorably marked by tragedy when she was only a few weeks old. Her young parents were both employed by pharmaceutical giant Quarmark—Christian as the head of marketing and Shannon as a rising chemist. With their careers on track, their next goal was to settle down and have children. They found their dream home quickly—a two-story Tudor-style mansion in a small town named Callowhill. They got pregnant on the first try—with twins. "They were classic overachievers," Trinity relates, smiling.*

"Twins?" Josie muttered. She had no idea that Trinity had a twin. She had known that Trinity grew up in Callowhill. It was a small town a couple of hours away, on the other side of Bellewood. In fact, the county seat was just about equidistant from both Denton and Callowhill. Josie stood and hastily prepared a cup of coffee for herself, returning to her laptop.

While many first-time parents might have been intimidated by twins, Shannon Payne says she and her husband never once worried how they would handle two newborns. "The day our girls were born was one of the happiest days of our lives."

The day our girls were born. Something gnawed at the back of Josie's mind, but she couldn't put her finger on it.

She read on: *Tragedy struck just a few weeks after the twins were born when a house fire destroyed their four-bedroom home. Their nanny was home with the twins at the time, but was only able to save one of them—Trinity.*

"My God," Josie said.

She skimmed over the rest of it—how the Paynes had never truly recovered from the loss of Trinity's twin sister, and how Trinity was glad she didn't remember anything because it would be too painful. A shiver ran down Josie's spine. She didn't know how a person could ever recover from the loss of a child. There was no doubt in her mind that it was an open wound that Shannon and Christian Payne would take to their graves. Josie felt a wave of sympathy for Trinity, and yet, she couldn't help but wonder if Trinity would have turned out less mercenary had she had the influence of a sister. Now they would never know.

She skimmed the rest of the article, but the only other new piece of information was that Trinity had a much younger brother called Patrick, who was still in high school in Callowhill. There was no mention of any love interests. Trinity didn't strike Josie as the type who would have time for a boyfriend. Josie had what she needed though—the names of Trinity's immediate family members. She opened a new tab and searched for a phone number for the Payne family in Callowhill. It was unlisted. Of course, with a daughter as famous as Trinity, the Paynes wouldn't want their number so easily accessible to the public.

Josie had only been suspended for a few hours. It was quite possible that no one at Denton PD had revoked her access to the police databases. Logging in to one of them, Josie pumped her fist in the air as her credentials were accepted. She searched for Shannon Payne first, banking on the hope that the Paynes still had a landline because cell service was spotty in the more remote areas of Pennsylvania. Luck was with her today.

Josie punched the number into her cell phone and listened to it ring eight times before the call went to voicemail, a female voice that sounded similar to Trinity's urging her to leave a message. At the beep, Josie said, "This is Josie Quinn. I'm the chief of police in Denton. I'm calling about your daughter, Trinity. It is very important that you call me back as soon as you get this message." She then left her number and hung up.

As she went to close out the browser on her laptop, the last paragraph of the alumni magazine article caught Josie's eye. *When asked if the tragedy of her sister's death has influenced her as a journalist, Payne smiles bravely, and a faraway look creeps into her eyes. "I think never knowing what really happened—who set the fire—will haunt my family forever and has definitely made me more diligent in my reporting. I will never stop until I have all the answers. It's just something that's in me."*

Josie looked at her cell phone and, realizing she had nothing to do while she waited for the Paynes to call her back, she opened another tab, pulled up a search engine, and typed in *Payne Callowhill house fire.* There were results with *Payne* and *Callowhill* in them, and *Callowhill* and *house fire*, but none with all three terms. Of course, Josie knew that Trinity was around the same age as she was, and if the fire had taken place a few weeks after her birth, that meant it would have happened in the late '80s—before the internet was a staple of daily existence. Back then, if the fire had made the news, it would have been in one of the county newspapers.

She finished her coffee and set off for the library.

CHAPTER 65

The Denton Library was a two-floor stone building designed by a local architect in the early 1900s in neoclassical style, complete with a grand staircase and large Doric columns. Josie had always loved the building; she had spent many hours as a teenager tucked away among the shelves, studying in the reverent hush that presided over the massive collection of books. In the intervening years, much of the building had been modernized, upgrading from tables to computer stations and expanding into conference and activity rooms. Josie explained to one of the librarians what she was looking for, and the woman led her to a computer station on the second floor.

"Would it be on microfiche?" Josie asked.

"Oh no, dear. We moved all that old stuff onto this new database. It's all computerized now. You'll see. We've got the *Denton Tribune*, the *Bellewood Record*, and a couple of the other local papers from the county. When you put in your search terms, it will trawl all of those papers, or only the ones you designate." The librarian reached across Josie and maneuvered the mouse until an image of an old *Denton Tribune* cover popped up next to a login bar. She typed in her credentials and gave Josie a short tour, showing how to do a search and narrow down the parameters.

Once the librarian left her alone, Josie glanced at her cell before setting it on the desk next to her—still nothing from the Paynes. Getting to work, it only took a few minutes to find two results. One was from the *Denton Tribune* dated October 4,

1987. It was on the front page and offered no more than Trinity had disclosed in her alumni magazine interview. The Callowhill fire marshal was quoted as saying the cause of the fire was still under investigation. Josie saved it and moved on to the next article, which was dated December 17, 1987. This article was from the *Bellewood Record*, on page four, with a number of county items that weren't newsworthy enough to warrant space on the front page. The headline read: *Cause of Callowhill Fire Arson; Police Open Murder Investigation.*

Josie skimmed the article, learning that the nanny who had rescued Trinity had died of smoke inhalation after going back into the house to rescue the other twin, making the case a double homicide. There were no leads and no suspects. Only a few months after the fire, the case had grown cold. The article ended with a quote from Shannon Payne that punched a small barb of pain into Josie's heart. "From the day my girls were born, I never left them alone. That was the only time I ever left them alone with the nanny. I can't help thinking that if I had been there, we could have saved them both."

From the day my girls were born. The amorphous shadow in the back of Josie's mind shifted, making itself known but not becoming clear. With a sigh, Josie saved the second article and went in search of the librarian to gain access to a printer.

As the woman clicked on several drop-down menus and selected a nearby machine, Josie asked her, "Uh, do you have kids?"

"I certainly do," the librarian answered. "A girl and a boy. They're grown now, of course. Why do you ask?"

"Oh, you looked familiar," Josie lied. "I thought maybe I had gone to high school with your daughter at Denton East."

"Oh no, dear," the librarian said, smiling at Josie. "I only just moved here from Pittsburgh a few years back. Maybe I just have one of those faces. Do you have children?"

Josie was glad the woman was chatty, and she wouldn't have to work too hard to bring up the subject she was really aiming for. "Oh no," Josie answered. "I mean, maybe one day. The world is a scary place these days. The thought of bringing a child into this chaos…" She trailed off, and the woman picked up the thread immediately.

"Oh, every parent feels like that, dear. When my daughter was born, I was terrified. It seemed like the world was worse than it ever was. Then, a few years later, my son was born, and it seemed even worse. But life goes on, and you manage."

"Thanks," Josie said. A large printer across the room whirred noisily as it spat out several sheets of paper. The librarian bustled over to it and picked them up. Josie thanked her again before she was called away by another patron. Settling back at her computer station, Josie pulled up the newspaper database again and searched the words *baby* and *adopted* for the years 1982 and 1983.

The shadow at the back of her mind had fallen away as she spoke with the librarian, revealing what had been bothering her. When Shannon Payne talked about her twins, she talked about the day they were born. When the manager at the Eudora told Josie about his drug-addicted son, he used the same language: the day his son was born. When the librarian talked about her own children, she too used the word *born*.

But when Josie and her team interviewed Sophia Bowen, she had said that she stopped working in the summer of 1983 "when we brought our eldest son home." Something about the phrasing had stuck in the back of Josie's mind, needling her, begging to be examined further. Maybe she was reaching. She was no longer chief and didn't have a police department to run to keep herself busy. Maybe she was just making things up to keep herself distracted from the fact that her life had fallen apart, and neither she nor the Denton PD were any closer to finding Lila Jensen. Perhaps Sophia Bowen had merely been referring to the day they'd brought their eldest son home from the hospital.

It was a long shot. She knew that. Adoptions weren't the

sort of thing that ended up in newspapers—not in the '80s, and not now. But if a prominent judge and his young bride adopted a baby, there was the tiniest possibility it would have been newsworthy on a slow day.

With time on her hands and a research database at her fingertips, Josie had nothing to lose.

Most of the results were articles having to do with changes to the adoption laws in the state, lawsuits, and adopted children searching for their birth parents. Her heart leapt as she found what she was looking for in an issue of the *Bellewood Record* from December of 1987—the same year as the fire that took the Paynes' daughter and their home. It was just a small piece buried on page eight of the paper next to the announcements of the schedules of various church services over the holidays.

Five Years Later, Alcott County's Manger Baby Plays Joseph in Live Nativity.

When he was only a few days old, little Andrew Bowen was the unwilling star of the Maplewood Baptist Church's outdoor nativity. Just before Christmas of 1982, someone left him swaddled in white cotton towels in the manger of the church's nativity scene. Residents of Alcott County were shocked by the discovery. The Manger Baby, as he became known after he was discovered, had been left in the freezing cold during an evening church service. Members of the congregation heard his cries as they left the service and called the police. Although the baby's parents were never found, he found a family with local judge Malcolm Bowen and his wife, Sophia.

The Manger Baby's case came across the judge's docket after he was placed in the foster care system. "As soon as I saw him, I fell in love," Judge Bowen recalls. "My wife and I were already trying for children, and I came home after seeing that baby for the first time and said, 'Sophia, what do you think about adoption?' Of course, she was on board immediately."

The Bowens were able to bring the Manger Baby home in the summer of 1983, when he was six months old. "It was the happiest day of my life," Sophia Bowen exclaimed. "I became a mother."

Five years later, young Andrew Bowen is thriving in his new home—he even has a little brother—and this year he will star as Joseph in the live nativity at the very same rural church where he was abandoned as an infant.

"We've made our peace with what Andrew's biological parents did to him. We've forgiven them, and we hope when Andrew grows up, he will too. We don't know what type of desperate situation the mother was in that she would give up such a precious little baby. What I know is that God gave us a gift," Sophia Bowen said. "Andrew made us parents for the first time. There is no greater gift than that."

Just in time for Christmas.

Knowing what she knew about Malcolm Bowen and Belinda Rose, the cheery, saccharine tone of the article made Josie's stomach turn. She thought of the photos of Andrew Bowen she'd seen in Sophia's home, and of the times she'd met him in his capacity as a criminal attorney in Denton. He was the spitting image of Malcolm Bowen, except blond. Was it possible that Malcolm Bowen had arranged to adopt his own son? Had Belinda left the baby in the manger?

Josie thought of the locket Belinda had returned with after she disappeared to give birth to her baby. It was one thing for her to go off and have the baby and then abandon him somewhere, but she had been gone for months, not days. Belinda Rose had had a plan. She had had somewhere to go. She had had help. Malcolm Bowen would have had enough power and influence to make sure that his own son ended up with him and Sophia.

On her phone, Josie googled Andrew Bowen's office number and called it. His secretary told her that he was in court. She left her cell phone number and asked that he call her when he was out. She was still reeling from her discovery about the Bowens when her phone rang in her hand. She recognized the number immediately and answered.

"Chief Quinn?"

"Mrs. Payne?" Josie said. "Shannon Payne?"

CHAPTER 66

Josie caught several glares from nearby library users and lowered her voice, pressing the phone to her ear, gathering up her printouts, and heading outside. "Thank you for calling me back, Mrs. Payne," she said.

A cool wind whipped up the steps of the library, so Josie moved behind one of the columns and out of the stream of people going in and out of the building.

Shannon Payne said, "I'm returning your call about my daughter. I talked to one of your detectives earlier. Is everything okay?" Josie heard her breath catch in her throat. "I guess it's not, or you wouldn't be calling—the chief of police. My God—"

"Mrs. Payne," Josie interjected before she became hysterical, "I'm sorry. I don't have any news. I was just calling to follow up and make sure that you, your husband, and your son are safe. I assure you that my team is doing everything they can to find Trinity."

She hated lying to Shannon, especially while she was under such stress and worried about her child, but trying to explain the current situation would take too long. Plus, Josie knew that it was true that Denton PD would do everything in their power to find Trinity—Gretchen and Noah were already several steps ahead of her if they'd already contacted the Paynes.

"Oh, thank you," Shannon said. "I certainly appreciate that. We're fine. I mean, we're not fine. We're worried about my daughter, but we're all accounted for and safe."

"Excellent," Josie said. "I just had a couple more questions, if you don't mind. Does Trinity have a boyfriend?"

Shannon laughed. "Oh no. She doesn't have time for that."

"Thought so," Josie said. "How about close friends? Anyone she would perhaps go and stay with if she needed to get away?"

Shannon was silent for a moment. Then she said, "I hate to say this, but Trinity doesn't really have time for friends either. That sounds terrible, but you have to understand, she's very career-driven."

Josie couldn't help but laugh. "Oh, I know, Mrs. Payne."

Shannon laughed as well, albeit a little nervously. "I guess you would. She's worked with you on a couple of cases, hasn't she?"

"Yes, she's been an invaluable resource."

"I gave Detective Palmer the names of all the people I could think of that she's friendly with in New York," Shannon said. "But really, if she needed to get away for a while, she'd come here."

"I understand," Josie said, throat tightening. If Trinity didn't have any friends, lovers, or other close associates she might run to in her time of need, then the likelihood that Lila was holding her against her will increased exponentially. Josie continued, "If you have any questions or you need anything at all, you can call Lieutenant Fraley or Detective Palmer. Of course, you're welcome to contact me as well, but they'll be actively working the case."

"Well, there was just one more thing," said Shannon. "Since I've got you on the phone."

"Oh? What's that?"

"Well, I don't know that it has anything to do with Trinity, but it's been bothering me." She stopped. For a moment, Josie thought the call had dropped. Then she added, "It's silly. I don't even know why I'm bringing it up."

"Go on," Josie said. "I'm listening."

A sigh. "Well, WYEP is running a story about a woman the

Denton PD is trying to locate. They keep showing her picture and saying she is a person of interest in a number of local crimes. It's quite an old photo, though."

"Yes," Josie said, wondering where this was going. "Her name was Lila Jensen, but she used the alias Belinda Rose for many years."

"I knew her as Belinda."

Josie's heartbeat skipped twice. "What?"

"My husband thinks I'm crazy," she said, laughing nervously.

"That's men for you," Josie replied. "Go on."

"She used to work for the cleaning service that came out to our house. In the mid to late '80s."

"Handy Helpers?" Josie asked before remembering that Handy Helpers had closed in 1984 after the death of its owner.

"Oh, no. I think they were called AB Clean. There were a few girls who used to come out, and she was one of them. After she started, things began disappearing from our home. Mostly my jewelry. I reported her to her boss, and he fired her. Not even a week later, our home burned to the ground. My girls were home with the nanny. They were only a few weeks old. Only Trinity survived."

"I'm aware of the fire," Josie said. "Did the authorities ever check her alibi?"

"They did look into it, they claimed, and said she had an alibi for the day of the fire, but I've always thought..." She trailed off.

Josie filled in the end of her sentence: "You think Belinda had something to do with the fire?"

A heavy sigh. "I don't know. I've never even been able to say it out loud until very recently. Like I said, the police told us that she was nowhere near Callowhill when the fire started. But it always bothered me. She was...there was something about her, something...dark. That sounds terrible. Really, I should just shut up. None of this has anything to do with my daughter. I'm probably just trying to distract myself—bringing up this old stuff so I don't have to think about where my daughter might be or what's happening to her." Josie heard her sob, then suck in several deep breaths. Then she added, "I don't know if I'm even making sense."

Josie leaned against the column and closed her eyes, the phone still pressed to her ear. "You're making perfect sense."

Shannon took in several more breaths. "Anyway, I just saw her picture on the television, and it gave me a shock. It brought back all the memories from the fire. It just hit too close to home. Losing a child, and now with Trinity missing..."

It was too strange, too coincidental. Belinda getting fired from cleaning the Paynes' house and then the fire soon after. All of it taking place the year Josie was born.

"I understand," Josie said. "I do. Listen, if you don't mind my asking, where were the girls when the fire started?"

"They were sleeping in their playpen in the family room. The nanny—before she died—said they were both asleep, and she'd just nipped to the bathroom for a moment. When she came out, the downstairs was filled with smoke. She said she could hardly see. She ran to the family room to get the girls, but only Trinity was still in the playpen. She scooped Trinity up and ran her outside. One of our neighbors had come out by then. The nanny handed Trinity to her and went back in. When the fire department arrived, they found her searching the house and made her come out. The police were always very suspicious of her. They never believed her story that only one of the girls was in the playpen. If she hadn't died, I think they would have tried to pin the whole thing on her. But if she had started the fire, why would she rescue only one of the girls, and then go back into the house? It makes no sense. She was lucky she survived for the few days she did after the fire. The fire department said my daughter was—" Shannon's words halted, and a high-pitched cry penetrated Josie's ear. She took several moments to recover herself, and Josie could hear her quiet weeping like a hundred thorns piercing her heart. Clearing her throat, Shannon said,

"The fire chief told us that she had been...incinerated in the fire. She was so tiny. We didn't even have any remains to bury."

Josie tried to speak—to say she was sorry, to utter some words of comfort or empathy. She wasn't a mother, but it had taken her only moments to bond with little baby Harris. Even though she saw him infrequently, she knew that if anything ever happened to him, she would never recover. And Misty would be utterly destroyed. Normal mothers—good mothers—loved their children. This was a fact Josie had always known intellectually, but never experienced.

"I'm sorry," Shannon said. "I shouldn't have brought it up. It's ridiculous. Like I said, I'm just deflecting or whatever psychologists call it so I don't have to think about the fact that my Trinity is missing."

"I'll find her," Josie said, her voice returning. This she could do. "I promise you, I'm going to find her."

CHAPTER 67

Lisette was in her usual spot in the cafeteria, sitting at a table working on a crossword puzzle as other residents drifted in and out. A pair of glasses sat low on the bridge of her nose, and her gray curls fell around her face as her head bent to the page in front of her. She looked up when Josie appeared beside her. "Sweetheart, how lovely to see you. In the middle of the day too." She craned her neck to look behind Josie. "Work again?"

Josie shook her head. Lisette must have seen from her expression that something was very wrong. Abandoning her puzzle, she stood and grasped both sides of her walker, pushing past Josie. "Come then, we'll talk in my room."

Lisette sat in her recliner while Josie perched across from her on the edge of her bed. "What's going on, Josie?" Lisette asked. "What's wrong?"

"Gram," Josie said, "I need to ask you some questions, and I need you to be honest. Promise me. If you do nothing else for me in this life, I need you to answer my questions truthfully."

Lisette gave a nervous chuckle. "Of course, dear."

"When I was born, was my dad there at the hospital?"

The faint smile on Lisette's face tightened into something strained. "No, he wasn't. Your mother—well, they'd been living together, and they got into some big fight. Your mother left. She was gone for months. Eli thought it was over. He never expected to see her again, honestly. He was about to move out of the trailer, had met another girl and gone on a few dates with her.

Then one day he came home, and there was your mother sitting on his couch with you in the crook of her arm."

A band of pain wrapped itself around Josie's skull. Throbbing began in her temples. "She just showed up with a baby one day?"

"Not just a baby. You."

"Dad didn't question the paternity?"

"Of course not," Lisette scoffed. "What kind of man would do that? Belinda said that she found out she was a few months along after she left him, and that she wasn't going to even tell him about you, but that once you came the guilt was too much, so she came back. She gave him the option—to be involved, or not. Naturally, your father wanted to be involved. He loved you the very instant he saw you."

Josie knew that there weren't DNA tests back in 1987—not the kind that were readily available to anyone in the public. These days, you could order a paternity kit online, swab your cheek, and mail it to a lab. But in the late '80s, if you had suspicions, you'd have no way of proving whether or not a child was your own.

"Did she say what hospital I was born in?"

"Oh, she had a home birth. Actually, she hadn't even sent away for your birth certificate until after she brought you home to your father."

"How old?" Josie asked. "How old was I?"

"Three months. She brought you home sometime in December; it was the most wonderful Christmas present we'd ever received!"

Under normal circumstances, Josie would smile, basking in the love her grandmother had for her. But at the moment, every muscle in her face felt frozen. The suspicion that had started growing during her conversation with Shannon Payne was still shrouded in her mind. To tear away the veil would mean shattering everything she knew to be true. Not to mention the absurdity of what she now suspected about the Payne fire and her own origins. She couldn't bring herself to think it, let alone say it aloud.

"Josie, why are you asking me these questions? What's wrong?"

Josie's voice trembled. "Did you know right away that I was someone else's child?"

Lisette went very still, holding her posture like a granite statue. "What are you talking about?"

"I don't look like Dad," Josie said. "And I don't look like you."

"You got your mother's looks," Lisette said.

"No," Josie said. "Both of us having black hair doesn't mean much. Gram, you knew, didn't you? You had to have known, or at least suspected, that I was not a blood relation to you and my father."

Lisette's face flushed. "Does it matter? Does it really matter? You're mine. You've always been mine. I didn't need a blood test to prove that, and you shouldn't either. Who helped raise you, Josie? Who fought for you? I battled like hell to bring you home with me."

"The deck was stacked, Gram. The judge you went before, Malcolm Bowen? He knew my mother, knew she was using an assumed identity. I was always leaving with her, no matter what happened that day."

"You don't know that. Judge Bowen was a good man, a fair man. When your mother finally left, he put the custody order through quickly and painlessly. He helped me."

"Judge Bowen was *not* a good man. Sorry to shatter your illusions, Gram. If he helped you, it was only because—" She broke off as her brain worked through it.

It was only a theory that Judge Bowen had been involved in helping Josie's mother, but Josie was sure that she had it right. She was certain that her mother had gone to him after Lisette first filed for custody and had him handle the whole thing quietly, using private mediation. Lila had had something on him—probably the knowledge that he had been having an affair with the real Belinda Rose as a minor. He wouldn't have wanted her exposing that secret, so he would have helped her. The only way that he would then turn around and help Lisette four years later is if Lila allowed him to, and Lila wouldn't have allowed Lisette to have custody of Josie after fourteen years unless...

"Gram, what did you do?"

"Josie Quinn," Lisette began in a scolding tone.

"Judge Bowen was in league with my mother. They wouldn't have let you have me unless you did something. My mother never did anything for nothing. What did you give her? What did you promise her?"

Lisette's head hung. "My sweet Josie."

"Just tell me."

With a sigh, Lisette said, "Fifty thousand dollars."

"What?" Josie's voice came out high-pitched. "Where did you get that kind of money?"

"Your father had a life-insurance policy. I didn't touch it after he died. I knew he would want me to save it for you to use for college or to buy your first home. But after the fire in the trailer, your mother came to me. She said she wanted to work something out. I think the police were really looking at her for burning the trailer down and for what happened to that poor boy, Dexter. I didn't argue. I offered her twenty-five thousand, but she had to leave and never come back. She wanted more. I told her for fifty she had to give me full legal and physical custody and never set foot in your life again."

Josie stood and paced the room. "Jesus, Gram."

"I had to. It was my only chance. I know it was a lot of money, but it was worth it. I had to get you away from her. I'm just sorry I couldn't do it sooner. The damage she did—Josie, I hope you know how sorry I am."

Josie held up her hands. "Stop. Just stop. I can't—I can't talk about that. I just—I don't—Gram, you knew I didn't belong to you all along. You worked so hard to get me, but why did you keep me? Why didn't you say anything? Did it ever occur to you that some family out there was missing me?"

Lisette gave a dismissive laugh. "A family? Please. Maybe some drug-addled man that your mother took into her bed for one night. Don't you see? For all I knew, whoever had really fathered you might be even worse than your mother. It was hard enough getting you away from her, especially after your father died. We were supposed to fight for you together. He promised me we would petition the court for custody. We were not going to be intimidated by her. He was going to spend every last dime he had, and I was going to help him. I'll never understand why he gave up. It wasn't like him at all. But then he was gone, and you were alone with that... that monster. All I knew was that I had to get you away from her."

"You could have said something," Josie said. "Told someone you didn't believe I was hers. Raised hell. Talked to Judge Bowen. Sent up red flags. But you didn't."

Lisette's eyes flashed. She pointed a crooked finger at Josie. "You're not listening to me. What if I had done that and we somehow figured out who your real father was, and he was worse than your mother? Have you never thought of that?"

"Not my real father," Josie said. "My real family. Gram, I think she *took* me from another family entirely."

"Josie, what on earth are you talking about?"

Josie knelt before her grandmother and held both her hands. "Gram, what I'm about to tell you is going to sound crazy. Or maybe, knowing what you already know about my mother, it will sound exactly right."

CHAPTER 68

Josie returned home, trudging into her kitchen and making another pot of coffee, although the way she felt, she doubted it would help—her limbs felt like they were moving through molasses. She hadn't felt so drained since she pulled little baby Harris out of the Susquehanna River six months ago. The day had been filled with a series of shocking discoveries, but she was no closer to figuring out where Lila and Trinity were.

Josie was so deep in thought that when she heard three loud knocks on her front door, she nearly jumped out of her skin. Through the peephole she saw Noah standing on her front stoop, both hands in his jeans pockets, his gaze fixed firmly on his feet.

She opened the door and stared at him. "What are you doing here?" she asked. "Did you find Lila? Trinity?"

He shook his head, still not looking at her.

She hated this awkwardness between them, and the last thing she felt like doing was discussing what had—and hadn't—happened between them the night before. But he was here all the same. "Would you like to come in?"

He stepped past her into the foyer, and she pulled the door closed behind them and motioned toward the kitchen. "I made coffee."

Only when he was seated at her table did he look at her. "I'm sorry about this morning—about Tara," he said. "I wanted to call, to warn you, but Tara wouldn't let us go."

"I understand," she said.

She set the coffee mug in front of him, and as she turned away, he touched her arm. "I was trying to figure out the best way to protect you."

Josie sighed and took a seat next to him. "Noah," she said, "you can't protect me from this. No one can. This fight has been a long time coming, and I'm the only one who can do it."

"No you're not," Noah insisted, his hazel eyes earnest. Seeing something besides hurt and confusion in his face instantly made her feel better. "Gretchen and I are going to help you. We already convinced the mayor that it's not you on that tape. We just have to find Trinity. We'll get this sorted out."

"Are you interim chief of police now?" Josie asked hopefully.

"The mayor doesn't trust me or Gretchen to be unbiased, which is probably smart on her part. She has this guy coming in. He's semi-retired. Has his own security firm. Used to work as a high-ranking police officer in Pittsburgh before that. He'll be the interim chief until further notice."

It was no surprise to Josie that Tara had someone waiting in the wings to take Josie's job. "Right," Josie said.

"Well, hopefully this guy is more reasonable than Tara."

"Nothing on Trinity?" Josie asked, turning back to more pressing matters. "I know Gretchen went to the hotel. Did you get her phone unlocked?"

He raised a brow at her, but didn't ask questions. "There were texts between her and an unknown number—a prepaid burner phone. We're trying to see if we can track down its location now. Whoever it was said they had information about her sister. We called Shannon Payne though—that's her mother—and her sister died as an infant."

"Yeah, I heard that."

"The messages were very cryptic, and after they stopped, there were a few phone calls back and forth, including one from the unknown number to Trinity's cell just before she ran out of her room."

"It was Lila," Josie said.

"But why? Why go after Trinity? And who the hell is this Heinrich guy? I couldn't find any connection between him and Belinda Rose or Lila Jensen. Although he's on the sex offender registry. Did you know that?"

Josie nodded. "Yes. He served almost ten years for molesting his thirteen-year-old niece."

"How do you know that?" Noah asked. "Was it one of your cases?"

"No, by the time I started at Denton PD, he was being released."

It had taken a long time for Josie to identify Heinrich as the man Lila had sold her to, and since nothing had actually occurred between them, there was nothing Josie could legally do to him. She'd worried that he would prey on more young girls once out of prison, but it had only taken a few days of surveillance to see that Heinrich was in no shape to assault anyone. Whatever had happened to him in prison had left him with a permanent limp and restricted range of motion in one of his arms. Most of the time he moved slowly, as though in great pain.

"I don't understand," Noah said.

The piercing pain in her temples was back. "There are some things I need to tell you right now."

The easy part was telling him what she had found out from Trinity's mother, and what her own grandmother had confirmed about Josie's birth—Josie's father hadn't been present when she was born. Lila had disappeared for months and then shown up unexpectedly one day with Josie. There was no actual proof that Lila had ever been pregnant or given birth, which meant there was a definite possibility that Lila had taken her from the Paynes.

Noah was on his second cup of coffee by the time she finished. His eyes had collected dark circles beneath them.

"I know it sounds insane," Josie said.

"No. I mean, yes. It does. Completely insane, but knowing everything we know now, I can see it. When all of this is over, you should take a DNA test. You can do them by mail now. Fast. My only question is why would Lila steal someone's baby?"

"Because it's the worst thing you can do to a woman."

"All because Shannon Payne got her fired?"

"Lila's reactions to things were never proportionate," Josie pointed out.

He downed the last of his coffee, and they sat in silence for a few moments. It pained her to bring up the last piece of the puzzle, but Josie knew she had to. Noah had supported her blindly in the face of the mayor's coup, and he was fiercely loyal to her—even after she had cut off their encounter so abruptly and clearly wounded him. He deserved to know everything, which meant telling him about Heinrich. "Noah," Josie said. "There's something else. Something I need to tell you. It's about Ted Heinrich."

He didn't say anything after she told him, and it didn't take long. The few words she could muster were inadequate to express the breadth and depth of what Lila had done to her and what was almost taken from her that day. Maybe that was okay, she thought. She had spent so many years pushing those feelings down and keeping them out of her consciousness, finally saying the words might make them lose a little of their power.

Josie watched the range of emotions pass over Noah's face as she spoke: shock, horror, pity, sadness, disgust, anger, and relief that Needle had intervened. She knew he was searching through the silence for something to say—anything.

She was relieved when Noah's cell phone rang. Slowly, without taking his eyes off her, he pulled it out and silenced it.

"Noah," she said softly. "You have to get that."

His eyes were intense, zeroed in on her with laser focus. "No," he said, "I don't."

They stared at one another. His phone rang again. Again, he silenced it. "Noah, it could be important."

He tapped his index finger on the table. "This is important. *You* are important."

She smiled. "Then help me. Answer your phone. It could be about Trinity. Or my mother."

"Lila," he said. "From now on she is Lila. She was not a mother to you."

"Lila, then."

His phone rang again, and he answered it, listening briefly and ending the call with, "I'll be there in ten."

Josie looked at him hopefully, but he shook his head. "Sorry. Nothing on Trinity. But Gretchen did pick up one of those teenagers working at the Spur Mobile store and got him to admit that a 'really weird old lady' gave him weed in exchange for giving out your new number, and that she 'did some other things' to get him to place the craigslist ads."

Josie stood up and walked him to the front door. "I knew it," she said. "I bet I know which one of those rotten little punks it was too. See what else you can get from him. If she came into the store, there might be video. Find out if she told him her name. Maybe we can figure out what alias she's using now."

Noah stood by the front door, smiling at her. "You got it, Boss," he said.

"Sorry," Josie replied. "It's a hard habit to break—bossing you around."

"I don't mind." He gave her a small smile, and her heart leapt.

CHAPTER 69

Josie's cell phone rang shortly after Noah left, breaking her thoughts. Those final moments with him had stirred up so many emotions within her, she was having a hard time keeping them down. She answered without looking at the number. A man's voice asked, "Is this Chief Quinn? Chief Josie Quinn?"

"Yes," Josie said. "This is Josie Quinn. Who is this?"

"Chief, this is Andrew Bowen returning your call—"

"Oh, yes. I called for two reasons. One is your mother—"

"Yes, my mother," he interjected. "She told me you called her and asked her to come in for a more formal interview. You should know that she's retained me as her attorney."

Josie suppressed a groan. "Let me guess, you have no intention of producing her for an interview because she's already told my detectives everything she knows. Does that sound right?"

He laughed. "Yep, that about covers it."

"And if that didn't work, you were going to cite her age and status in the community and argue that there is no reason to bring her into the police station like some kind of criminal."

More laughter. "Want to tell me how I'm going to handle my next trial too? I'd really like to know if I win or not."

"Sorry, I'm not psychic," Josie said. "Just used to dealing with criminal defense attorneys. So tell me, Mr. Bowen, if your mother hasn't done anything criminal and has nothing to hide, then why not bring her over for a cup of coffee to answer a few more questions?"

She heard what sounded like him taking a drink. Then he said, "Okay, Chief, what are you really hoping to get here? You

questioned Mrs. Bowen about the murder of a girl she barely
knew that happened over thirty years ago."

"I wouldn't say they barely knew one another," Josie said.
"Several people we spoke to said they were quite close. Your
mother even admitted that she became good friends with
Belinda after your father took an interest in her. They felt sorry
for her because she was a foster child."

"So what?" Andrew said. "Sure they were friends, but
according to my mother—and this was confirmed when you
and your detectives came to visit with her—Belinda Rose went
missing in 1984. That was almost a year after my mother left
the courthouse to be a full-time mom. What do you think she
knows that she isn't telling you?"

A lot, Josie thought. She didn't believe for a second that
Sophia didn't remember Lila, but she still couldn't figure out
why she would lie about it. Josie could see her lying about her
and her husband's relationship with Belinda Rose. Perhaps
Sophia had found out that they were having an affair. Whether
it was before or after they became friends was anyone's guess,
but Sophia had stayed with her husband for decades, raised his
children, and played the role of dutiful wife. Admitting that she
had knowledge of her husband's affair with a minor over thirty
years ago was probably not something she wanted to do. But
why lie about knowing Lila?

"Look," Andrew was saying, drawing Josie out of her
thoughts. "My mother is a good woman. She was a faithful
wife and an excellent mother. She is active in her church and
does a lot of community service and volunteer work. She's done
a lot of charity work in this county to help local foster children.
I just don't understand why you are dragging her into this
investigation when she has nothing to do with it. You're going
to have to help me digest that. Otherwise, I would definitely not
recommend that she meet with you or any of your detectives
again. Certainly not at the police station. Now, what was the
other thing you called about? Is it a different case?"

For the moment, Josie abandoned the topic of the formal interview.

"It was a personal question," Josie said. "Nothing to do with a case."

There was a beat of silence. Then he said, "Okay, I guess. Can't promise I'll answer, but go for it."

"When you were growing up, did you ever have . . . extra teeth?"

"Supernumerary teeth?" he asked.

"Yes," she said. "Exactly."

"Err. Yeah, I did. My mom took me to have them removed as soon as they grew in. She was always worried I would grow more, but nothing ever came of it. We had to go to a special oral surgeon in Philadelphia. Apparently, it's pretty rare."

"I've heard that," Josie said.

"How on earth did you know about that? What's this about?"

"Wild guess," Josie said. "I'm sorry, Mr. Bowen. I've got to go. It's an emergency."

CHAPTER 70

Darkness was creeping in as Josie pulled up in front of Sophia Bowen's house. A single downstairs light glowed through one of the living room windows. Josie waited to see if anyone was coming or going, and when she was relatively sure that Sophia was home alone, she went to the front door and knocked. Sophia answered wearing a pair of tan slacks and a pink button-down blouse that flared at the waist. Her smile froze when she saw that it was Josie. She started to close the door, but Josie jammed a sneakered foot between the door and its frame. Sophia kept on pushing, but Josie pushed back harder.

"I know about Andrew," she said. "I know that he is Belinda Rose's son. She had an affair with your husband, and Andrew was the result."

Sophia's hands went slack against the door. Her gaze dropped to her feet as Josie pushed her way into the foyer and closed the door behind her. "Why did you lie?" Josie asked.

Sophia took a moment to collect herself and then lifted her chin and glared at Josie. "You have no right to come here, barging in and making such outlandish claims. I'd like you to leave now."

"Or what? You'll call the police? Listen, I don't care about your husband's affair. I don't even care that you lied to your son and told him he was adopted when he's not. What I care about is finding Lila Jensen. I know that you remember her. Hell, I know you've been in touch with her."

"I haven't—I haven't been—"

"Save it," Josie said. "Lila has been wreaking havoc on my life for the last month. She's done things it would be impossible to do without help. Sure, it was easy enough for her to find a couple of dumb teenage boys to carry out simplistic pranks or to rely on her old drug buddies for other things, but now she's moved on to more elaborate schemes. Schemes she would need a lot more help for—money, a place to stay, a place to hold someone. You live all alone in this big house. You have money to spare. You're the perfect target for someone like her. So tell me, what does she have on you that would make you help her?"

Sophia's face was ashen. She twisted her fingers together, her eyes darting around the room. "I didn't want to help her. I really didn't. She's not here, if that's what you're after. She wanted to stay here, but I told her absolutely not. I hadn't seen her in over thirty years, then a month ago she showed up on my doorstep wanting money, a car. I told her I couldn't do it, but she threatened me."

"She knew about your husband's affair with Belinda Rose," Josie said. "She was going to tell Andrew that he wasn't really adopted. That his father wasn't the saint everybody thought he was."

Sophia spread her palms in a helpless gesture. "What could I do? I didn't want her to destroy Malcolm's memory, his legacy. What does it matter if he slept with some girl thirty years ago? He did the right thing. He made sure that Andrew came to him and that he was a good father. Why destroy that now? And Andrew, he looked up to his father so much. He became a lawyer because Malcolm was a lawyer. It was just a little bit of money she wanted. That was all. What's a little bit of money compared to my son's memory of his father?"

"How much?" Josie asked.

Sophia folded her arms over her chest.

"How much?"

"Twenty thousand," Sophia muttered.

"Jesus," Josie said. "You gave her twenty thousand dollars?"

"It was a small price to pay."

"Why did she come back? Why is she here? Why now?"

Sophia said, "She wouldn't say, but I think she might be sick. She didn't look well. I asked her the same thing you're asking. All these years. I thought all of that was behind me. She said she had some scores to settle and she didn't have much time left. I said, 'Time for what?' and she said that wasn't my business."

"Where is she?" Josie asked. "Where is Lila now?"

Again, Sophia looked all around the room, refusing to settle her gaze on Josie. She was like a small child. If she didn't look directly at Josie, maybe Josie wouldn't acknowledge her.

"Tell me!" Josie snapped.

Finally, Sophia sighed. She walked over to a table near the back of the foyer and picked up a purse. "I'll take you to her."

"Just tell me," Josie said.

"It's pretty remote," Sophia said. "If she sees just you and not me, she's likely to bolt—or come after you."

Josie didn't want Sophia coming along, but she couldn't argue with that logic. If there was even the smallest chance of finding Lila and rescuing Trinity, Josie had to take it. "Fine," she said, "but I'm driving."

CHAPTER 71

They drove in silence, broken only by Sophia giving Josie directions to an old abandoned textile mill near the Susquehanna River. She parked the Camry along the access road and went to search the trunk for a flashlight. She made a show of riffling through the array of items that filled Sergeant Lamay's trunk while Sophia waited in the passenger seat so that she could fire off a quick text to Noah. If Lila and Trinity were there, she would need backup.

Textile mill with Bowen, she sent. He would figure it out.

The two of them walked along the old access road in darkness with only the moonlight to illuminate their way. If Lila was on one of the upper floors, Josie didn't want her to spot the bobbing flashlight beam. Sophia, in two-inch heels, kept stumbling along the cracked asphalt. "Slow down," she hissed at Josie.

"No," Josie said simply. "You keep up."

By the time they reached the southern entrance of the mill, Sophia was sweating and huffing out breaths. Josie stared up at the behemoth—five floors of old yellowing brick and smashed-out windows like empty eye sockets staring down at them. Josie felt a tickle along the back of her neck. "Where is she?" she asked Sophia.

"The third floor," Sophia answered. "That's all I know. This is where she said she was staying."

For twenty thousand dollars, Lila could have done a lot better, but not many places would let you keep a hostage on the premises. "You go first," Josie said, and she pushed Sophia through the creaky doors.

Once inside, she turned on the flashlight and swept it around the cavernous room. Broken glass, garbage, and other debris littered the floors. Old equipment sat abandoned like dilapidated sentries. A rat scurried just out of view as they walked through the place looking for the stairwell.

"Over here," Sophia said, pointing to a set of double doors to their left. Graffiti and rust marred the paint on the doors, and a blackish fluid leaked from the wall above, over the door handles, and onto the floor. "Open it," Josie said.

In the peripheral glow of the flashlight, Josie saw the look of disdain that Sophia gave her as she riffled in her purse. "We don't have time for this," Josie said.

A tissue appeared in her hand, and she used it to cover the doorknob before pulling it open. The door groaned behind them as they entered the stairwell. In the silence of the huge building, it sounded like the roar of a jet. The concrete steps crumbled beneath their feet, and Sophia stumbled again, grasping desperately for the railing. Josie kept the flashlight pointed ahead and her ears pricked for any sounds above them. They had gone up two flights of steps when Josie suddenly realized that she no longer heard Sophia's labored breath behind her.

Instinctively, her free hand reached for her gun, but of course it wasn't there. She curled both hands around the long handle of the flashlight, but it was too late. She was yanked back by her shoulder, down the steps, tumbling into darkness.

CHAPTER 72

Josie fell and fell until she stopped with a thud on the landing they'd just cleared. The back of her head ached, and her right wrist throbbed. Searching around her in the dark, she realized she'd lost the flashlight. It must have broken on impact, because not even its beam was in sight. Feeling her way along the wall, Josie found the railing and pulled herself to her feet. Pain shot through her left ankle, and she stopped for a moment to try and listen over her thundering heartbeat for Sophia. Then she felt the cold, steel circle of a gun barrel against her cheek, and Sophia's icy voice in her ear.

"Don't move."

Josie put her hands in the air even though she wasn't even sure that Sophia could see her. She blinked several times, trying to acclimate her eyes to the absolute darkness of the stairwell. High above them on one of the upper flights of stairs, a thin shaft of moonlight crept in through one of the broken windows.

"If this is about your secrets," Josie said, "no one is going to hear them from me. I'm only interested in stopping Lila."

"Oh, this is about my secrets all right, but not the ones you think."

Josie shifted her face fractionally, nudging the barrel of the gun back slightly toward her ear. She could just make out Sophia's angry glittering eyes in her periphery. "You sure you know how to use that gun?" she asked.

Sophia pushed the barrel hard into Josie's cheekbone. "A rich old lady, living alone? You're goddamn right I know how to use this."

Josie didn't doubt her. "What is Andrew going to think if his mother kills the chief of police?"

"He's going to think I had no choice. Don't you worry. I'll cover this up just like I covered up Belinda's murder. Except this time, the secrets will stay buried."

Josie felt a cold shock go through her. "What are you talking about? You killed Belinda?"

"Of course I did," Sophia spat. "She was a whore, pretending to be my friend while she screwed around with my husband."

Playing for time, Josie asked, "You said you left the courthouse long before she died. You had Andrew. Did you know then that he was Belinda's?"

"I didn't know anything. I was blissfully unaware of what a disgusting pervert my husband was. Did you know he screwed every young woman who came into that courthouse? I think he even had an affair with Lila, but I could never prove it. I had no idea what he was doing. Belinda and I were good friends. Great friends. I trusted her, and I believed him when he told me he was trying to be a father figure to her."

With each word, Sophia dug the barrel of the gun deeper into Josie's cheekbone. Josie lowered her hands slowly and tried to shift away from Sophia, but she clamped a hand down hard on Josie's shoulder. Josie had to keep her focused on her story and not on the gun she was holding to Josie's head.

"You really believed your husband was trying to help Belinda because she was a foster kid?" Josie asked.

Sophia humphed. "I was young and stupid. I loved my husband, and I wanted to believe him. Then Belinda disappeared for a few months, and when she came back, she started seeing that teacher, Mr. Todd. She was more reserved those days, but we were still friends, so she confided in me—every detail about her relationship with Todd. I didn't think there was anything to worry about between her and Malcolm."

"But then Andrew came along," Josie said. She tried to take a step, and Sophia, lost in tales of the past, moved with her.

"Yes, Malcolm came home and said he had seen a little boy who was up for adoption and fallen in love with him—would I adopt? We could do for this little boy what no one had done for my good friend, Belinda. Well, I met little Andrew, and I just fell in love with him. I was living the dream. A full-time mother. No more typing and getting coffee for these asshole judges and lawyers. Answering phones and filing. So tedious and boring."

"If you didn't know that Belinda was ever even pregnant, how did you find out about the affair?" Josie asked. The barrel of the gun had slid slightly, and she could feel Sophia's hand tire with the effort of holding it up for so long.

"It was Valentine's Day, 1984. Malcolm was working late. I put little Andrew into the stroller and walked him in the cold over to the courthouse. Pushed him right up to Malcolm's chambers' doors, and then I heard them. I heard them . . . screwing. I hid in the stairwell and looked through the window in the door, waiting to see who it was. Imagine my shock when Belinda walked out of Malcolm's office, looking rosy-cheeked and satisfied with her buttons done up wrong."

So Belinda had broken off her affair with Lloyd and Damon Todd's father to pick back up where she'd left off with Malcolm Bowen.

Sophia lowered the gun to Josie's waistline as she spoke, reducing the pressure and seemingly taking some pleasure from getting it all out at last. "I didn't confront them. What would be the point? I hustled the baby home, put dinner on the table, and tried to get on with my life. But I just couldn't forget." She paused for a moment, taking herself back. "A few weeks later, I visited the courthouse during regular hours and ran into Lila. She could tell something was wrong immediately, so we went outside for a smoke break, just like old times, and I told her that I had seen Malcolm and Belinda. She said that she suspected he was probably screwing her before she'd disappeared too. Two years he was carrying on with that girl. That nobody. We had only been married for three."

"So you decided to take matters into your own hands," Josie prompted as, distracted by her memories, Sophia let the gun fall to her side. Relief flooded through Josie at having the barrel of the gun finally pointed away from her. She dared not make a move and break the trance. Noah and the cavalry would be there any minute.

"It was Lila's idea," Sophia explained. "She came up with a plan to lure Belinda out to a playground on the outskirts of Bellewood. She thought I'd just confront her, maybe throw a few punches. But when I saw her there, I just lost it. Two years. Right under my nose. Malcolm probably only adopted Andrew so he could get me away from the courthouse and they could carry on more freely. I hit her."

"With what?" Josie thought she heard the sounds of cars over asphalt, but she couldn't be sure. "With what?" she repeated.

"It was a bar from one of the jungle gyms; there was some storm damage and one of them had broken down. Belinda kept going on about how Malcolm loved her more than me, and that it was only a matter of time before he got rid of me. She would be eighteen in six months—all she had to do was wait, and then he would divorce me, take the baby, and start a whole new happy family. I didn't even know that Andrew was *her* baby until that moment. The lies. My God, the lies. I picked up the bar and...I didn't mean to kill her."

"But you did. How did she get buried in Denton?"

"Lila took her. We put her in Lila's trunk, and she said she would help me cover it up if I helped her with something else."

"Helped her how?" Josie asked.

"She wanted money. She said her boss was...molesting her. She needed to get away. So I agreed. She took Belinda's body and the money, and I never heard from her again. Until last month."

"You didn't give her money," Josie said. "Your husband did. What did you tell him to get him to pay her off?"

"I told him everything. He had a choice: turn me in and

become the judge whose wife murdered his underage mistress, or pay Lila and make the entire thing go away forever."

"He chose his reputation."

A loud bang sounded from below them, followed by shouts. In the moonlight, Sophia's eyes gleamed with anger. She raised the gun back to Josie's face. "What did you do? Who did you call?"

Josie didn't answer. Instead, she turned toward the gun, knocking it out of Sophia's hand and punching Sophia square in the face. Sophia stumbled backward, crying out as she fell. Josie dropped to her knees, searching frantically around the debris-strewn landing for the gun. One of Sophia's hands clamped around Josie's damaged ankle, making her cry out in pain. Josie kicked out, but Sophia had already pulled herself up and was looming over Josie. In her hand was the gun that Josie was searching for. She held it by the barrel, and before Josie had a chance to react, she brought it down hard onto Josie's head.

The stairwell tilted, and Sophia's shadowy form went out of focus. Josie tried to stand, but her legs wouldn't work. Next thing she knew, Sophia's hands were under her armpits, pulling her up the flight of steps she had just tumbled down. Josie willed her limbs to fight back, but there was no response.

She was dragged quickly through a side door, and the sounds of boots pounding along concrete and the shouts she had heard earlier faded. The moonlight was brighter on the third floor, but still, Josie couldn't seem to get her vision to clear. "Stop," she mumbled. But Sophia kept dragging her along; she was surprisingly strong. Finally she dropped her, and Josie rolled onto her back. A giant soft-flow dye machine loomed over her, a vast network of piping, nozzles, and pumps surrounding a massive cylinder so large that one would need a ladder to climb to the top of it. The tubular chamber had long since rusted, leaving a gash down the middle of it. Josie watched as Sophia slipped in and out of focus, poking her head into the jagged opening of the cylinder and turning back for Josie.

"No," Josie said, her heart hammering. "I can't…" she tried. "I can't go in there."

Sophia ignored her plea, dragging her closer and lifting and pushing her uncooperative body through the hole in the dye machine. The jagged metal edges of the hole scraped against Josie's back, pinching through her jacket and T-shirt and painfully scraping away skin. Her arms and legs tried again to fight Sophia off, but Sophia seemed to be everywhere at once inside the cylinder, pulling her deeper into the darkness.

"I can't…" Josie tried again.

Sophia laid her out flat on the cold rusted metal and lay down beside her. When Josie tried to speak again, Sophia clamped a hand over her mouth. "Now shut up," she told Josie, "'cause we're going to be here awhile."

Panic burned through every cell in Josie's body. She tried to get her bearings, to hold onto some piece of herself that understood that the darkness couldn't hurt her—just as Ray had always told her—but she couldn't. She was a young girl again, in the closet, spinning and falling through a dark abyss without end.

"I said shut up," Sophia hissed, pressing her palm more firmly over Josie's mouth. As Josie's breath came faster and faster, her hands reached up, trying to pry Sophia's hand away from her face. Sophia took her hand away momentarily, but all that came out of Josie's mouth was a high-pitched noise—she was hyperventilating. Josie felt her arms being tucked against her sides, then she felt Sophia straddle her, pinning her in place and settling her weight across Josie's middle. Sophia's hand was across Josie's mouth again. Josie's chest burned with the effort of trying to take something more than the short, shallow gasps of sheer panic. With each moment that passed, she took in less and less air.

Finally, mercifully, she passed out.

CHAPTER 73

Josie was awoken by the intense pounding in her head, like someone was driving spikes into her temples. She dared not open her eyes as her mind searched for some thread that would lead her back to reality. Where was she? How had she gotten there? Where was she last?

She focused on her senses. Her mouth was painfully dry, her lips pasted together. It seemed as though every inch of her body ached. It only took a small attempt at movement to realize she was hog-tied—hands tied behind her back and then bound to her feet, which bent behind her, her heels pressing into her buttocks. The air around her was warm though, and her cheek rested against something surprisingly soft.

Not the dye machine.

Then it came back to her: Sophia Bowen, the textile mill, her team breaching the doors on the first floor, the struggle in the stairwell, being stuffed into the bowels of the old machine. How many hours had Josie spent in there? The very thought brought bile to the back of Josie's throat, and she choked out a series of coughs. Her eyes snapped open. She was lying on a carpeted floor, her face next to what looked like a bed—the box spring set right onto the floor without a frame. Sunlight streamed from somewhere overhead, though she couldn't turn her body to see.

For just a moment, she was so grateful to be out of the dark hole Sophia had put her into, she thought she might cry. Taking several deep breaths, she tested her restraints again. She was stuck, everywhere except her head, which she lifted and turned in the other direction, coming face to face with Trinity Payne, whose swollen, bruised face lay inches from hers. Dried blood crusted at the corner of her lips, her nose looked crooked and smashed, and a wheezing sound came from her as she breathed.

Josie felt a surge of relief, despite their circumstances. If she was breathing, Trinity was still alive. Josie called her name a few times, but she didn't stir. Josie wiggled closer, trying to touch some part of her face against Trinity's, but she could barely move. She puckered her lips and blew air at Trinity's face. After the fourth or fifth try, Trinity's mouth twisted, and her eyelids fluttered open as far as they could. Trinity attempted to speak, but nothing came out. Licking her lips, she tried again, her voice scratchy but audible this time. "What are you doing here?"

"Where is here?" Josie asked.

"I don't know," Trinity said. "I'm not sure."

"I saw you on video at the body shop."

Josie thought she saw a tear leak from the corner of one of Trinity's eyes. "I didn't want to do it. She made me."

"Lila?"

Trinity made an attempt at shaking her head but stopped immediately, wincing and sucking in a sharp breath. "Barbara Rhodes."

The name was familiar. Why did Josie know that name?

"How did she get you to do it?" Josie asked.

"First she called me and said she had a story for me—the fire that killed my sister. She said she had proof of who'd really set it—someone from the cleaning service my mom used—then she hinted that my sister wasn't really dead."

"My God," Josie said.

"I didn't want to upset my mom in case it was bullshit, but she knew things, details I only ever heard my parents talk about. She made me meet her a few blocks away from the hotel. Said I had to walk, no car, no bag—she was afraid I'd hide a weapon—and she made me promise I wouldn't bring my phone. She said she didn't want me recording her or sending information from my phone until she knew she could trust me. She said she would give me ten minutes, and if I wasn't there in time, she would be gone forever. I thought she might be dangerous, but when I showed up, she was just this fat old lady. She wasn't even armed, and she was so nice. I didn't think she was…"

Trinity broke off as a cough erupted from her body, spraying blood from her lips onto Josie's face. "Sorry," Trinity said as the coughing fit receded.

"It's okay," Josie said. "You didn't think Barbara was a threat?"

"Right," Trinity said. "I got in her car, and we started driving. She mentioned some diner, and I knew the one she was talking about, so I thought it was okay. When it became apparent that she wasn't taking me there, I confronted her. That's when she told me that if I wanted the story, I had to do something for her."

"You killed Ted Heinrich for a story?" Josie couldn't keep her voice from rising.

Trinity looked as though she was trying to shake her head. "Not a story—and I didn't kill anyone. When she told me what she wanted me to do, I told her she was crazy. I told her to pull over and let me out; I'd walk back to my hotel. She pulled over. I got out. But she came after me. We were on this quiet little mountain road. No one around. We had a fight. She won. I woke—I don't know where. Could have been here. Tied up. She told me I would do what she said, or my family would die. She had help, Josie. She was facetiming with some guy who was outside my parents' house. She told me if I didn't do exactly what she said, she would kill them all. My parents and my little brother."

"How old is your brother?"

"He's only sixteen. This guy was following him around.

Taking photos of him. I don't know who he was, but I was terrified, so I did what she said. She drove for what seemed like hours and then parked a block away from the body shop. Some other guy pulled up in an Escape. She told me to get in, drive to the body shop, and go inside. As soon as they left me alone in it, I checked the glove compartment. It was your car. I knew then that whatever she was doing had something to do with hurting you. Then when I got inside the body shop, she was already there. She came in through another entrance—in the back. The owner was already tied up. He was in bad shape. She made me watch while she tortured him. She said if I tried to run away, that's what would happen to Patrick. She told me to drive back to her car, and her friend would take the Escape off my hands. He tied me back up, put me in her trunk, and left in your car. I was in there for hours just trying to figure out why they were involving you. Why both of us? Then I thought about why she'd contacted me in the first place—telling me my sister might still be alive. There's always been such a resemblance between us. Surely you've noticed it too?" There was a hopefulness to Trinity's voice.

"Yeah," Josie said. "I noticed."

"So then I thought maybe what she said was true—that someone from the cleaning service burned our house down and took my sister. And maybe my sister was really alive after all. And…and maybe it was you."

Only a DNA test would tell them for sure, but Josie felt in her heart and her gut that Trinity was right. They were sisters. "What's my…what's my real name?" Josie asked.

Something that looked like a smile stretched across Trinity's battered face. "Vanessa. Vanessa Anabelle Payne."

Josie groaned. "I like Josie better."

"Very funny."

It was still too much to wrap her head around. Her entire life was a lie. She'd been taken from her family and raised in poverty by a woman whose cruelty knew no bounds. All the while, her actual family was only two hours away in an affluent small town, mourning her loss. Every time she thought about it, the room seemed to spin. She brought the subject back to Heinrich. "This woman—did she tell you why she was targeting the man in the body shop?"

"No. She just said I shouldn't feel sorry for him. I tried to stop her, but she said if anything happened to her, her friends would hurt Patrick. I should have tried harder. I should have tried to save that man." Tears leaked from Trinity's eyes. A bloody snot bubble popped in her nostril.

"It's okay," Josie said. "It's okay. You did the right thing."

"It was disgusting. The smell. She made me watch."

"Stop crying," Josie said as more liquid leaked from Trinity's nose. "You can barely breathe as it is. I need you to keep it together."

"I can't," Trinity blubbered.

"You can, and you will. We need to find a way out of this."

"Yeah, right. How are we going to get out of this?"

"Have you tried shouting for help?" Josie wondered.

"How do you think my face got like this?" Trinity replied.

Again, Josie tested her bindings, but there was little give. Already in the short time she had been awake, her shoulders and legs began to ache.

"She's not going to leave us here like this," Josie said. "At some point she's going to have to move us. That will be our chance."

"Not if she's got one of her friends with her."

Josie didn't respond. Somewhere nearby, a door banged open and closed. Muffled female voices traveled toward them, getting increasingly clearer.

"Don't ever summon me again." The sound of Lila's voice after so many years sent a shudder through Josie's body.

The second voice was Sophia's. "I had no choice. If it weren't for you, I wouldn't be in this damn mess. We had a deal, and you went back on it when you showed back up here, so I'll summon you whenever I please."

Josie heard what was most definitely a slap, then a gasp, and what sounded like a tussle—grunts and thuds and then glass breaking. So, Lila had come to the mill and helped Sophia transport her.

"...and I'll use it. Get away from me. Get back..." It was Sophia. The sounds of struggle had stilled. Josie imagined she must have pulled her gun. Sophia added, "Now, you'll clean up this mess you made, and you'll leave Denton once and for all."

"Not without my money," Lila said.

Josie expected Sophia to protest or threaten Lila some more, but all she said was, "Fine. Come see me after you've finished whatever this is you're doing."

"Oh, I've got a few more people to visit after this," Lila said.

"Why? Why are you doing this? Why can't you leave the past in the past?" Sophia cried.

"Because I ain't got much time left."

"What did these people ever do to you?" Sophia asked.

"They think they're better than me, that's what. I'm through being treated like dirt."

There was a heavy sigh. Then Sophia said, "You're paranoid. No one thinks they're better than you, and that's not a reason to ruin people's lives."

"Says the hoity-toity bitch who lied and paid me off to keep her and her husband's reputation clean," Lila shot back. "Now put that thing away."

There was a beat of silence. Then Sophia said, "Malcolm told me what was in your file before he destroyed it. He and Mrs. Ortiz had quite the shock over it."

Lila's voice was hard and menacing. "You better leave now before I change my mind about killing you."

CHAPTER 74

Josie waited for Lila to come into the room where she and Trinity were sandwiched between a bed and the wall, but she didn't come. Trinity fell back to sleep, her broken nose whistling. Josie racked her brain, trying to figure out where Lila would be keeping them, her mind still addled from the pistol-whipping Sophia had given her. She couldn't tell if hours or minutes were passing. She thought about calling out to Lila, but she didn't want to draw her attention until she had some kind of plan. She was just drifting off when the sound of a phone ringing came from another room. Again, she heard Lila's voice. "Hello? Yeah, this is Barbara. Okay, I'll be right over." Then there was the sound of a door slamming. Lila had gone out.

Again, Josie wondered why the name Barbara was so familiar to her. Then she remembered arriving at the trailer park the day the Price boys had found human remains. The neighbor who had been watching them, who had called 911, was named Barbara Rhodes. Josie hadn't met her because she'd already been interviewed and sent home by the time Josie got there.

Belinda Rose. Barbara Rhodes.

"Son of a bitch," Josie said. She wiggled closer to Trinity, rocking her body from side to side until one of her elbows nudged Trinity. "Wake up. Trinity, wake up!"

Had Lila been under Josie's nose all along, now posing as Barbara Rhodes? Noah had interviewed her the day they found the bones and not long after seen the sixteen-year-old photo of Lila Jensen that Dex had given her. Why hadn't Noah made the connection? Trinity had said Barbara was overweight and old. It had been sixteen years; perhaps Lila looked markedly different.

"Trinity," Josie said. "I think I know where we are. I think we're in the trailer park."

Trinity stirred with a soft moan but didn't wake up.

"Trinity. Wake. Up. Lila's out. We're in the trailer park. I think we should scream. Someone might hear us."

Josie thought of the little Price boys living next door with their mother. She took in a deep breath and started screaming at the top of her lungs. She screamed until her throat ached and her lungs could take no more, periodically falling silent to listen for anyone who might be coming. There was nothing.

Trinity's voice was barely audible. "No one will hear you. Don't waste your time."

Josie knew she was right. Josie had grown up in this very park, and no one had heard her screams then either. Or if they had, they hadn't come to her rescue. "If she hears you," Trinity added, "she'll hurt you."

"She's already hurt me," Josie said and filled her lungs to scream some more.

CHAPTER 75

She shouted until there was barely anything left of her voice. Next to her, Trinity wept. At long last, as her cries receded into helpless croaks, Josie heard a door open and close, and heavy footsteps approach. She heard another door swish open, and the air in the tiny room changed. Josie's heart paused, and then kicked back into motion. "Josie," Trinity whispered. "I think I wet myself."

"Shhh," Josie said. "I'm going to get us out of this."

Josie had to crane her neck to see a fat pair of ankles beneath the hem of a white cotton dress approach. She had just enough time to notice Lila's feet were crammed into a pair of ugly, black flats before she was yanked up by the bicep and tossed onto the bed. She fell on her back, her hands and feet crushing painfully beneath her. Lila's face loomed above her.

Josie saw immediately why Noah had not recognized her, how he couldn't possibly have recognized her as the woman in the photo Dex had given her. Now in her sixties, Lila Jensen's long, silky black hair had gone shock white. Gone was the sheen, replaced by a straggly mane of thick, dry strands that tumbled down her back. She had gained weight. A lot of weight. Her flesh spilled out from the shapeless white dress draped over her form. Her once smooth, youthful, pale skin was stretched taut from the added pounds, her cheeks so chubby they seemed to swallow her eyes. Sophia had said Lila was sick, and Lila herself had said she didn't have much time. Josie wondered with what. Cancer perhaps?

"Little JoJo," Lila said.

It was the eyes that gave her away, though. They narrowed as Lila smiled the smile that had filled Josie with unbridled terror for as long as she could possibly remember. The little girl inside of her recoiled, but the adult inside her—the chief of police—fought back.

"My name is Josie," she said.

Lila cackled. "No. It's not. That's not even your name." She kicked out a leg, and Josie heard Trinity grunt. "Hey princess, what's your little bitch sister's name again?"

There was only the sound of Trinity weeping.

"Why are you doing this?" Josie asked, trying to draw Lila's attention away from Trinity. "Why did you do it? You took away my life. Everything. My real mother thought I was dead. My whole family. Why?"

"Why not?" Lila said.

"You could have walked away," Josie said. "At any time."

Lila's face flushed, and her eyes glowed with anger. She pointed a pudgy finger to her chest. "You think I get to walk away from this life? Is that what you think? That I ever had a chance to walk away? All those godawful foster homes with their degenerate foster parents? What a joke. I wanted to walk away. I wanted to run, but I couldn't. Everyone else got two parents, money, loving homes. Bullshit. I got nothing. Even that slut, Belinda. She got to live in a nice foster home with a woman who loved and protected her girls. What did I get? Every shitty home I went to, someone hurt me, and no one did a damn thing about it. When I left the homes, it didn't stop. Why should other people get to live perfect lives while I get shit on over and over and over again?"

Josie watched in perfect stillness as spittle flew from Lila's mouth. She had a feeling that Lila had been waiting a very long time to unleash that particular tirade. When she finished, Josie asked, "But why *me*? Why did you take me?"

"Because I could. You were there. I kept waiting for the

police to come for you, and they never did. Then I didn't know what the hell to do with you, so I came and found Eli. I knew he would take care of you if I told him you were his. Except he went and fell in love with you, didn't he?"

"He thought he was my father," Josie said. It hurt to say it out loud; Eli Matson was the only father she had ever known. Her memories were old and out of focus now, but what she remembered most about her father was how much he had loved her and how safe she had felt whenever she was with him.

"He was mine. He was supposed to love me more," Lila said. "After I gave him the baby he so desperately wanted, he turned against me, he hated me in return. How's that for sense?"

Josie remembered her father uttering those words in the hospital after her mother had taken a knife to her face: "I hate you." The battle for Josie had started a while before that, but that was the first time she'd ever heard him say those words. Other memories came flooding back to Josie. The conversation she had heard from her bedroom the night her father killed himself was eerily similar to the exchange she had heard earlier between Lila and Sophia when they had been arguing— suddenly Lila's tone changed completely, became calmer and a little nervous. Josie's skin prickled, goosebumps erupting all over her flesh. She might not have believed it before, but after what she had learned about Lila in the last few weeks, there was no doubt in her mind now that she was capable of something that unthinkable.

"Did you kill my father?" Josie asked quietly.

Lila laughed. "Took you long enough to figure that one out. A fine detective you are."

"Why?" Josie asked, incredulous. "You could have left me with him and gone away. Started over somewhere else. And my gram—" Here Josie's voice cracked, thinking of the grief and confusion that Lisette had carried around with her for decades, thinking Josie's father had given up on them.

"You're not listening to me, little JoJo," Lila said. "He got what he deserved. He betrayed me. He said he loved me, but he didn't. I didn't mean to kill him. Not at first. But then we were walking out in the woods to 'work things out' after I showed him the gun I got from Zeke, and I just did it. I waited for the police to arrest me, but they believed me when I said it was a suicide."

"And you kept me because you didn't want Lisette to have me," Josie said.

"You were a little bitch, but you had your uses," she replied, smirking.

"Until my grandmother paid you to leave. Why did you come back? Why after all these years did you feel the need to ruin my life? And Trinity's?"

Lila glanced down to where Trinity lay at her feet. "Two years ago, I'm sitting in the waiting room of a doctor's office watching the TV. There the two of you were—being interviewed about all the 'good' you did up in those mountains. You're a famous police chief. The other one is a famous reporter. Then they call me back to the exam room and tell me I've got cancer. That's not how things were supposed to end." She kicked out again, and Josie heard Trinity yelp. "And this bitch. Every time I turned on the television, I saw her face. Your face. I couldn't go without making sure you knew what it felt like to be me. You don't get a happy ending while my insides rot to hell."

"Then why did you dig up Belinda?" Josie asked. "It was you, wasn't it? You got the boys to find her. That's why there were so many foxholes."

Lila nodded. "Took those little idiots a week. I didn't think they'd ever find her. I needed money."

"You squeezed Sophia Bowen for twenty thousand," Josie pointed out.

"Yeah, but there's this experimental treatment I could get if I had enough money. It might be my only chance. I can't get that much from Sophia. Maybe close to it, but it wouldn't be enough. I pulled every con I could think of, but I was running out of time. Then I remembered Belinda kept saying she had a big payday—she just had to cash it in. She always said that. She begged for me to help her when Sophia was after her, and she said she would share it with me. I didn't pay her any mind back then. She was a stupid kid. But then I remembered that locket she always wore, and I thought, 'Holy shit, did I miss that?' Sophia always said it was cheap costume jewelry, but I got to wondering, what the hell was Belinda always talking about? Did she mean the locket? So yeah, I paid a couple of kids to dig her up."

"You have the locket," Josie said.

"I tried to sell it, but turned out Sophia was right. It was cheap costume jewelry. All it had inside was a lock of hair. Stupid bitch. All that for nothing."

It must have been Andrew Bowen's hair. Judge Bowen had given Belinda the locket and had obviously promised he would take care of Andrew. The "payday" Belinda had bragged about was what she could get by threatening to expose the judge.

"Anyway," Lila said, "I think I can get it from Sophia now, especially after that business in the mill the other night. I saved her ass again. I depleted my funds with these little projects of mine." At that, she laughed again and reached down, pulling Trinity upward. "The drug lackeys around here got expensive since I was here last."

Trinity cried out in pain as Lila dragged her toward the door. "What are you doing?" Josie asked, unable to keep the panic out of her voice. "Where are you taking her?"

Lila dropped her onto her side, and Trinity's body made a loud thud. Her strangled cries turned into an angry shout. "Leave me alone, you old twisted bitch!"

"What are you going to do with her?" Josie asked.

"You'll be joining her soon enough," Lila answered. She bent toward Trinity, eliciting more screams from her, and slowly untied her feet. She pulled Trinity upright, but she fell down immediately, her legs useless from having been tied in the same position for so many hours. "You better learn to walk real quick, princess," Lila told her. When Trinity's legs collapsed under her once more, Lila sighed, slid her arms under Trinity's armpits, and dragged her out of the room.

Josie's chest felt like it was being crushed. "Trinity!" she screamed.

"Josie!" came the answer.

There was a series of grunts and a couple of thumps, the front door opening and closing again, and then silence.

Lila was going to kill Trinity.

Josie opened her mouth and started bellowing at the top of her lungs once more.

CHAPTER 76

Josie had no sense of how much time had passed, but suddenly a face floated above her. Not Lila. A boy. It took her panicked brain a moment to process what she was seeing. She tried to remember which boy was which. The shaggy-haired one was older. Was he Troy or Kyle?

"Kyle?" she croaked.

He nodded. In his hands, he held a long gun with the words RED RYDER emblazoned on the stock. A BB gun. His simultaneous innocence and bravery brought tears to her eyes. "Can you untie me?"

He nodded again. Carefully he placed the gun onto the bed next to her and helped her turn onto her stomach so he could work at her bindings. He struggled for several minutes, until Josie could feel hot drops of sweat falling from his face and landing on her arms. "Go get a knife," she told him. "From the kitchen."

Wordlessly, he left and came back, then started gently sawing away at the ropes. Both of them kept silent, listening for Lila to return. Her hands came free first, allowing her to flip onto her back and stretch her legs out in agony and ecstasy. Kyle handed her the knife, and she quickly sawed through the ropes binding her feet. "Thank you," she told him.

He snatched the gun up from the mattress and motioned toward the door. Josie couldn't help but smile. He wanted to go in front of her, to protect her. "I'll go first," she said. Then she stood up and fell right to the floor. She hadn't been bound as long as Trinity, but her legs were numb and weak. Kyle helped her stand and tucked himself under her left arm. Together, they hobbled out to the living room of the trailer, where they found a kitchen table covered with fast food wrappers and prescription pill bottles. On the couch sat a laptop and two cell phones.

Outside it was dark, with only the golden glow of the exterior light over the Price trailer's front door. The air was cool, and after several deep breaths, Josie's head started to clear. Leaning on Kyle, she flexed and tested each leg until she could stand.

Kyle pointed to the dark wooded area across the street. "They went into the woods. Come on."

He took a few steps toward the forest and stopped, turning back to her. "Aren't you coming?"

Josie wanted to squeeze him, but instead she smiled again. "Kyle," she said. "Thank you for saving me, but I can take it from here. I do need your help with one more thing though. I need you to go inside, wake up your mom, and have her call 911. Tell them that your neighbor was holding two kidnapped women next door—a reporter and the chief of police—and tell them she took us into the woods. Can you do that?"

He nodded solemnly.

Josie laid a hand on his shoulder. "And then I need you to stay here and wait for the police, okay? So you can point them in the right direction."

"I can do it," he assured her.

"Thank you," Josie said. She waited until he was inside the trailer before she took off into the moonlit woods.

CHAPTER 77

Josie's muscle memory kicked in the moment her feet hit the trail. When she and Ray were teenagers, they had met in the woods during the night countless times. Her legs carried her into the heart of the forest without conscious thought. She was halfway to where they had found Belinda Rose's remains—where her father had been murdered—when she stopped, trying to steady her breathing and listen for the snap of twigs or the rustle of brush. All that came to her were crickets chirping and the low, mournful hoot of an owl. Her heart was pounding so hard it felt like it might jump right out of her body.

Once her eyes adjusted to the darkness, trees and rocks took shape around her. The moonlight was stronger here than it had been in the warehouse, filtering through the canopy of trees overhead. As quietly as possible, Josie found a nearby rock, hopped onto it, and swung her body up onto the low branch of a tree. Bear-hugging the branch, she used her vantage point to search the nearby forest. She thought she saw the flutter of crime-scene tape from where they had excavated Belinda Rose in the distance. To the left of it was movement, and then she heard what sounded like a wail. Trinity. She was still alive.

Josie lowered herself back down and ran in the direction of the crime scene, her stiff legs working more quickly now. The wail became louder as she approached the hole from which Dr. Feist had excavated Belinda's remains. She slowed to a halt.

Suddenly, pain streaked across the back of her shoulders, and she went tumbling forward into the black hole, landing face-first in a pile of loose dirt. As she rolled to her side, her arm brushed against something fleshy. Feeling around, she found one of Trinity's elbows. Josie's fingers scrabbled over Trinity's prone form, trying to get to her ties. "Trinity!" Josie whispered, clutching the hard knot of her shoulder. "Trinity, I'm here."

Above them, moonlight reflected off Lila's pale face, and the edge of a shovel gleamed in her hands. A pile of dirt hit Josie's face.

She was going to bury them alive.

Josie abandoned her efforts to untie Trinity and struggled to her feet, feeling around the edges of the hole, trying to find a foothold. Her fingers closed over a tree root protruding from the dirt wall, and she put a foot on it and hoisted herself up. Lila was there waiting, the shovel raised high above her head. She brought it down as hard as she could, but Josie rolled to one side, narrowly avoiding it. She stumbled forward, her foot catching on a rock and sending her flailing. She broke her fall with both hands and felt the end of the shovel whiz past her head. Josie scrambled to turn onto her backside as Lila swung the shovel again. Josie kept backing up as fast as she could, fear closing her throat, but the shovel caught her forearm this time, causing a sickening crack and a white-hot streak of pain through Josie's entire arm. Instant nausea rocked her body. Pulling her lifeless arm in close, she shuffled further backward, trying to put some distance between them again.

Lila raised the shovel one more time, laughing maniacally. "Come on, little JoJo. I've been waiting a long time for this. Stop running. Be a good girl."

A pop sounded, and Lila froze. The shovel fell to the ground as her hands flew to the side of her head. "What the hell?" she muttered.

Another pop burst through the night. Then another, and another. Each time, Lila jumped as though startled. Josie spun around, searching the woods for the source, her addled brain

taking a moment to figure out what the popping noise was—
Kyle Price's BB gun. Josie scrambled to her feet and picked up
the shovel with her good hand. She raced toward Lila and took
a wild swing that made contact with Lila's back—a solid kidney
shot. She fell to the ground. Josie pulled back and swung again
but missed. Lila reached out and wrapped a hand around Josie's
ankle, trying to pull her off balance. Josie brought the shovel
down again. It glanced off Lila's shoulder with just enough
force for her to release Josie's leg.

Josie turned and ran away from her, trying to make her way
back to Trinity.

"Stop, JoJo," Lila gasped. "I'm your mother, remember?"

"You're not my mother," Josie said over her shoulder. "You
took me away from my mother."

"I raised you."

"No, you hurt me, you abused me, you tried to sell me.
You're not a mother."

Lila's voice was getting closer. "I'm the only one you
ever had."

"Are you out of your mind? You tried to ruin my life, and
you just tried to kill me."

Josie turned, and Lila was right there. She raised the shovel
over her head, but Lila grabbed it. As they fought over it, Lila
changed tactics, huffing, "I've got money. I'll give you money.
Give me the damn shovel. We'll bury the reporter together and
go our separate ways. No one has to know. Come on, I'm dying.
I don't want to do it in prison."

"I don't give a shit what you want," Josie told her. "It's over.
You're over. You're finished ruining lives. I'm going to make
sure you rot in prison every day for the rest of your shitty life."

Josie won the tug-of-war, sending Lila off balance. She
stumbled backward without falling, and Josie turned away to
flee just as one of Lila's arms shot out, pushing at the small
of Josie's back. The ground rushed toward Josie's face. She
dropped the shovel and tried to break her fall with her good

hand. As soon as she hit, she rolled. She lost sight of Lila, but she kept moving so Lila couldn't zero in on her. Footsteps sounded close by, but then Josie heard the pop of the BB gun again.

"Knock it off!" Lila shouted.

Pop. Poppoppop.

Getting her bearings, Josie stood again. Lila was turned partially away from her, her eyes searching out the source of the BBs. The shovel hung loosely in one hand. Beyond her, Josie saw two sets of crime-scene tape around the other holes the Price brothers had dug. Holding her broken arm against her side, Josie planted her feet into a runner's starting position, tucked her chin, and bolted as fast as she could. She shoulder-tackled Lila's torso, and the two of them flew through the air into one of the empty holes, Lila's fleshy body cushioning Josie's fall. Josie heard her struggling for air, the wind knocked out of her. Sweat poured off Josie's brow as she struggled with one good arm to turn Lila's body over and push her face into the dirt. She sat on the backs of Lila's legs and screamed for Kyle to go get help.

Flashlight beams cut through the trees. Josie heard shouts and the sound of boots pounding along the forest floor, then Noah's voice, which brought tears to her eyes. "Josie!"

"Here!" she shouted back.

Her staff rushed in. What seemed like a half dozen of them stood over the hole, shining their flashlights down on her. "Trinity's over there," she said. "In the other hole. One of the other holes. She needs help."

"We'll get her," Noah said. Josie heard more boots pounding the ground. Shouting. The night was awash in flashlight beams. Two of her officers climbed into the hole with her and Lila. They secured Lila's hands behind her back and then lifted Josie up, out of the hole, and into Noah's arms.

CHAPTER 78

Josie dozed in a vinyl chair beside the bed they'd given Trinity in Denton's emergency room. Trinity was badly dehydrated, with wounds on her wrists and ankles where Lila had bound her. Her face was swollen and covered in various shades of blue and black and green. Her nose was broken, just as Josie had thought, and a CT scan of her head had revealed a small hematoma, but she wouldn't need surgery. A couple of her ribs were broken, and two of her fingers, but she would survive.

A hand touched her shoulder, and Josie bolted upright, an involuntary cry escaping her lips. "It's okay, Boss," Gretchen said softly. "I told them I'd come get you. You've got to go back for pre-ops now. Noah will be there with you."

Josie's arm was badly broken. She'd undergone a full exam and various x-rays on her arrival in the ER—she would need surgery. The nurses wanted her to wait in her own curtained-off area, but she'd refused, instead keeping vigil by Trinity's bedside. Josie glanced over at her sister and back at Gretchen. "When will her parents be here?"

"Soon," Gretchen said.

Josie stood up and let Gretchen hook an arm through hers, guiding her out into the hallway and off to another set of cold, bright, sterile rooms. Josie was numb and silent as she changed into a hospital gown and let the nursing staff take over. Hands probed her, taking her blood pressure and temperature, sliding in an IV, sending medication into her veins that made her feel relaxed and drowsy. She was grateful for the slow tranquility that overtook her. When Noah appeared by her bedside, she smiled broadly and reached for him with her good hand.

He took it and grinned back at her. "Well," he said, "I see whatever they're giving you is better than Wild Turkey."

She laughed. Or at least she thought she did.

Then they were wheeling her down a long hallway. They passed Trinity's room, and Josie saw Shannon Payne clutching her daughter and weeping into her matted hair. Even in her semi-stupor, Josie was struck by the resemblance between herself and Shannon Payne. How had Lila gotten away with it all those years, passing Josie off as hers? It didn't matter now. The worst was over. Lila was going to prison. Josie closed her eyes, her mind too tired to think.

When she opened them again, she was in a cavernous room filled with people rushing around. The air was freezing. A nurse with a skullcap pressed a vial of medicine into her IV. "I'm gonna ask you to count backward from ten in a minute, hon," she said. "Then you're gonna have the best sleep of your life."

Josie smiled at the nurse. That was exactly what she needed. She opened her mouth to say "ten," but sleep arrived first.

CHAPTER 79

Josie perched on the edge of the hard plastic chair the county jail had provided. The walls of a cubicle closed her in on both sides. Thick glass separated the visitor's room from the inmate room. It wasn't thick enough, Josie thought as Lila Jensen was marched up to the seat across from her. The guard left Lila cuffed and pushed her down into a chair. Lila shot him a dirty look as he said something Josie couldn't make out. He walked off, standing in the corner of the room, hands clasped together at his waist, eyeing Lila like she might jump up and attack someone at any moment. But there were only two other inmates with visitors, and each one of them were seated several slots away.

Lila's face was saggy and yellow. Josie couldn't tell if the jaundice was from the struggle in the woods or because her liver was failing her at last. She had refused to tell the doctors at Denton Memorial where she had been treated for her cancer or what her alias had been before she was Barbara Rhodes. A local oncologist was able to determine that she had ovarian cancer. She'd had at least one surgery, radiation, and chemotherapy, but the cancer had returned, spreading through her body. They gave her two months to live. Josie thought she was just mean enough that she would probably outlive that prognosis—maybe even by years. Josie still wasn't sure what would give her more pleasure—knowing Lila was dead, or knowing she was suffering in prison.

Lila smiled at Josie and picked up the phone receiver on her side of the glass.

Josie's right arm was casted and in a sling, so she used her left hand to pick up her own receiver and press it to her ear.

"Didn't think I'd see you again, JoJo. 'Cept on TV. I'm tired of seeing your face, to tell you the truth."

Josie was tired of seeing her own face on television as well, but it was unavoidable. Trinity was a correspondent for a national news show, and she now had the story of a lifetime. Rumor had it the network was working to find an anchor position for her, so hungry were they for her and Josie's story.

Josie got right to the point. "I want the names of your accomplices."

"What do you mean?" Lila asked.

"You know what I mean. Anyone who helped you with, what did you call it? Your 'projects.' Anyone you paid to place craigslist ads or break into my house or stalk Trinity or her family. Or move Trinity. Or take my car to Ted's Body Shop and then drive it back to where he found it."

Lila laughed, dark blue eyes glittering. "No," she said.

"I can make you more comfortable in here," Josie offered. She hated to do it, hated to even offer it, but what she hated more was the thought of nameless, faceless people all over Denton who had helped Lila carry out her twisted plans.

"Fuck you," Lila said. "You think I'm going to give you your happy ending, JoJo? No, you're not getting it. Not from me. You made a choice out there in those woods. You could have let me go."

"I made a choice?" Josie asked incredulously. "I never had a choice. Ever. You took that away from me when I was only a few weeks old."

"Oh, you want to play that game? Who had the worse childhood? You don't want to know what happened to me."

Josie leaned forward. "You're wrong. I do want to know. Your foster-care file was destroyed. There is nothing left. I don't even know where you came from."

Lila considered this for a moment. Then her hand tightened around the receiver. "I'll tell you what, JoJo. You're a detective, right? Big-time chief of police and all that. I'll give you a clue. You figure it out before I die, and I'll give you those names."

"What is it?" Josie said.

Lila hung up the phone and stood. Behind her, the guard startled, hand on his gun, and took a small step toward her. She leaned forward, opened her mouth wide, and breathed along the glass until it fogged. Then with one finger, she traced a series of letters and numbers into the spot she had made.

OY9555

Then she turned away and signaled to the guard. Josie watched the message fade as Lila Jensen was led back into the bowels of the jail.

CHAPTER 80

Josie dozed on Noah's couch, nestled in a blanket, the remote in her good hand. She was watching *Ally McBeal* reruns while she waited for her pain medication to dull the throbbing in her arm. She had been back to her own house, replaced the kitchen window, repainted her bedroom walls, replaced all the bedding that had been destroyed, and bought a new jewelry box. But she didn't feel right, not as safe as she did right now in Noah's home, where no hungry reporters waited outside, shouting and vying for photos and any comment she might make. At Noah's she felt hidden and out of harm's way. He had assured her that she could stay as long as she needed. He had tried to be there with her as much as possible, but there was so much work to be done to wrap up Lila's case that he was only home a couple of hours at a time.

The remote dropped from her hand when she heard the front door open and close. She blinked the fatigue away and smiled as Noah entered. He grinned back at her, placing the large wooden box in his hands on the coffee table and then planting a kiss on her forehead. "How do you feel?" he asked.

Josie lifted her cast. "Like someone broke my arm with a shovel."

"I'm sorry," Noah said.

Josie shrugged. "It'll heal."

"Did you figure out Lila's message yet?"

She shook her head. "I'll sleep on it. It'll come to me. What's that?"

Noah tapped a hand on the box. "We found this in Lila's trailer. I thought you might want a look at it."

Josie threw the blanket off her lap and lowered her legs to the floor, moving to the edge of the couch. "Silverware?" she asked. The box looked like an old box Lisette used to have where she kept her expensive silverware set. She'd given it to Josie and Ray when she'd moved into Rockview. Josie remembered because she and Ray had argued over it. Josie thought they should use the silverware, because what else would you do with it? Ray thought it was too fancy to use on a regular basis. The box was still sitting unused in Josie's garage.

"No," Noah said. "I mean, I think that's what used to be in here, but now it's—I don't know. You have a look."

Josie reached forward and lifted the lid. The inside was lined with dark-red velvet that was worn in many places. There were several pieces of jewelry, including jewelry that Needle had taken from Josie's home. She sifted through the pieces until she found what she was looking for. Tears filled her eyes as her fingers closed around her old engagement ring, then the pendant Ray had given her when they'd graduated from high school. On a normal day, the sight of them would have been like a spike in her heart, but now they filled her with joy. They were relics from the life she had made in spite of all that Lila had done to her. Symbols of the great loves of her life thus far.

She set them aside and sifted through various newspaper clippings, including one about the Payne house fire. There were also photos—of men, mostly, including Josie's father. There were other trinkets that had little meaning to Josie, whose import she couldn't guess. Belinda Rose's locket was there with the tiny piece of Andrew Bowen's hair inside. "You'll have to get this to Andrew Bowen," Josie said.

"Of course," Noah replied.

She picked up a long purple scarf wrapped around something soft and unraveled it. A gasp escaped her throat. "Oh my God."

In her hands, his small face covered with rust-colored blood stains, was Wolfie.

CHAPTER 81

Josie sat at a table in the back of Komorrah's Koffee, her black hair tied in a ponytail and covered with a baseball cap. She had managed to evade the press, even though she wasn't that far from the police station, where several reporters had taken up residence, hoping to catch someone coming or going who might have information about the sensational Lila Jensen case. It was going to take months for the fervor to die down.

Wind chimes positioned over the front door tinkled as Gretchen entered. Josie smiled and waved her over. Gretchen slid into the booth across from her and pulled a file from inside of her jacket.

"Did you get it?" Josie asked.

Gretchen pushed the file across the table. "Yeah, I got it. It's all there."

Josie's fingers brushed the edge of the folder. "Did you read it?"

"I did."

Josie flagged the waitress over and Gretchen ordered a large coffee. Josie had already purchased several pastries, and she pushed the plate across the table toward Gretchen, spinning it so that the pecan-crusted sweet roll was positioned just under Gretchen's nose. Gretchen eyed the pastry as though she were sizing up an enemy. "We're about to discuss toxic mothers," Josie said. "You're going to need it."

Gretchen laughed and picked it up, taking a hearty bite. A small piece of pecan hung from her bottom lip. "You better have one too, because Lila Jensen's mother is the mother of all toxic mothers."

Josie selected a cheese Danish and ate it in three bites. Gretchen savored her roll more slowly, appraising Josie as she ate. "Have you cried yet?"

Josie shook her head. She wiped her hands on a napkin and sipped her latte.

"You'll need to cry," Gretchen said matter-of-factly. "I mean, just do it. You've got to release some of that pressure."

Josie nodded.

"Did you meet with the Paynes?" Gretchen asked.

"Sort of. They came to the hospital. My grandmother suggested a dinner party. Them and my people. She thinks more of a party atmosphere will be easier for me."

Josie had barely been out of surgery when Shannon and Christian Payne, together with their son, Patrick, had burst into her room. Shannon had gathered Josie up into her arms, holding her, crying and whispering things Josie couldn't remember. Christian and Patrick had hung back, the teenager looking uncomfortable and awkward while his father stood stoically, silent tears streaming down his cheeks. Two days later, Trinity had shown up with a mail-in DNA test, and she and Josie had sat cross-legged on the hospital bed, spitting into tiny vials and laughing like teenagers.

Josie put a palm over the file. "Will you tell me what it says?"

"Of course," Gretchen said. She sipped her coffee and then folded her hands on the edge of the table. "You were right. The clue that Lila gave you was an inmate number. Lila Jensen's mother is serving five life terms in maximum security."

Josie's eyes widened. "Five life terms?"

"She's listed as Roe Hoyt, but that's just the name she was given after she was found."

"What are you talking about?"

"Roe Hoyt lived alone in a shack in the woods high up in

Sullivan County. No electricity or running water. The land was technically owned by the state, so she wasn't living on any type of family land. They think the shack was an old game warden building—a place the wardens could stop and take shelter if they found themselves out that far. No one had been out there for years."

Josie asked, "Who found her?"

"Hunters," Gretchen said. "They were put off by her because she didn't talk much except to make noises—one of which was the word roe, which is how she got her name. She was wild-looking, dirty, unkempt. They might have left her alone except she had a little girl."

Josie felt a sinking feeling in her belly. "Lila."

Gretchen nodded. "The hunters said she looked to be about five years old. She was running around the woods buck naked like a feral animal. They tried to take her with them, but she attacked them. So did Roe. So they went back to civilization and got the authorities. Police came and took them both into custody. When they searched the shack, they found the remains of five infants."

"Jesus," Josie said.

"Lila went into foster care. Her first foster mother named her Lila and gave her their last name—Jensen. She was delayed, had a lot of behavioral problems. The Jensens couldn't handle her, so she was shuffled from foster home to foster home. This isn't in that file. I got this from Alona Ortiz. She read Lila's foster-care file before Malcolm Bowen destroyed it."

"She told you?"

"The DA isn't interested in prosecuting Ortiz. She made a deal to tell everything she knows and testify against Lila and Sophia. She was the one who helped Belinda, by the way, the first time she ran away from Maggie Lane's house to have her baby. Bowen paid her off to give Belinda a place to stay until the baby came. Then he made arrangements for Andrew to go into the foster-care system and greased some more palms so he could adopt him. Anyway, everything bad you can imagine happening in a foster home happened to Lila Jensen."

"My God," Josie said.

She tried to picture Lila as a small child. Feral, forced into a world she didn't understand filled with people she couldn't trust. Had she even had a chance?

Gretchen tapped the file. "You can keep this. One day, you'll be ready to open it."

They each sampled another pastry, and the waitress refilled their coffees. Changing the subject, Gretchen asked, "Did Tara talk to you?"

"Yeah. She took me off leave and said that I could return to my post as chief when my medical leave was finished. I told her no."

Gretchen choked on the Danish she'd just stuffed into her mouth. She coughed and spit into a napkin. "What?"

"I don't want to be chief," Josie said. "I never did. Tara only wants me back now so she doesn't look bad for firing me after I found out my whole life is a lie. I told her to appoint another detective position, and I'll go back to doing what I was doing before Chief Harris died."

"What did she say?"

"I don't know," Josie said. "I stopped listening after 'you've got some nerve.'"

Gretchen laughed. "She'll come around."

CHAPTER 82

The smells of pasta sauce and garlic bread filled Josie's house. From her place on the living room couch, she could hear the sounds of dishes clinking and the kitchen faucet running. She could hear Ray's mother and Misty talking and laughing, although she couldn't make out what they were saying. Harris was fast asleep on Josie's chest, his head turned toward Lisette, who sat next to Josie on the side of her casted arm, stroking Harris's fine blond hair.

"Smells good," Lisette commented. "Mrs. Quinn said Misty made the pasta herself. Homemade pasta! Who knew the stripper could cook?"

"Gram!" Josie admonished.

Lisette laughed, one arthritic finger stroking Harris's rosy cheek. "You're strange bedfellows, you two."

"I'm just helping her out," Josie said. "She's not so bad. I get to spend lots of time with little Harris here."

A blast of cool air announced Noah's arrival. He closed the front door behind him and looked around, his eyes landing on Josie. He grinned. In his arms was a large bag. "I got three different kinds of wine," he said from the foyer. "I wasn't sure what kind of wine went with meeting your long-lost daughter you thought was dead after thirty years."

"The answer is all of the wine," Josie said.

Noah laughed and headed off to the kitchen. Lisette elbowed Josie, her eyes sparkling. "You're getting to spend a lot of time with that handsome fellow too, aren't you?"

"Slow your roll, Gram, we're still work colleagues."

"So? You don't outrank him anymore, right? You and Ray were married, and you both worked for the Denton PD. It's not an impossible situation."

"Not now, Gram," Josie said, but she couldn't keep the smile off her face. Harris stirred, and Lisette lifted him from Josie's chest, cradling him in her arms. Josie stood and peeked out the windows.

"Don't be nervous," Lisette said.

Josie turned from the window. Not being nervous wasn't an option. It wasn't possible. There were no guidebooks or tutorials for this scenario. She didn't know if spending more time with her blood relatives excited her or terrified her—a little of both, really.

Josie sat back down beside Lisette. "Gram, are you okay with this? Really? I don't have to pursue this."

Lisette raised a brow. "Nonsense. You can't walk away from your family."

"But you—"

Lisette squeezed Josie's knee. "I'll always be your grandmother. You'll always belong to me. But now you'll also be theirs, and that's okay. Truth be told, I'm happy you've found this out."

"Happy?"

Lisette nodded. "I'm not getting any younger, dear."

"Gram."

"One day I'll be gone. That day will be sooner rather than later. I feel at peace knowing you've got people to look after you."

Josie leaned her head against Lisette's shoulder. "Thanks, Gram."

A moment later, the doorbell rang. Josie hopped up and walked into the foyer. She looked back toward the kitchen. Noah, Misty, and Ray's mom stood in the doorway, offering smiles of encouragement.

Josie took a deep breath and opened the door.

A LETTER FROM LISA REGAN

Thank you so much for choosing to read *Her Mother's Grave*. If you enjoyed it, and want to keep up-to-date with all my latest releases, just sign up at the following link. Your email address will never be shared, and you can unsubscribe at any time.

https://lisaregan.com/

Thank you so much for returning to the fictional Pennsylvania city of Denton to follow Josie Quinn on her latest adventure! I hope you'll stick around for more as Josie returns to her position as detective and takes on more exciting cases.

I love hearing from readers. You can get in touch with me through any of the social media outlets below, including my website and Goodreads page. Also, if you are up for it, I'd really appreciate it if you'd leave a review and perhaps recommend *Her Mother's Grave* to other readers. Reviews and word-of-mouth recommendations go a long way in helping readers discover my books for the first time. As always, thank you so much for your support. It means the world to me. I can't wait to hear from you, and I hope to see you next time!

Thanks,
Lisa Regan

LisaRegan.com
Facebook.com/LisaReganCrimeAuthor
Twitter @LisaLRegan

ACKNOWLEDGMENTS

First and foremost, I must thank my amazing readers and faithful fans! Thank you so much for your enthusiasm and passion, and for sticking with me on this wonderful journey. Thank you to my husband, Fred, and daughter, Morgan, for your infinite patience and unending encouragement. Thank you to Nancy S. Thompson, Dana Mason, and Katie Mettner—my first readers and some of the best writing friends an author could ever ask for! Thank you to my parents—William Regan, Donna House, Rusty House, Joyce Regan, and Julie House—for your constant support. Thank you to the following "usual suspects"—people in my life who support and encourage me, spread the word about my books, and generally keep me going: Carrie Butler, Ava McKittrick, Melissia McKittrick, Torese Hummel, Christine & Kevin Brock, Laura Aiello, Helen Conlen, Jean & Dennis Regan, Marilyn House, Tracy Dauphin, Michael Infinito Jr., Jeff O'Handley, Susan Sole, the Funk family, the Tralies family, the Conlen family, the Regan family, the House family, the McDowells, and the Kays. Thank you to Lilly Billarrial for the goody-goody line. Thank you to the lovely people at Table 25 for including me, encouraging me, and teaching me. You know who you are. I'd also like to thank all the lovely bloggers and reviewers who read the first two Josie Quinn books for taking a chance on my work and spreading the word!

Thank you so very much to Sgt. Jason Jay for answering all my law-enforcement questions so quickly and in such great detail that I can get things as close to authentic as fiction will allow.

As always, I must thank Jessie Botterill for her continued brilliance, patience, and faith in me, as well as the entire team at Bookouture. You are miracle workers, all of you, and I feel so blessed and grateful to be working with you.

I'd like to thank the incredible team at Grand Central Publishing for their hard work and everything they've done to bring this series to so many new readers. In particular, thank you to Kirsiah McNamara, Alli Rosenthal, and Ivy Cheng. It's been a dream working with all of you!

ABOUT THE AUTHOR

Lisa Regan is the *USA Today* and *Wall Street Journal* best-selling author of the Detective Josie Quinn series as well as several other crime fiction titles. She has a bachelor's degree in English and a master of education degree from Bloomsburg University. She is a member of Sisters in Crime, International Thriller Writers, and Mystery Writers of America. She lives in Philadelphia with her husband, daughter, and a Boston Terrier named Mr. Phillip.

LisaRegan.com
Facebook.com/LisaReganCrimeAuthor
Twitter @LisaLRegan